SOCIETY IN INDIA

Change and Continuity

DAVID G. MANDELBAUM

Society in India

VOLUME TWO

CHANGE AND CONTINUITY

UNIVERSITY OF CALIFORNIA PRESS

BERKELEY, LOS ANGELES, LONDON

University of California Press
Berkeley and Los Angeles, California
University of California Press, Ltd.
London, England
© 1970 by David G. Mandelbaum
ISBN: 0-520-01895-8
Library of Congress Catalog Card Number: 70-99952
Printed in the United States of America
3 4 5 6 7 8 9

To Ruth

Contents of Volume Two

PART V *Village, Region, Civilization*

CHAPTER 19

The Village: Separate Hearths
and Common Home

A JATI cannot stand alone. Its people necessarily cooperate with some people of other jatis; commonly they compete with still others. The main locale of this cooperation and competition is the village. The groups involved are primarily the families and jati-groups of the same village and its vicinity, rather than whole jatis of a region. To a villager then, his village is far more than just a collection of houses, lanes, and fields; it is a prime social reality. To the student and observer it is a principal unit for the understanding of the society. Yet some observers have doubted the significance of the village either as a corporate group or as a useful unit for analysis (e.g., Dumont and Pocock 1957, pp. 25–32; 1960, pp. 88–89).

These doubts arise, in part, in reaction to the exaggerated notions of village autonomy that once were current. They may also stem from the complexities of the relationship between the multi-jati village and the multi-village jati. Moreover, village discord is apt to strike the observer's eyes and ears more stridently than does village concord.

The standard quotation, often reprinted, on the Indian village as a monolithic, atomistic, unchanging entity is from a report by Sir Charles Metcalfe, one of the founding administrators of British rule in India. The passage begins, "The village communities are little republics, having nearly everything that they want within themselves and almost independent of any foreign relations." It goes on to tell that wars pass over it, regimes come and go, but the village as a society always emerges unchanged, unshaken, and self-sufficient. Later writers of considerable influence, among them Sir Henry Maine, Karl Marx, and Mahatma Gandhi, reiterated this idea and suggested that the village was so perduring because it was so self-sufficient (Metcalfe 1833, p. 470 or 1832, p. 331; Srinivas and Shah 1960).

When modern field studies came to be made, however, they showed quite a different situation. An Indian village typically is hardly a republic; it has certainly changed from time to time; and it clearly was not and is not self-sufficient. The whole nature of traditional society militated against the independent isolation of a village. In earlier days there was a good deal of coming and going among villages, even though roads were poor and travel dangerous. Marriage affiliations were commonly made between families of different villages, and each marriage would set in train a lifetime of visiting between the two families by the married couple and at least another generation of such visiting by their children.

Such visiting still continues, as do other long-standing reasons for frequent movement among villages. Economic needs send people in and out of the village. Few villages have a complete roster of resident specialists. Senapur, near Banares, has twenty-four jatis, but a family requires services provided by from thirty-five to forty jatis. So there is constant movement for work and trade. Each local area is a kind of labor pool; some villages in it utilize the surplus labor of others; villagers with special skills circulate through the locality (Opler 1956, p. 7). Certain services are available only in the nearest towns. Bricklayers and lime-workers, goldsmiths and coppersmiths, florists and genealogists tend now to be found in towns or larger villages.

Markets are a major reason for travel within a locality. It is a rare place where no one is outward bound for market weekly, unless the village is itself the seat of a market concourse. A good many villages have been involved in an interregional market economy for centuries, producing crops that were transported across regions and states (Srinivas and Shah 1960, pp. 1376–1377).

There are also the religious attractions of other places. A village ceremony may bring visitors from hundreds of other villages. In every region there are holy places to which people go on fixed days or at any time when impelled by a pressing need. And there is the magnetic pull of the great centers of pilgrimage which draw millions yearly.

All these movements have been intensified and sped up in recent decades. New reasons for travel—education, administrative business, litigation—have augmented the traffic. To be sure, not every villager travels; many a village woman seldom leaves her neighborhood and some men stir forth only occasionally. But for most of its people the village is not by any means an isolated unit. Villagers are closely bound into a larger social sphere and have long been so joined. For example, Opler writes that the articulations of Senapur people with other communities and far-flung places is "not a recent development or a consequence of modern systems of communication or transportation. They rest on ancient practices and patterns" (Opler 1956, p. 8).

Just as a villager is bound to many other people with multiple strands—deal with one person and processions of others follow—so his village is linked by many ties to other villages, towns, cities. A village is not a neatly separable social and conceptual package but it is nonetheless a fundamental social unit. When an observer first comes to live in a village, the internal cleavages claim attention at once—in the very settlement pattern, in the daily avoidances, in the division of labor and of power—so that the signs of village solidarity tend to be overshadowed.

Village Solidarity

Yet such solidarity typically exists and comes alive for certain purposes and under certain circumstances. Villagers live close to each other; they see each other and interact more frequently than they do with people of other villages. They share the same familiar lifespace and share also common experiences of famine or harvest bounty, of flood or epidemic, of village fast or festivals. A village is usually an administrative and revenue unit. This in itself provides some common experience in the school, in the post office, in revenue collection. A man commonly has his closest economic associates within his village—as patrons or clients or workers or customers—with whose help he makes his livelihood.

When a man goes outside his village, he is apt to be identified first of all by his village rather than by jati or other reference category. As two strangers meet at a weekly market or in town and begin to talk, one of the first questions they may ask of each other is, "To what village do you belong?" Long after a family has emigrated to a town, its members still know and can identify themselves by their ancestor's native village. In Maharashtra, Mrs. Karve reports, the village is called "White mother earth," the habitation area being so distinguished from the black fields, and a man uses this term in taking a solemn oath. If he is excommunicated he must beg forgiveness of all in the village before he can be taken back (Karve 1958a, pp. 83, 87).

If a village gets a reputation in its locality for a particular characteristic, all those in it are then dubbed with a common label, whether as simple, or hard-working, or tight-fisted. These stereotypes do not ordinarily have great importance, though a quarrelling mother-in-law and daughter-in-law, perhaps even husband and wife, may belabor each other with the less complimentary epithets of their native villages. Sometimes the village reputation becomes a more serious matter. Carstairs tells of an incident in a Rajasthan village in which a youth, urged by companions as a dare, ate a bit of human feces. This became known immediately, with sad results for the boy. Even more, all in the village came to be known as being from the place "where they eat feces" (Carstairs 1961, pp. 105–106).

The immediate judges and enforcers of jati ranking are the people of one's village. They follow the standards of the region and the civilization and will not depart too widely from these norms. Nonetheless, it is they who perform the acts and give the opinions that place a person's jati in a particular local niche. As we have seen, this varies from locality to locality. Thus in Bisipara village the washermen are ranked among the clean jatis, but in the neighboring Boad territory, in the same district of Orissa, they are considered untouchables (Bailey 1963b, p. 129).

There may also be certain differences in rank assignment from village to village in the same close locality. When a man of Ramkheri village, for example, attends a ceremony in a nearby village, he observes the rank order of the place where he is a guest, although it may differ from that in Ramkheri. But he does so within certain limits. One such limitation is that a guest will not take food from anyone from whom he would not take water in his own village. That is, a guest may adjust his conduct to the extent that he may take food from a person from whom he would ordinarily accept only water. To illustrate this variation from home practice, one Ramkheri villager cited the example of two men, one of Rajput and one of farmer jati, who went together in a wedding party to another village. The two could not eat in one line at home, but in the other village this was done. "We shall also eat in one line; and it will not be a matter for our Ramkheri caste councils, because it is the custom of that village." The author comments that a man going across the boundary to another village automatically sheds his status as a resident of his own village and can conform to the commensal rules of the host village. In this respect "the village is very much a reality" (Mayer 1960, pp. 49, 159). In other parts of India as well, the village, in minor but still appreciable degree, is the arbiter of its own ranking practices.

Out of these common standards, identifications, and practices comes an allegiance to one's village that is expressed in many ways. One way is through the feeling, held widely though not universally, that all in the village share something of a kinship bond. This is directly shown in the fictive kin relations and the village exogamy that we have noted for North India. In the south also, a marriage can be of concern to the entire village. This is particularly true in a small village like Gopalpur where, Beals writes, a marriage is seen as a victory in the competition among villages. Every marriage of a child of Gopalpur activates more kinship ties and facilitates future alliances for the people of Gopalpur. "For this reason, the village as a whole must sanction any marriage that takes place between Gopalpur and any other village, and the village as a whole undertakes the responsibility of ensuring that people from other villages get value received when they arrange a marriage in Gopalpur" (1962, p. 28).

Not all villages of South India, by any means, display this kind of interest. In some, especially where there is a vast social distance between highest and lowest, those at the top could hardly care less how the Harijans mate. But even in such places the topmost are still concerned that no one in their village should bring an evil reputation to it.

Village ceremonies are commonly an expression of village solidarity. In the region of Gopalpur this is explicitly demonstrated in the festivals called *jatras*, given by all in a village to honor their village deity. The host families invite relatives from other places and regale them with food and entertainment. Wrestling matches between teams from different villages are a principal feature. As each contestant grapples with his opponent, he is cheered on by his teammates and fellow villagers. Young men of all jatis (save the very lowest and perhaps the Brahmins) participate as teammates for their home village, their usual differences and cleavages forgotten for the occasion. Two men who had sworn to murder each other took part on one such team, their sworn intentions dropped for the sake of village victory. "In the hand wrestling as in other aspects of the jātra, intra-village differences of status are minimized in order to create a representation of village unity" (Beals 1964, p. 107).

A jatra festival is supposed to show the host village as a good, friendly, and cooperative place in which to live. Those who succeed in establishing a favorable reputation for their village gain advantage in marriage negotiations as well as in trade and employment. Hence most people in a village try hard at festivals to please the guests as well as to honor the deity. Women visitors "exist inside happiness" at these occasions, in good measure because fathers and elder brothers provide a plentiful supply of drink to their daughters and sisters who come back for the festival. Far into the night groups of women gather, sing, and pass the bottle.

The men guests, for their part, do not really want to be convinced that their hosts' festival is better than their own, so there is a great deal of criticism and faultfinding. "Visitors leaving a jātra talk about 'our village,' and about how well 'our village' behaved, and about the superiority of 'our village jātra.' " This competition between villages occasionally becomes so intense as to lead to riots.

Beals notes that a village that actually is free of serious conflict does not need to demonstrate the fact at great cost. Hence a village advertising its state of harmony by holding a jatra may be one that is not particularly harmonious. Yet in staging a successful festival, the people of a village build up and demonstrate—to themselves as well as to others—their village loyalties (Beals 1964, pp. 109–113).

Village solidarity rites are common to many parts of the land. In Ramkheri, for example, there is a ceremony at which all forty-four shrines in the village are honored in succession as the concern of the entire village (Mayer 1960, pp. 101–102). Where a local deity is worshipped as the tutelary spirit of the whole village, there are special rites in which all villagers may take part. In Senapur the village deity is supposed to protect all its people and animals from external dangers. But he (or she) does so only "if they are willing to cooperate by obeying the accepted religious, moral, and spiritual discipline of the community"; at least once a year each family must worship the village deity (R. D. Singh 1956, p. 11).

Particularly dramatic expressions of village unity vis-à-vis supernatural forces occur in the cattle-curing rites, called *Akhta*, which are held in parts of North India. As described for a village of Delhi State (Freed and Freed 1966), during this rite the whole village is sealed off from the outside world for forty-two hours. No one may come in or go out, not even a bus may pass through. Every soul in the village must observe stringent taboos on the use of iron, wheat, and salt, and all must abstain from other customary activities as well. The daily routine of every inhabitant is abrogated; each one must be aware of and concentrate on the rite.

The ceremony is held when there is an epidemic among the village cattle. Its purpose is to cure the sick animals and to ward off disease from all the useful domestic animals of the village. The rite begins after dark on the first day when a group of men visit each house and cattle shed spreading smoke from a pot of burning incense and cow dung. The incense is believed to have cleansing and purifying powers. On the next morning every animal in the village —cattle, camels, pigs, donkeys, even chickens (though not, apparently, dogs and cats)—is collected at a given place and then driven in three circuits around the village with much shouting and splashing of water.

Following the herd comes a man holding the pot of burning incense. After the last round he runs through the motley herd and on across the fields to bury the pot in the land of another village, symbolically transferring the disease from his own village to another. In the ceremony that the Freeds witnessed, the pot was buried on what was probably government-owned land; if the people of another village had come to know of an intention to plant the pot in their grounds, they would have been "ready with sticks" (Freed and Freed 1966, pp. 682–689).

The whole rite symbolizes the village as a defensive unit against malevolent supernatural forces. Villagers stand together then, apart from all the rest of the world. Together and alone they marshal their collective strength through collective discomfort. Together, without distinction of jati rank, they perform the prophylactic rites for their animals and ritually transfer the evil influence from their corporate body into that of another village.

There had been opposition to performing this rite in the village where the Freeds were living because such practices are contrary to the teachings of the reformist religious movement, the Arya Samaj. Most families of the dominant landowners are followers of this movement though only a very few observe all its precepts meticulously. One man said that his father was against it because if the village held Akhta, the observers would consider them foolish people (Freed and Freed 1966, pp. 682–683). The Freeds replied that they had never seen Akhta and would like to see it.

Later, after more cattle had died, the village council decided to hold the ceremony, though in somewhat modified form, to conciliate some of the objectors. This rite is generally being held less often than formerly, not only because of reformist opposition, but as much because other means of coping with the threat of epidemics are becoming known and used.

Village festivals of all kinds are fading out in a good many places (cf. Nath 1962) partly because internal dissensions make it difficult to arrange for them and partly because alternative events and channels have become popular. But even when the ritual manifestation of village unity diminishes, that unity may be shown in other ways.

One common way to show village unity is to repel incursions by outsiders. If the forces of government threaten all in a village, or if strangers attempt to harm a fellow villager, or if the people of another village assault one's own, fellow villagers may well rise to the joint defense. An example of this occurred in Rampura, near Mysore City, when the state agricultural department ordered that fishing rights in the village tanks should be auctioned off. The villagers had been fishing in these tanks whenever they wanted to, and they felt that this order was an encroachment on their rights. So when a government official came to the village and opened the auction there were no bids. The villagers had seen to it that no one from their village or from any other place could approach to buy their rights (Srinivas 1955b, p. 32).

A similar episode occurred in Wangala in Mysore when the Revenue Inspector announced the auction of an acre of good land because of delinquent taxes. The land belonged to a poor man who had suffered a series of misfortunes. Land is precious and scarce in Wangala and ordinarily, eager bidders would not be lacking. Yet the leader of a rival alliance declared that no one should attend the auction because "to bid at such an auction would be supporting the Government against a man of one's own village." This was decided at a panchayat meeting; the auction was later canceled and arrangements were made for the owner to borrow enough to satisfy the tax arrears. Village (and jati) unity overrode factional differences (Epstein 1962, pp. 143–145).

Two such incidents are told for Shamirpet, near Hyderabad. One day some soldiers from a nearby cantonment rode into the village in two army trucks and began loading firewood belonging to a villager. It was obvious that they did not intend to pay and when the owner remonstrated, they beat him up. Word of this spread quickly through the village; men armed with staves came rushing up to stop the looting. At this the soldiers retreated and threatened to come back with reinforcements to destroy the whole village; they did not.

On another occasion, water for Shamirpet fields was diverted under cover of night to the fields of Aliyabad, a nearby village. "Next morning an organized team from Shamirpet attacked Aliyabad." The Aliyabad people said that the water had been diverted by mistake; probably they had bribed the guards and had overreached themselves by not allowing any water at all to flow into Shamirpet. "But in the dispute itself the two villages had forgotten their internal differences and dissensions and each of them had acted as one body" (Dube 1955b, pp. 210–211).

These three villages, Shamirpet, Wangala, and Rampura, appear to have relatively little internal friction. So their people may be more likely to rally defensively than would those of a deeply divided village. But even a fractious village has a certain unity simply because it is a node for the activities of its inhabitants. Typically, as was shown above, the village is where a man grew up, where his close kin live, where his work partners and helpers are, where his friends are found, where he worships, where he is known and placed. He shares with his village neighbors the lore of the village, that detailed inside knowledge that no others have.

It has been said that the village is a unity because of its extensions, not in spite of them (Singer 1956b, p. 4). That is, the villager's relations with other people take place so largely in the context of his home village that he is socially and psychologically involved with the village as a whole. This is not to say that the village is always or even usually a unified community; it is to say that it is important to its people.

Some observers have stated that a villager participates in two kinds of unity, one "vertical," the other "horizontal"; the village is the vertical unit and is made up of horizontal layers, each of which is a jati. This may be too static a view of a villager's affiliations and actions. His support of one or another social group varies by context and by circumstances.

Thus in Rampura there are occasions when many men of the village stand together, as they may in a fight against another village during a festival involving a number of villages. Yet a Brahmin of Rampura would not be likely to be attacked there by the enemies of his village because he has a special ritual position as a Brahmin. An untouchable or a Muslim of Rampura would be involved in the fight more because of his attachment to a particular patron who was also in the fray than because of village patriotism. The same three groups, Brahmins, Muslims, and untouchables, are not given important formal roles in the annual village ceremony of Rampura but still their cooperation is sought in staging the ceremony (Srinivas 1955b, p. 33).

Just as the occasions for "vertical" unity do not necessarily engage every last man and group, so the occasions for "horizontal" unity do not necessarily bring in every man and family of the jati-group. Loyalty to jati sometimes conflicts with loyalty to village. An elder participating in a village council, as we have noted, must sometimes tread a narrow line between what is good for the village and what is to the advantage of his jati kinsmen. The common suspicion is that kin ties are placed over all, but one test of an able leader is whether he can somehow reconcile the two, preserving the public good while not neglecting the cause of his kin.

The relations among jatis in a village are ways of "being together separately," as Beals puts it. That phrase applies to the human condition anywhere; each person is an individual in his family, a member of one group in a collocation of groups, a part of a local society in a larger social order. But for Indian villagers the togetherness and the separateness are largely carried on in the same locale, with much the same set of people and with the ritual separations pervasively significant. Separation often is a ruling concern, yet separation must always be mitigated by the fact that a jati cannot exist by itself. In Gopalpur, "The belief that jatis are related to each other, like brothers, and that all jatis provide essential services for each other creates a unity within the diversity of jatis" (Beals 1962, p. 41).

A village is clearly an important and viable social entity to its people, who also take part in the larger society and share in the pattern of the civilization. Hence the question raised by some students of Indian society as to whether the village is an isolable unit for study requires no absolute answer. In some ways it is, in others it is not. The people and culture of the village should be studied both in their local milieu and in wider perspective (cf. Marriott 1955b, pp. 171–182).

Settlement Patterns and Solidary Relations

Two important influences on village solidarity are local geography, especially the settlement pattern, and local economy, particularly the means of land management. These affect the ways in which the people of a village pull together or do not, yet it should be emphasized that the feeling for one's village is usually strong whatever the geographic or economic variations may be.

There are three main types of settlement pattern. Most common is the nucleated village, a tight cluster of houses surrounded by the fields of the villagers, perhaps with an outlying hamlet or several satellite hamlets. A second type is the linear settlement, in which houses are strung out, each surrounded by its own garden or compound, with little or no physical demarcation to show where one village ends and where another begins. This type occurs in Kerala, in Konkan, and in the delta lands of Bengal (Miller 1954; Karve 1958a, pp. 74–75; Nicholas 1963; Mencher 1966). The third type is simply a scattering of homesteads or clusters of two or three houses, again with no necessary physical indications of the limits of any one village. This type is found in hill areas, as in the Himalayan foothills, in the highlands of Gujarat, and in the Satpura range of Maharashtra (Shah 1955b; Karve 1958a, pp. 76–82; Nandi and Tyagi 1961). In each type, both houses and fields are included in the people's definition of village.

Despite the blurring of geographical markers in the two latter types, the people of such villages know who belongs to their village and what it takes in. This may or may not coincide with the government's definition of where the bounds of a particular village lie, but the villagers themselves know who belongs to what village grouping. Thus in Sirkanda, in the Himalayas, about half of the villagers live outside the central settlement, mainly in field houses (called chans) which are some distance from the village nucleus. These outlying people readily identify themselves as belonging to Sirkanda and are so identified by others. "This in spite of the fact that they no longer reside in the village, that other villages may intervene between them and Sirkanda, and that they may be surrounded by the chans of other villages" (Berreman 1963, pp. 34–35, 260).

So also in northern Kerala where the line of houses of one village merges into another and the outsider can see no obvious boundaries. "The boundaries are nevertheless known to residents, and social relations are generally more intensive within than without" (Miller 1954, p. 411). In parts of the Bengal delta, houses line the higher ground at the edge of the waters; a village there is one segment of a long chain of houses, yet is a distinct social entity. In two such adjoining villages in Midnapur district, some houses of one village can only be reached by passing through a part of the other village. People of one are served by jatis of the other; men of one village own land in the other; at the boundary, adjacent families on both sides consider themselves to be part of the same neighborhood, "Yet the villages are quite distinct from one another." Each has its separate headman, its own meeting pavilion, its own temple. Each is maintained as a separate jural segment; its people convene their own council in settling disputes (Nicholas and Mukhopadhyay 1964, pp. 15–22).

In all three settlement types the village is an important social unit. But having said that, we must also emphasize that settlement patterns—and the factors that go into the making of them—affect social organization. For example, the dispersed villages of Kerala are more loosely organized than are the compact villages of Madras (Mencher 1966, pp. 143–146).

The effect of settlement pattern on village organization is further shown in a comparison of a linear village of the Bengal delta with a nucleated village of West Bengal. The nucleated village, called Chandipur (Murshidabad district), has one hundred sixty houses and one thousand people crowded in about five acres of habitation site. The other village, Radhanagar, has about one hundred houses along some twenty miles of winding settlement chain. Both villages share a generally similar culture although the nucleated village is much older and most of its land is held by the locally dominant Brahmins. The other village has recently been reclaimed from the waters; its settlers are mainly people from middle and lower jatis who dared settle on this frontier because of their hunger for land. Landownership is much more evenly distributed, there are fewer jatis of artisans and servants, there is less social interaction because of the dispersal of the houses, and less elaborate distinctions are made in caste ranking.

The contrast in political organization between the two is particularly marked. When a dispute is to be settled or a public decision made in the village of the delta frontier, the headman calls together a council and "eight or ten prominent men are sure to attend every meeting because no decision can be taken without them." In older Chandipur the headman is much more the supreme authority; he is by far the largest landowner in the village, the head of the most powerful faction of the ruling jati. He decides who is guilty, he decrees beatings and collects fines. "Others may come to watch and influential men may even express opinions, but it is the headman who makes decisions" (Nicholas 1963, p. 1195). Such concentration of power is not likely to develop under the greater dispersal of land ownership and of habitations in Radhanagar. The village is a viable unit in both instances, but a strung-out or scattered village is less amenable to close control than is a tightly packed huddle of houses.

The layout of a village generally reflects something of its social structure. Harijans commonly live in a separate quarter, removed from the main site by some open space and equipped with a separate water point, thus forming a distinct hamlet. Where there are two sizeable Harijan jati-groups, each tends to have its own locality. Nowhere in the Andhra villages observed by Mrs. Karve do the two main Harijan jatis there, the Malas and the Madigas, live in one section of mixed housing; she finds this true, also, of the Harijan jatis of Maharashtra (1958b, p. 137). Not only Harijans but any other jati-group may inhabit a separate hamlet for particular reasons of village history.[1]

The central village is typically divided into several sections, which may be formally demarcated as wards or more vaguely recognized as separate neighborhoods. In either case, particular jati-groups or lineages tend to reside in each section, giving some social distinctiveness to the several parts of a village. The distinctions are very marked in Sripurum village of Tanjore, where the three main social levels are mirrored in the residential pattern. The Brahmin jatis all live along one long street; the Adi Dravidas (the untouchables) live across a main road and jatis of the middle blocs labeled "non-Brahmins" are located between the two. The Brahmins' street is their exclusive domain, others do not enter it unless they have some particular business there. Nor do Brahmins ordinarily set foot in the Adi Dravidas' street; if they do they must bathe before resuming normal activities in their houses.

People of the three divisions are quite segregated from each other except in economic interchange. Most of the village land is owned by Brahmins; most Adi Dravidas are landless laborers; the non-Brahmins are mainly tenants and artisans. So the residential divisions parallel division of jati rank and economic class (Béteille 1962, p. 142). Social and physical separations have been particularly strong in Tanjore district villages because the Brahmins as dominant landowners could enforce rigorous ritual separation (cf. Gough 1955, pp. 47–52).

A family in most parts of the land prefers to live near its close relatives, partly because of the convenience of freer interchange in food and in all manner of things, but also because there is mutual protection in living together, especially for the smaller, weaker groups in a village. "A man feels safer in the *keri* (ward) of his

---

[1] The number of these satellite hamlets is said to be larger in eastern India, from eastern U.P. to Bengal, than elsewhere (Nath 1961, p. 142; see also Spate 1954, pp. 171–181).

caste," Srinivas says of Rampura in Mysore and this is widely so (1959a, p. 5). If there are many families of a jati, those of the same lineage cluster together. If there are only a few, the cluster includes the whole jati-group. Villagers have said (and I, for one, have reason to believe it is true) that even the dogs know their ward and try to chase out animals or strangers who amble in from elsewhere (cf. Smith 1952, p. 54).

The social ties of neighborhood are illustrated in the account of the wards of Ramkheri village (Mayer 1960, pp. 132–139). There as elsewhere a ward contains its own social nuclei. The participants in each nucleus may be found sitting on special platforms where the men smoke of an evening, or on favorite verandahs, or in work-shops, or simply at good vantage points from which to see what is going on. To find a man, one goes to his accustomed leisure ground in his ward. Since women stay closer to home than do men, their daily interchange is all the more restricted to their own quarter of the village. They usually make good use of the trip to the well where women of various wards may gather, but there is a limit to the time that can be spent in this refreshing way. At harvest time, those whose fields are contiguous or close share one threshing floor and this provides an informal bond among villagers of different jatis in Ramkheri.

A good deal of informal cooperation normally goes on between neighboring households. People borrow utensils or staple foods from their neighbors in the ward and men exchange daily labor. Neighbors attend the minor household rituals of a family, those rites that do not bring in a large visitation of kin from other places. They also help in those rites where nonkin are necessary, as in a bridal procession, when women are needed to sing songs for back-ground music and to provide foreground badinage.

Although neighbors do not necessarily belong to the same alli-ance, there is some tendency for an alliance to be centered in a particular quarter, partly because lineages and jati-groups tend to be similarly centered. Propinquity can breed enmity in village India as elsewhere, but, in general, village neighbors are likely to share at least some neighborhood interests and loyalties within the bounds of the whole village (cf. Dhillon 1955, pp. 43–45; Nicholas and Mukhopadhyay 1964, pp. 27–29).

Economic and Other Influences on Village Organization

A key factor in the relations among the families and jatis of a village is the nature of landownership. The following chapter deals with the kind of village in which one jati-group owns most of the land and thereby controls much of the village. Economic aspects of such control are illustrated in a comparison of two villages in Uttar Pradesh that are similar in area, in the number of jatis, and in general culture. In one, Madhupur, families of the dominant jati own 82 percent of the land and have long ruled the village. The other, Ramapur, has two leading jatis, the boatmen and the Brahmins, each of which derives considerable income from pilgrims to nearby Allahabad. These two jati-groups are at about the same economic level, and neither owns much land; most of its village lands were held by an absentee landowner at the time of the study. Though there is theoretically great ritual distance between the Brahmins and boatmen, social distinctions are not actually as sharply made in Ramapur as they are in Madhupur, where one jati-group dominates. There the dominant landowners kept other jati-groups in strict subordination and quelled attempts by lower jatis to raise their status (Opler and Singh 1952, pp. 188–190). Though jati relations in different villages are set in the same frame of ritual hierarchy, differences among villages in distribution of economic power make for considerable differences in these relations.

The effect on ritual relations of economic power is also shown in a brief comparison by Alan Beals of six villages in northern Mysore (1962, pp. 84–97). Though the six are only a few miles apart, there are notable differences among them. One is markedly conservative, another clearly progressive; jati lines are sharply drawn in one and in another they are more relaxed. In one, called Chintanhalli, there is a particularly great gap in wealth between the landowners and the rest of the villagers; that village has the most authoritarian social structure of the six. Chintanhalli lands are irrigated, are very productive, and are much too expensive to be purchased by farmers with little capital. Its garden crops require continuous, intensive labor. The landless laborers cannot oppose the landlords in organized, open conflict, because the landowners can defend their position too well with beatings and arrests. The laborers do express themselves through theft, murder (three in five years), and migration. This kind of conflict is not common in the region, and Beals concludes that it rises from the unusually great economic disparity in this village. In those villages of the sample with less disparity in wealth, there is also less rigid and pervasive stratification. Thus gross differences in wealth within a village, as in Chintanhalli, seem to make for more rigid stratification and authoritarian dominance. These conclusions are drawn from the preliminary study of only six villages. They are worth testing much more extensively.

Two other villages of Mysore are included in Beals's comparative observations. One village illustrates the effect of a peculiar ecology and of a strong sectarian religion; the other illustrates the influence of a nearby city. The first village, called Elephant, is situated in an isolated hill enclave. Most of the inhabitants are Lingayats, members of a sect-based jati. The Lingayat religion, more than the jati, seems to dominate in the village. "The people consider themselves among the last upholders of jati purity in an impure world." The village is a theocracy ruled absolutely by its priest and a few influential men. These rulers sometimes argue among themselves, but they permit little conflict, sin, disobedience, or theft in their village.

Elephant also "bears a peculiar cross" in that its men have to be especially considerate of their wives. There is no drinking water available in the village during the dry season, and water has to be carried up five hundred feet, over a mile of steep stone staircase, from a valley below. Families do not want to marry their daughters into so difficult a place. So the men of Elephant make the special concession of helping with the carrying of water and of wood. "Wives are treated with the greatest circumspection, for should one leave, it would not be easy to find another" (Beals 1962, p. 91).

The other village, called Namhalli, is dominated not by a sect dating from the twelfth century but by a telecommunications factory dating from the mid-twentieth century. Namhalli, as has been noted before, is near the city of Bangalore, and as the city has grown the village has become a quasi-suburb. Buses come every day to pick up and deliver the villagers who work in the factory. Yet, although Namhalli has been considerably affected and has recently benefited by the extension of the city, it is still essentially a village and the people follow the basic patterns and values of village life.

Beals writes that the villagers in Gopalpur, Elephant, and Namhalli share the same culture. "They all recognize the significance of jati, they all believe that it is sinful to disobey one's older brother, and they all hope to marry their sister's daughter" (1962, pp. 92–96). These clues indicate that proximity to the city for centuries did not greatly alter the usual village standards; proximity to and employment in factories has affected the villagers, as will be noted in the following chapter, but has not as yet altered these characteristics.

Urban influence does not seem to have affected village social structure greatly, although a strong impact of modern urbanization may yet come. In a review of the impact of urban areas on village life, Lambert concludes that the principal changes in village life do not stem from urban sources particularly but follow on general changes in the society. The social structure, he finds, is most sensitive to changes in land rights and the effect of the urban areas is "less than might be expected" (1962, pp. 129, 138–140).

This is further illustrated in Majumdar's study of Mohana, a village just eight miles from Lucknow. Two miles of rough cart road separate Mohana from a paved highway to the capital city and during the rains these two miles of mud discourage travel. Nonetheless, there is considerable contact with the city for trade, marketing, worship, and education. Yet the social order of Mohana does not differ appreciably from that of other villages of the region that are much farther from the city and have fewer contacts with it. The people of Mohana see themselves as villagers, supporters of a better, simpler, more pious way of life than they think prevails in the city. They may seek help from those who have special knowledge of the town and they may admire them for their experience, but most "regard the village as distinct and socially distant from the town" (Majumdar 1958a, p. 329). There may not be that much difference between town and village society, but many in Mohana believe there is, and are staunch for the village ways.

A factor that does carry great potency for change in village society is the advent of irrigation. This is well documented in the comparison, noted several times before, of two villages in Mysore—Wangala whose fields received irrigation, and Dalena whose lands did not. In Wangala the managers of the sugar factory took charge of most economic matters relevant to growing the new cash crop. As Wangala farmers prospered by producing sugarcane, they had no reason to venture beyond the village, and they intensified their local society and culture. In Dalena, no such farming potentials were created, no outside experts were provided, and the men had to seek opportunities outside the village if they were to keep pace with the increased prosperity of the more favored villages of the locality. They did seek such outside support and quite successfully. In doing so, they have given up some of the traditional goals, or at least modified them, and have taken to ways and standards that they have met in the town. This has indeed affected village social relations, but less because of the inherent attraction of the town than because of the economic forces that sent Dalena people to town (Epstein 1962, pp. 311–335).

Only a beginning has been made in classifying types of village social structure. The earlier studies, like those of Maine (1881) and Baden-Powell (1896), served their authors' purposes but are no longer adequate. Bose (1958c) has noted certain indices for classification including the degree of concentration of artisans or tradesmen and patterns of social change. Alan Beals has classified villages in relation to internal conflict; his guidelines have been adopted in Bernard Cohn's survey of dispute resolution to distinguish four village types. The first is the small village of only one jati. The three other types are multicaste villages with, respectively, a single head, a dominant jati, and no single dominant jati (Cohn 1965, pp. 83–98). The nature of village leadership is a salient element in this typology. The appointed officers of a village may or may not assume leadership roles but the functions of each office are important ones in maintaining the village community.

Village Offices: the Headman

The social establishment of a village normally includes an official headman (or headmen) and a keeper of land records, the accountant. Both are agents of external authority, appointed by government and answerable to it. The headman is a member of the village who has specified duties and receives some pay for fulfilling them. He is usually a landowner, or at least one of the more substantial personages in the village. As a permanent resident he is subject to whatever social pressures his fellow villagers can exert on a co-resident. The accountant, however, need not be a member or old resident of the village, and in some states, the Punjab for example, it was official policy that he not be posted in his own village. In such places, and wherever the accountant is a sojourning stranger, the power he can wield for his own purposes tends to be great.

The headman's office goes by various names; its official functions are much the same throughout India. He is first of all the collector of land taxes. For doing this he receives a commission on the total amount collected or gets some rent-free land for his use. Secondly, he is the local link with the police. He is charged with keeping order in the village, and if some disorder occurs, it is he who must report it forthwith to the nearest police station. If the village employs watchmen, he supervises them; if the police require a weekly report, he has to send it in, naming any strangers in the village. Should a fight be in the making, he is supposed to try to break it up, and if he foresees an outbreak of violence he should call in the police before it occurs. In some places he reports the vital statistics; everywhere he must look after visiting government officials and should give them the impression that their orders and desires will evoke quick response. He is expected to act as the representative of the villagers when they want something from the authorities.

The position of headman is usually hereditary, though government officials can remove a headman for cause and shift the office to another family. The appointing officials may decide that there should be more than one headman—in Ramkheri village there are three, each responsible for a different part of the village. In Maharashtra, there are usually two, the revenue headman and the police headman. In the Kondmals region of Orissa, the village headmen have the police function, but the taxes are collected by a headman who has charge of a number of villages (Bailey 1957, p. 148).

With the headman's official duties go nonofficial functions. A headman may not be one of the actual leaders of his village or even of his jati-group, but the fact of his connection with police and officials can give him an advantage. In village eyes it endows him with potent influence, as it often does in fact. Police and other officials regard a cooperative headman as their man in the village and they are inclined to listen to him and to back him.

Because of this aura of influence, a headman may be called on to arbitrate disputes. He sits on the traditional village council, and is likely to be its chairman, insofar as there is a chairman. Often he leads in village ritual, functioning for all the inhabitants. This is especially true in the larger ceremonies in which all the villagers collectively stand before the gods (cf. Mayer 1960, pp. 112–114). When a group goes from the village to the district headquarters with a request for some village project, or attends on a political notable, or seeks a favor of a high official for the village, the headman is expected to be with them.

The actual influence of a headman depends partly on his personal abilities and social qualifications, which are quite like those we have noted for an alliance leader, and partly on the social structure of his village. Thus in Kumbapettai of Tanjore district, the headman is a nonentity. He is one of the dominant Brahmins there and they do not take kindly to any special preeminence of one of their number. They traditionally ruled the village without need for an effective headman (Gough 1955, pp. 43–44). In contrast, there is the headman of Chandipur in West Bengal. As the richest man of the ruling jati, he runs the village like a rustic dictator (Nicholas 1963, p. 1195). Supreme, also, but more in village esteem than in actual power, is the headman of Gopalpur in northern Mysore. Beals notes that the average villager of Gopalpur sees the headman as one who is wise and admirable and in every way superior. They take their disputes to him to be settled and are glad to obey him, even though many realize that he has a good many faults. For them he is "our Gauda," our headman. "Gopalpur creates its Gauda because the village has a need for a superior being, one beyond the ordinary"; that his life is really one of "loneliness, misery and fear" is of little concern to them (Beals 1962, pp. 53–63).

Most headmen are not ciphers or autocrats or presumed paragons. They are more often like the headmen of Shamirpet in Andhra or of Ramkheri in Madhya Pradesh, well-to-do men of respectable lineage and eminent jati. Their jati need not be ritually high but is almost always one that is powerful and respected in the locality (Dube 1955b, pp. 45–46; Mayer 1960, pp. 96–97). Such headmen maintain their influence by consulting with jati or alliance leaders on any issue of consequence; their power is tempered by the need for support from the leaders of their own and of other jatis. The appointment of a headman from among its members generally strengthens the power of a jati-group that is already strong. The office supports its power and can be used to increase it.

As new agencies for social and economic development come into a village, the headman does not have quite so strong a hold on communication with governmental authority. Other villagers come to have regular contacts with officials. The headman's grip weakens further when more villagers become educated enough to deal effectively with officials. Nevertheless, the village headman is usually someone to be reckoned with in village life. A visitor who ignores him may be resented not only by his close partisans but also by those villagers for whom he represents the village as a whole community.

Village Offices: the Accountant and Others

The accountant's office is quite a different one, more narrowly restricted to the one function of keeping the land records. It is one of the very lowest ranks of the government bureaucracy and is about as poorly paid as is the post of schoolteacher. The accountant is officially subordinate to the headman, and yet in his own sphere he may be one of the most powerful men in a village. This is because he is the sole guardian, sometimes the only interpreter, and the single recorder of the official documents that give rights to land.

The ordinary villager, as Lewis observed in Rampur, has no way of checking on the accuracy of the accountant. In order to challenge any record that he makes it is necessary to go through extremely costly and time-consuming litigation, perhaps up to the High Court (Lewis 1958, pp. 330–337). Moreover, any changes in the records which the accountant slips in without the owner's knowledge, may become legal if they remain unchallenged for a period of years— four years in the Punjab, five or seven in other states. Since even a literate, well-educated man cannot easily follow the accountant's quite technical details, a villager can hardly afford to antagonize the accountant.

The power of the accountant is vividly sketched in the Wisers' study of Karimpur village, east of Agra. There the accountant's records include the crop grown on a plot of land, its value, and the various rights held on it. He notes all changes in ownership, inheritance shares, mortgages, rents, and sales. Because many in the village cannot read and check his accounts, he possesses "powers which he, as a low-grade agent, could hardly be expected to disregard." In one case he could threaten, by indirect but unmistakable hints, to drop the name of one of the five owners of a grove. The unfortunate one had to pay something to him, else in a few years the omission of his name from the record would cost him his rights in the grove. "The possibility of its detection amid the masses of records are slim. Once when such a discrepancy was noted by an examining officer, the accountant blamed the carelessness of his assistant."

In another case a widow rented out her land for a term of five years. While she was on a lengthy visit to her relatives, the accountant transferred title to the land to the renter for a payment of fifty rupees. In this instance the widow took the case to court and, showing unusual diligence, won back the land. But the accountant was only reprimanded (Wiser 1963, pp. 107–111).

An accountant's common tactic is delay. If a man needs a copy of his title to some land, or if a sale or a mortgage must be recorded, the accountant can easily claim that he is swamped with work and hold off until the additional fee he demands, beyond the usual unofficial fee he always gets, is paid. In Rampur the purchase price of a plot is commonly recorded at a much higher price than was actually paid. This is a kind of title insurance because others may later challenge the sale and claim prior ownership on some legal technicality. But even if they win the case, they must give back to the purchaser the price which was recorded. The entry of this inflated price calls for another emolument for the accountant (Lewis 1958, pp. 332–333).

So villagers try to keep on the right side of the accountant. He gets gifts of grain, vegetables, milk, and fuel; often he has a good house rent free. For special transactions he gets a cow or a buffalo or even land. Some of his bills may be forgiven by a village merchant who is also a landowner. It is not only the small tiller of the soil who treats him with respect. Large landowners, even high officials, are sensitive to his power.

An officer of the Indian Civil Service, Mr. B. S. Grewal, in discussing this subject with me, told of calling on the Speaker of the Punjab Legislative Assembly in the days before independence. This eminent personage, knighted by the King-Emperor, was sitting on a cot beside a village man and was addressing him respectfully by a highly honorific title. After the villager had gone, the host explained that his visitor was the accountant in his ancestral village, where he owned land. Without the accountant's good graces, even he would be at a loss in his village. Mr. Grewal added that from his experience as Financial Commissioner of the Punjab in the 1960s, he found that the accountant was then still a very powerful figure in Punjab villages.

An accountant, for his part, can remind the villagers that he has to bear extraordinary expenses. In Karimpur, the accountant had to pay his immediate superior the equivalent of a month's salary. He had to appear before officials at district headquarters and this required more expensive dress as well as travel expenses. More to the point, however, is that his official association with educated people gives him motivation to improve his status, to give his sons an education, and to marry his daughters expensively into educated families.

Though at a disadvantage in any dispute with the accountant, villagers are not entirely helpless. They may take the records to court, as the Karimpur widow did, and get them corrected or, as happened in a village of Poona district, the villagers can get the accountant transferred. The accountant in Poona had overreached himself by using the office for the improvement of his jati as well as of his purse. He was a Harijan and he provided a public celebration on the birthday of the Harijan leader, the late Dr. Ambedkar. He procured contributions from non-Harijans for the purpose, but he soon was removed (Orenstein 1959, p. 421). And in Rampur, accountants "who overstep themselves are in danger of being killed by disgruntled groups" (Lewis 1958, p. 332).

The accountant in Rampur is in a special position of strength because he happens to have some of the functions performed by village headmen elsewhere. He is the sole representative of the revenue department in that village and is the main contact between villagers and other government officials. In other places, where the office is hereditary and the incumbent is a resident of the village, as is true in South India generally, his unofficial powers seem to be much diminished (cf. Srinivas 1955b, pp. 6, 12). Presumably he can aid one alliance rather than another, but apparently he does not levy tribute quite so heavily as does an accountant who is posted to a village for a few years and feels he must mine the territory while he can.

The new programs of land reform and of consolidation of holdings have given fresh opportunities to the accountant. Where there is a maximum limit to the amount of acreage a family can cultivate, it is he who can report the distribution of holdings that is to the family's best advantage. And when tenants receive rights to a plot after cultivating it for a certain number of years, the accountant can see to it that the actual period does not become a matter of record. When Mrs. Wiser returned for another look at Karimpur after thirty-two years, land was even more difficult to obtain than before, and one of the ways of getting it was "by bribing the village land recorder to alter a record" (Wiser 1963, p. 155).

Yet the accountant's monopoly is being weakened as more men can read the records and more dare complain to higher officials about a faked record. And when the accountant is drawn into responsibility for village welfare, his powers change. Thus in Wangala the accountant is a hereditary official of a Brahmin jati, as is common in that part of Mysore. His superior officer, called the Revenue Inspector, can join with the village accountant in giving or withholding favors. He can turn a blind eye to the cultivation of waste lands belonging to the village; he can be permissive about overdue taxes or illegal land transactions.

In recent years, however, the Inspector and his staff have been given the task of encouraging villagers to be progressive. For this an Inspector needs the cooperation of the villagers and on such cooperation depends his promotion. So for weeks before a scheduled visit of the Deputy Commissioner of the district, the Revenue Inspector, in his city clothes, was seen persuading the villagers—who in this prosperous place are not much concerned about official visits—to sweep the street and put up a decorated arch of welcome. At this time the Revenue Inspector is most amenable to requests from the villagers. On one occasion he had to meet a quota of land to be given as part of a Bhoodan campaign for voluntary redistribution of land. A deal was arranged whereby two acres of useless land were donated, and one acre of the village's common land, potentially very productive, was quietly transferred to a magnate (Epstein 1962, pp. 142–143).

Such stirrings among revenue officers, however, are still small, and in very many villages the accountant retains a good deal of negative power to hamper land and crop transactions and positive power to augment his income. One effect of these powers has been to lift the status of the local jati from which accountants are recruited. Moreover, the accountant's role has commonly been understood by villagers as that of a government servant who is alien to the village even though he resides in it and has power over its inhabitants. This may have set a pattern for such newer roles as that of the tubewell operator, also a government servant, also an alien, and also one whose power must be parried with cash.

The schoolteacher is another government employee who has long been a fixture in many villages. He too, is often a stranger who temporarily resides in the village but, except when he is a person of outstanding personal ability, he generally has little power or influence in the place where he teaches. A schoolteacher may be dedicated to his profession, but his pay permits little concentration on it. He must scrounge about for extra jobs—writing petitions, tutoring, keeping a store. If a teacher has land in his own village he is usually off just as soon as his school duties are over to look after it. The schoolteacher could be of much more consequence both for the village and for the whole society if he were a more effective link between the village and the larger culture, as other functionaries act as links between village and government. But the educational administrative system is such that the schoolteacher is more often a part-time caretaker of children than a full-time agent of the civilization.

There are other village servants, such as watchmen, scavengers, a number of functionaries to serve visiting officials; they are commonly given the use of land in return for their services (cf. Dube 1955b, pp. 51–53). Their duties have more to do with the inside organization of the village than with its relation to the wider society.

Villagers Together and Apart

Day-to-day relations between people of different jatis are usually economic and ritual transactions rather than friendship or other voluntary exchanges. A man's economic dealings are centered in his village and the villages of the close vicinity. As has been noted, any one village does not usually include all the needed specialists. The locational aspect of jajmani relation is illustrated in an account of Sherupur village (Faizabad district, U.P.); most of the thirty-five persons who render jajmani services for Sherupur do not live in the village itself, but in settlements within a two-mile radius (Gould 1964, pp. 26–28).

A landowner maintains relations with some specialists who live at a distance. One may be the genealogist who, in some parts, appears periodically to bring his register up to date, extol the merits of the line, and collect his fee. There may be a goldsmith in town to whom the householder regularly goes when he needs jewelry. Often there is a roving beggar or holy man who makes the rounds of his own begging circuit. But all these are occasional relations; the main locale for economic interchange and ritual services is within the village and its close neighborhood.

Considerations of local supply and demand affect this interchange as we noted in discussing jajmani relations. When the one barber in Totagadde in Mysore died leaving no successor the landowners searched about for a replacement, found one, and installed him in the village. He then demanded and received several increases in pay. The village leaders reluctantly agreed to his demands rather than go to the trouble of finding yet another replacement (Harper 1959b, p. 770).

In Shanti Nagar, near Delhi, the supply of barbers is limited because barbers find more lucrative employment in the city. The only person available to shave the village men, when I visited the village, was an eleven-year-old boy. He fulfilled the duties of his jati with on-the-job training and while he was doing so, Stanley Freed observed, a good many of the village notables would appear with bloody, hacked faces after their morning shave.

Sometimes the supply is greater than the demand. In Sirkanda, for example, the artisans have lost a good part of their clientele because of the competition of bazaar goods and have had to turn to such ancillary occupations as brewing illicit liquor. The competition among them for clients has made for bitter hostilities among artisans (Berreman 1962b, p. 390). The classic case of oversupply is that of weavers. They became superfluous all over India as cheap factory-made textiles became available. Many had to become landless laborers and in some areas their jati status declined as a result of their impoverishment (cf. Baines 1912, pp. 62–64).

Supply and demand also operate at the other end of the social scale. There is typically an increased demand for the services of Brahmin priests where families of lower jatis prosper. One characteristic act of their mobility efforts is to secure priestly services that they previously could not get because they were too poor in purse and too polluting in jati practice. Conversely, the services of Brahmin priests may be dropped, as the Jats of the Delhi area did under the influence of the reformist Arya Samaj movement. The priests there had to turn to other occupations (Lewis 1958, pp. 77–78). Such continual adjustments in jajmani services, whether of Brahmins or of washermen, have been worked out in the context of the village locality.

Most of a villager's informal social relations are characteristically with others of his jati or of a jati of the same bloc as his. There are usually few voluntary associations that might foster friendship across jati lines. The possibility of such friendships depends partly on the size of the village and of the jati-group as well as on the rigor of social separation. In contrasting two villages of different size, the smaller village of Gopalpur with its larger neighbor Gannapur, Beals notes that "In Gopalpur, friendships are frequently developed between people belonging to different jatis; in Gannapur, friends tend to come from the same jatis" (1962, p. 87).

Friendships across the main jati blocs are virtually unknown in Sripuram in Tanjore district, where people of each of the three main divisions keep rigorously apart. Friendships are made between men within each division and not between men of different divisions. Several young schoolteachers of different Brahmin jatis in the village are friends, but "I have not come across a single instance of such personal friendship within the village between a Brahmin on one hand, and a non-Brahmin or an Adi-Dravida on the other" (Béteille 1962, p. 145).

Much the same situation is shown in the responses to a questionnaire survey on relations within a village carried out by Karve and Damle in three Maharashtra villages (1963). Though the three are very different from each other, the survey results in all are quite similar.[2] In residence patterns, the "nearest neighbors tended to be

[2] One of the three villages, Vorkate in northern Satara district, is a "typical Maratha village with many castes," nucleated in form and located in relatively flat terrain. The second, Ahupe in Poona district, is a more scattered village in hill country; its people are largely of a jati that is "semi-tribal." The third, Karal on the coastal strip of Ratnagiri district, is a dispersed village of separate garden-compounds with no single jati in the majority, unlike the other two villages. Included in the survey also were

agnates or affinal kin. The larger circle of neighbors consisted of caste fellows. Then came other touchables."

Each Harijan jati occupies a separate section, segregated from the other untouchable jatis as from the houses of "touchable" jatis. A villager has most interaction with those who are kin as well as neighbors, next greatest is with those of the same jati or jati bloc. Tenants are mainly of the same jati as their landlord (except in one village), but the borrowing of money and other economic transactions are not so much confined within the jati. Jajmani relations—called *balutdari* in Maharashtra—were then being carried on in all three villages, though the traditional pattern was changing. A majority of those interviewed found them useful and necessary. When a family needs help, whether in the field or in the home, it gets help first from kin in the village, then from jati fellows, and only for a few particular needs, such as medicines, from any others.

Almost every family entertains guests or gives hospitality to fellow villagers, but the guests are almost entirely from one's own kin and jati. Friendships are with people of one's own jati "except extremely few genuine friendships across the caste." [3] And in these few friendships, the man of lower jati may be entertained with tea and food in the house of his higher ranking friend, but he washes his own dishes and they are kept separately from those of the household (Karve and Damle 1963, p. 73).

In all, a very large part of a man's, and even more of a woman's, social relations in these Maharashtra villages are with his kin and within his jati-group. "Thus we find that most of the intercourse of an individual was confined to kin-groups and the inter-group intercourse was regulated by the caste code" (Karve and Damle 1963, pp. 71–75). Some friendships are maintained between people of different echelons of rank, but the difficulties in the way of doing so are considerable in these as in most other villages, so that most friendships are between villagers of about the same social level.

---

families from a modern farm colony near Poona. In all, members of 343 families were interviewed.

[3] From the tables given by the authors, it appears that 230 villagers of touchable jatis answered a question asking each respondent to name six friends. Of these, 155 named friends only in their jati, 63 included names from other touchable jatis, 3 named only kinsmen, while 9 (just under 4 percent) gave some names of untouchables (Karve and Damle 1963, pp. 236–239, 475–476).

This is also noted in Gumperz's discussion of communication in Khalapur (Saharanpur district, western U.P.). Khalapur villagers of all jatis came into regular contact with those of other ranks, but "interaction among different groups is limited to certain neutral spheres." Free discussion and interchange of opinion go on mainly in the social nuclei of men who regularly come together in a certain man's house or other place. There are no comparable places or occasions for frequent daily communication. Even the communications for development workers and other agents of government are mainly transmitted through these groups.

Such a social nucleus is usually, but not always, made up of men of the same jati. Gumperz comments that "intercaste friendships are fairly frequent among touchable classes with roughly similar positions in the hierarchy" (Gumperz 1964, pp. 91–92). In another account of Khalapur, close friendships are said occasionally to cut across "caste group lines, though they never existed, so far as we know, when ritual distance between two men was very great" (Minturn and Hitchcock 1966, pp. 32–33).

These close friendships in Khalapur frequently begin in school and are maintained by former classmates in adult life. This is becoming increasingly common through the land, and as educational opportunity widens so does the likelihood that a man's fast friends will be drawn from a wider circle than that of his jati. So is it also with broadening economic participation. As economic participation becomes less closely bound to jati occupation, so do mutual economic interests bring together men of different jatis. But these trends are not yet very far advanced and the intimate interchange and free cooperation of most village men are still mainly with jati fellows and status compeers.

Even so, an Indian village is not the "sink of localism," of invidious discrimination and ruthless exploitation, that Dr. Ambedkar, revered leader of the Harijan movement, said that it was, nor is it the harmonious, resilient "little republic" that Sir Charles Metcalfe supposed it to be (Ambedkar 1948, p. 39). It is home for those who live in it. Despite the many allegiances that each one in it has with kin and jati mates in other villages, with specialists, mentors, or patrons in towns and other centers, and in spite of the deep and sometimes bitter cleavages among its inhabitants, it typically remains a real community. As McKim Marriott has written after depicting these fractionating forces, "But I am still compelled to go on to say that the village of Kishan Garhi is like a living thing, has a definable structure, is conceptually a vivid entity, is a system—even if it is one of many subsystems within the larger socio-politico-religio-economic system in which it exists." Marriott goes on to tell how Kishan Garhi, like most other Indian villages, is a vital nucleus of economic activity, a main nexus of social activity, a principal stage for political striving (1955b, pp. 176–178).

Our preference for the term "villagers" for most of the people included in this study is founded on just these functions of the village in Indian society.

CHAPTER **20** The Village: Internal Regulation

Iɴ those villages where one jati-group is clearly the most powerful, its leaders and panchayat are likely to manage the whole village. They may not be able to manage themselves very well; as we have seen, a dominant jati-group may well split into bitterly opposed alliances. Nevertheless they characteristically unite against a threat to their controlling power and so maintain their joint control over the other villagers.

In villages where no single jati-group is in firm control, several jati-groups or alliances vie for local power and, on occasion, unite for the village welfare. The arena for such contests and the vehicle for village solidarity is commonly the village panchayat. The panchayat, for a village as for a jati, is better understood as a pattern of dialectic, decision, and action, rather than as a formal political body with clearly defined duties. A panchayat helps in crystallizing and formulating village opinion; it is an agency for maintaining village order and is often also a means of reflecting and eventually legitimating changes in the local order. A dominant jati-group exerts control through its panchayat.

Dominant Jatis

In his listing of the "dominant castes" of India, Baines classified them as a special kind of landholder (Baines 1912, pp. 42–46). Although land is usually the basis of their position, their power rises not from one but from a combination of forces. For a jati to be truly dominant, its members must not only be numerically strong in the village or locality, but they must also be prepared to exert their economic and political power. They are able, if necessary, to field a band of determined men who will discourage dissidents by force

(Srinivas 1959a, pp. 1–2). Usually they are of respectable ritual rank. Nowadays some of them are likely to be educated enough to deal with officials and so to facilitate the holding of power. Importantly, they think of themselves as entitled to rule the village. Some jati-groups that are numerically large in their villages are nevertheless not dominant, not so much because their members are deficient in economic strength and social status but mainly because they lack a self-image as rulers.

The families of a dominant jati-group usually control a good proportion of the village land.[1] The ruling landowners tend to feel that they really are the village and all others in it are there only as their dependents or hangers-on. "In a sense, then," Lewis says of Rampur near Delhi, "the other castes, even the Brahmins, are in the village at the sufferance of the *Jats*" (1955, p. 155). It is possible to speak of "the" Jats in the village—even though there are deep factions among them—because they can stand as one if they see a real challenge to Jat authority and will unite against any who dare challenge Jat supremacy.

Because they control the principal means of production, the dominant families can dispossess other villagers of their livelihood. Thus the dominant Rajputs of Khalapur can threaten to take away house sites, fodder supply, even latrine areas from other villagers (Minturn and Hitchcock 1966, p. 48). The dominant Thakurs of Senapur determined not only the kinds of service that their clients should give them, but also what these clients were required to give to each other (Rowe 1963, p. 42).

In Rampura near Mysore City, each patron of the dominant Okkaligas is a combination of master to his clients, landowner to his tenants, creditor for village debtors, and main employer of a retinue of dependents. He thus holds a multiple economic grip on villagers of all jatis (Srinivas 1955b, pp. 26–31). This jati-group is firmly in control. Its leaders settle disputes, both small and large;

[1] The Brahmins of Gamras near Kanpur are both ritually highest and numerically largest in their village, but, as was noted earlier, they are not the dominant group. They are relatively poor, fifth among the village jatis in per capita income, and they are internally at odds. K. N. Sharma writes in a personal communication that only two of the Brahmin men are listened to respectfully by other villagers on secular matters.

In another village of U.P., Karimpur in Etawa district, the Brahmins do control much land and they also control the village (Wiser 1963, pp. 14–19).

they plan and oversee joint activities; they represent the village to outside authorities. A disputant who deliberately tries to take his quarrel outside the village for settlement is declared guilty of slighting the local patrons. "His action is, in effect, a declaration of 'no confidence' in them, and he will soon be made to realize that he has incurred their wrath. Nemesis is swift in an Indian village when people are bound to each other by a multitude of ties" (Srinivas 1959a, p. 9). Also, magnates in other villages are likely to support the local patrons, whose help they may need in arranging a match, securing a loan, or keeping their own political premises tidy.

These Okkaliga leaders—whose jati is classed as Shudra—rule over the local Brahmins, yet they take care to show formal respect to them. When a Brahmin of the village is in difficulties, he is apt to go to one of the Okkaliga patrons for help and advice. Should a Brahmin challenge the power of the village leaders he may be called to task. The headman of one village of the region once disciplined an arrogant Brahmin priest by imposing a boycott on him. "The high ritual position which this Brahmin occupies does not free him from the secular control of the dominant caste" (Srinivas 1959a, p. 8).

So strong and esteemed are the Okkaliga patrons of Rampura (Srinivas uses the term "Peasant" for their jati name; we take his terms for this and the other jatis) that they are asked to settle affairs internal to other jatis. When a Lingayat priest brought two loose women to live with him, the indiscretion was really his own affair and that of the local Lingayat jati. But when these women tried to join with the proper wives of other Lingayat priests at a ceremony it was too much. One of the Lingayat priests appealed to the Okkaliga headman to see to it that the loose women did not join in the sacred cooking, and the headman did indeed stop them.[2]

Similarly, the Peasant elders of a nearby village arranged the terms by which a Muslim divine would serve his congregation. When later these Muslims could not agree among themselves, they

[2] Rampura has had an unusually stable and firm village government, Srinivas observes, because the two principal Peasant leaders have been friends rather than opponents. Their fathers were also powerful men, but they were enemies and headed two of the main factions. Friendship between the two present leaders was founded "in the teeth of their fathers' opposition" and has resulted in advantage for the village as well as for the jati-group (1959a, p. 7).

informed the Peasant elders that they would thenceforth bring their disputes to them. "This highlights a feature of rural social organization in this area, the council of the dominant caste tries to create a structure of authority within each group it has to deal with, though its efforts frequently fail" (Srinivas 1959a, p. 12). They feel responsible for village government because of their paramount position and so they try to devise ways of maintaining the several parts of the village order.

Still, they do not attempt to reach into every dispute. When a council of washermen from several villages met in Rampura, no Peasant leader attended, holding that the matter under dispute was for the washermen to thrash out among themselves. The untouchables of the village try to settle their own disputes without recourse to their patrons. The patrons in turn are very reluctant to have untouchable children in the school and to allow them to improve their position. They want to keep the cheap labor and the menial services that the untouchables provide (Srinivas 1959a, pp. 4, 8–9).

On occasion the dominant landowners may interfere drastically in another jati's domestic affairs; a patron is especially likely to intervene if one of his favorite clients is in danger. Srinivas mentions one Okkaliga panchayat that imposed two fines on a fisherman accused of making false charges against a kinswoman. The larger fine was to go to the Okkaliga common fund and the smaller to the fisherman's jati council. They also threatened the fisherman with expulsion from his own jati if he repeated the allegation. Such a threat is quite extraordinary; the leaders of one jati are rarely in any position to impose outcasting in another. The powers and presumption of this dominant jati are unusually great (Srinivas 1959a, p. 11).

Another example of a strongly dominant jati-group is that of the Brahmins of Kumbapettai village in Tanjore district. Their rule has been loosened in recent years, but they were still the actual managers of the village when Kathleen Gough studied the village in the 1950s. Their council would intervene in disputes within other jati-groups. In family quarrels in the other jatis, if one of the parties to the quarrel was not satisfied with the judgment of his own elders he would carry the matter to his Brahmin landlord. That patron then would consult with other landlords whose clients had an interest in the matter and together they would arrange a settlement.

The dominant jati-group can also impose collective punishment.

The lower jatis of the village have strong organizations for the speedy settlement of disputes, and this is partly because the over-lords may punish the whole jati-group if a quarrel among them results in serious trouble. These Brahmins do not have a strong jati organization of their own, but "the fact that they are the administra-tors is itself a source of unity among the Brahmins." No matter how acrimonious their own disputes may be, they generally unite against offenders from the lower groups. Thus when some Harijans broke the traditional order of precedence at the harvest festival in 1952 and drove their cattle through the streets before the non-Brahmin jatis did so, the Brahmin elders fined all the Harijans of the village collectively. As in Rampura, these dominant landowners try to keep agents of their authority within each jati-group. They reserve the right to depose a headman of a lower jati if he displeases them in any way (Gough 1955, pp. 44–47; 1960, pp. 37, 47–51).

Yet dominance is always tempered by dependence. A ruling jati-group needs the help and services of the other villagers; patrons can-not afford to alienate their clients completely. Even in so tightly controlled a village as Kumbapettai, the power of Brahmins is limited in several ways. A Brahmin offender who has trespassed in the Harijan quarters or who has been caught in sexual relations with a Harijan woman may be punished by the Brahmins themselves. These Brahmins may even look the other way if a youth of higher jati is beaten by those whom he has offended. Another constraint on their power can be felt when a tenant of low jati is pushed beyond the limits of endurance by a repressive landowner. He stands before the temple and invokes the curse of the goddess on the oppressor. Brahmins who know that they have pressed too hard greatly fear the curse. As do other dominant landowners, these claim to have a kind of paternal affection for their tenants and servants so long as the lower jatis stay in their traditional place (Gough 1960, pp. 49–50).

In Khalapur at the other end of India, the dominant jati of Raj-puts is also strongly entrenched. They too recognize their depend-ence on the jatis who serve them. In one instance they gave way a bit to a complaint from a sweeper who had been beaten by a Rajput whose potatoes had been damaged by the sweeper's cow. The sweepers of the village stand together; they perform services that the Rajputs are very reluctant to lose. Hence the sweepers were able to extract the semblance of an apology from the Rajput who had done the beating (Minturn and Hitchcock 1966, pp. 48–49).

There are always some limits to the power of a dominant jati in its village, but how greatly that power is constrained by dependence on other jatis rests in good part on the strength, unity, and will of the subordinates.

Dynamics of Dominance

The three examples of Rampura, Kumbapettai, and Khalapur are all villages that are managed by a strongly dominant jati-group. There are many villages in which no single jati-group is dominant over the others.[3] Thus in Bisipara in Orissa, two jati-groups confront each other as rivals for leadership. In other places one alliance of jati-groups competes for power with another alliance (cf. Bailey 1960b, p. 260; Nath 1962, p. 1877; Atal n.d., pp. 5–6).

Such competition occurs in Ramkheri (Dewas district, Madhya Pradesh), where the Rajputs are the traditional leaders but their authority is not overridingly powerful. They own more land, animals, and equipment than do members of any other jati-group and are also the largest employers. But there are rich families in other jatis also, and a few other jati-groups are nearly as well off as the Rajputs. The Rajputs, with 12.9 percent of the population, are second numerically to the Khatis, farmers who made up 19.8 percent at the time of the study. (The Okkaligas of Rampura constitute nearly half their village, the Brahmins more than a third of Kumbapettai.)

The village headman in Ramkheri is a Rajput; Rajput elders are called on to help in judging disputes between jati-groups, but elders of other jatis are also asked to help. The Rajput leaders do not interfere with affairs internal to another jati, as the dominant leaders of Rampura do, nor is there any particular stigma, as there is in Rampura, about taking a dispute elsewhere than to the Rajput elders—even to the courts. These Rajputs are allied with nine other jatis in Ramkheri whose people follow their lead and emulate their manner. As against these allies, there is another set of jatis in the

[3] In a survey of five regions of India, Marriott characterizes the upper Ganges region as one in whose villages "political and economic powers are generally diffused among many independently acting families" (1960, p. 39).

village, of which the Khati farmers are the most prominent, who are vegetarian and who in general follow an ascetic-ritual style of life rather than the Rajput model (Mayer 1958a).

The traditional Rajput leadership is being challenged, mainly by rising men of the oil presser (Teli) and farmer (Khati) jatis. The Rajputs are becoming concerned with consolidating their old adherents and with attracting new allies (Mayer 1960, pp. 125–131). Although the Khatis are well based for leadership, only a few of their men seek to supplant the Rajputs. As a group the Khatis prize jati exclusiveness and purity; they emphasize thrift and work. The Rajputs pride themselves on their largesse and are always ready to drop their own work when some village activity is going on. The Rajputs think of themselves as civic leaders and rulers; the Khatis, as yet, do not. Mayer suggests that when some of the Khati villagers become headmen and civic leaders, the interests of other Khatis may well be different. "The behavior of a village caste group may, in fact, be found to vary with the responsibilities (and dominance) it has in the village" (1958a, p. 414).

The dynamics of dominance in a village parallel the dynamics of eminence within a jati. Given the pervasive perspective of hierarchy and the belief that one's own group is worthy of higher rank than it presently enjoys, a locally strong jati-group tends to reach for dominance over the other villagers. Once the members of such a group acquire a good measure of dominance, they feel impelled to consolidate and strengthen their control against potential challenge. To gain and to hold paramount power in a village, they need economic strength; in the traditional village economy strength resides in land.

All are not equally ambitious to rise and become dominant. Most of the Khatis of Ramkheri are not particularly interested in becoming big fish in the village pond. Yet at any given time some men in a village are seeking greater power. That power, once acquired by some families, tends to be extended to their jati-fellows in the village because powerful men are inclined and expected to favor their kinsmen. They also encourage the idea that one can be a leading influence in the village. Thus some Rajputs of Ramkheri are poor and insignificant men, yet they stand on their group's political prestige. These poorer Rajputs take care to act publicly in the manner of their leading lights. If one of the chief Rajput leaders is present at a meeting his jati-fellows defer to him, but when no influential Rajput is present, the lesser Rajputs take over and assume direction of discussion. Since Rajputs attend to village affairs more assiduously than do men of other jatis, they are apt to take charge of whatever concerns the whole village. "For the Rajputs, village leadership was a caste thing, for the other castes it seems to have been the role of one or two 'big' men of their caste" (Mayer 1960, p. 113; 1958, p. 425).

Once a jati-group can unitedly exert economic power its men tend to seek control of village political and ritual matters. "The more forms of dominance which a caste enjoys, the easier it is for it to acquire the rest" (Srinivas 1959a, p. 3). Its leaders may intervene in the internal affairs of other jati-groups and its council may assume jurisdiction over everything that concerns the village. Because of this tendency, some observers have said that the solidarity of the village is only the solidarity of its dominant group (Dumont and Pocock 1957b, p. 29). This is not really so, for the people of a village like Gopalpur can show considerable cohesion on occasion, although there is no strongly dominant jati-group in it (Beals 1962, pp. 33–41; 1964, pp. 103–104). Even stronger statements on the importance of the dominant caste have been made by F. G. Bailey. "The traditional system contains one dominant caste which alone has a corporate political existence: the other castes are its dependents and are not politically corporate" (1960b, p. 191, also pp. 169, 258–259; 1961, p. 12). This is not always so, as several case examples cited in this chapter illustrate. Thus in Khalapur in U.P. and in Rampura in Mysore, both villages with a strongly dominant jati, there is still scope for councils of other jati-groups and jatis. These councils regulate their own affairs and can have some effect on village affairs.

In Khalapur there are more than thirty jati-groups, each with its own panchayat. Each council tries to protect its members' interests and to uphold "its pattern of social behavior and religious values." The village council of Khalapur takes a wider jurisdiction, over disputes between people of different jatis and over cases of theft and other breaches of village peace and order (Retzlaff 1962, pp. 18–21). Neither in Khalapur nor in most other villages traditionally dominated by one jati does the dominant jati wipe out all independent corporate action by the subordinate groups. Such action has indeed been confined largely to their internal jati affairs. But the

evidence does not support Bailey's view that the traditionally dominant jati was the sole corporate political entity in a village and that
this was completely different from the modern situation in which
any large jati can be a corporate political body (Bailey 1960b, p.
191). A dominant jati may now find it more difficult to encroach
on the internal affairs of subordinate jatis or to cut them off from
a voice in village affairs quite so completely as was formerly possible. It is still true, however, that a dominant jati's coercive powers
can yield a kind of forced solidarity that otherwise may be lacking.

A dominant jati-group that is not Brahmin does not usually try
to demote the Brahmins from their high ritual status. Their leaders
may take charge in ritual matters, as in determining the order of
precedence at a ceremony, but they generally do so with some
display of deference to the officiating Brahmin. They do not seek
to usurp his ritual role and sacred status. For the most part, they do
not want that role for themselves, although they esteem it. The
local Brahmin is the symbol and often the exemplar of the principles
of purity. In honoring him they honor the ritual principle by
which much of their domestic and social behavior is regulated. "The
dominant caste," Dumont and Pocock write, "is consciously subject
to Brahmanic axioms but once the latter have been accepted and
the Brahmins have been 'fed,' the less conscious royal model comes
into play" (1957b, p. 33).

A paramount jati is likely, as has been noted, to separate into
competing alliances. Where no single jati-group is preponderant,
an alliance includes families of several jati-groups. In the long run
there is a continuous process of challenge and response among village groups, not only in a Toynbeean sense, but also in a direct face-
to-face way. The challenge comes from those who have been subordinate and who have gathered enough strength to think that they
can strike for higher place. The reaction may wreck the challenge;
the superiors and their descendants may continue to rule in the village and the region for centuries, but a driving force in the system is
that new challenges continually arise as new sources of strength are
found by potential challengers.

This dynamic favors the emergence of a dominant jati in a local
system. In older settlements of the delta region of Bengal, for
example, one jati has commonly risen to be the dominant one; in the
newer villages on recently reclaimed lands clear dominance, even

when one jati is numerically strong, is not so evident (Nicholas 1963, p. 1189). Yet even in these relatively egalitarian frontier villages, the people's cognitive expectations are for hierarchy and that inclines their village organization toward stratification and dominance.

Thus in Radhanagar village (Midnapore district) 86 percent of the population of some 600 are of about the same ritual rank, indeed 77 percent of the village belong to the same Mahisya jati. There is not much differentiation in wealth among the village families, yet they regard their community as stratified (Nicholas MS. 1967, p. 7).

In their annual village festival several of the villagers are made into "temporary Brahmins," as Nicholas puts it, so that there may be a proper sacred hierarchy. Evidently the few and poor Brahmins resident in the village do not suffice for the hierarchical needs of this grand occasion (Nicholas MS. pp. 18–20). Nicholas points out also that in adopting token dowry payments and in the conduct of panchayats, the people of this village demonstrate their inclination toward hierarchy. "When the principal men of the village, acting as judges, mark themselves off as 'superior' to the general public, they take an important step toward legitimating the decisions which they hope to reach" (Nicholas MS. p. 32). Both in ceremonial and in panchayat activities, Nicholas finds, the people of this village believe that social hierarchy is necessary for legitimate social activity and that without it such events are imperfect and ineffective.

Village Panchayat

The elders and leaders of a village assemble in panchayat to cope with problems internal to the village and to deal with external threats or opportunities. If the internal order of the village is challenged, the council sessions serve as an arena for ascertaining public opinion and mobilizing power alignments. If a change in the power structure has clearly been accomplished, the village panchayat provides a means of publicizing and of validating the change. A panchayat is also gathered to face external incursions. Increasingly, a village panchayat takes on some of the entrepreneurial functions urged by government agencies.

Modern political leaders have placed very high importance on village panchayats as means for grass-roots political participation.

This is reflected in H. D. Malaviya's scholarly and comprehensive volume on village panchayats in India, written under the auspices of The Economic and Political Research Department of the All India Congress Committee. In it the author mentions that the very last document Gandhi signed was a draft constitution based on panchayats (1956, pp. 254–255).

The form and procedure of a traditional village council is like that described above for a jati council. It consists of all those men whose participation is needed for the assembly to reach a judgment that will hold. The number of participants depends on the nature of the issue for which a meeting has been convened. A falling out between two retainers of different landlords may require only an *ad hoc* meeting of the patrons to straighten out the quarrel. But a problem that seriously affects the whole village, one that perhaps endangers the reputation of all in it, requires a convocation of many of the household heads.

When there is a strongly dominant jati-group, its panchayat tends to be also the panchayat for the whole village. Their leaders decide both jati and village affairs. Elders of other jatis may attend a session but more as givers of evidence or receivers of information than as full participants. Where no one jati-group is paramount, a broader representation of leaders is needed for effective judgment. This broader base still does not include all groups and classes. Harijans usually attend only to serve as messengers. Women very rarely participate. And certain jati-groups may not want to participate. In Bisipara, the shopkeepers keep aloof from the village council in which the other touchable jatis participate. Their interests lie mainly beyond the village and they neither associate nor dissociate themselves with village affairs (Bailey 1957, pp. 192, 203).

The influence exerted by village leaders rests on the same attributes that were mentioned for jati leaders; most village leaders are the men of greatest influence in their jati as well. Typically they have the qualifications of wealth and family support, suitable age, and a history of proper use of their wealth; they also have time and interest for village affairs. A leader gains in influence if he is an effective speaker and if he presents himself as a firm, reliable yet humble person, or at least one who is not voraciously ambitious. To be effective, a village leader must balance off competing claims and should be able to switch personal styles, now being the loyal kinsman to a relative, now the amiable helper of authority, and altogether the friend and guardian of the whole village (cf. Hitchcock 1960, pp. 267–268; Minturn and Hitchcock 1966, pp. 15–16).

Assembled in panchayat meeting, the village leaders seek to redress ritual offenses, to calm secular disputes, to organize group enterprises. A jati-group council has similar functions, but the two have differing though overlapping jurisdictions. The jati-group council takes cognizance of cases having to do only with their own jati practices or only with their own members. People of other jatis, especially the higher ones, are not particularly concerned with such matters.

The difference between the two jurisdictions is illustrated in Rampura by the kinds of questions that each kind of council typically entertains. The jati-group council, Srinivas writes, considers such questions as: "Should R be thrown out of caste for having sex relations with an untouchable woman?; and, should J be granted a divorce from M?" The village council takes charge of such questions as these, "Who stole grass from X's field?; who set fire to Y's straw rick?; and, is Z speaking the truth when he says that P owes him a hundred rupees and not fifty?" (1959a, p. 7).

Some village councils assume executive and legislative as well as juridical functions. Thus over one year the council of Bisipara village in Orissa arranged for the regular cleaning of public places, saw to the upkeep of a temple, organized the repair of a dam, and decided on invitations to a village festival. It abolished certain perquisites of washermen and barbers, and it transferred rights to provide music from one Harijan jati to another. The council also listened to complaints by a herdsman against a washerman.

Though this is a vigorous council, there are some affairs over which it will not take jurisdiction. When a young Brahmin quarreled with his mother's brother, the council tactfully refused to intervene and simply put off discussion of the matter. Should a village man have "an indiscreet liaison" with a woman of lower rank, then it is his jati-group and not the village that takes notice and prescribes action. His indiscretion endangers the jati not the village; only his jati fellows will share in his defilement. The woman's jati may ignore her or, if the group's sense of self-respect has been touched, may punish her. But the affair is not normally turned into a dispute between two jati-groups; each is concerned only to discipline its own members. If, however, the woman has been taken by violence and against her will, that is quite another matter; it is comparable to any other kind of assault and can be taken to the village elders for redress (Bailey 1957, pp. 191–195).

An especially heinous misdeed may be taken up by both village and jati councils. Some offenses are so enormous that the reputation of the whole village as well as of the transgressor's jati is imperiled by them. As we mentioned on page 280, in Shamirpet incest in a family is one such crime, the killing of a cow (almost always accidental) by a Hindu is another. No single jati-group is dominant in Shamirpet yet the village council, at the time of Dube's study, was a strong one. It took over matters that might otherwise have been for a jati council. Because the village panchayat is sufficiently aggressive, "it has arrogated to itself a considerably wide range of powers" (Dube 1955b, p. 55).

In northern Kerala, two tiers of village panchayats were maintained because of the special rigor of jati separation in that region. The lowest jatis of a village were under the jurisdiction of the local Tiyyas, then small tenants and laborers (toddy-tappers by traditional occupation), who were themselves subordinate to the landowning Nayars and Nambudiris. The Tiyyas took some responsibility for maintaining order among the low jatis. Cases that could not be settled by the Tiyya elders were taken upward again to the landowners. One of the reasons for this delegation of dominance was that the distance pollution then observed in Kerala made it difficult for an arbitrator of higher rank to come close enough to a dependant of lowest rank to find out what the case was all about (Miller 1954, p. 413).

In addition to internal, judicial functions, a village panchayat commonly takes external, executive responsibilities, especially when the defensive unity of the village must be rallied. A panchayat is a means of gathering, consolidating, and giving effect to public opinion. If all in a village feel themselves threatened, public opinion is readily consolidated, especially, as we have seen, against the forces of government or of another village.

In Bisipara, for example, a post office had been experimentally established for five years. At the end of the period the Postal Department found that the office was running at a loss and decided to close it. The villagers not only would be inconvenienced by this;

they also would lose the prestige of having a post office in their own village. They petitioned against the decision, and the postal authorities replied that the service would be continued if the village would make good the loss for the five years past and guarantee that there would be no loss in the future. The village council met; no hint of faction divided them over this issue. "They replied by asking this question: If the post office had made a profit over the past four years, would it have given the money to the village?" (Bailey 1957, p. 193.) The author does not tell us whether the council succeeded in this effort, but he makes plain that all sides in the village were as one against the postal officials.[4]

Procedure in a village council follows that outlined in Chapter 16 for a jati or jati-group panchayat. Discussion of a problem is usually continued until a consensus satisfactory to all (or almost all) of the most powerful men is reached. If it appears that no agreement is possible at a session, the council meeting disbands and another is called later when some change of view may have come to pass (cf. Retzlaff 1962, pp. 23–25). One such change may result from the very act of arguing, as we have noted for the jati council of Chamars in Senapur; it occurs also in village councils. Even if a side loses its case, the act of venting its grievance and stating its justification apparently makes it easier for the members of the losing side to give their consent, albeit reluctantly, to a judgment that goes against them. Their tacit consent is usually necessary because voting on a proposition "with a majority carrying the issue and thereby binding the minority to that agreed decision, was and still is completely alien to the system" (Retzlaff, p. 24). A decision, if it is to stick, must have the consent, even though it may be reluctant or unspoken, of the main groups involved in the dispute.

After such general consent is obtained, the leaders try to enforce the decision. The powers they command are of the same kind that

---

[4] Other Bisipara cases that are discussed without reference to jati or factional interest are those in which the issues and the evidence are so clear-cut "that there can be little debate about who is in the right and who is wrong." Thus in the case of a young man who wrongfully abused a widow, there was no dissent in the council about fining him because he was obviously at fault. He belonged to a faction opposed to that to which the widow belonged, and perhaps that was why the matter was not brought before the elders of their common jati. In the village council hearing no factional consideration entered (Bailey 1957, pp. 193–194).

we have noted in the jati panchayat. They can impose penalties and fines and occasionally physical punishment. They can decree that the offender must provide a feast for the villagers before he is fully reinstated. Should the culprit refuse to submit to the judgment of the council, they can coerce him in many ways, as we have seen that a jati council may do. His axe may disappear, his cow get lost for days, his crop may be trampled. The services of washerman or carpenter may be stopped—or rendered so badly that it might be better to have none at all. His hay rick may catch fire, and he himself, however wary, may be waylaid on a dark night and beaten painfully. Nonviolence has been an important doctrine in the intellectual centers of the civilization and has a certain place in village ideology; violence has been a potent sanction in village as in jati politics.

The most dire penalty in the power of a village council, however, is not retributional violence, but the expulsion of the offender from village society. One who is so cut off is not necessarily also cast out of his jati; he may find shelter with jati fellows in another village. For gross transgressions, the offender may be cast out by both his village and his jati councils. A village council is inclined to go along with a jati council's strong verdict. But jati members are less apt to follow the village council's lead against a jati fellow.

Village leaders must show a high degree of outraged unanimity if their ostracism is to be successfully imposed and honored in other villages. Bailey found that in Bisipara such strong unanimity is evoked only in exceptional cases, as in the punishment of persons found guilty of keeping malignant spirits. In one such hearing, the defendants had to take a prior oath that they would abide by the council's decision and not call in government authorities to evade punishment if they were found guilty. "The plaintiff in such a case cannot get justice (as the village conceives justice) out of a Government court: the case must be conducted within the traditional juridical system." Four men were found guilty and fined. The one who had the largest fine, a washerman, demurred and was boycotted until, after two months, the council reduced the amount of the fine and he then paid it (Bailey 1957, pp. 157, 262–263).

When the village boycott of a man is effective, it is a most potent means of counterchange; yet occasionally an offender refuses to recant. He may feel strong enough to hold out, as some have done for jati boycotts (see pp. 300–304 above). A case of this kind occurred in Ramkheri when a prospering oil presser came in conflict with the Rajput leaders of the village mainly about some grazing land that he had begun to cultivate against their wishes. The economic issue did not come to a head directly but was fought out over quite another matter, about the kind of dramatic performance that should be staged at the Holi festival. The Rajput leaders decided to put on a much bawdier kind of play than some others could approve. After a confrontation on this matter, those who objected to the racy performance were threatened with ostracism. They all gave in with the exception of the oil presser, who had had a number of previous quarrels with the Rajput elders. He refused to yield and was boycotted, ostensibly because he would not agree to the choice of the play, actually because he was challenging the established powers.

At first no one would smoke with him or invite him to ceremonies; no craftsman or laborer would work for him. But he managed to keep going, and when Adrian Mayer was in the village, some four years after the boycott had been declared, he had survived and had partly broken the sanction. His lineage mates came to his domestic rites, which was excused because the ritual duties of agnatic kin are acknowledged to be paramount. But others had also resumed relations with him, "people who have ambitions of leadership in the village, who resent the present dominant group because of this, and so show their independence by accepting the invitations of the boycotted household" (Mayer 1960, p. 124).

Village Alliances and Changes in Power

Such resistance to panchayat decree usually indicates a change in power relations within the village. A successful challenge by one family encourages other challengers, who may well consolidate their forces against the previously ruling group to form a new or newly strengthened alliance. Participants in multi-jati alliances within the village, like those within a dominant jati, support each other for a variety of reasons.

One common reason for mutual support is economic; the dependents of a patron are also likely to be his adherents in village disputes. Another is kinship; the closer kin of a leader or challenger are apt to be his supporters. Jati is another factor in alignments; when alliance leaders who are of different jatis confront each other, each is likely to be backed by his jati fellows in the village unless they are his declared rivals. Common residence in the same neighborhood or ward occasionally impels a man to join one alliance rather than another. Having a common foe in the village is a great alliance binder.

Enmity within a jati-group and consequent adherence to rival alliances is illustrated among the potters of a delta village in West Bengal. The families of a potter lineage quarreled about marriage and land; four households came to be boycotted by the others of the lineage. These four then joined the alliance of the village headman, separating themselves from the alliance to which most potters belong, which opposes the headman and his jati. The jati of the headman, the Mahisya, is strong in this village. The Mahisya are cultivators, who elsewhere in the region rank fairly low and are ritually inferior to the local potters, but in the Mahisya-dominated villages, the potters are placed lower than Mahisyas. "The Potters feel that the Mahisyas have usurped all the positions of power and authority in the society, and they are subject to the will and whim of the dominant caste" (Nicholas and Mukhopadhyay, 1964, p. 29). Yet some potter families support Mahisyas because of the quarrel in a potter lineage.

Allegiance to a multi-jati alliance can be shifted just as adherence to an alliance within a jati-group can be. A man does have some option in his alliance affiliation. Usually only a strong personality or a highly incensed man will dare oppose the group to which his close kinsmen and jati fellows belong, but this does occur. Examples of alliance shifts can usually be found wherever opposed village alliances exist, as they do in a great many villages. Malcolm Darling, who knew Punjab villages well cites a knowledgeable estimate given to him in 1930 that only about 25 per cent of the villages of Rawalpindi district were free of deep factional splits and most of those only because they were too small to support rival sides (1934, pp. 41–42).

Alan Beals has analyzed some of the variables in factional conflict (1965, 1966). One variable is village size. From a survey of conflict in thirty villages of Gulbarga district, Mysore, Beals suggests that opposed factions cannot exist unless the village community is large enough to be divided into two viable segments. Villages of less than fifty households, he finds, do not support opposed alliances. "Life in such an infinitesimal community may provoke insanity or flight, but it is not likely to provide a suitable setting for party conflict" (1965, p. 18). Further, Beals finds that prolonged factional opposition will occur if the landowning jatis contain more than fifty households and represent over 50 percent of the village population (1965, p. 19). These tentative conclusions from a limited survey have to be tested against wider evidence, but they are in keeping with similar findings that were noted in Chapter 15 (Reddy 1952, p. 258; Singh 1961, p. 9). They indicate one possible variable in the incidence of village conflict.

An impressive case study, which highlights a different set of forces, is given in the previously mentioned account by Beals of conflict in Namhalli village, only a few miles from the city limits of Bangalore. Namhalli in 1952 had 603 persons living in 106 households; by 1960 it had 542 persons in 113 households. Economic conditions had improved in that short span so that more people worked and lived outside the village (hence the population decline) and more could set up separate households. With economic improvement came a marked betterment in village cooperation and a decrease in village conflict. When Beals lived in Namhalli in 1952, the village was in a condition of pervasive factionalism in which almost no villagewide cooperation could be managed. Hostility among the villagers was rife. An attempt to stage a village festival in 1952 ended in a series of grand quarrels between two alliances, which lined up some jati-groups against others and which split some of the larger jati-groups.

The year 1952 was a difficult one for the people of Namhalli. The period of prosperity that had begun in World War II had come to an end. There was a severe drought; some realized that opportunities for outside employment were shrinking and the traditional agricultural economy of the village could not possibly support the enlarged and continually swelling population. No fresh solutions were proposed. "On the contrary, old patterns of conflict merely became intensified, to the point where almost every meaningful interpersonal relationship became affected" (Beals and Siegel

1966, p. 128). The old patterns for resolving conflicts, within the family as within the village, could not be used effectively; mutual distrusts and enmities remained rampantly unresolved.

However, even when village cooperation was at a low ebb as it was in 1953 and 1954, most of the men rose to the common defense when there was threat of robbery by outsiders. They collaborated also when such major crimes as rape or poisoning were suspected. But the ordinary work of village maintenance was not done.

This condition continued until 1958 when several fortunate trends greatly eased the tensions. Jobs became available in nearby factories and bus service was provided to them. Agricultural income rose, partly because of the expanded market in the city. A new way of raising capital for village needs as well as for personal requirements, the chit fund, was successfully adopted (Beals and Siegel 1966, pp. 136–138).

By 1960, when Beals again studied the villagers, the roads were well maintained and the wells promptly cleaned. Although the village festival had not been resumed, there was less conflict within the village and more cooperative activities. The kind of close solidarity that used to be expressed in the village festival may no longer be required. "In the same way, village unity, being no longer a condition of survival, had ceased to be expected" (Beals and Siegel 1966, p. 138).

This Namhalli example illustrates how antagonism between alliances in a village can change over time and that alliance members can change toward a more solidary condition, just as individuals can change their alignments and drop old enmities. Alliances are not required features of village social structure as families and jatis are, but they are very common elements in it. Moreover, there is something of the same feeling about factional opposition in a village that there is about fraternal opposition in a family. Both are generated by forces in the social system and many villagers take part in them. Yet these same men, when their own particular quarrel is not in question, decry the prevalence of rivalries. Thus in Gopalpur where opposed groups are called parties, "Lineages, jatis, clique groups, and neighborhoods are regarded as desirable by people in Gopalpur; parties are considered to be a symptom of social disorder —the village divided against itself" (Beals 1962, p. 44).

The struggle for village power is not unique to village India.

Wherever there is power there is contest for it. The contest in Indian villages is sharpened by the prevailing perspective of hierarchy, which sees any strengthening of one's status rivals as a demeaning of one's self and one's side. Therefore any proposal or act of a rival that may redound to his advantage, even if it may also be of advantage to the whole village, is likely to be obstructed by his opponents. The situation in Senapur in the 1950s was like that of Namhalli in the early 1950s, when no faction and no leader or group of leaders was strong enough to organize the village for any sort of constructive action. Yet each faction was strong enough to block any decisive action on the part of the opposing groups (Cohn 1955, pp. 68–76).

Such impasses are very familiar to those who have worked in Indian villages. Yet there are also many villages, more like the Namhalli of 1960, in which villagewide enterprises for the common good are regularly carried on. We have noted that in Rampura in Mysore two of the most powerful men are allies and friends rather than rivals and enemies, to the benefit of the village; in Bisipara in Orissa two jati-groups are in confrontation, yet a number of joint enterprises are accomplished; in Shamirpet in Andhra the village council is an effective body, even though there are factional rivalries in the village.

An effective village council fulfills both short-range and long-range functions. At any one time it maintains village order and helps keep the particular social order of the village. But as that social order changes the panchayat sessions reflect the new social facts; the council eventually validates the changes, adapts them to the local society and the society to them.

In the recurrent process of maintaining village order a council has power to act in such matters as theft and assault, working in conjunction with or in evasion of the official police. Ceremonies of the annual cycle are arranged by the council. These are mainly agricultural and protective rites for the whole village. (Rites of the life-cycle are staged by kinsmen rather than by the village.) The council also looks to the relations among the jati-groups, especially to those status claims which seem to threaten the village order, as when Harijans try to reject their traditional, polluting services and to take on higher practices.

If the village council (in which Harijans rarely figure) does not itself take positive action, its members may tacitly condone any violent action taken. Thus the Balahi of Khargan and Khandwa districts of Madhya Pradesh, in the 1940s, were able to ride buses and trams, to send some of their children to school, even to draw water from a few village wells put in by government. Nevertheless, they were usually confined to separate residential sections of a village and often were not allowed to walk freely in the streets of higher jatis. In some villages a Balahi did not dare to wear a clean shirt or a waist cloth draped in the style used by the higher groups. Further, "several cases are known of Balahis who have received a severe beating because they refused to eat carrion or the leavings of a high caste dinner" (Fuchs 1950, pp. 58–59).[5]

The economic as well as the ritual rise of a Harijan is often resisted. Thus the stoneworkers of Gopalpur, who are categorized as "unclean meat eaters" because they will eat pork (though not beef), are ranked close to the bottom of the local hierarchy and have to live separately on the outskirts of the village. Yet by the 1960s some had acquired land and had achieved a middle economic position. There is far more friction, however, when a stoneworker tries to improve his economic position than when a man of higher rank tries to do so. When a group of stoneworkers bought some good land (their other lands are inferior) and one of their men began ploughing it, a number of higher ranking villagers attacked him with clubs and beat him severely. The attackers apparently had little to fear from council action because "repercussions are likely to be slight when a Stoneworker is beaten" (Beals 1962, pp. 37–39).

Such violent reactions probably are triggered by deep symbolic meanings as well as by direct economic or ritual rivalry. We have suggested that Brahmins generally receive at least lip homage from others in their village because they exemplify the purity principle by which all villagers—in some degree—regulate their lives. It may also be that Harijans exemplify the pollution principle, the inseparable counterpart of ritual purity, which equally is used to govern

---

[5] The author adds that the Balahis treat people of jatis "a shade lower than their own" with equal severity. "The Balahis are the first to complain if in school their children have to sit with children of a lower caste and they keep their distance from a Mehtar more carefully than any member of a higher caste" (Fuchs 1950, p. 59).

conduct. In the person of Harijans, other villagers have constant proof of the detriment of pollution. So long as they must guard themselves against pollution and yet be defiled by it daily, they are likely to resist allowing the exemplars of permanent pollution to divest themselves of that status because that brings into question a fundamental postulate of their social and personal life. The special inertia against Harijan rise will be considered again in the discussion of social mobility.

Although a village council helps to maintain order in the village and the social order of the village, the same order of power and rank is not preserved indefinitely. In the long run there are shifts and adjustments; some groups rise, others fall. Some of the lower and subordinate manage to garner secular resources and use them to raise their ritual rank. The village council is one locale in which this process becomes openly acknowledged and, if successful, where it is clearly validated.

This process is illustrated in Wangala in Mysore where the village council must include the heads of the major lineages in the dominant jati of "Peasants" (Vokkaligas). Eight lineages are regarded as major, and the participation of their elders is considered essential for a valid council judgment. Other Peasant lineages and households in the village are of lesser importance in council. One of these minor lineages came to be a major lineage through the efforts of its leader, one of the richest and most influential men in the village. His father had acquired wealth and this leader increased his patrimony. Through his economic strength he could exert pressure in village politics.

Being intelligent and purposeful, he was able to establish a firm political following on the basis of his economic strength. He spoke up in council meetings, and as a number of the council members were in debt to him they listened when he spoke. He became an integral part of these meetings and, without any particular discussion of the matter, his lineage has become recognized as one of the major lineages because he is clearly a major member of the council. This case shows, as the author notes, that economic mobility is based more on the individual's achievement while political mobility is more closely involved with a man's group (Epstein 1962, pp. 119, 127–128). It also indicates how the economic success of one man can benefit his kinsmen in the village.

This can occur for a whole jati-group as well as for a lineage. When one member becomes exceptionally prosperous, he is likely to see to the welfare of his jati fellows in the village, at least to the degree that they are his staunch allies rather than his challengers. Together they can use their wealth to take positions of greater influence in village politics. Over time their economic strength and new political influence are reflected in, channeled through, and therefore validated by sessions of the village council.

Such sessions can be very stormy because in them the throes of adaptation to changing circumstances are worked out. The forces for change may arise within the village or may impinge, as they often do, from outside the village. We look next at the external relation of the village, that is the regular relations of villagers with networks and centers beyond their village bounds.

CHAPTER 21

The Wider Ties of Village:
Centers and Regions

Oᴜᴛꜱɪᴅᴇ the circles of his kin, his jati, and his
village, a man carries on more intermittent social relations that are
nevertheless of high importance for him and for the whole social
system. Most men make regular trips to a nearby market, occasionally visit more distant sacred places, sometimes have direct contacts
with government officials. Specialists from outside come into the
village; there are merchants and hawkers, touring religionists and
peripatetic beggars, inspecting officials and policemen on circuit.
Some men in each village take link roles, connecting the village
community to the wider spheres of economics, religion, and government.

Each of these wider spheres can be described separately by the
analyst for purposes of descriptive clarity. But each is also part of
a larger whole and the nexus should not be neglected. In previous
chapters jati and village have been examined separately, but we
should note again here that the two are component subsystems
within a local social order. A villager usually moves without difficulty from one subsystem to another, taking the roles appropriate
to each as the situation warrants. For some purposes, especially
those of hearth and home, he acts as a member of his family and jati-
group. For certain economic, jural, and defensive purposes, he
acts in the capacity of a fellow villager. Occasionally he may be
uncertain about the proper role to take, as when he wants to join
an alliance opposed to that of his lineage mates. But in general
the obligations of each set of relationships are not greatly in doubt.

Neither is viable without the other; each provides necessary
inputs for the other. For the village community, the jatis provide
and maintain the main components, the jati-groups. For the jati,

the village provides the social matrix of specialization each jati requires. Thus village and jati are indeed separate when used for certain purposes by the participants and when analyzed with reference to those purposes by the observer. In other contexts of action and of analysis, the two are reciprocal subsystems within larger systems. The next larger systems, in turn, can be described as separate entities, but they should also be understood as subsystems within a total field of society and culture.

Main elements in these larger contexts are the relations among villages and especially between village and center. Kinship bonds, as has been noted, require much travel among villages. Within a closer radius, jajmani exchanges necessitate many short trips. People circulate to attend panchayats and other jati affairs.[1] There is usually constant coming and going among the people of several contiguous or nearby villages (cf. Smith 1952). Within such village clusters, whenever news and influences from a center reach one village they are quickly known in the others. Influences from various centers are regular and important factors in village life and in the lives of most villagers.

Centers and Hinterlands: Villagers and Townsmen

Almost all in any village have been to the nearest market center, which is usually within a few hours' round-trip journey; a good many will go there regularly. Within a similar radius, if not in the same location, there is usually a holy place that attracts the villagers on ceremonial occasions or for personal exigencies. The nearest administrative center and the modern educational and medical facilities may not be so close but they also attract villagers from many villages roundabout.

Each local center has a hinterland of clientele and each is in turn part of the hinterland of a larger center. The trade center of

[1] For two adjoining villages in Faizabad district, U.P., thirty-three specialists come from six different hamlets within a two-mile radius. The eight settlements form a jajmani unit although they fall within five different village administrative units (Gould 1964, pp. 20–27).

The circulation occasioned by jati affairs in Rampur, near Delhi, includes council meetings in a unit of four villages and in the larger unit of twenty villages. These in turn belong to a league of 360 villages (Lewis 1958, pp. 29–31).

smallest scope in a locality is usually the market held once a week in some convenient open space. Surajit Sinha studied such a market in Singhbhum district of Bihar at intervals over ten years (Sinha *et al.* 1961, pp. 131–163). It is held weekly at a village called Bamni. Customers come from about a five-mile radius, most of them from within three miles of Bamni. Some of them visit other weekly markets as well; there is one on Sundays three miles away and another on Saturdays four miles away. There are twelve weekly markets in the 634 square miles of the subdistrict; Bamni is among the largest of them.

Products of the immediate locality—vegetables, lentils, fish, pots, sweets—are sold, as well as goods brought in from other places—cooking oil, salt, kerosene, tobacco, onions, matches, and sugar. Some buyers also bring their own produce to sell or barter. Most sellers come from a greater distance than do the buyers.[2] Goods and services of some sixteen artisan jatis are available as well as products handled by specialized traders of still other jatis. In this part of Bihar, an average number of jatis in a village is only about six.

The Bamni market, like others of its kind, also serves political, recreational, and general societal purposes. During the time when Sinha observed it, the most powerful local leader customarily sat on a cot in the market surrounded by his close associates, the influential village headmen in the locality. An ordinary farmer did not dare go near that cot, much less sit on it. Gentry of the higher jatis could speak with the leader on nearly equal terms. "All people attending the market would immediately recognize him as the lord of the land and as representing the peak in the regional power hierarchy." In this market, villagers could plainly see who the main leader was and who were his closest associates (Sinha *et al.* 1961, p. 154).

A good many of the visitors, especially in the slack season for farm work, came only for the fun of meeting friends at the market. New contacts could be made there. Given a few encouraging clues,

2 Some merchants cover a circuit of 7 markets within 10 miles of Bamni; those who deal in manufactured goods come from places more distant, from as far as 20 miles away. A sample of the people at the market showed that buyers came from 24 different villages, sellers from 52. Those who visited principally to buy represented 19 jatis among the 125 people interviewed, sellers represented 32 jatis among 314 interviewed (Sinha *et al.* 1961, pp. 142–144).

a young man knew how to proceed. A girl's coy smile could easily bring her a fond pinch in return, and should that produce nothing more discouraging than a gay frown, a gift of betel chew and perhaps more intimate exchanges followed. Older people sought out their friends and relatives to exchange news and gossip; they did not seek to establish new social relations at the market.

Jati considerations were not central in market transactions but they were not entirely irrelevant either. While visitors to the Bamni market patronized tea stalls, sweetshops, and betel-chew sellers without much concern for the stricter avoidances of their home villages, yet none of these vendors were Harijans. Tradesmen were of many jatis. The main cash product, *lac*, was handled by traders of twenty-one different jatis. Manufactures, however, were sold or serviced mainly by artisans of the jatis traditionally involved with them. "From all these it becomes clear that even today, a greater part of material transactions in the market closely follow the traditional division of labour in terms of caste" (Sinha *et al.* 1961, p. 140).

Traders now come from a wider range of jatis than before, but in general the functions of markets like Bamni continue. Local products are sold or bartered; commodities from afar are on sale; specialists find the customers they need and villagers find there the full assortment of specialist jatis. As travel improves, the smallest markets lose attendance to the larger, but a market like that at Bamni flourishes. It is much more than a center for economic transactions. It is a chief place for recreation and a main node of local communication.

Beyond such local markets are those of wider scope. There is a larger market center nine miles from Bamni; it is a Tuesday market located on a railway line and a paved road. This draws more tradesmen from greater distances than does Bamni and also more buyers, possibly because it is the only cattle market in the subdistrict. While Bamni market draws from some fifty villages, the cattle market at Balarampur brings buyers and sellers from about 600 villages (Sinha *et al.* 1961, pp. 157–162; see also Patnaik 1953; Mukerji 1957).

Larger markets are often specialized. A marketing study of a Punjab locality showed that the farmers were inclined to take their wheat to one market, *gur* to another, and cotton to a third (Neale et al. 1965, p. 166).

There are, in addition, periodic centers that attract great numbers. They are mainly religious fairs and festivals during which a village or town honors its special deity. Thousands, even hundreds of thousands, then throng to the celebrated place. With them come merchants, hawkers, dealers, amusement purveyors in numbers. The report on fairs and festivals in Gujarat in the 1961 Census of India lists 1521 annual fairs in that state, with an estimated attendance of more than seven million (Trivedi 1965). Other accounts of fairs and festivals in the 1961 Census volumes (Part VII-B of each volume) testify to similar numbers.

Major influences flow from the permanent centers, the main towns. The district headquarters is usually a center for trade as well as of administration. It is often also a center for educational and medical services and of religious observances.[3]

A villager's visit to town follows patterns familiar to him. His dealings in the town bazaar are much like his dealings with a village shopkeeper. He worships in the great temple using the same ritual idiom that is appropriate in the village shrine. This familiarity does not mean that a villager is an easy participant in town life or that he feels completely at home in town, but rather that there are typically established relations with villagers and a regular place for them in the town setting.

Towns and cities are ancient in India and the relations between townsmen and villagers are also of ancient standing. Townsmen in the traditional centers have not been so very different from villagers in their social organization and general way of life. The Jatavs, leatherworkers of Agra City, for example, organized themselves in groups of related households that resemble the localized lineages of the villages, save that the emphasis was more on common locality than on lineage affiliation. Such a group maintained its own headman and panchayat; it was a unit of close cooperation

[3] Of a total of 310 districts in India, 216 were larger than 4,000 square miles and had more than a million population in the 1951 census. Each district is administratively divided into subunits, called *taluka* in some states, and a *taluka* is further subdivided into groupings of villages, called by various terms, *hobli* in Mysore, *firka* in Andhra (Rao and Bhat 1960, pp. 3–9).

and of frequent interaction. Several of these groups constituted a *mohalla*, a section of the city that was the functional equivalent of a village in that it was a unit for personal identification, for actual and fictive kinship, for panchayat functions, and a unit of exogamy (Lynch 1967, pp. 143–150).

Such common ground between villager and townsman of similar social level does not usually induce visiting villagers to want to settle there unless economic need impels them to take work in a town. But a villager's visits to a town are eased by the ample precedents for such trips, by the experienced companions or suitable guides he can generally find for his first ventures into that wider world, and by the traditional similarities between town and village culture.

True, what is part of everyday routine for a townsman may be a special occasion for the visiting villager. Many a villager looks forward eagerly, from one visit to the next, to the delights of the town—whether the heady distraction of shopping, the exaltation of grand ceremony, or the more mundane pleasures of cinema and restaurant. In the context of the town and under cover of anonymity a man from the village may relax his jati's standards for dining and drinking, and for personal contacts.

These visits are made more by men than by women. A woman does not often travel beyond the villages of her kin. She may go to the local market and on great occasions to a festival or a pilgrimage center. But the contacts between centers and village are mainly in the keeping of the men.

Link Roles

Regular contacts between village and large center are maintained by those villagers who take on link roles; some do so because of ascribed office or jati occupation, others for personal gain. One official link role is that of the village headman who is required to transmit information, requests, and orders between the village and governmental authority. He is expected to be spokesman for the villagers to official authority and also the agent of that authority in the village.

Other bridging functions are performed in the regular course of a jati's calling. A tradesman brings goods into the village, acts as a broker for the crop or as agent for a broker in town. A Brahmin priest is supposed to share in the learning developed at the great centers and some are indeed learned enough to bring scriptural ideas and stories to their village clients.

Link roles can be lucrative and so ambitious men seek them. An energetic man of almost any jati may try to be a broker for village products. Those who are exceptionally successful may have considerable influence as wealthy men in their jati and as entre- preneurial innovators for the village. One Oraon tribesman who had been hired by a merchant and so was able to learn about the ways of the market, enriched his own locality when he introduced potato cultivation and also a more efficient way of trapping (D. P. Sinha 1963; 1967).

On another level of linkage are the religious-esthetic brokers who come into the villages. Some are themselves villagers who organize a dramatic company and stage plays in the villages of their vicinity (cf. Hein 1958). Cultural specialists from the centers are imported for grand occasions. A wealthy magnate may bring in a famous performer for a wedding or festival; a renowned sage may be brought as an act of merit.

One of the most famous of Madrassi performers of song and recitation, Saraswati Bai, had been an artist for forty eight years when Milton Singer interviewed her in 1955. She frequently per- formed in villages before audiences of thousands. "I have not spared a single village and not a single village has spared me." Her presentations combined devotional lessons with dramatic per- formances of great esthetic appeal (Singer 1958, pp. 361–364). Traveling performers and sages have linked villagers to the artistic and religious centers for centuries, disseminating the ideas and precepts of the larger civilization (cf. Singer 1964; Geertz 1960). In the nineteenth century these ties were strengthened by improved travel, railways, postal services, and printed matter. More recently the ties have been enhanced by cinema and radio.

Another type of middleman is the self-appointed agent of liaison with government who offers his services for a fee. Such experts— there is commonly at least one in a village—claim special knowl- edge of bureaucratic ways or special advantage with an official, if only with the peon who guards the magistrate's door. One such middleman is mentioned by Srinivas in an account of a family dispute in Rampura village of Mysore. This man, called Kulle Gowda, urged that the family register a deed of partition, rather than settle the dispute without formal legal action, pointing out all the advantages to the members of the family in doing so. He was interested in having these legal steps taken because it would mean one or two trips to town for him as the family's representative. "The brothers would have to bear the expenses of these trips, and besides, Kulle Gowda would be able to charge them other expenses, real or imaginary—the clerk to be paid a certain sum for doing the work quickly, and so on" (Srinivas 1952b, p. 18).

Some years later, when I was with Professor Srinivas on a day's visit to Rampura, Kulle Gowda told us of a trip he had taken not long before to the city of Madras. He had lifted his sights considerably by then for he described how he had interested a movie magnate in a script on village life that he was writing and trying to sell.

Village and center are thus linked by many agents and channels of communication. What is transmitted through them is another matter. One of the few studies which bear on this question is by Y. V. Lakshmana Rao (1966). He has examined the different kinds of communication in two villages of Andhra Pradesh and has found a marked differential between the relatively abundant and diverse communications of the prospering village and the sparse communications of the economically stagnant one. Further studies of this kind will illuminate the detailed processes of modern relations between village and center. For the society and civilization as a whole, however, it is clear that the traditional networks of communication have brought about certain broad effects.

Regions: of the Observer and of the Participant

The broadest effect of these long established networks is that certain root concepts and practices, such as the varna concept and the purity-pollution practices, have come to be shared across the subcontinent. Other concepts and practices have become characteristic of particular parts of the subcontinent, mainly because closer communications are possible within geographic barriers than across them. To be sure, mere frequency of social interaction does not automatically create cultural resemblances; much depends, in

India as elsewhere, on the nature of the relations and the views of one another held by those who are in communication. Nevertheless, cultural similarities within a region indicate that there has been relatively closer social interaction within its borders than across them.

The term region here refers not only to a geographic tract but also to common characteristics of culture and society held for some length of time by the people of a territory, especially as such traits are contrasted with features characteristic in other parts of the larger geographic entity. Two kinds of social-cultural regions should be distinguished. One kind includes those delineated by trained observers; the other includes those which the people in the society perceive and which may command their loyalties, identifications and actions. The two are not mutually exclusive categories, although the regions denoted by analytic observers are not necessarily recognized by those who live within them.

The inhabitants of an observer's region may be quite unaware that they all belong to a territory in which important cultural and social elements are shared. Thus the four main zones of kinship practices formulated by Mrs. Karve for all of India (1953, 1965) are very useful taxonomic concepts for social scientists, but few, if any, residents of the respective zones have any notion that they can be so classified.

On the other hand, if a number of people strongly feel that they share a regional identity, that in itself is a common feature, which observers must take into account. Government authorities may denote a new political entity, which then may become one of the importantly perceived regions for the people within it (cf. Schwartzberg 1967, pp. 90–91).

Taxonomic regions can summarize a great deal of information and so can be useful for economic and social planning as well as for a general understanding of cultural distributions and social processes. The nature of such regions depends on which traits are selected as significant and what purpose the formulation is intended to serve. Any village and each family can be subsumed within differently postulated regions, each valid for its purpose.

To take just the matter of religion, Srinivas has noted that the people of Coorg—a relatively small but geographically and culturally distinctive hill district between Mysore and Kerala—can be classified as practicing a special variety of Hinduism as contrasted with that practiced in adjoining areas. In a larger view, their Hinduism belongs in one region with that carried on in the larger tract comprising "Malabar, South Canara, and Coorg Proper." That, in turn, belongs to a region he calls "Peninsular Hinduism," which itself is part of the vast region of "All-India Hinduism" (1952a, pp. 213–215).

The geographic spread of what is denoted as a region thus varies according to the criteria and purposes selected by the analyst. For certain criteria and purposes the whole subcontinent can be treated as one region, as Emeneau has done in respect to certain linguistic traits and as Kroeber has done in regard to civilization (Emeneau 1956; Kroeber 1947). For other purposes a tract like Coorg, which at the time of Srinivas' study had less than 200,000 people (fewer than 50,000 of them speakers of the Coorg language), living in a hill territory of some 1500 square miles, can validly be considered a separate region, both to the observers and to the participants. Even much smaller tracts and populations can usefully be denoted as regions for still other purposes. The present discussion deals mainly with regions of larger compass, those that take in very large blocs of the Indian population and terrain.

In previous chapters major differences have been noted in social organization between northern and southern India—more accurately between Hindi-speaking people of the upper and central Ganges Basin and the Dravidian speakers of the southern part of the Indian peninsula (cf. Karve 1965, pp. 242–252; Srinivas 1956b, pp. 218–219; De 1967, pp. 66–68).[4]

These differences are basic, yet in the distribution of other traits the north-south division is not so clear or so important. For example, Bose and Sinha have traced variations across the country in 14 material items having to do with village form, house types, diet, dress, utensils, and carts. Cohn's analysis of these data shows that three of the traits have quite a mixed distribution; six fall into an

[4] An interesting sidelight on North-South differences comes from a World War II study in military psychiatry. Dr. A. H. Williams reported that his patients from North India tended to show different symptoms from those shown by patients from the South. The South Indians, both Hindu and Christian, had more schizophrenic symptoms. The soldier patients from North India more often had other psychiatric disorders (Williams 1950, pp. 139, 167).

east-west classification, and only five into a north-south division (Bose and Sinha 1961; Cohn 1967, pp. 19–21).

Three macro-regions of India have been formulated by Selig Harrison in his book on political unity and diversity. "The political history of India can be viewed as the history of three large geographical arenas—North, Deccan and South—set off from one another by profound physiographic differences" (1960, p. 15). The principal criteria Harrison uses to distinguish those macro-regions are historical and geographic. They are historical in the sense that they are based on continuities in broad political development and on the present awareness of those continuities. They are geographic in the sense that the morphology of the landscape inevitably affects communications, and the nature of the communications, as has just been noted, affects (though it does not determine) the nature of cultural resemblances and social loyalties.

The most detailed mappings yet made of the regions of India have been done on the basis of geographic and economic criteria. The 1965 report on regional development by the Registrar General, Ashok Mitra, generally follows Spate's comprehensive treatment of Indian regions and adds data from the 1961 Census of India (Mitra 1965; Spate 1954; A. T. A. and A. M. Learmonth 1958). The projects for a National Atlas and for the new India Gazetteer use a similar outline. Additional criteria have been taken into account in J. E. Schwartzberg's map of the cultural regions of the subcontinent which utilizes linguistic and other cultural variables as well as physiographic and economic features (1967, pp. 102–111). This work is being advanced by the author and his associates in the project for a historical atlas of India.

Such maps do what maps are intended to do, they illustrate variations and gradients of the social terrain. They can, for example, illuminate regional differences among groups bearing the same name and status. They can summarize the influence of a dominant jati; they can trace isograms of social structure.

Some regions are stamped with the characteristics of a strongly dominant jati. Thus in the parts of the Punjab (now Haryana) where Jats are dominant, they typically make up most of the village community, with few other jatis represented and those few having a relatively small population. This characteristic may well stem from Jat landowning customs that assign almost all the village land only to Jat lineages (Pradhan 1965; Schwartzberg 1965, pp. 488–489).[5]

Another example of the regional influence of a dominant jati is from Dewas district of Madhya Pradesh. Rajputs are strong in many villages there, but are not dominant in all. Other jatis that have dominance are generally allied to Rajputs. Mayer comments that "where the caste which may most clearly be called dominant does not control all or even the majority of villages in a region, these other villages will tend to be under the authority of castes which are sympathetic to it, and which adopt its ways in order to identify themselves with it, and then become its commensal equals and allies" (1958a, p. 419).

A few studies have taken social structure as the main criterion in regional mapping. Marriott has analyzed the degree of caste elaboration in five selected regions, examining the number of jatis and the consensus about their ranking rather than jati customs and functions. This study indicates that among the five areas, there is most elaborate ranking and greatest consensus about rank in Kerala. In decreasing order of rank elaboration and consensus are the Coromandel, the Upper Ganges, the Middle Indus, and the Bengal Delta areas. Although questions remain about the causes and correlates of these variations, the structural differences of jati ranking among the five areas have been indicated (Marriott 1960; Cohn 1962; 1967, pp. 8–9; Mandelbaum 1962).

Another feature used for mapping Indian regions is their historic character. Some have been nuclear centers of influence over long periods; others have been route areas; and still others have been relatively isolated (Cohn 1967, p. 12). Whatever criteria are selected, the analyst does well to heed Schwartzberg's comment that what should be of prime concern is not the periphery of a region but its core, that part in which the variables defining it are well expressed (1967, p. 94).

Of all the observers' classifications, the most generally useful are

[5] As was noted in earlier chapters, the ranking of a jati can vary from place to place. Thus in much of Midnapore district, West Bengal, the Mahisyas are in the large majority, outnumbering the local herdsmen and potters. The order of jati ranking follows this fact. "Like the Potters, the Herdsmen generally in Bengal rank higher than the Mahisyas but must accept their dominance in Midnapore" (Nicholas 1965, pp. 37–38).

the major linguistic groupings. Mrs. Karve has noted that the contiguous territory inhabited by speakers of a main language and its dialects also shows relative homogeneity in social organization, in material culture, and in religious practices, as contrasted with the practices of another linguistic region. She has used such regions extensively in her analysis of kinship organization, and other scholars have made similar use of linguistic regions (Karve 1951, p. 1; 1965, pp. 1–6; Srinivas 1962, p. 98; Stein 1967, p. 42; De 1967, pp. 52–54).

These linguistic regions have come to be much more than useful taxonomic devices for scholars and administrators; they have become potent participants' regions as well. Some popular leaders have taken their linguistic region as a main category for self-identification for political and cultural symbolism. Many now perceive it as an important unit, all the more because state boundaries have been redrawn to adhere more closely to linguistic boundaries.

Regional Identification and Situational Context

A villager recognizes and feels potentially identified with a whole series of regions and other groupings; which of them motivates his action at any given time depends on the situation, especially on the context of confrontation with those of other regions or groups (cf. De 1967, pp. 52–56). Thus a person may see himself as a member of a particular lineage, alliance, jati, village, village cluster, district, state, language region, and nation. But he does not perceive and cannot participate in all at once.

When a dispute between his village and another is in question, he is likely to act as a village member; when he believes that the rights of those of his language are jeopardized, he may rally with others of the same language. Srinivas comments that solidarity with one's group, whatever it may be at a particular juncture, seems to require a certain amount of rivalry with parallel groups. So a man is a member of his jati vis-à-vis other jatis and a Hindu when in confrontation with non-Hindus. Similarly, he is an Indian in relation to non-Indians, so that "irrespective of his village or caste or region he reacts like an Indian when the problem of Goa or Kashmir crops up. . . . Tensions and conflicts at a particular level maintain the identity and separation of groups of the same order but these groups can and do unite at a higher level" (Srinivas 1962, pp. 110–111).

This process has been noted several times in preceding chapters. What needs to be clarified by future research is the sequence of choices that a man commonly faces and the points at which he must select among alternate loyalties. The pattern of such choices changes over time and as a villager's social space and intellectual horizons expand through wider experience and education, he finds himself aware of more potential identifications than his forefathers could recognize.

A person becomes especially aware of his region when he is out of it. Surrounded by people of different speech and manner, he typically feels in need of friends of his own kind. Migrants to a city, as was noted, generally find shelter and help from city residents from their own locality. A hotel manager in a northern town once told me that he enjoyed especially friendly relations with a university professor of the town because both of them were from Kerala. Regional clubs are common in the major cities, places where a man far from home can come to speak his home language, to meet his regional compatriots, and to enjoy familiar food, gossip, and humor.

Regional self-identification is usually strongest in a geographic enclave that is relatively isolated from outsiders but whose people are quite conscious of outsiders. An extreme example is a village of Kulu district north of Simla in the Himalayas. It has some 500 inhabitants who are so cut off by mountains from the rest of the world that they speak their own language, maintain their own customs, and have very little identification or contact beyond their remote wild glen (Rosser 1960).

A pocket of some 10,000 people exists in the hills along the Madras-Mysore border near the Kauvery River. For centuries the people of this enclave had little contact with outsiders; their lives and loyalties were concentrated within the villages of their hill territory. They were nearly self-sufficient economically; marriages were rarely contracted out of the territory; their leaders managed their own political affairs. Yet, as in other isolated parts of India, they were culturally a part of the main. There were several jatis among them and the dominant Lingayats carried on a full sectarian way of worship and conduct. In their infrequent contacts with outsiders they presumably felt themselves to be very much the distinctive inhabitants of a distinctive territory; inside the territory, jati differences were maintained (MacLachlan and Beals 1966).

Jati differences have been maintained in other isolated hill tracts. While the intensity of social relations within an enclave provides a base for special territorial identification and customs, it does not do away with cultural and social distinctions among the jatis of the enclave. The four peoples of the Nilgiri Hills of South India were largely isolated from villages on the nearby plains until the mid-nineteenth century. Together they formed a separate social system; there were constant, even daily, relations among members of the four groups, yet they remained completely distinct both culturally and socially (Mandelbaum 1956).

How and with whom a person identifies regulates the ways in which he shapes his conduct. He takes certain groups and categories as reference models to emulate. Other groups he sees in negative reference and is unwilling or unable to be like them. In later chapters reference models are considered in relation to social mobility. The mention of reference models is relevant here in that regional groupings in India often carry either positive or negative reference in the eyes of other people.

This reference behavior is exemplified in Berreman's account of Sirkanda village in the Himalayan foothills, located within a day's journey of the town of Dehra Dun in one direction and of Mussoorie in another. Sirkanda villagers speak Pahari, the distinctive language of a thousand-mile-long belt of the Himalayan hills; they share the major cultural features of Pahari speakers; they think of themselves as Paharis as against the people of the towns and the plains villages. They feel at a disadvantage when they have to deal with non-Paharis because they believe that the others are more knowledgeable and sophisticated than they are. "As a result, Paharis do not identify themselves as people who can learn or benefit from the ways of people of the plains"; they have frequent contact with non-Paharis but have taken over relatively little from them (Berreman 1960b, pp. 775–780, 783).

Their regular visits to large centers have had little effect on them because the town is too strange, the town traits too alien for any great cultural impact. Sirkanda men usually go several times a year to Dehra Dun or Mussoorie for marketing or other purposes. But their visits are usually brief and often uncomfortable sorties. They have no one to stay with in town and must bunk down in a temple or shop unless the visitor can get to a Pahari village before dark. Trips are scheduled, when possible, so the traveler can stay the night in a friendly village rather than in the alien cold town. Moreover, hill villagers feel conspicuous in the large centers because of "their rusticity and distinctive dress, language, and behavior." They are sensitive lest they be objects of ridicule. All this is not conducive to ready adoption of town manners.

By contrast, the Sirkanda people have much more intense and frequent interchange within their own hill locality, an area of some sixty settlements within a four-mile radius of Sirkanda. Eighty percent of all marriages are contracted within this locality; two markets are within it and the most important annual fair for these villagers takes place in their own territory. So there is considerable cultural homogeneity among the people of these 60 settlements. Their jatis are relatively few, with most people belonging to the higher jatis. There are cultural differences among the jatis, but they are not very great, partly because families of the lower jatis have been thinly dispersed among the settlements of the higher jatis. This is quite unlike the Nilgiri situation, in which each group was concentrated in its own settlements and so could maintain and develop its own cultural bent.

A few hours' walk from Sirkanda across a watershed to the north, there is another enclave whose people have somewhat different customs and are suspected by the Sirkanda villagers of practicing witchcraft. Both factors impede social relations between Sirkanda and these people. The Sirkanda people have more cordial relations with villages to the east of them, where the better lines of communication lie, than with those to the north and west, where there are not only more difficult geographic and cultural barriers but also a sharp dialectic boundary (Berreman 1960b, pp. 778–781; 1963, pp. 294–318).

What is illustrated among these hill people holds true elsewhere, that the wider social relations of a villager are directed by both objective and subjective factors. Objectively, there are the facts of geography, economics, social divisions, or cultural similarities. Subjectively, there are the identifications that a person makes of himself and of others. With some groups he feels able to identify, at least on some level, able to cooperate with them socially in some situations, and able to learn from them in some contexts. Others are defined as outsiders or enemies or aliens, with little likelihood of social cooperation or cultural assimilation. Migrants to a new region have usually resisted such assimilation, clinging tenaciously to the speech and customs of their original region. Thus the Tamil-speaking Brahmins who moved into Kerala have long continued to use Tamil as their home language (cf. Iyer 1909; Béteille 1962).

Influences of the region of residence do in time erode the practices of the region of origin. Mrs. Karve, however, once witnessed this process in a Maharashtrian village as it was occurring. A jati council of Gujars had been convened to judge a case of cross-cousin marriage, which was prohibited by their own jati tradition but practiced by their present neighbors. The Gujars are a pastoral group whose main locale is to the north of Maharashtra. These Gujars had maintained the marriage patterns of their northern brethren; their panchayat still imposed a fine for cross-cousin marriages. But this was on the way to being changed; a Gujar elder commented to Mrs. Karve that "One cannot resist the customs of the land in which one lives. After all a fish cannot wage a feud against water" (1953, pp. 9, 162).

Regional Change and the Rise of Regionalism

The region changes over time. One contributing factor is that centers rise and fall, their clientele and hinterlands shift. The town of Deoli in Rajasthan, for example, formerly the capital of a Maharana's state, has become an empty shell since the ruler's power was assumed by the present government. Its residents are now part of the political hinterland of the district headquarters rather than actors at the right hand of state power. The old feudal loyalties are now disintegrated (Carstairs 1957, pp. 15–27). Other towns have risen in influence. Thus the commercial importance of Bolpur in West Bengal has steadily increased as it has grown—from a small village to a railway station, to a rice market, to a milling town—until it has become a trade center for a large area (Bose 1958a, p. 151). As Bolpur grew, the nearby river port, Supur, declined (Fukutake et al. 1964, pp. 103–140).

The people of any one village normally participate in centers of several different kinds. Thus Ramkheri village is seven miles from the district headquarters town of Dewas in Madhya Pradesh, and so the villagers go to Dewas to trade and for governmental and political business.

Dewas and its village hinterland are, in turn, part of the larger tract known as Malwa which contains the religious centers of Ujjain and Manud, respectively some thirty and one hundred miles from Ramkheri. The fame of Ujjain is ancient; its location fixed the prime meridian of Sanskrit geographers. Its temples still draw throngs of worshippers, among them people from Ramkheri. That center and that religious identification have not changed for the Ramkheri villagers. Nor have the commercial attractions of the city of Indore, twenty-two miles from Ramkheri, lessened for them. What has changed for them is that the new administrative and political center at Bhopal has become important. Bhopal is now the capital of the state of Madhya Pradesh. As the people of Ramkheri become increasingly engaged in larger political affairs, some of their leaders have become increasingly involved with officials and politicians whose center is at Bhopal (Mayer 1960, pp. 11–14; 1962, pp. 271–276; Spate 1954, p. 578).

Beyond the rise and fall of particular centers, the general trend for villagers is toward wider experiences and broader social horizons than they previously had. This induces broadening of jati boundaries through the kind of caste associations that are discussed in later chapters. Those who take active part in such associations become aware of the greater political arenas of state and national affairs. In those arenas one's region is in competition with others and regional allegiance is likely to be a powerful rallying influence, reaching on occasion into the villages as well as to the political centers.

"Regionalism" has become a major political factor for several reasons. One is simply the creation of the independent nation within which sectional interests vigorously compete for shares of the nation's substance and for symbols of regional eminence. Another is the growth in importance of the regional languages, in the number of people educated in those languages, and their increased self-identification with the language and the region. This began in the nineteenth century when local leaders deliberately propagated indigenous regional speech, literature, and practices as ways of opposing the language and influence of the elite, whether they were English and colonial, or Persian and Mogul (cf. Cohn 1967, pp. 21–25; Brass 1967; McDonald 1968; Srinivas 1962, pp. 98–103; Irschik 1969).

The regional language is only one of the speech forms commonly used by villagers and townspeople. For each of three levels of interaction—within a village cluster, within local centers, and at regional centers—there is, as John Gumperz has noted, a corresponding level of language. More marked linguistic differences occur between adjoining regional languages than between dialects of adjoining village clusters. This linguistic separation between regions is another element in sharpening loyalty to region.

In a village and its close vicinity, the people usually speak the same dialect although particular jatis may use a special variation of the village dialect in their homes.[6] The regional dialect, as distinct from the village dialects, is used over a larger area. It is "the native language of small town residents" and is spoken by villagers when they visit the local centers. They use it to communicate with townspeople and with other villagers whose dialects differ from theirs.

There are variations between one town and another in the region, Gumperz notes, but these are minor in comparison with the much greater differences among the village dialects. Some of these regional dialects have in the past been literary languages much as Braj Bhasa, spoken around Agra, Avadhi spoken around Lucknow, and the Konkani spoken around Goa. At the present time literary works are written mainly in a regional language rather than in these regional dialects (Gumperz 1957, pp. 72–73).

The regional language is that which is used, in literary and colloquial versions, at the principal center, usually the capital of the state. The literary form is the more elegant version taught in the higher schools, and used in writing and formal speeches. The colloquial form is spoken by the uneducated in the main center

---

[6] The Sweepers of Khalapur village have a distinctive dialect which they use with each other; two other untouchable jatis in the village have their respective dialects. There are six dialectic variations in all, each used by a different group of the village. But all in Khalapur also know and use the dialect that is standard in the locality (Gumperz 1957; 1958; Gumperz and Naim 1960).

and by the educated in home usage and for special purposes, as in humor or to underline verbally a certain kind of message. The regional language is the usual speech of the educated people throughout the region. Townspeople in the smaller centers know both the regional dialect and the regional language quite well, but at home they speak the regional dialect.

The transition between one regional language and the next is sharpened by the way each is taught—as a separate language and culture vehicle—in the schools. But the dialects intergrade in complex ways. Gumperz gives a hypothetical example of two villages, A and B, on either side of an administrative border, such as the one between Bengal and Bihar. The dialects of the two close-lying villages may differ very little, but in village A the regional language will be Hindi and in village B it will be Bengali. "A villager from A can easily talk to a friend from B in the local dialect, however the two will not be able to exchange letters unless one knows both languages" (1957, p. 76).

The range of a regional dialect is commonly also the span of jati endogamy. Apart from border areas, even people of considerable education and wealth tend to marry within the area of the regional language. All other kinds of social interchange also decrease sharply across the spatial edge of a regional language.

Linguistic differentiation is an old feature of Indian civilization. In ancient Sanskrit drama, the parts were written in different languages and dialects for characters of different social status. It seems likely that there were commonly regional language cliques in the courts of ancient kings. But linguistic regionalism has been given a new importance by modern developments. What were mainly observers' regions of classification have increasingly become participants' regions of identification.

The linguistic regions of India were comprehensively mapped by Sir George Grierson in the Linguistic Survey of India, a work that began in 1898 and was concluded with the publication of the final volume in 1927. Long before that, learned men in India had a general knowledge of the major linguistic divisions. At the religious supercenters pilgrims from any corner of the country could be directed to that quarter where others of their regional tongue could be found. But the social force of linguistic identification did not develop greatly until communications within the regions improved, until the regional language was propagated for educational, literary, religious, and political purposes, and until local political leaders felt a need for supralocal alliances in order to swing political weight.

Regional interests have lately been seen as so opposed to national unity that some commentators have considered this opposition as a major, perhaps the greatest, issue confronting the nation (Harrison 1960). Some tensions between local loyalties and larger interests exist in all complex societies; they have been constant issues in all great states. Both kinds of identification and loyalty are necessary and some conflict between them may well be inevitable. The question is not whether such tensions should exist at all but rather how well the social system provides for their management.

Regional Loyalties and Wider Identifications

The management of conflicts of loyalty has had to be worked out anew in recent decades, particularly because of the rise of new political units since Independence. It has not been easy. Material resources are scarce in relation to expectations of regional political leaders and there is severe competition among sectional interests. There is also the general inclination to rank social units of all sorts, regions included, so that the people of one see themselves in status competition with those of others.

Villagers usually participate in regional rivalries only indirectly, through those who fill the link roles with the centers. But villagers often engage in similar rivalries at a more local level. Their several kinds of affiliations are not necessarily mutually destructive forces. A person does feel that he is a member of a particular jati, village, region, state, and religion "but these loyalties can represent a hierarchy of values and are not necessarily inconsistent with being a citizen of the Indian Republic" (Srinivas 1962, p. 110).

There is a traditional basis for the larger national identification. It is the idea, mainly engendered by Hindu religion but shared by those of other religions as well, that there is an entity of India to which all its inhabitants belong. The Hindu epics and legends, in their manifold versions, teach that the stage for the gods was nothing less than the entire land and that the land remains one religious setting for those who dwell in it. That sense was and is continually confirmed through the common practice of pilgrimage.

In most villages there are likely to be some who have been on pilgrimages, perhaps to distant centers. A count in one village, Sherurpur in U.P., showed that 49 pilgrimages had been made among a total population of 228. The nearest religious center is 20 miles away and it had attracted 28 pilgrimages; the other pilgrimages were to centers from 100 to 540 miles distant. Men and women higher in rank traveled more; villagers of the four higher jatis had made nearly twice as many pilgrimages as were made by those of the other four jatis of Sherurpur (Gould 1959, pp. 10–13).

Sacred centers range from those that attract visitors from a few score miles, to those that bring devotees from an entire linguistic region, to the great supercenters that draw people from all parts of the land.[7] A graphic, enlightening account of a pilgrimage to Pandharpur, a main center for Marathi-speaking people, has been written by Mrs. Karve. She tells how vivid a learning experience it was for the pilgrims. All recited the poetry of five centuries every day of their long march together. That poetry embodies a basic religious philosophy; "People speaking many dialects sang the same verses and thus learned a standard language. Their learning was achieved in a massive dose but without pain or compulsion."

The days of the pilgrimage are a joyous time; at halting places along the route there are continual performances by members of the vast moving congregation in music, dancing, drama. Some of it is bawdy, for all levels of esthetic and intellectual taste are represented. The bereaved and the suffering feel able to unburden themselves to their fellow pilgrims and so find relief. "The whole atmosphere was full of joy." Yet, as Dr. Karve observes, despite the comradeship of the pilgrimage, pilgrims of widely different jatis kept separate, especially in eating (1962, pp. 19–23).

Pilgrimages to the supercenters reinforce religious precepts but also impress the pilgrim with the vastness, the diversity, and— seemingly paradoxically—the oneness of the society. When I met the Indian anthropologist, L. K. Anantakrishna Iyer, shortly before his death in 1937, he had just returned from a long circuit of the

---

[7] The seven supercenters usually include five in the state of Uttar Pradesh —Banaras, Prayag (Allahabad), Mathura, Hardwar, Ayodhya—and Draraka in Gujarat, and Conjeeveram in Madras. Some Hindus include Ujjain in Madhya Pradesh or Nasik in Maharashtra in the list. There are still other variations on the list of the seven most sacred places (Bharati 1963).

great sacred places of pilgrimage. Even so learned and experienced a scholar as he was impressed afresh with the deep unity of Indian society and culture, and he spoke eloquently of that unity.

A villager is also likely to return from a distant pilgrimage with an enhanced sense of the India-wide tenets of his religion and society. He has seen a variety of custom and a diversity of peoples —yet all gathered for the same purpose, acting on the same assumptions and focussed on the same rites and symbols. Some of the rites specifically underline the social unity of the whole country, as when a pilgrim to Rameshwaram in the far south, bathes in the sea and then takes a pot of sea water to be emptied into the Ganges (Srinivas 1962, pp. 105–106; 1966, pp. 22–23, 130–132; Bharati 1963).

Perhaps pilgrims can readily assimilate the idea of the whole India because of the very fact that they consort with others of their region in the great center. They are received by local guides who cater to visitors of their kind, so they are not totally bereft of their regional moorings in the vast strange concourse. Even a scholar who sojourns in Banaras for years can live and study with others of his region and language. "A priest from the region of Maharashtra," Cohn and Marriott write, "who travels a thousand miles north to Banaras for learning the Vedas resides in a Maharashtrian school and studies Sanskrit under Marathi-speaking teachers . . ." (1958, p. 7). Regional custom and cuisine are quite compatible with transcendental rites and concepts.

Members of other religions, Muslims, Jains, Sikhs, Christians, go on pilgrimage to their own sacred places. They too experience an amity and identity there that surpasses locality. In a later chapter the social orientations of villagers of these religions will be discussed.

A sense of national identity is now consciously inculcated in all Indians through education, through national ceremonies and observances, through the mass media, through the speeches and examples of prominent national leaders. Many in India had been prepared for this secular message by the tradition of their religion. Either they themselves or someone they knew had been personal witnesses to dramatic displays of conduct that transcended local and regional affiliations.

There has not been in India the kind of dichotomy between

rural peasantry and the town elite and literati that prevailed in some other civilizations. Jati specialization in the villages paralleled specialization in the centers. A village Brahmin could consider himself as pure ritually as a Brahmin serving in a renowned temple and as worthy of reaching the highest pitch of scriptural learning if he had the ability to do so. Village tradesmen maintained commercial links with higher centers; they could and some did become great merchant tycoons if capacity and fortune favored. So also with able men of the warrior-ruler tradition. More than a few founders of dynasties were village bred and battle elevated.

In this respect the society of closed jatis was, in some degree, open. Within their jati's calling, whether religious, mercantile, or military-governmental, talented villagers occasionally did move from their village to live in a center. Only a very small proportion in the higher jatis did so, but many who remained in the village maintained regular ties with a large center. The vast mass of cultivators, artisans, and laborers lived their lives within a narrow locale. However, people and influences from the centers came into that locale, and the villagers themselves might have experienced the vivid lessons of the pilgrimage. Those lessons bound village to center and center to village in the shared concepts of the civilization.

CHAPTER **22** The Villager and Some Perennial
Problems of Civilization

W<small>ITHIN</small> the village and outside it, Indian villagers
have to cope with problems that are inherent in any civilization.
Some of them have been noted above, such as those arising from
specialization and from the relations between village and center.
There are other constant forces that pose perennial problems in any
complex society and in the culture of such a society, that is to say,
in a civilization.

To begin with, there are forces from the encompassing natural
systems of biology and ecology. Every social system, whether relatively complex or simple, rests on these natural systems. The people of a civilization, however, direct and exploit these forces to a
far greater degree than do primitives. These natural systems can be
called "parasocial systems" in the sense that they constantly and
directly impinge on social relations.

In India as in most of the world man's control over biological and
ecological forces has greatly increased in recent times. This has
been possible because of the establishment of global social-cultural
systems, as of technology and science. These newer systems may
be termed "megasocial systems" in that they surpass any one national society and affect all of them.

Within each complex society there are certain problems characteristic of such societies. One basic problem is that of providing for
both broad personalized relations and narrower impersonalized relations. We discuss here a duality in role relations in Indian villages
arising from this perennial problem, especially in economic, political, and religious activities.

Yet another problem indigenous to civilization is that of providing legitimate special roles for exceptional persons. Discussion of these roles leads to a general consideration of role definition and of fields of action among Indian villagers. Much of the discussion of this chapter applies not only to villagers but also to modern-educated, mainly urban people as well. A person's leeway of choice in his roles and field of action brings the discussion to the subject of the following chapters, the study of social and cultural change.

Larger Systems of Biology and Ecology

Both biology and ecology are usually treated as parameters in social analysis; that is, they are taken as constant factors in studies of social interaction and culture change. And it is not only the analyst who takes these forces as given. Villager and observer alike assume that there will be a flow of infants into a society, that they will grow up through the biological stages of the life-cycle, that the sown fields will yield and the seasons properly turn. But under certain circumstances these systems cannot be taken as parameters because forces from them obtrude strongly into the social routine.

Villagers deal with such obtrusions, say epidemics or crop failures, as best they can through empirical and supernatural means. The observer has to deal with such obtrusions by expanding his frame of analysis, by taking direct account of forces that he ordinarily relegates to other scientific fields. Thus illness can be taken as a parameter in the study of village society until we have to account for those social changes that result from the decrease in the incidence of fatal illness and the consequent rise in population.

Expanding the frame of social analysis to include such topics as demography, disease, genetics, and the biological life cycle also limits opportunities for neatly circumscribed well-integrated analyses. This matter of the scope of one's inquiry has been discussed in respect to social anthropology generally by Devons and Gluckman (1964) and by Bailey with specific reference to his work in India (1964), both with inclinations toward clearer circumscription rather than expansive exploration. In the present discussion, we can only acknowledge, and that all too briefly, the social potentials of these parasocial factors.

Among the most powerful of such factors are those of ecology, which in this agrarian culture mainly involves the technology of land cultivation. The subsistence basis of jati and village is postulated on plough agriculture. Those in India who use a different kind of cultivation, usually maintain a different kind of society. There are a good many tribal peoples living in remote, usually hilly, areas who practice swidden or "slash-and-burn" cultivation. The wild growth on a plot of land is cut down, burned over, and seeds sown in the ground fertilized by the ashes. Since the fertility of such soil declines sharply after a few seasons, the cultivator leaves it and begins the cycle again by clearing a new patch of overgrowth.

Swidden agriculture can be quite an effective way of adapting to a hill-jungle environment through a "canny imitation" of the natural landscape rather than by a bold reworking of it as in wet-rice cultivation. But the yield of swidden agriculture is always quite limited. Additional increments of labor or capital do not proportionately increase the crop, as they do with rice cultivation. The estimates of the number of people who can subsist on swidden fields range from 20 to 50 per square kilometer. Whatever the number in any particular locality, the carrying capacity of swidden land is far below that of ploughed land (Geertz 1963, pp. 15–37). Swidden agriculturalists in India typically maintain a tribal rather than a caste society, perhaps because caste organization implies a certain density of population that swidden methods cannot sustain. Some tribal groups do use ploughs or have a combination of plough and swidden methods, so the adoption of plough agriculture is not a sufficient cause for adopting caste organization although it does seem to have been a necessary condition for its historical establishment (cf. Bailey 1960b, pp. 63–68).

This subject is examined more extensively in the later discussion of tribal societies, and the symbolic importance of the role of swidden cultivator is noted there. The point here is that the one kind of relationship to the land provides a viable subsistence base for caste society while apparently the other does not. Swidden cultivation is rarely, if ever, the principal support of a caste village.

Another kind of ecological influence affects the intensity and flow of social relations. This influence has been noted in the previous discussion of village settlement patterns, particularly in Nicholas' comparison of two villages of West Bengal whose people have quite the same culture but who live in two markedly different terrains (1963). One village is situated on the marshy, low-lying land of the active delta where houses must be strung out in long lines along the embankments, the only feasible house sites. The land has been newly reclaimed; each village is a kind of frontier settlement. As was noted in the discussion of village settlement patterns, social interaction within this village is relatively limited, jati composition and jati relations are relatively simple, and there is very little dominance by one jati over the others. The other village is in an area of ancient habitation, termed the "moribund delta." The settlement is in the usual compact cluster, permitting a good deal of jajmani and other social interchange within the cluster. The jati order is much more complex and rigid than in the frontier village; in this part of Bengal dominant jatis are common.

Not all of these differences are direct outcomes of the ecology. The marshy, frequently flooded terrain does dictate the strung-out settlement pattern and this does impede frequent interchange among fellow villagers; the relative simplicity of the jati order is a more indirect result. Those who are attracted to this new ground are mainly from the lower jatis of cultivators and are often from the poorer families among them who do not have enough to live on in their home villages. Better-off cultivators, artisans and other specialists are not usually drawn to a chancy frontier locale. The delta ecology limits certain kinds of relations and encourages others. It limits social interchange and fosters a relatively simple jati order.

A similar ecological contrast, on a broader scale, is given in Joan Mencher's comparison of Kerala and Madras as ecological and cultural regions. Kerala is a well-watered land, lush and green, whose villages consist mainly of spatially separated homesteads. Most of Madras has less adequate and dependable rainfall; irrigation works were built there in ancient times.[1] Villages are nucleated, partly because of the requirements of water management. In the compact Madrassi settlements, village organization can be tighter than in the dispersed houses of a Kerala village (Mencher 1966, pp. 137–152).

As for caste organization, Mencher says that "ecological factors have led to an elaboration and development of a relatively constant

[1] The shift to intensive irrigation cultivation, as Dr. Mencher notes, fosters the kind of monumental social adaptations that have been discussed in many works, notably those of Karl Λ. Wittfogel and Julian H. Steward. A brief note on this subject by Henry Orenstein suggests some of the main activating forces in these changes (Orenstein 1965).

caste system in somewhat different directions" (1966, p. 163). In Kerala, the direction was toward authority focused on person-to-person relations, toward jati and rank proliferation, toward small, weak states and toward rigid spatial standards of pollution because of the close proximity of different jatis in a small homestead. In Madras the ecological influences made for group-to-group authority relations, less jati proliferation, larger bureaucratic and state organizations, and less need for stringent distance pollution (Mencher 1966, pp. 163–165).

As villagers take up modern agricultural technology and gain greater control over ecological forces, such traditional differences among regions are being modified. The new technology requires multiple, dependable social ties in order to assure supplies of water and fertilizer, of vaccines and transport, of all the complex flow of goods and messages that modern agriculture demands. Since the government provides much of the frame for these new economic and social relations, villagers have to be increasingly involved with government officials in all regions. The spread of modern agricultural technology seems, in the short run, to be terribly spotty and agonizingly slow, but in the long run it is likely to be steady and massive. Great changes in agricultural methods bring notable changes, in India as elsewhere in the world, in social relations.

As for biological factors, the consequences of the new social controls over disease have been much discussed in the demographic literature and need only be mentioned here. These controls have been made possible by the megasocial system of medical science and have been mainly implemented by governmental agencies. Their success makes necessary new social adaptations of many kinds, a principal one being for greater controls over the biological forces of procreation.

Modern science and technology are affecting every phase of Indian village society. We return to this theme later, but now turn to three of the subsystems of village society.

Dual Functions in Economics, Politics, and Religion

Villagers have traditionally distinguished religious, political, and economic activities in the sense that there are separate specialists and social patterns for each of these subsystems. Each includes two sets of functions and roles, one for the more local, personal, and immediate purposes, the other for more distant, societal, and long-range purposes.[2]

In economic relations, there is on the one side family production and internal village exchange, and on the other the flow of village-center trade. Cash crops, such as cotton, turmeric, and areca nut, have been traded through centers for centuries.[3] Different styles of behavior go with differing economic functions. The jajmani relationship, as we have seen, tends to be a multiplex bond in which two families share a long series of rights and obligations. They share in ceremonial as well as economic exchange, their association implies broad mutual support as well as specific transactions. In contrast, the trade relationship between villager and town merchant is more narrowly confined to the transaction itself.

These distinctions are not always clear cut. Thus certain tasks are arranged on a specific contract or cash basis even between jajmani associates. Conversely, many a villager has a personal relationship with a town merchant. In Totegadde village of Mysore, cash transactions have long been used in marketing the traditional crop of areca nuts, yet multiplex role relations are still important (Harper 1959b, 1961). In general, economic relations within the

---

[2] A similar distinction has been made by Srinivas and Béteille (1964) in contrasting a person's "close-knit" network of relations within the village to the "loose-knit" network outside his village.

[3] Because we are apt to think of wide-ranging trade as a recent development, it is well to recall that such trade is ancient and integral in Indian culture. The people of the Indus civilization, dating from the third millennium B.C., maintained trade links with Central Asia, Northeastern Afghanistan, Northeastern Persia, and South India. Indeed the whole existence of this civilization depended on a regular trade between hinterland villages and centers. The main centers such as Mohenjo-Daro and Harrappa, were key elements in the development of civilization. The large grain storehouses at these sites indicate that the concentration of specialists was made possible by the establishment of regular commerce with a wide hinterland (Wheeler 1953, pp. 28–33, 58–62). The classical manual of statecraft, the *Arthasastra,* of perhaps the third century B.C., details the duties of the official who supervises trade. In more recent times, nineteenth-century accounts show that there was a considerable amount of indigenous interregional as well as village-center trade. The temporary blocking of the flow of cotton into the English markets as a result of the American Civil War brought sudden, though temporary, prosperity to cotton growers in India (Kautilya 1951, pp. 104–106; Drekmeier 1962, pp. 276–277; Srinivas and Shah 1960; Leacock and Mandelbaum 1955).

village are more often carried on through roles of multiple function, while in extravillage relations, the roles are likely to be more restricted to narrowly economic functions.

In political functions there is a duality between the politics of power within the village and the maintenance of administration by state authorities. We have previously discussed the characteristic political contests within a village and the manner in which agents of the state were kept out, insofar as was possible, of intravillage relations. Villagers rendered to agents of the state the revenue and deference that was their due; they did not want them meddling in the village nor did they usually think of themselves as active participants in state affairs. This is reflected in the differences between villagers' behavior in their own panchayats and in formal law courts. In the one milieu villagers emphasize the settlement of conflict, in the other the emphasis is rather on worsting an opponent. The two spheres are complementary in many ways: advantageous contacts with administration make for power in the village; dominance in the village helps to smooth relations with state administration.

In religion the duality is between the transcendental and the pragmatic functions, between those beliefs and practices that deal with the needs of society and those that are more directed to the immediate needs of the individual (Mandelbaum 1966, pp. 1174–1179). The transcendental complex is used to assure the long-term welfare of society, the maintenance of the social and of the sacred systems, and the proper transition of individuals from stage to stage within these systems. It is concerned with the ultimate goals of man. The pragmatic complex is used for personal benefits and local exigencies—to cure a sick child, for success in family ventures. The one is connected to religious centers far beyond the village as well as to places of worship within the village; the shrines of the other are mainly within the locality. Different forms and practitioners attach to each, as was previously noted in Chapter 13.

The transcendental deities are conceived as being universal in scope, their message for Hindus given in Sanskrit texts, their rites and ceremonies staged in a regular round. The practitioners of the transcendental complex are mainly, though not exclusively, Brahmins, and are hereditary priests of high jati rank. They are accorded prestige because of their jati and its calling and they are presumed to be exemplars of ritual purity.

The deities of the pragmatic complex are considered to be local in power and in residence. Their messages and stories are transmitted in the folklore of the vernacular. Some of their rites are cyclical but a good many are impromptu, staged when an urgent need arises. Some of their practitioners are priests, religious technicians, but they are generally shamans also, who become possessed by the deity and through whom the deity speaks, something that does not usually happen with the Brahmin priest and the high gods whom he serves. The shaman's calling is an achieved rather than a hereditary one. Any prestige that a shaman gains through his powers accrue to him alone, not to his jati. He is often of low jati and his clients are not bound in jajmani relations to him as a Brahmin priest's often are. They call on him as their need arises and their desire inclines. The pragmatic practitioner is not an exemplar but rather a demonstrator of the presence and powers of the local deities (Mandelbaum 1964, pp. 8–11).

The two complexes are used in complementary relation, each for its own purposes. Traditionally there was little rivalry between them. The Brahmin priest did not decry the services of the shaman, and the shaman, whether in possession or not, did not revile the services of the priest and his gods. Doctrine did not pit one against the other as might seem likely from a literal reading of scripture. The transcendental doctrines of karma, of the soul being held in moral account from one transmigration to the next, and of maya, of the immateriality of the flesh and all earthly things, did not prevent a Brahmin or any villager from trying to enlist the help of the local godlings to cure his sick child and for similar mundane but urgent purposes.

Each complex is clearly distinct from the other, but neither is kept as an absolutely exclusive category. High gods may be invoked for quite pragmatic purposes; local deities may be petitioned to look after transcendental affairs. A local deity or ceremony can gradually be assimilated into the scriptural pantheon and identified with Sanskritic rites. Conversely, a god from the scriptural roster may be transformed, by the people of a particular locality, into a pragmatic and local spirit. Marriott has discussed these processes under the terms universalization and parochialization (1955b, pp. 211–218). These transpositions change the particular details within each complex; they do not usually do away with the distinction between them.

In religion, as in economics and politics, people of different social levels participate in different ways. Those of poorer and lower jatis have less to do with transcendental rites and more to do with the pragmatic. This is in part because pragmatic needs press urgently upon them, in part because they have little responsibility for, or freedom to engage in, matters of larger and longer concern. Yet they do participate to some extent in the worship of transcendental gods, just as villagers of high jati, especially women, seek benefits from the pragmatic deities.

The worship of the high gods, as was noted in the previous chapter, takes many villagers to distant places. The regional centers are part of the general transcendental pattern, sometimes specifically designed after a supercenter. Thus the town of Wai in Maharashtra was built up to be a kind of "Southern Banaras," its temples, festivals, and bathing ghats consciously modeled after similar places not only in Banaras but in other important religious centers as well (Cohn and Marriott 1958, pp. 6–7).

Non-Hindus maintain a similar religious duality. There is, moreover, considerable mutual use of local deities by villagers of different formal faiths. So Hindus and Muslims alike pray for favors at the tomb of a particularly revered Muslim whose spirit is thought to watch over a locality; Muslims in turn may seek the aid of a Hindu shaman (cf. Beals 1962, pp. 47–48).

The same duality is seen in art, which is inseparable from religion in village life. Traditional art forms are integrally connected with religion and the major ceremonial occasions also provide for esthetic performance and enjoyment. Folk dancing, for example, goes with ceremonies of the local deities and the literary arts and architecture are in the province of the transcendental complex.

Education once was part of religion, specifically for the maintenance of transcendental religion. In pre-British times, education was loosely organized, confined to the higher jatis, directed to maintaining traditional ways and learning. It was so heavily weighted toward preservation of the sacred word, that a child's education characteristically began with many months, even years, of nothing but sheer rote memorization. Over many centuries that system of education effectively fulfilled the purposes for which it was intended. The scriptures were preserved intact, the learning was transmitted unimpaired. After the establishment of the British regime (and far more under the independent government), education has become widespread, more formal, more organized, and secular. It is now intended as a prime means of innovation rather than as the great instrument for conservation.

With the enormous expansion of modern, secular education, educational administrators have had to face difficult problems involving, among other things, the duality of role relations. Many educators believe that education ought to be carried on through personal rather than impersonal relations between student and teacher. Yet with masses of young people now being educated, impersonal mass roles rather than personal multiplex roles have to be taken.

Such tensions between differing role requirements are inherent in complex societies; individuals require at least some personal, noncontractual, supportive, multiplex relations, but the demands of maintaining a complex society impel toward impersonal, contractual, simplex roles.[4] Different civilizations have evolved different ways of coping with this tension. Kinship roles usually provide much of the personal dimension; the duality in kinship roles in India has been noted above, some of the agnatic roles rather paradoxically being more impersonal than certain affinal roles. The dual sets of roles in economic, political, and religious activities are the means evolved by Indian peoples for meeting a problem inherent in all civilizations.

Special Roles

Another perennial problem of complex societies is the kind of role to be accorded to persons who do not fulfill the normally expected

[4] The disparity is acutely felt in medical services. Thus in an analysis of medical practices in Sherurpur village, Gould writes, "The peasant sees hospitals and clinics as places where he will be compeled to wait endless hours in congested anterooms, castigated and mocked by officious attendants, and finally examined and treated by a doctor who will show no personal interest in him whatsoever." But the same villagers welcomed modern medical services when "medicine was being integrated into patterns of social interactions which they understood and which did not drain from them every ounce of their self-respect as the price of being benefited by what the modern world has to offer" (Gould 1965b, p. 208).

roles. Some social provision is usually made for the accommodation of exceptional personalities. These include men who insist on carrying out the ideal precepts of religion so literally as to impede ordinary social relations. In India, Hindu nonconformists may take special, and honored, roles in which their singular personality does not clog the normal processes of social life.

A man who wants to do so may cut himself entirely loose from his local society and completely vacate all his roles and statuses within it. He becomes a *sanyassin*, a religious devotee who consecrates himself to deity, takes no social responsibilities, lives by alms, and often wanders about without fixed home. Scripturally such a role is enjoined at a certain stage in life for men of the three highest varnas; in practice a man of almost any jati can throw off his ordinary costume and identity, and take on the ochre robe and the asocial character of the sanyassin.

A man who did not fit in with his society, who "was out of joint" with the social institutions, Nehru wrote, became a sanyassin (1946, p. 249). The lack of fit may rise from a powerful vocation for religion or for any number of other reasons, but whatever their motivation such men are considered to be outside the social norms expected of others and they act in that way. One of the early European observers, Barbosa, wrote in the sixteenth century that these devotees did not observe food or touch taboos (Dames 1918, p. 232).

This freedom from expected norms still obtains. On becoming a sanyassin a man discards the insignia of his previous identity, a Brahmin puts off his sacred thread, cuts off the tuft of hair that the orthodox wear. Occasionally the family of such a man conducts funeral rites to mark his symbolic departure from earthly affairs. And when a sanyassin does actually die, he is buried, in the sitting position proper for religious meditation and dedication, rather than cremated (Ghurye 1953; Karve 1953, pp. 297–298). These persons are both pure and polluting. Carstairs tells that in Deoli town in Rajasthan a Brahmin will bow down and clasp a sanyassin's foot, but will not sit to eat with him, even if he had been of the highest caste before becoming a sanyassin. By leaving taboos behind and associating with persons of the lowest castes, "he carries a threat of pollution for one who is still committed to the dialectic of pious

observance versus defilement which is inescapable in everyday life"
(Carstairs 1957, p. 102).

Some sanyassins settle into one place rather than wander, and
direct their efforts toward religious-social improvement as well as
to their personal salvation. Such an ascetic came to a village of the
tribal Reddi along the Godavari River and there established an
ashram, a religious retreat, in a garden he laid out. His reputation
as a holy one spread to towns far from his retreat in the jungle-clad
hills, and visitors of wealth and high rank came to him from afar to
share in the merit of his presence. He required his visitors to contribute toward the welfare of the Reddi and when the anthropologist Fürer-Haimendorf was in that village in 1943, the sanyassin had
founded an organization for the "poverty relief" of the local tribal
peoples (1945, pp. 269–275). Two decades later a young anthropologist drawn to visit the village because of its anthropological
rather than sacred renown found the ashram and its founder still
in vigorous condition.

Other devotees remain in their home villages, especially those
who take on this role in their later years. Some who discard personal
ties at a relatively young age remain in the region of their home,
sometimes attached to a village temple, and despite their worldly
nonattachment, still exert influence over the villagers, especially
women, to the point of taking a strong though usually indirect hand
in village politics (Gough 1956, pp. 838, 842). K. D. Gangrade has
studied a village in the Delhi district in which the sanyassin resident
in the village temple exerts a strong, though covert, influence on
alliance politics.

A modern monastic order of sanyassins, the Ramakrishna Mission, is directed toward works of social welfare as well as to the
spiritual elevation of its members. It is quite unlike the traditional
orders—the term "monastic order" implies much more organization
than they usually had—whose members would preach to the laity
and answer their questions but would not engage in social enterprises. The scholar, Agehananda Bharati, tells how he came to India
from Vienna, where he was born Leopold Fischer, to join the Ramakrishna Order. But after a novitiate of two years he left that group
because of doctrinal and other differences and was initiated as a
sanyassin by a venerable monk of one of the traditional orders. His

account of his experiences as a wandering mendicant vividly illustrates the relationship between itinerant sanyassin and villagers
(1961, pp. 157–173).

Although the disengagement from society is not necessarily total
severance, almost all sanyassins live a life of overt asceticism. Of
this religious dedication, N. K. Bose writes, "The price demanded
from the individual was indeed heavy. He had to surrender all the
benefits normally derived from collective life. Only when he was
prepared to put up with the starkness of such a life, was he assured
a degree of freedom and prestige not enjoyed even by the sacerdotal
caste. The sanyassin was put beyond the operation of social laws"
(1953a, p. 181).

Not all the mendicant devotees are universally respected; villagers may grumble, especially when a number of them come
through their village, that the holy state is becoming a kind of
racket for some. Nor does every man who takes to the role stay
with it until death. Some, either replenished with spiritual achievement or depleted by sparse alms and rigorous wanderings, revert to
their previous social niche. But a man who feels stifled by social
duty can still become a sanyassin and thereby attain social release
as well as spiritual gain. "We may imagine," Bose concludes, "that
this safety valve was responsible, to a certain extent, for the stabili-
zation of the Hindu order of society. Those who suffered from a
feeling of oppression, could escape and leave the organization itself
to work as before" (Bose 1953a, p. 182). Individuals who might
have created considerable friction in a local system could in this
way remove themselves from it.

While the sanyassin is not a member of any social group his
role is recognized as moral and legitimate by the society he has renounced. Dumont and Pocock note that this holy state "counterbal-
ances in a way the existence of castes and is rightly included in a
definition of the system" (1957a, p. 17). One who deliberately cuts
himself off from every social group must, nevertheless, keep to certain social prescriptions for the role, as in style of dress and of hair
and in ascetic practices: A sanyassin casts himself in a zero social
role but that role nonetheless has social position, social shape, social
weight. The role of alienation itself is part of the system of society.

Roles and Fields of Action

Roles are not straitjackets; a villager has room for some individual variation even in the more rigidly prescribed roles. A woman's roles generally allow for less variation than do a man's, a young bride's far less than a mature matron's, but all role behavior is subject to the actor's personal touch. All role behavior is also subject to social change. When actors in large numbers begin to alter particular role behaviors in consistent directions, they thereby begin the course of social change. A role, as formulated by the observers, includes both expected behavior and the actual behavior with specified others as that behavior is regulated according to certain norms (cf. Gross *et al.* 1958, pp. 48–67; Parsons 1961, pp. 41–43; Banton 1965).

Moreover, a person switches his style of behavior as he takes different roles. The same man who feels constrained to be a rather aloof father to his adolescent son commonly shifts to being a more friendly, supportive person when another youth, his sister's son, comes into view.

The expectations held about any particular role are far from uniform. A certain minimum agreement is necessary in order to maintain interaction but beyond that minimum there often are considerable differences of view (cf. Levinson 1959). In the traditional jajmani roles, patron and artisan typically take differing views of what should be tendered by the other, the landowner stressing loyalty and devoted service, the artisan stressing the protection and regular rewards due him from the patron. The artisan tends to have a grander notion of the importance of his position than does his patron. What is important for the maintenance of jajmani relations is that there be just enough agreement so that the exchange of goods and services can continue.

A person's field of social action includes those role relations that he carries on commonly and centrally, as with his family, and those that are more occasional and peripheral, as with a town merchant or a priest of a distant temple. In addition to the actual field of interaction there is the potential field—those roles that a person may possibly actuate under certain circumstances. Actual and potential fields of conduct are illustrated in the distinction between kin of cooperation and kin of recognition, which was noted in respect to the uses of kinship. The former are kinsmen with whom a person maintains actual relations and the latter are more distant kin, either genealogically or geographically distant, with whom kinship interaction may be established if one of the potential kinsmen becomes wealthy and ambitious enough to expand his field of actual kin, or if both of them do.

A person's kinship field changes over time as births, marriages and deaths alter its composition; it may be changed also through voluntary extensions or contractions. The combined kinship fields of the members of a jati-group (the kinship region, as Mayer calls it), include all those "populations within which marriage can take place without enquiries as to credentials of membership" (Mayer 1962, p. 268). Rising families may expand that kinship region, making marriage alliances farther afield than before, or they may contract their endogamous circle by hiving off from the larger jati and deciding to marry only with those families who meet new and higher standards.

A villager may activate his potential roles in any aspect of his life. The extent to which he can do so is dependent on a series of conditions, attributive, cognitive, motivational, expedient. Attributive factors constrict the possible roles that can be taken. Men of the lowest jatis had, and to a considerable degree still have, a very constricted range of roles, actual or potential. They could not take overtly active roles in village politics; they were debarred from large parts of the transcendental complex of religion; they were usually too crushed by poverty to be able to take any but the most elemental economic roles.

Cognitive factors also delimit the range of possible roles. A villager's fields of conduct are obviously limited to the roles he knows about or can know about. Not all of those he knows are open to him or attractive for him, but he cannot take on new roles unless he knows something about them. People whose education, travel, and information are very limited have small role potential; those whose horizons of experience and knowledge are wider have greater fields for potential relationships.

Motivation to expand one's roles and relationships is not in short supply, at least, not among some men of almost any village. The process requires a firm base of material and social resources; an ambitious villager is commonly in middle age by the time he has established a base above that which he inherited. Hence much of his role expansion is done through his children, by enlarging their potential fields by means of formal education and by arranging socially advantageous marriages for them. Expediency in marshaling resources for a particular purpose is characteristic of such men. They are able to translate potential relationships into actual services, to command loyalties of diverse kinds and to bring them to bear on specific issues. A successful alliance leader in a village commonly does this, gaining his ends—whether to calm a dispute or add to his land—by calling forth support from people of different jatis, lineages, and interests.

The people who are called upon, and respond, in order to help a man achieve his purposes constitute his resource network (Sharma 1963). The term "network" has also been used for those people in a group's actual field of social relations who are deployed by the members of the group for certain purposes (cf. Jay 1964; Mayer 1962; Srinivas and Béteille 1964). Through the contacts of his resource network, a man may reach far beyond his usual field of relationships. Village leaders have long manipulated these resource networks to gain their ends, but in recent times the reach of such a network from the village can be remarkably extended.

Thus in Sripuram village of Tanjore district in Madras, a Brahmin landowner wanted to have his son admitted to an engineering college in the city of Madras. He proceeded first through his own father, who practiced law in the nearby town and who had as a client an eminent businessman, a non-Brahmin in Tanjore city. The landowner from the village could thus discuss his problem with the businessman who, in turn, had influential business associates at the state capital, Madras. Through these city magnates the village landowner was put in touch with a member of the committee of the college to which his son was later admitted (Srinivas and Béteille 1964, p. 166). Such manipulation of social resources for one's family is laudable by traditional standards, but in the context of a modern establishment it is open to criticism by other standards, criticism that is expressed in such epithets as favoritism, nepotism, or even corruption.

Village, Civilization, and Change

These four chapters on the village have examined salient features of internal and external relations, the ties among village, center, and region, and villagers' responses to certain problems of civilization. The overarching concept of Indian civilization consists in large part of the fundamental, prevailing ideas about man and society; some of these have already been discussed, others will be noted in succeeding chapters. Scholars have sketched the outlines of the civilization, but much of the analysis remains to be done (cf. Raghavan 1956; Brown 1961; Singer 1964). It is an analysis needed for comparative studies of civilizations as well as for an understanding of Indian civilization (cf. Kroeber 1944, pp. 480–686).

The idea of Indian civilization is known in villages, but it is not a concept that is in the fore of villagers' perception. However, when there is confrontation with people of other civilizations, this latent concept—now couched in modern nationalist terms—becomes an important force, as it did in the struggle for national independence.

The village, in sum, is a basic feature of the civilization and continues to be a viable community for its inhabitants. A person's village provides him with one source of his self-identification, with a nexus of his activities, a stage for his status, and an arena of conflict. Observers can view it as a system comprising component jati-groups and functional activities, and also as a subsystem of larger social systems. The people of a village have used the panchayat pattern to facilitate interchange and effect counterchange. Alliances are commonly important to a village system, though villagers are usually reluctant to avow that alliances are proper and legitimate factors in village life.

Those of any one village have ties with people in many other villages and centers. Their relations with centers are important cohesion factors in maintaining the precepts of the civilization. These precepts, together with the other elements of the society and civilization, have been altered over time and are now in a vast process of change.

In the preceding chapter it was observed that a villager can choose to identify himself with one or another of his groups and groupings

according to the context of action in which he is involved at a particular juncture. In the same way he has some choice in selecting
one role or even one subsystem of action rather than another in
order to gain his purpose. The choice of system for action and
selection of role within a subsystem is often quite clear and straightforward to the participant. For one of the dominant "Peasant" jati
in Wangala, as Mrs. Epstein writes, it is the context of a social situation that determines to which unit he feels and expresses his allegiance. "In his everyday economic activities he regards himself as
a farmer or farmhand; on ceremonial occasions he acts as a member
of a faction; in his relation with other castes and untouchables in
Wangala he acts as a member of the Peasant caste; and in his relations with the Administration he acts as a Peasant of Wangala"
(1962, p. 145).

But there are other occasions when the choices are not so clear
and when alternative possibilities can be manipulated. Thus Bailey
tells of a villager of Bisipara who is an untouchable by jati, a minor
official by appointment, and a quite affluent trader by his own efforts. His trade is carried on with men of the Kond tribe who are
rated as a clean jati by the neighboring Oriyas. When this man,
Nrusingh by name, visits Konds in his capacity as a minor official
he overplays that role, hectoring them more than do other minor
officials who are not untouchables. The Konds, on their side, "do
not hesitate to rub in Nrusingh's untouchable state." But neither
wants to allow their mutual animosities to stand in the way of their
trade relationships; their other roles do not contaminate the roles of
buyer and seller. The Konds may treat Nrusingh in any one of his
three capacities but not all three at the same time because the roles
are in some situations contradictory. "In every situation the actors
have an element of latitude and may choose the way they will behave in order to further their own ends. The Konds can humiliate
Nrusingh by treating him as an untouchable or they can flatter him
by treating him as an official, whichever suits their purpose" (1960b,
p. 209).

Whether Nrusingh is humiliated or flattered signifies very little
even in his own small remote village, but the principle and fact of
choice among roles and systems is of the highest importance in such
villages and essential to an understanding of the whole social system.

We have so far focused on the main roles, groups, and systems of village society, on the rules of the social game. Although changes and choices have necessarily been mentioned before, we now turn to a more detailed examination of the dynamics of the social order.

PART **VI** *Recurrent Change Through Social Mobility*

CHOICES, decisions, alternatives, confront a villager when he comes to take responsibility, whether for his family or lineage, for his jati or village. A man is then impelled to be something of a manipulator of his culture and society as well as a creature and carrier of it. To be sure, the actual decisions may privately be influenced by the women or the younger people, but the men, the heads of family, the elders and leaders, must give the signal and initiate action.

Some kinds of decisions occur only a few times in the lifetime of the decider and may set in train a series of events that he does not foresee or desire. But from the wider perspective of the observer most of these decisions can be seen to lead into cycles which are regular processes of the social system. Such cycles follow on decisions to choose one girl rather than another as a bride for one's son, to keep a joint family together or to part, to join in an alliance affray or to remain aloof. The cycle of family growth and dispersal is one kind of recurrent change.

Our main interest in the chapters of the following two sections is with recurrent change in the social order through jati mobility, religious regrouping, and the movement from tribal to caste society. We begin with jati mobility, looking first at the underlying pressures toward status competition among jatis, the conditions required for a successful mobility campaign, the cultural adaptations that ambitious villagers typically make, and the social tactics they use to secure their purposes.

Competition Among Jatis

Recurrent change among jatis arises from consistent efforts by members of lower jatis to raise their ranking. The higher jatis usually oppose them in order to preserve their own superior rank, but some of the lower do succeed in time in raising their status. Occasionally a higher jati may fall in rank. Such shifts are positional not structural changes. The social structure remains quite the same even though one group now is accepted as higher than its former superior and its members outrank those of a previously higher set (cf. Srinivas 1965, p. 8).

The political contests involved in this process in village India have been called routine politics by F. G. Bailey in contrast to the "politics of change"; this contrast is like that which Max Gluckman has drawn between rebellions and revolutions in African societies. Routine politics are repetitive, in the sense that whichever side wins, similar conflict at once emerges, and the system goes on as before. "The logistic, factual, and jural rules of this type of conflict are such that when one group wins it is immediately faced with a similar conflict, where the same rules apply, and so on down the infinite corridors of structural time, until something happens to change these rules" (Bailey 1965, pp. 23–24).

The "corridors of structural time" are also corridors of power, because repetitive politics are basically about power, about who gets what and who controls whom in the local system. Village political contests were traditionally expressed as disputes about jati rank and as struggles about the insignia and prerogatives of rank. Men who accrued wealth or new political resources typically tried to translate them into a gain in ritual rank in order to legitimate their rise and fix it against the passage of time. In that sense jati mobility included both economic and political mobility.

Status contests, as has been noted, can be carried on as vigorously within a jati as among jatis. But such internal contests are usually superseded by united defense if the rank of the jati as a whole is at stake. A prospering man normally tries to enhance the standing of his family and lineage within the jati. But unless that jati can command a suitable degree of local respect, his gains are incomplete. He is likely to try to band together with his jati confreres to raise the jati, and—as they see it—to restore it to its proper place.

Individual mobility, by itself, is limited and ephemeral. It is limited because even though a man may become wealthy and personally powerful in his locality, his neighbors of higher rank still deal with him according to the ritual attributes of his jati. It is ephemeral because members of a rising family must find brides and grooms for their children from comparably eminent families. Unless other families of their jati have risen in similar proportion, the status gains of one family may fade away after a generation. Hence mobility in rank must be collective if it is to be fruitful and durable (cf. Srinivas 1966, pp. 44-45).

The drive for collective mobility is of surpassing concern to many villagers because they believe that greater power and material rewards are won by those who succeed in gaining higher rank. The grounds for this belief are particularly clear to members of the lowest jatis. The people of an untouchable jati are usually landless and are highly dependent on the will of the landowning patrons. Other jatis commonly resist the acquisition of land by untouchables lest on becoming less dependent, they no longer will consent to do polluting tasks. Untouchables who can somehow lift themselves to a higher social level may be freed of many economic and personal shackles. Untouchables can aspire to higher ritual rank because they share the pervasive ideas that one's own group is entitled to higher place in the social hierarchy than others accord it and that the higher position is worth struggling for.

This valuation of self and of society is an important factor in the striving for jati mobility. The people of a jati typically hold to an origin myth that tells of their descent from noble or divine ancestors, or from some of each kind. These accounts not only reflect the common self-image, they also serve to justify efforts to regain one's noble and rightful heritage.

Villagers cherish two different origin myths, one for the society as a whole, the other for their own jati. The account for the whole society is that discussed previously of the four varna categories as given in *Manu* and in other scriptural sources. The people in each of the four categories are fixed by that account in their respective rank, the order is immutable and the ranks are not competitive one with another. The scriptural concept of *dharma*, of one's sacred duty, asserts that each person should fulfill, dispassionately, the obligation of his station in life. That station is given to him for the duration of one lifetime as a result of his soul's *karma*, the supernal merit or demerit that his soul has accrued in previous existences (cf. Karve 1961, pp. 91-101).

The other account, that of one's own jati origin, does not contradict the first in any single particular, but taken in conjunction with it encourages constant competition among jatis. Their jati myth assures the members of a lower jati that they really belong to a higher rank; hence, if they are truly to perform their sacred dharma, they must struggle to get that loftier rank formally and permanently acknowledged by others. The myth also implies that they must keep jatis below them in the proper lowly position to which local society and their respective karma assigns them.

The reigning, ideal principle is that of social immutability while the ruling, actual principle is that of social competition among those close to each other in rank. Some observers, basing their views on the ideal principles, conclude that caste in India is essentially a noncompetitive system (cf. Leach 1960, pp. 6–7; Bailey 1963a, pp. 121–122). Others see an apparent paradox or contradiction between the ideal rule and the actual condition (cf. Pocock 1964). To the villagers, little contradiction is involved; each principle is applied where it is relevant for oneself and one's group. Jati rivals do not worry much about the validity of their opponents' story of origin; it is the validity of one's own that must be fought out and justified in the village arena.

Competition among jatis may well be ancient, but only a few historical studies of the subject have yet been made. Rivalries among ancient guilds resembled contemporary jati rivalries. There is evidence of jati mobility from the Gupta period, as when silk weavers, perhaps still organized as a guild, moved across to another region and rose to new, more respectable occupations (Thapar 1966, p. 153). In medieval South India, there seems to have been considerable social mobility by families. This too was accomplished mainly by geographic mobility. New land was available for cultivation (as it was in many parts of India well into the nineteenth century); ambitious people could move to a new place, put untilled land under the plow, become landowners in a new settlement, and so establish a new social identity for themselves. This obviated some of the intense rivalry of more recent times, when new lands were not so readily available (Stein 1967).

A seventeenth-century report by the Dutch missionary, Abraham Roger, mentions jati rivalries quite like those of the twentieth century. Roger lived in Pulicat, north of Madras, from 1631 to

1641. In one passage he describes the jati called "Wellala" and then notes, "The other castes I shall not here set forth according to their order, for that there is no unanimity among them as to which precedeth, but each mightily claimeth and pretendeth that his own caste is best" (translation by L. H. Gray in Jackson 1907, p. 244).

From the more ample European sources of the eighteenth century come numerous references to competition for jati rank. In his review of these sources, V. P. S. Raghuvanshi cites examples from various parts of the subcontinent, commenting that some of the South Indian accounts "look as if there were a constant scramble for superiority among the various trading, artisan, and cultivating castes at certain places" (1966, p. 167).

The Abbé Dubois, who lived in South India for some thirty years at the end of the eighteenth and the beginning of the nineteenth centuries, tells of a quarrel between "Pariyas" and "Chucklers" that threatened the peace of a whole district. The dispute concerned the right of the Chucklers to wear red flowers in their turbans on ceremonial occasions (Dubois 1928, pp. 26–27). Such antagonisms between two untouchable jatis have been carried on in modern times as well, for example between the Malas and the Madigas of Andhra. Similar rivalries are found at every social level; the landowning Kamas and Reddis in Andhra have been such rivals (cf. Frykenberg 1963, pp. 2–5; Harrison 1960, pp. 206–213).

Even the top jatis of a local order are likely to jostle for higher status among themselves. If there are several Brahmin jatis within a village, each may claim and strive to be the highest. Sripuram village of Tanjore district holds 12 separate jatis of Brahmins, in a Brahmin population of 341 (Béteille 1965, pp. 72–79). They are differentiated by the language used in the household (Kannada, Telugu, or Tamil), by priestly occupation (of the Siva and Vishnu temples), and by doctrinal affiliation (several jatis of Smarthas and several of Iyengars). Most of them oppose the non-Brahmins' drive for political power in the village, but they are divided among themselves and indeed believe that the present decline of Brahmin power is a result of their disunity.

The evidence, however, is that they are not any more at odds now than they were in the past. Béteille indicates that in the 1880s "they quarreled bitterly among themselves over ritual and other matters." As for the present order of rank among these Brahmins, "it is doubtful whether a definitive answer can be provided even after detailed consideration of political, economic, and other 'interactional' features" (Béteille 1962, pp. 143–144).

Brahmins in all regions naturally emphasized those stories that reminded others of their sacred obligation to acknowledge Brahmin superiority with proper respect and gifts. These were not always and everywhere readily forthcoming. In parts of the Punjab, for example, a good many Hindus gave little more than lip service to their local Brahmins (cf. Tandon 1961, pp. 76–77).

Yet Brahmin jatis were acknowledged as belonging to the highest varna among all Hindus and among many they were supported with material gifts as well as with gestures of respect. Nevertheless the Brahmin jatis were not, and are not, immune to status competition. Where several live in the same locality, claims and counterclaims of higher status among them are commonly pressed. Harijans may have more at stake in their push for mobility, but the competitive drive animates people at all levels of village society.

Conditions for Mobility

Aspirations for jati rise are common; achieved aspirations are much less common. To achieve a rise usually takes time measured in generations. Ambitious members of the jati must first be able to command ample wealth and power. The process typically begins when a good many families of a low-ranking group secure such resources, usually through long and hard efforts. They use them to improve their ritual purity and then to secure public acceptance of their claims. Mere reform of jati practices, in itself, does not usually bring about much gain in rank.[1]

Wealth and power are used for jati gains in ways similar to those noted above in the status competition among families, lineages, and alliances within a jati. Assets in the political system, such as friendly connections with officials, facilitate gains in the economic system.

---

[1] The Mala of the Telengana region of Andhra, for example, do not eat pork or carrion as do other untouchables in these villages, yet they are firmly classed as untouchables "and rank only just a little higher than the carrion-eating Madigas" (Dube 1955c, p. 190).

And those who amass wealth are inclined to develop political connections to make their wealth more secure. Both economic and
political assets are typically invested in the higher form of village
security, namely augmented jati status.

Occasionally an able, persevering man, even though of poor
family and lowly jati, becomes rich. Such success stories are widely
known, though the number of such instances is small. Even an
untouchable can become relatively wealthy; one such man in Bisipara village in Orissa became a middleman in the sale of hides. He
began with nothing and prospered until he came to own land
worth more than that held by all the others of his jati-group
(Bailey 1957, p. 159).

But a few wealthy men do not make a mobility campaign; that
requires concerted use of wealth and power by many families. It is
helped along if they can mobilize enough force and courage in
their villages to withstand threats of violent reprisal (cf. Srinivas
1959a, p. 4).

A whole jati can gain in wealth when favorable economic opportunities open in the jati's occupation. One historic example is that
of the Kayasths, a jati-cluster whose members are widespread over
North India and whose traditional occupation was that of scribe.
Writing was not an accomplishment highly prized by Brahmin
scholars of earlier ages, who saw it as a useful device but one mainly
necessary for clerks and merchants; a true scholar committed scripture to memory. When the Mogul emperors established administrative procedures based on written records kept in Persian, the ability
to use these records became important and lucrative. Many Kayasths, following their traditional occupation of scribes, became
proficient in Persian. A good many of them showed high ability and
intelligence and were appointed to influential posts. Their capabil-
ities became all the more useful during the British regime; a number
of Kayasth families rose high in public service as well as in education and wealth. Thus strengthened, eminent men of several
Kayasth jatis fought long legal battles to have their social rank
recognized as being above the Shudra category to which earlier
tradition had assigned them (Bhattacharya 1896, pp. 175–191;
Baines 1912, pp. 38–40; Karve 1961, p. 45).

A more recent instance of jati rise through occupational opportunity is that of the Noniyas of Uttar Pradesh. Their traditional occupation was the extraction of salt and saltpeter from saline soils. Since the handling of salt for profit is ritually a dubious business, they were ranked quite low. In Senapur elderly villagers recalled in the 1950s that when they were children the Noniyas were "almost untouchable," and Bhattacharya noted in his all-India survey that "generally they are regarded as semi-clean Sudras" (1896, p. 265). During the last part of the nineteenth century some Noniyas prospered greatly. When better salt than theirs became available, they turned to other kinds of work with earth: some took to agriculture, others to building watercourses, wells, tanks, roads, and to making bricks and tile.

When the British greatly expanded irrigation facilities, roads and other public works, there was a great expansion of demand for the skills that the Noniyas possessed and for the bricks they produced. Some Noniyas became contractors to government and grew wealthy. A small but powerful Noniya elite arose; these families campaigned vigorously for higher status. "The changing opportunity structure in colonial society, with the emergence of a newly prosperous group within the caste and the resulting incongruence of their ritual and economic ranks led to the founding and financing of a self-conscious caste mobility organization" (Rowe 1968, p. 70). In Senapur they are now placed by the dominant Thakurs as ninth or tenth from the top among the twenty-four jatis of the village, well above their earlier rank.

In some villages of eastern Uttar Pradesh, the local Noniyas are almost entirely landless and are still heavily dependent on landlords of other jatis. These poor Noniyas see the organization for Noniya improvement "as a distant and not very real entity." By contrast, there is a small group of well-to-do men in Bombay, also of Noniya extraction, "who would appear to the superficial observer as well-established, middle-class professional men of a Kshatriya caste" (Rowe 1968, p. 68).

There is a saying among Indian Muslims which, in various versions, expresses the relation between growing wealth and mounting ambition. It is told about weavers or butchers or other low-ranking groups. "Last year we were weavers, this year we are Shaikhs, and next year if the harvest is good we shall be Sayyids" (cf. Misra

1964, p. 170; Ibbetson 1916, p. 10; Baines 1912, p. 63).[2] Wealth makes augmented purity possible; enhanced status may then follow. The reverse does not hold. Many a group has purified its practices and still remained poor and lowly. Greater purity is usually costly, requiring the giving up of previous sources of income or the assuming of expensive new customs. Such assumption, if seen as a threat by those in a higher niche, raises opposition and hostility, which has to be countered by still more expenditure.

Gains in political power have usually opened the way for economic advantage and eventual rise in jati rank. In medieval India, rulers of low social origins were commonly accorded Kshatriya status after they seized power (Stein 1968, p. 79; Panikkar 1956, p. 8; Srinivas 1966, pp. 30–42). To capture or found a state, a freebooter had to have staunch allies, usually his clan and jati mates. Once he was installed in power, his comrades-in-arms became wealthy landowners. They then could afford the appurtenances of higher ritual rank and could quell any opposition to their claims.

A ruler's grace and favor could also affect the status of jatis other than his own. In some princely states this influence continued into the late nineteenth century. A British official who had served in Punjab hill states wrote that "it is within the present writer's own experience that the Raja of Lambagraon . . . readmitted to the twice-born status certain Kolis who had been ousted from it more than a century earlier by the Raja of Kangra, as a punishment for disrespectful behavior." He noted also that the Rajas of Chamba similarly had conferred the right to wear the sacred thread, with a step up in social rank, in return for gifts or special services (Maynard 1917, pp. 93, 97). This occurred in the South also; in the same article, Sir Sankaran Nair is quoted as giving an instance from sixteenth-century Kerala. The Charmas, "a servile caste," had been raised to the station of the military Nayars by the Maharaja of Cochin as a reward for military services (Maynard 1917, p. 93; Srinivas 1966, pp. 40–42).

When the British took over direct rule, they refused to intervene in caste affairs in this way. Hence manipulation of political power

[2] A similar Tamil saying is "Kallan, Maravan, and Ahamudiyan by slow degrees become Vellala. Having become Vellala, they called themselves Mudaliyar" (Béteille 1965, p. 98).

for jati mobility became more circuitous; it was done through long litigation about jati prerogatives or through the education of sons who might become government officials. Their positions then enhanced the prestige of the jati, even though as officials they might not bestow more tangible rewards.

Special Resistances to Change in Jati Status

There is a certain inertia to jati ranking, as was noted in discussing village power relations. Untouchables find it particularly difficult to move to the other side of the untouchability barrier, as the Holerus of Totagadde village in Mysore have found. As in most areas, the landowners there were strongly opposed to allowing untouchables to own land. One Holeru recalled that the elders of his jati were even fearful of going to speak to a Brahmin (Harper 1968, p. 57). They had neither the skills, the education, nor the capital which might enable them to be anything other than unskilled laborers.

Nevertheless these Holerus have in recent decades thrown off some of the more degrading practices. They no longer eat beef, they will not remove dead cattle, they will no longer supply wood for funeral pyres. But these reforms are depreciated by the Havik Brahmins who are dominant in this village. On one occasion a Havik loudly asserted, in the hearing of his Holeru worker, that the Holerus were dirty and degraded because they ate beef. When the anthropologist to whom he was speaking questioned this, the Havik asked his servant if the statement were not true. The reply was that the Holeru council had prohibited the eating of beef for jati members some thirty years before. The Havik triumphantly said, "You see, I told you that Holerus are a dirty caste—they used to eat beef" (Harper 1968, p. 36).

Holerus are further bound into lowly status through their very quest for respectability. A Holeru family feels that it must give elaborate weddings for its children, each costing the equivalent of from one to two years of a man's income. The money usually is advanced by a Havik landowner; in return the Holerus pledge themselves as indentured laborers for years. Harper notes that of all things in the world, they value most that of which they have the least—prestige—and they strongly believe that a group's rank is in part based upon the elaborateness of its marriage rites (1968, p. 61).

They delude themselves. It is true that in staging a lavish wedding a Holeru family demonstrates how completely it shares in the values of the higher jatis. But despite such demonstrations and notwithstanding the reform of their customs, Holerus remain at the bottom of the local hierarchy. The landowners continue to advance marriage expenses to Holerus because they need field hands at peak demand periods and that is one good way of insuring a reliable labor supply. A good many Holerus are in constant debt and so are bound fast in the nethermost depths of social rank. But they are beginning to revise their mobility tactics and may yet succeed in narrowing the social gap between themselves and the other villagers.

As an untouchable jati must overcome special resistances in order to rise, the fall of a Brahmin jati is slowed by special inertia. If a Brahmin family loses its means of livelihood, its members may turn to performing some less honorable priestly tasks, such as funeral rites, or may act as priests for prospering families of lowly jatis who had not previously been able to afford the services of Brahmins. In Kumbapettai village of Tanjore district the dominant landowners are Smartha Brahmins; none of them would act as household priests for families of low rank.

In this region there are also Telugu-speaking Brahmins who traditionally were household priests to the local aristocracy. When the princely courts and courtiers were dispossessed, many of the Telugu Brahmins had to officiate for lower groups who "in their efforts to rise in the ritual hierarchy, were glad to employ impoverished Brahmins as household priests." One such Brahmin came to Kumbapettai in 1947, rented a house there and "ekes out a livelihood by conducting marriage, funeral and ancestral rites for those non-Brahmin families of the village who care to pay his fee" (Gough 1960, p. 31).

Brahmin jatis whose members officiate professionally at funeral rites or who take clients of low status are ranked lower than other Brahmins. Those euphemistically called Mahabrahmans, "great Brahmins," were considered to be so impure that in Punjab villages of the nineteenth century they were not allowed to come inside the village gate save for funerary purposes (Ibbetson 1916, p. 221). However, the contemporary Mahabrahmans of Ramapur village near Allahabad, mentioned previously, are very favorably situated because the sacred center there draws many worshippers who require their services for the memorial rites which are best completed at that holy place. A Mahabrahman of that locality is apt to be relatively wealthy, but in spite of his Brahmin status, most Hindus treat him in some ways as an untouchable and will not accept water and food from his hand. "He may not live in many villages" (Opler and Singh 1952, p. 185).

There are jatis of so-called "degraded" Brahmins in most parts of India (cf. Bhattacharya 1896, pp. 118–131). Generally they are recognized to be Brahmins, entitled to wear the insignia of their varna, to officiate at rites, especially funerary rites, to receive gifts due to Brahmins, but yet they are Brahmins who must be kept at a social distance by most other villagers. To be taken as Brahmins worthy of higher esteem, they would have to give up officiating at funeral services and this they are presumably reluctant to do because it is so lucrative. One such Brahmin jati obtained a rescript in the nineteenth century from a revered religious leader which certified to their true Brahminhood. Despite this document, their village neighbors continued to treat them as before (Bhattacharya 1896, p. 93).

An entire Brahmin jati may decline in status. The Gayawal are the main temple priests at the great pilgrimage center of Gaya. In recent decades they have come on hard times. Others have encroached on their clientele and the total number of pilgrims has fallen off considerably. The Gayawal have lost income and, from the evidence of L. P. Vidyarthi's account, they have diminished in ritual rank as well. They are still indubitably Brahmins, but are no longer as respected and influential as they once were (Vidyarthi 1961, pp. 86–110).

Impoverished Brahmins may descend to giving less prestigious services but they rarely, if ever, drop below the Brahmin category. Even a man who is cast out of a Brahmin jati may still, somehow, maintain his status as a Brahmin. One such case, recounted by Bhattacharya, is that of the ancestor of the Tagores. When this Brahmin was made outcaste, he left his village and settled in the town of Jessore. His descendants moved to Calcutta, which was then a kind of new frontier. Caste credentials were not too closely examined. The new elite there considered that "A Brahman is a Brahman though outcasted by his clansmen" (1896, p. 122). The

Tagores were able to establish themselves and rise to the top of the new secular elite though, as is noted in Chapter 25, it was a very long time before they were fully accepted as unblemished Brahmins. It was possible for them to remain Brahmins, but difficult to restore their former ritual standing among orthodox Brahmins of Bengal.

Personal Ambitions and Systemic Counterchange

In sum, social mobility is possible at all social levels, though it is more feasible for some jatis than for others, more propitious under certain circumstances, and more eagerly sought by some men than by others. Ambition to improve one's status is very common though some villagers display relatively little and others display little else. An ambitious man does not neatly differentiate among the various levels of his social aspiration; he tends to see the rise of his family, of his lineage, and of his jati as being all of a piece. Specific efforts for one or the other advance may have to be directed in different ways, but he hopes that a status rise at one level will advance efforts in the others. The basic conditions for a successful rise are similar at each level as is illustrated by the previously noted examples of lineage mobility in Wangala village and of the mobility of hypergamous sections among the Patidars of Gujarat.

In Wangala, Scarlett Epstein observes, the main contests result from an imbalance between the secular and the ritual status of lineages in the dominant jati. The size of a family's landholdings can shift drastically in a relatively short time. A man can build an estate in his own lifetime or conversely, a large estate can be dissipated in a few years, fragmented among numerous heirs. Formal lineage status is hereditary; descendants of eminent lines cling tightly to their hereditary lineage rights when their material fortunes decline. The rivalry between the "conservative" and the "progressive" factions in Wangala stems from such imbalance and since ritual status is regarded as the ultimate criterion of social status, "the 'progressive' faction is led continuously to bring its ritual status in line with its economic dominance" (Epstein 1962, p. 132).

Similar contests occur among the hypergamous sections, the "village circles" of the Patidars of Kaira district in Gujarat. Each jati-group belongs to one of these circles, and a daughter should be married into an equal or higher village circle. As a family prospers, it invests its wealth in symbols of prestige, especially buildings, and tries to contract the most prestigious marriages possible in its hypergamous range. Sometimes a family becomes wealthy enough to break into a new marriage bracket and others in its village try to do the same. They may succeed if the whole jati-group has prospered. "When any particular village makes more money as a result of a few good years of tobacco harvests, it may well endeavor to cut its ties with the other villages of its marriage circle and attempt to be included in the next highest circle" (Pocock 1957b, pp. 22, 29–30).

Efforts to raise one's lineage or jati-group do not preclude efforts in behalf of the whole jati. Each effort is made in the context suitable for it. Lineage leverage is tried when only jati brethren are involved, jati leverage is used when confronting other jatis. Promoting a whole jati is the more arduous task, if only because jati fellows who are scattered in many villages have to be mobilized and directed.

The goals of a jati campaign are to have the higher jati status ritually legitimated by local Brahmins, affirmed by all villagers in daily life and on ceremonial occasions, and confirmed, if necessary, by village panchayats.

The members of a rising jati have made good their claims when those who formerly would not eat with them or accept cooked food from them, now do so. Mayer notes that in Ramkheri the commensal seems to be the key relationship for a moving caste to establish, "for besides having ritual significance, it is reciprocal" (1956, p. 142). Eating together is a public and unmistakable gesture.

To attain these goals, the people of an aspiring jati usually have to reform jati practices and refurbish the jati origin myth. Villagers in India are no more versed in their actual history than are villagers anywhere, and they may ignore what they do know when it reminds them of what they would rather forget. But they are far from indifferent to statements about their past that can be enshrined in myth. Myth and customs may be suitably adjusted in a generation or two if economic conditions favor and unified efforts avail, but the opposition of higher jatis often lasts longer. And even when a jati has seemingly clinched a higher place, the memory of its former, lowly position is apt to linger on with the other villagers through more than one or two generations.

Those who try to raise their jati status are in one sense attempting to alter the local system. Those who resist their efforts are applying counterchange pressure to restore the previous order of that system. But in the larger view, a mobility drive is a way of bringing about closer parity between a jati's secular powers and ritual status. It is thus a means of restoring a local system to the state toward which local caste orders in India repeatedly gravitate, namely to eliminate great disparity between a jati's secular power and its ritual rank.

In that wider sense then, a prospering jati's struggle to rise is part of the counterchange of the system, although on the local ground it is the opponent's efforts that appear as counterchange pressure. The acts intended to disturb an existing, static order of rank, simultaneously serve to maintain the dynamic, adaptive system of jati relations.

CHAPTER 24 Cultural Adaptations and Models for Mobility

As the families of a jati, in sufficient number, accrue a strong power base, and as their leading men become united enough to move together for higher status, they typically step up their efforts to improve their jati customs. They try to abandon demeaning practices and to adopt purer and more prestigious ways. They usually want to drop their old name for a better one.

A modern instance of this traditional process, that of the Yadavas, has been illuminatingly described by M. S. A. Rao (1964). This example illustrates a mobility effort which combines traditional and modern modes of disengaging from degrading customs and associating with respectable practices. The term Yadava has been taken by many different jatis, mainly of North India, whose traditional occupation was cattle keeping. They now maintain a national organization which has published a well-edited and well-produced volume entitled *The Divine Heritage of the Yadavas* (1959). The book was originally written by V. K. Khedkar, a schoolteacher who rose to be private secretary to a Maharaja, and was later revised and enlarged by his son who was a surgeon. It argues that the jatis whose occupation was cattlekeeping and milk selling are descended from the deity Krishna through a number of royal dynasties.

These jatis, among whom Ahirs are a widespread and numerous contingent, have usually been held in considerably less glorious repute by their neighbors. While an occasional warrior of a pastoral jati did establish his own state and dynasty, cattlekeepers are ranked in many localities among the lower blocs of the Shudras. This was partly because they wandered about with their cattle and so their purity practices (so the explanation ran) could not be checked; partly because they performed castration operations on animals, and, perhaps mainly, because they were involved in the sale of milk (Baines 1912, pp. 56–58). The production of milk for one's family is entirely proper, but economic transactions in the sacrosanct product are thought to be unseemly. A cow's milk, like mother's milk, should be for one's children, not for customers and cash.

As some herdsman families became prosperous in the late nineteenth century, the campaign to take the Yadava name and Kshatriya style was begun, backed largely by a new business elite. Some men from these jatis, long accustomed to trading at cattle markets, became successful city tradesmen; others, who had traditionally contracted for the care of animals, became wealthy as contractors to government for the same purposes.

The book by Khedkar combines a traditional origin myth and a highly modernized improvement campaign. It postulates divine and noble ancestry for a good many jatis in several language regions covering hundreds of thousands of people who share little more than a traditional occupation and a conviction about their rightful prerogatives. The editor's introduction begins by giving the credentials of the authors, including the eight British diplomas, degrees, and certificates garnered by Dr. Khedkar. The editor also tells that the authors' manuscript was corrected, revised, and brought up to date by one Professor and two Assistant Professors of Indian History from the University of Allahabad. (It must be said that a very modern apparatus of historical scholarship is shown in the footnotes and references of the text.) A final chapter, added to the original manuscript by Dr. B. N. S. Yadav, states that the ancient Yadavas upheld "republican ideals" as against imperialist movements. The writer concludes that "In this way we find that in the hoary past the Yadavas were associated with a political ideology which is considered to be progressive" (1959, p. 200).

This contemporary mobility drive was preceded by many earlier struggles carried on separately in various localities. At one stage Ahirs in the Punjab and U.P. joined forces to improve Ahir status (Marten 1924, pp. 231–232). Parallel but independent efforts were being made at about the same time in other linguistic regions. Representatives of the separate organizations met at Allahabad in 1924 to found the All-India Yadav Maha Sabha (the "great league" or "great assembly" of Yadavas). This association has published a journal ever since, and its resolutions urge that all adherents conduct themselves in a life style befitting the name Yadava.

Certain components of this improved life style are quite like those traditionally prescribed by the jati panchayat of almost any ambitious group. Jati fellows are told to discard demeaning practices, particularly the eating of meat and drinking of liquor. They are urged to take on prestigious customs and symbols, one of which is the wearing of the sacred thread. When a good many Ahirs in Bihar actually began to wear the sacred thread there was intense, sometimes bloody, opposition from the dominant Bhumihars and Rajputs (Marten 1924, pp. 231–232; Lacey 1933, pp. 267–268; Rao 1964, p. 1440).

Other reforms urged by the Yadava Sabha are more rooted in modern social and political conditions than in the traditional ideals. Thus the delegates to Yadava Sabha conventions have frequently resolved that dowry payments among their members should be lowered, the age of marriage of their children raised, the duration and cost of weddings lessened, and marriage alliances between families of different Yadava jatis increased. The wealthier brethren are encouraged to contribute to Yadava welfare causes and, as M. S. A. Rao reports, "They gave liberal donations to build schools, colleges, hostels, hospitals, and temples, to scholarship funds and toward the expenses of running caste journals and of holding conferences and meetings" (Rao 1964, pp. 1441–1442). With popular elections, opportunities opened to put fellow Yadavas in office in constituencies where Yadavas are numerically strong. By 1964 there was a "sizable group" of Yadava legislators in both the Bihar and the Uttar Pradesh assemblies, and some twelve members of the central legislature were Yadavas. At the top, "there is an Ahir Minister in the Union" (Rao 1964, p. 1443).

A new proposal for Yadava improvement came as a result of the fighting of 1962 in the Himalayas. One company that fought gallantly was the 13th Kumaon composed entirely of Ahirs. One hundred fourteen of this company were killed; their brave stand received wide sympathy and admiration in the Indian press. It stimulated the Yadava Sabha to press for the formation of a Yadava or Ahir regiment in the Indian Army (Rao 1964, p. 1440).

The modern Yadava campaign includes many more people, uses

more rationalized techniques, and seeks broader achievement than
a more traditional effort waged by a single jati to improve its local
lot. But in essence the modern campaigners follow similar patterns
of action for similar purposes. On the one front they must disen-
gage themselves from low jatis and their demeaning customs.
Hence there is still the plea to give up meat and liquor. On the
other front, they seek to associate themselves with the more prestigious customs and groups. Putting on the sacred thread is a
gesture of self-association with the category of the twice-born,
although this symbol no longer is as important to young men as it
was to their fathers and grandfathers. Refining the jati's origin
story is another traditional move. Other reform proposals associate
the rising group with the educated and modern elite.

Change of Name and Customs

In both the older and the newer means of cultural adaptation for
jati mobility, a characteristic step is to change the name of the
group. Either a respectable term is added to the old name, or an
entirely new name is proposed.

A case in point is that of a sheepherding jati of the Poona district
in Maharashtra. A number of families in this jati have become landowners and have given up their rather lowly former occupation,
claiming the occupation of landowner, soldier, and village headman, and assuming the sacred thread. Known formerly as Sagar
Dhangar, the latter being the term for shepherd, they now call
themselves Sagar Rajputs. Orenstein reports a speech given by an
official of their caste organization, who cited the "historical" reasons
that they are not Dhangars and should not be so called. He demonstrated, to the loudly voiced satisfaction of his fellows, that they are
really Rajputs (which links them to the mythology of the martial
nobles) and also Marathas (which links them to the dominant jatis
of Maharashtra). The historical contradiction involved in their
claim to be both was as irrelevant to his appeal as the fact that
historically they were neither. His peroration was, "Then tell
everyone that you are Marathas!" (Orenstein 1963, pp. 6–7).[1]

[1] In this locality both terms are used to mean all jatis whose men follow
the Kshatriya model. The term Maratha may refer either to a specific jati
of the Maratha cluster or to any "high caste whose rank was more secularly

Similarly, in parts of Bengal the dominant cultivators are called Mahisyas, a name that has come to be the standard term for them only in the past fifty years. "Previously in Midnapore and still in parts of Bengal where they are not dominant, they are known by the despised name Kaibartta or Hali Kaibartta (ploughing Kaibartta) in order to distinguish them from the lower-ranking Jali or fishing Kaibartta, with whom they now admit no connection" (Nicholas and Mukhopadhyay 1962, p. 19). Such name changes are an old story in India. In eighteenth-century Gujarat, members of the Kunbi group who became landlords and revenue collectors were called Patidar, the title for revenue officials. This title carried such great prestige that in time Patidar became the name of the jati-cluster (A. M. Shah 1964b, p. 90; Srinivas 1966, pp. 35–38; Pocock 1955, p. 71).

When a decennial census was established, it provided a new arena for mobility efforts, especially in the matter of name changes. At the time of the first nationwide census, taken during 1867–1871, some groups formally registered their claims to a grander name than that commonly given them. Two jatis of cultivators in Madras, for example, asked to have varna terms affixed to their jati name, Vaishya in the case of one, Kshatriya in the case of the other.

In the 1901 Census, information was collected and published on the relative ranking and varna affiliations of each jati. This had the effect of certifying that the Census was indeed an arena for mobility struggles and precipitated a new phase of the competition. Many aspirant jatis thereupon concentrated their mobility efforts on the census operations. By 1911, census officials were inundated with petitions for name changes and other status certifications; one officer reported receiving about 120 pounds of petitions from the districts he covered (O'Malley 1913, p. 440).

A count of the claims for higher rank in four census regions of the 1931 Census (United Provinces, Bengal and Sikkim, Bihar and Orissa, Central Provinces and Berar) shows 175 such claims, of which 80 are to Kshatriya status, 33 to Brahmin (including two

---

based as against those whose rank was based more on ritual purity." The specifically Maratha jatis are traditionally soldiers, landowners, cultivators, and the newly ascendant. Sagar Rajputs emulate this reference group in certain ways (Orenstein 1963; 1965a, pp. 143–146; also see Karve 1961, pp. 44–45).

untouchable jatis claiming Brahminhood), 15 to Vaishya. There were 37 requests for new names without specific varna reference; 9 Muslim groups asked for new labels. Twenty-three groups entered more than one claim; a few claimed two or three prestigious names, perhaps in the hope that one would stick (Srinivas 1966, p. 99). In the 1941 Census and thereafter, the listing of jati and varna names was largely eliminated, terminating the use of the census as a tool for jati mobility.

Only certain elements of group custom are deliberately altered for mobility purposes. A great part of the jati's life style is kept quite the same, partly because of economic necessity and habitual response, partly because the members of an aspiring group see no need to make completely sweeping changes. If they are farmers seeking to be known as Kshatriyas rather than as Shudras, they commonly take pride in their work on the land, perhaps seeking to add a bit of martial luster to their yeoman status or to be known as overseers as well as tillers. Their aspirations do not require that they abandon farming. Many of the artisan jatis too, are not necessarily eager to give up their respective crafts, but rather to have traditional carpenters (or masons or whatever) recognized as practitioners of a high-ranking calling. Rising families do not try to change those domestic practices that have no deleterious implications (cf. Marriott 1959a, pp. 67–68).

All agree that certain practices degrade the practitioners. Hindus who seek a social status above the lower echelons avoid the eating of beef or of any carrion meat, the disposal of corpses or carcasses, the handling of products of dead animals (particularly cows), and the disposal of excreta. Muslims have different but parallel standards. Although there is solid agreement about what should be avoided, there is less consensus as to what should be emulated. Alternate models of prestigious conduct are available; different strategies for social rise are possible, and a combination of models may be feasible.

In sorting out the processes of mobility, it is useful to distinguish reference categories, that is, general principles for proper conduct, from reference groups, actual exemplars of conduct. A main reference category is that of the "twice-born" varnas in the three classic variants. Another is that of modern, educated, elite conduct. Each

category is invoked in certain contexts and has particular appeal at
certain stages of mobility. Commonly the two are combined, as
when a jati organization exhorts its members to become strict vegetarians and also to be zealous proponents of college education for
the children. The reference principles are usually interpreted according to the living example of a prestigious reference group.
These are people whose life style can be seen and copied by those
who seek similar rank, privileges, and respect.

Varna as Reference Category

"Twice-born" is a generalized category. Ambitious families of
Shudra or Harijan category select one of the three varna models to
emulate, but all three models share common elements. The general
label for the three is from the scriptural sacrament of the second
"birth," the *Upanayanam* rite, at which a boy is formally separated
from his preinitiation status and takes a last meal as a child, with his
mother. He undergoes a token transition status, acting for a few
moments or hours as an ascetic student bound for the great religious
center, Banaras. He is incorporated into his new status when he
receives a sacred verse from his spiritual mentor and is invested with
the sacred thread worn across the left shoulder (cf. Kane 1941, pp.
268–316; Stevenson 1920, pp. 27–45). All birth rites proclaim a
child's legitimate membership in society; this rite of second birth
endows a boy with an important aspect of his full status and
identity.

In religion, the "twice-born" are expected to show greater concern for the transcendental complex than do other folk and to have
less to do with the pragmatic complex. Rites conducted by any of
the "twice-born" should not, and rarely do, include blood sacrifice.
If they want to propitiate local deities by such sacrifices they
should contribute indirectly or vicariously. They are expected to
follow the main tenets of Sanskrit scripture more closely than do
others; their customary diet is supposed to be more pure than that
of the lower orders in their locality. Those of Kshatriya status
need not be vegetarians and teetotalers, but they still do not eat the
lower forms of flesh, especially beef, nor do they offer alcoholic
liquor in religious ceremonies. They usually have closer jajmani
relations with local Brahmin priests than the lower jatis can have.

Closer adherence to scriptural teachings entails more stringency in family relations, especially for women. A girl should become a wife as early as feasible and a mother as soon as possible. Her fate depends on her husband; as a wife no divorce is open to her, as a widow no remarriage is possible. "Among Hindus generally, there is a preference for virginity in brides, chastity in wives, and continence in widows, and this is especially marked among the highest castes" (Srinivas 1956a, p. 484). This last phrase is important. It is not that people of the upper varnas can claim exclusive rights to these family practices, as traditionally they did to the sacred thread, to the initiation sacrament, and to Sanskrit learning; it is rather that they should carry out these practices in purer fashion than do others.

The division between "twice-born" and all other Hindus was reflected and probably reinforced by the way in which British courts interpreted Hindu family law. For the purposes of British-Indian law there were only two kinds of Hindus, the "twice-born" and the Shudras. Any Hindu whose jati did not qualify as being of the three upper varnas had to belong in the fourth. The converts to Hinduism and untouchables were classed as Shudras. One kind of law was enforced for Shudras in matters of marriage, succession, and adoption and another kind for the "twice-born." The chief legal tests for the higher category were whether the sacred thread was customarily worn and whether marriage ceremonies followed Sanskritic patterns. If there was evidence that widow remarriage, inheritance by illegitimate sons, and divorce were allowed this was taken as an almost decisive index of Shudra status. In various legal decisions, other criteria were mentioned as indicating membership in the higher rank. These pronouncements tended to focus the reform efforts of mobile groups on these criteria (Derrett 1963, pp. 28–29; McCormack 1963, pp. 68–69; Galanter 1963, p. 545).

The process of cultural adaptation to these higher standards has been called "Sanskritization" by M. N. Srinivas. He defines the term as "a process by which a 'low' Hindu caste, or tribal or other group, changes its customs, ritual, ideology, and way of life in the direction of a high, and frequently, 'twice-born' caste" (1966, pp. 1–45; 1952a, pp. 30–31; 1956a). The concept has been a fruitful one, which has stimulated a number of further explorations (e.g., Chanana 1961b, Gould 1961b, Barnabas 1961, Singer 1964, van

Buitenen 1966), but the earlier formulation of it has drawn criticism, notably that there has been great regional and historic variation in the content of "Sanskritic Hinduism" (Staal 1963).

That is quite so. Sanskrit scripture is vast; different sources lay down differing standards for conduct; the same source has been held by different interpreters to sanction different action. The Bhagavad Gita testifies to this (Edgerton 1952, vol. 2, p. 103). In Sir Edwin Arnold's translation of the relevant passage it is rendered as follows:

> "Look! Like as when a tank pours water forth
> To suit all needs, so do these Brahmins draw
> Texts for all wants from the tank of Holy Writ.
> But then, want not! Ask not! Find full reward
> Of doing right in right.

Doing right, as we have seen, is taken by many to mean trying to raise one's jati rank; their superiors in rank usually view such striving as being quite wrong.

Yet most villagers agree that certain canons of conduct should be followed by those who legitimately count themselves among the "twice-born." These standards have long been upheld by the higher jatis and they do underlie the many varieties of Sanskritization. These themes of conduct are repeatedly brought home to villagers, as has been noted, through religionists of many kinds, visiting entertainers, itinerant preachers, revered mentors. Some of the most effective agents of Sanskritization, paradoxically, have been devotees of anti-Brahmanical sects. In their missionary zeal, these sectarians reached into groups which were not already imbued with the scriptural standards for the "twice-born" and were sometimes as successful in implanting these ideas as in making converts to their opposing sect. This was true for Lingayats of Mysore in earlier centuries and for the Arya Samaj in North India in the twentieth century (Srinivas 1966, pp. 21, 101).

Mrs. Karve has commented that among the illiterate people of Maharashtra, there is far greater knowledge about the literary tradition of the last seven centuries of this land than among the people who have received their education in schools and colleges. Through village channels there has been effective communication of the "fundamental theoretical framework underlying the social structure" (1961, pp. 117–119). This is true in other parts of India as well; religion remains a propitious code for communication (Gumperz 1964).

People of the "twice-born" varnas are thus differentiated from the rest of society by standards that are based on scripture and accepted by most villagers. When a group becomes resentful enough about being classed as Shudras or Harijans, powerful enough to do something about it, and united enough to launch effective action, its members change their personal habits and jati manner to conform to a particular varna model. The model is also a marker. If such a group can succeed in being accepted by their neighbors as a jati of the higher varnas, they have arrived. Untouchables do not usually try to become Shudras; they aim for one of the higher categories, most frequently Kshatriya. Those classed as Shudras do not often use that term for themselves, though other villagers do (Karve 1961, p. 47); when they gather strength for a mobility leap, they generally aim for one of the "twice-born" categories, rather than for higher place among Shudras.

Which category is selected by those of an aspirant group depends on such factors as their origin myth, the attraction of a locally dominant group, and on calculation of the most feasible strategy for status gain. Whatever model is chosen, the general requirements for each are well known throughout village India. In simplest terms, jatis classed as Brahmins are expected to stress purity, piety, learning, and priesthood more than do others in their locality. Kshatriyas, for their part, emphasize honor, virtue, force, and masculinity. Vaishyas pride themselves on steadiness, thrift, intelligence, as well as on purity and piety.

These various features are known in the remotest corners of the land because, together with the basic "twice-born" standards, they are presented, assumed, and repeated through all the media of the civilization—in sacred stories and plays, in local tales and anecdotes, in the information picked up by pilgrims, in the talk of genealogists and other professional visitors to the village, in daily interchange. A villager knows from his everyday experience that there are considerable variations of occupation and custom in every varna category. Yet certain directives for behavior are postulated for each varna category and they do regulate the conduct of those classed in it or of those who aspire to be so classed.

Kshatriya Models

The warrior-ruler model of the Kshatriya has been the most popular for ambitious men of lower jatis. It best accommodated those who cut their way up with their swords in earlier centuries (Karve 1965, p. 116). Under the Pax Britannica, it remained a popular and feasible model. In the sample from the 1931 Census, there were 80 claims to Kshatriya status made by lower groups, as against 33 claims to Brahmin and 15 to Vaishya standing (Srinivas 1966, p. 99). Those who proclaim themselves as Kshatriyas are expected to be ready to use force to gain their honorable purposes and to be zealous in defense of their honor. It does not much matter, for purposes of the Kshatriya ideal, if they be slow in learning, lacking in wealth, deficient in ascetic piety. In those jatis whose men pride themselves on their warrior tradition, the beau ideal of the Kshatriya is absorbed from childhood; a youngster learns it from his elders' frequent reference to the glories of their own kind and to the craven conduct of others. It is lovingly and lengthily depicted in stories and dramas from the Epics. A man of true Kshatriya breed should be easy to anger, hard in combat, magnanimous in victory, freehanded with his possessions, closefisted with his honor.

Rajput jatis have particularly upheld and cherished their Kshatriya character. A sketch of the martial Rajput as seen in Khalapur village ninety miles north of Delhi, is given by John Hitchcock. He writes that a Rajput who faithfully follows the warrior tradition looks a bit old-fashioned now to the educated young men of his jati, but even they share some of his attributes. The older Rajput still dresses the warrior part, with a long mustache and a high turban; he goes always armed with a heavy, wire-bound staff, which he stands ready to wield with skull-cracking skill. He considers himself to be one of the rulers of society by birthright and natural endowment, and "regards it as his duty to see that the proper relationships between all castes are maintained, and that the hierarchical order of society is preserved." He takes great pride in his warrior ancestry and has fine scorn for all who do not share his heritage and tradition. If he acts rashly, he explains it as a sign of his valor; if he grasps for power, it is evidence of his destiny to be a ruler. As for ritual piety, he "regards it as a kind of warrior's dispensation that he is permitted to hunt, eat meat (except of course for beef), drink liquor and eat opium" (Hitchcock 1958, pp. 216–221).

Other Rajputs across northern India take a like Kshatriya posture. In a Gujarat village the Rajput overlords are described as being dedicated to the achievement and maintenance of power; they proudly say that a Rajput who bears an insult commits a thousand sins (Steed 1955, pp. 114–115). In a Madhya Pradesh village the local Rajputs run village affairs and are considered to be "the prime Kshatriya caste" (Mayer, 1960, p. 63). According to a description of the Rajputs in a Rajasthan town, "their traditional duties are to rule, and to fight" and although they did not have much good to say for their hereditary ruler "every Rajput insisted on his loyalty to him: if it came to fighting, even those families which were out of favour would claim the privilege of carrying arms in his support" (Carstairs 1957, pp. 106–107).

A Bengali version of the martial style is the Ugra-Kshatriya jati, Ugra meaning "hot-tempered." They are characterized in Lal Behari Day's novel of 1872 about his village in Burdwan district as "a bold and somewhat fierce race, and less patient of any injustice or oppression than the ordinary Bengal raiyat." An account of the same village as of 1962 quotes this passage and comments that the Ugra-Kshatriyas ("a strong, courageous community") still show the same characteristics. Their origin myth (from *Manu* X.9.)[2] told of their descent from a Kshatriya man and a Sudra girl, and so they were not given unequivocal Kshatriya standing, but "they are now claiming themselves to be Kshatriyas and are trying to acquire the status of the twice-born themselves" (Basu 1962, pp. 24, 36).

Bold, ambitious, pugnacious men have found little difficulty in taking on Kshatriya attributes. No great revisions of diet or of routine are required in doing so. People of the Kshatriya category are not expected to be as stringent about food, drink, and ritual niceties as are Brahmins, nor as skilled in trade or crafts as are Vaishyas. What is required is a display of force and fortitude, useful qualities in any event in a struggle for higher rank. Ambitious cultivators frequently own to these qualities, and the Kshatriya ideal is based on control of land.

Moreover, it is not difficult to construct a mythical or even his-

[2] The same myth episode was used to explain the origin of the Coorgs in South India (Srinivas 1952a, pp. 33–34, 219–220; Hopkins 1884, p. 306).

torical association with warrior ancestors. During millennia of
battles many warrior bands rose to power and many also were
toppled and dispersed. A genealogist can usually manage to find one
such forgotten ancestor for an ascendant group (Srivastava 1963,
pp. 264–265). K. M. Panikkar indeed concluded that practically all
Indian rulers had been successful fighters who were then elevated to
Kshatriya rank. "Every known royal family from the time at least
of Mahapadma Nanda in the fourth century B.C. belonged to non-
Kshatriya castes" (1956, p. 8). So sweeping a statement may be
doubted by other historians and challenged by proud scions of the
former princely houses, but there is no doubt that once a group
fought its way to power, it was likely to be reclassified from
Shudra to Kshatriya status.

Such reclassification has occurred in many a village scene. In the
village of Gaon of Poona district, for example, two jatis assert that
they are Kshatriyas. One is Maratha, of the jati-cluster dominant in
the region. The other is known as Sagar Rajputs, whose change of
name was mentioned above. They are dominant in Gaon village
and its vicinity. Other villagers of Gaon tell that not so long ago
(as the older people well recollect) the present Sagar Rajputs were
Dhangars, shepherds by traditional occupation and Shudras by traditional classification. They grew in strength and ambition to the
point where they were able to change their name, declare their
Kshatriya status and wear the sacred thread. One of them hired a
genealogist who proceeded to trace their ancestry to a chief officer
in the armies of the great Maratha leader, Shivaji. Those of the
Maratha jati in Gaon, much longer and more securely established
in their warrior repute, are apt to sneer at these claims. And the
Sagar Rajputs have not fully adopted certain Kshatriya practices,
particularly the ban on widow remarriage. They counter Maratha
aspersions about this by accusing Marathas of covertly allowing a
widow to be unofficial wife to her dead husband's brothers. Most
of the other villagers take the Marathas' view about Sagar Rajputs'
claims, but they do so more in private than openly because the
Sagar Rajputs are quick to take offense and ready to beat up the
offender (Orenstein 1965a, pp. 145, 159).

Yet Marathas themselves have not always been universally accepted as Kshatriyas. In the nineteenth century they were labelled
as Shudras by some Brahmins (*ibid.*, p. 145). Mrs. Karve cites an

account, dated 1697, of the elevation of Shivaji to the category of Kshatriyas. A Brahmin found a suitable genealogy for him and counseled that the sacrament of the sacred thread be performed as was the custom of the northern Kshatriyas. "So in a sacred place Shivaji had the thread ceremony performed on him and was made a pure Kshatriya and then crowned King in the year 1674" (Karve 1961, pp. 43–44; 1958a, p. 88).

In the Dravidian-speaking regions, there were not many jatis that had long-standing claims to Kshatriya or even Vaishya standing (cf. Dubois 1928, p. 15). The Nayars of Kerala, warriors by preference and profession, were classed as Shudras by the Brahmins of the region, and only the ruling lineages among them were known by the term Kshatriya (Mayer 1952, pp. 26–27). During the nineteenth century, several Tamil groups began to declare Kshatriya affinities. One of them, the Padayachis, petitioned for the title of Kshatriya at the time of the first census in 1871, and by the 1891 Census, they had produced a book on their rights to the name and rank. To judge by their ranking in Tanjore district, their efforts have not been wholly successful; there they still are placed below the jatis they were trying to surpass (Béteille 1965, pp. 87, 97).

The Coorgs are an example of a people who have effectively secured their reputation as Kshatriyas, as was noted earlier, despite certain lapses from the usual Kshatriya standards. They were a compact body of warriors and landholders and as they became more closely incorporated into the mainstream of the civilization they retained these characteristics, fitting well into the category of Kshatriya (Srinivas 1952a, p. 33).

Brahmin Models

Some ascendant groups take to the Brahmin rather than the Kshatriya style. They stress ritual purity and purifying ritual, they become more meticulous about avoiding pollution. They do not have to perform priestly services or acquire scriptural learning because many Brahmin jatis do not provide such services and a great many Brahmins have little learning. A Brahmin jati needs mainly to be more ritual-directed and purity-focused than are the other local jatis. Their degree of purity is always relative to the practices of the others. Many Brahmin jatis are strictly vegetarian, especially those of the South and those of Vaishnavite sects. There are also many Brahmin jatis of North India whose members do eat meat and fish (Sharma 1961a), but they do not eat the more defiling kinds of meat and although their diet is not vegetarian it is still at least as pure as the customary diet of jatis in their locality, and usually more so (cf. Carstairs 1957, pp. 115–116).

As for learning, the ideal of the scholar was wholly fulfilled by relatively few Brahmins. Yet the ideal was and is revered by Brahmins more than among other village jatis. Kshatriyas may consider a very learned Brahmin, one who has a whole Veda in his memory or who is accomplished in scriptural exegesis, as worthy of respect but scarcely of emulation. Brahmins and would-be Brahmins see the scholar's pursuits as an exalted version of their own; Kshatriyas do not. In the traditional Brahmin view the earth belonged to Brahmins, but Kshatriyas were allowed to rule it so that Brahmins could avoid the necessity of taking life and could devote themselves to ritual (Ingalls 1958, p. 212).

Those who aim their mobility efforts in a Brahmin direction need not stress power over others but rather control over their own group so that its members are uniformly disciplined to Brahmanical standards. This discipline is a standard theme in the pages of caste journals. N. K. Bose gives a characteristic example from a Bengali caste journal of 1908, the journal of the Namashudra, cultivators and boatmen, who despite their name have waged a long struggle to win recognition as Brahmins. In translation this passage reads, "prompted by envy or anger, people may dislike us; but if one observes our clean Brahminical way of life as practised generation after generation, they will have to admit unanimously that the Namashudra caste is descended from the ancient sages and *Rishis*, i.e., from pure Brahmins."

Another Brahmin-oriented group in Bengal are the Yogis, weavers by traditional occupation. Their caste journal began advocating Brahminhood from about 1911; by 1921 the priestly section among them claimed Brahmin status and in the Census of 1931, the leaders of the jati claimed that all Yogis were properly of Brahmin status. Discrepancies between Brahmin standards and Yogi practices were thrashed out in their publications. The question whether Yogis who had taken the sacred thread could still be farmers was answered with a clear "yes," but on the former Yogi custom of allowing widows to remarry there was some disagreement. Those who took the stricter Brahmanical line wanted to forbid it, but other members of the jati were not so sure, perhaps because they saw new respectability for the old practice under modern Western influence (Bose 1958b, pp. 86–88).

Some jatis emulate the Brahmin model without campaigning actively for Brahmin rating; others take the warrior-ruler model without trying to be known as Kshatriyas. In two of the jati blocs of Ramkheri village in Madhya Pradesh, for example, the several jatis of each bloc are accepted as being about equal in ritual rank; both blocs are ranked just below the local Brahmins. The people of one are vegetarians and teetotalers, those of the other eat certain kinds of meat and drink liquor.

The leading jati among the vegetarians is that of the farmers (to use the author's terms), the other vegetarian jatis are gardeners, carpenters, smiths, tailors, and Bairagi. All these are most confident of the superiority of their style of life. Mayer notes that "They are supported in their contentions by the emergence of popular Governments since 1948 which are dominated by vegetarian castes, and they look forward to national policies which will eventually ban all animal slaughter and so bear out their superiority" (1960, p. 45). Whether the government has actually been so dominated or whether such influence may long continue does not affect the confidence that these jati-groups have derived from the Gandhian movement and its political consequences. They are oriented to the Brahmin mode yet do not claim membership in the Brahmin category.

Rajputs are most numerous in the other bloc and set the tone for the seven jati-groups who are their firm allies in the village. These allies consider the vegetarians to be "weak and effeminate" and take pride that theirs is the style of the former Rajas and, as they believe, of the meat-eating rulers of Western countries. They scoff at the farmers' prudence and exclusiveness. Rajputs are more generous, civic minded, and outgoing; they present a model that men of lower jatis feel they can readily emulate. The origin story held by these jatis lets them circumvent the question of old Kshatriya status. It is the story of the god Parasurama who scoured the country, looking for Kshatriyas to kill. In their flight from this supernatural scourge, Kshatriyas took to different occupations as a disguise.

Hence when Parasurama came upon a Kshatriya working as a gardener, he spared him and that man's descendants became the gardener jati. Rajputs alone carried on their martial occupation; the others can then claim to be ex-Kshatriyas if they wish, or avoid the question as many do (Mayer 1960, pp. 44–45, 60–62, 88).

A similar example from South India is from Sripuram village, Tanjore district. There, also, two blocs of jatis display different life styles, one prizing force and rule without raising the Kshatriya banner, the other following a more ritualized pattern without claiming to be Brahmins. Each set is known by the name of its leading jati, Kalla and Vellala respectively. Kallas are described as being physically larger and as having a distinctive "domineering" appearance. "They can be distinguished particularly from the Vellala group by their close-knit organisation (their 'tribal' character, as some call it), the comparative unimportance of Sanskritic elements in their culture, and their tradition of lawlessness and violent life which still makes them feared by the generality of people" (Béteille 1965, p. 84). Vellalas follow a more ritualistic, "Sanskritic" style of life and proclaim themselves as Vaishyas. While the Kallas are the more important politically, the Vellalas are the more influential ritually (Béteille 1965, pp. 82–85; Gough 1956, p. 827).

Artisans, in many villages of the South, show a special kind of mobility striving. The five allied jatis of artisans have made long and insistent claims to being Brahmins. They say that they are Brahmins of a special and most superior kind, descended from the god *Visvakarman*, builder and architect of the heavenly realm. Included under the collective title of *Panchala* are jatis of goldsmiths, copper and brass workers, carpenters, stonemasons, and blacksmiths. Through much of the Tamil-, Kannada-, and Telugu-speaking areas, these artisans are allies. They tend to spurn the proper Brahmins, those so recognized by the rest of the local society, and they do not seek priestly services from them, relying instead on priests of their own jatis. They disdain Brahmins as a reference group, but identify thoroughly with Brahminhood as a reference category.

Men of these jatis wear the sacred thread; they are so ritually meticulous that they will accept food and water from few if any other jatis; they use Sanskrit gotra names for their clans; they observe scriptural sacraments; some of them have even studied the Vedas. Yet despite all their scriptural ways, they are not taken as equal to proper Brahmins by their neighbors. In some places even untouchables will not take food and water from blacksmiths, though they are vegetarians. Perhaps the very audacity of their claims has led to special discrimination against them (Epstein 1962, pp. 162, 294; Srinivas 1955a, pp. 22–24).

Their claims are not new. Accounts of the seventeenth century hint at them (Jackson 1907, p. 243; Ghurye 1961, p. 6). Dubois noted at the beginning of the nineteenth century that the five classes of artisans "refuse, in some districts to acknowledge Brahmin predominance." They were also principal partisans of the Left-Hand faction, arrayed against the Right-Hand faction of the higher Shudra jatis and their allies (Dubois 1928, pp. 23–25). Reports from the beginning of the twentieth century note their continued assertions that they are Brahmins of the purest water and highest degree and the continued response of their neighbors that they are no such thing (Baines 1912, pp. 58–60; Thurston 1909, Vol. III, pp. 106–125).[3]

These artisan jatis of the South adapted culturally to the Brahmin category but failed socially. Perhaps they were able to keep themselves ritually isolated and relatively pure because they had a grip on the economy. Without the services of carpenter and blacksmith, other villagers would have difficulties in farming and without the services of goldsmith, coppersmith, and stonemason, other parts of village life would be impaired. Hence when blacksmiths took on the sacred thread, other villagers could not maul and harass them lest the next harvest suffer for lack of tools and repairs. Yet the artisans did not have enough power to compel others to respect their claims. For several centuries there was a standoff. The local systems worked quite well, these artisans and cultivators maintained jajmani relations with other jatis for economic purposes only. The unresolved controversy apparently was not a great impediment to the functioning of the local caste systems.

[3] Baines notes similar tendencies among artisans of Bengal and Maharashtra, though these claims were more modest and less militant. More recent studies from these two regions indicate that some artisans continue these assertions (Nicholas 1962, p. 130; Orenstein 1965a, p. 212). Artisan jatis of the Gangetic plain have not generally advanced such claims.

Vaishya and Shudra Models

The Vaishya model, like the Brahmin, is ritualized, stringent, and ascetic, but it includes, as the Brahmin does not, a mandate to engage in a mundane occupation, commerce. (cf. Srinivas 1966, pp. 31–32; Carstairs 1957, pp. 119–120). Those who seek Vaishya status can keep any clean occupation and still show their Vaishya affinity whenever they market their produce or open a shop.

The Telis of Orissa, traditionally oil-pressers and ranked as Shudras, have insisted that they are really Vaishyas whose trade was halted by external circumstance; they had to fall back temporarily on the less respectable occupation of extracting vegetable oils. In the resolutions passed by the Teli caste organization there is regular mention of this origin story.

The resolutions also include rules about the kind of trade proper for Telis. For example, they may sell betel leaves but may not sell betel prepared for chewing. The former is a respectable wholesale trade carried on by growers, the latter smacks of the petty peddler's traffic. "Those of our caste who earn their living by cultivation of betel leaves, may sell leaves at the plantation. On no account should they carry baskets of betel leaves to distant markets either on their heads or in bullock carts." A resolution taken at another meeting allows for selling betel leaves in a shop but not "by wandering from place to place." Several resolutions indicate that some Telis continue to carry on inferior kinds of trade, and they are urged to transact only the more honorable kinds of trade, those suitable for people of Vaishya status (Patnaik and Ray 1960, pp. 31–32, 34, 42).

Farming as well as trade is permitted for Vaishyas. The Vellalas, farmers who lay claim to being Vaishyas, stress the purity of their practices rather than the pursuit of commercial profits (Béteille 1965, p. 97; Gough 1956, p. 829; Thurston 1909, p. 366). But other jatis take to the Vaishya category just because of its mercantile feature. The numerous and influential Patidars of Gujarat are shifting from Kshatriya to Vaishya affiliation, as we noted above, mainly because of their increasing involvement in trade and because of the high prestige that businessmen have come to have in Gujarat.

The term Patidar, meaning landowners who had a particular kind of tenure, became the name of the jati-cluster. For several generations Patidars proclaimed themselves as Kshatriyas; they argued that they, like the local Rajputs, wielded political power. Like Rajputs, they supported genealogists to create and keep ancestral records and they became fond of the blood-and-thunder recitations of the bards. But in recent generations, a good many Patidars have been giving up the genealogists and their tall tales. They now prefer to have the same status as the local Baniyas, the trading jatis who are indubitably Vaishyas. When the kingly model was dominant in their region they adhered to it, but it seems a bit obsolete to them now that many Patidars have been successful in trade. Both Baniyas and Patidars took to English education at an early date; both have prospered and, in general, have adapted to modern conditions more successfully than have people of the traditional Kshatriya jatis of Gujarat. Hence a number of Patidars see little to gain by clinging to the old kingly model and have shifted their adherence to the model which is now more suitable, realistic, and profitable (Shah and Shroff 1958, pp. 268–270).

The fourth varna, the Shudra, is rarely taken as a goal for mobility, though presumably an untouchable jati could try to rise by claiming Shudra status. In the sample taken from the 1931 Census, twenty-six untouchable groups gave themselves Kshatriya status, five claimed Vaishya, and two even claimed Brahmin titles. Thirteen untouchable groups demanded to change their jati names without giving a particular varna. None in this sample of 148 claims argued for Shudra status (Srinivas 1966, p. 99).

Not all rising Shudra jatis lay claim to a higher varna. One such group, the Mahanayaka Shudra of Puri district in Orissa, convened caste assemblies in 1935 and again in 1959. In the published reports of these meetings there is no mention of superior varna. There are, however, many resolutions for improvement and reform, as for more meticulous birth ritual and stricter endogamy, against pre-puberty marriage, for the education of poor boys of the jati, and against demands for exorbitant dowry gifts, like a gold ring or a bicycle (Patnaik 1960a, pp. 81–118).

Both traditional and modern elements are typically included in such resolutions; recommended ritual improvements are from the "twice-born" repertoire, educational uplift is from the modern sector. There are other reference categories used by particular groups. As we shall note in a later chapter, rising Muslim families attempt reforms in special Muslim terms while also calling for secular improvements and purer practices much as do ambitious Hindu families.

Reference Groups

When jati brethren change their ways to raise their status, they not only adopt a reference category but also follow the specific example of a reference group, a life model. They insist, however, on keeping their own group identity. They do not want to merge with those whose rank they esteem and whose ways they emulate. They feel no need, therefore, to copy all features of their reference groups, but only those they need for better rank. The standards of behavior for the reference *categories* are learned, indirectly as it were, from books, rituals, tales, schooling, dramas, and latterly from movies, newspapers, magazines, and radio. The standards of the reference *groups* are vividly seen as enacted in life.

The life style of a strongly dominant group generally influences others in its area. We have mentioned the example of Gujars in a Maharashtrian village who were changing their marriage patterns to conform with the ways of the locally dominant Marathas. Some of the Brahmins of Maharasthra also follow the Maratha practice of cross-cousin marriage, even though it is against scriptural prescriptions and is contrary to the common practice of Brahmins. Excommunication for this offense was decreed in the eighteenth century under the Peshwa government but such marriage arrangements among Brahmins are still known (Karve 1953, pp. 9, 17, 162; Raghuvanshi 1966, p. 149).

In Gujarat, Rajputs are taken as a prime reference group by the jatis known as Koli. The term Koli, as A. M. Shah and R. G. Shroff explain, once covered about a quarter of all Gujarati Hindus and refers to an assortment of people who owned little land and who were presumably of tribal origin. In recent years, prosperous Kolis have employed genealogists who provided ancestral records linking them with Rajput history and prehistory, and ultimately showing divine provenience. They have taken clan names and some of the marriage customs of Rajputs, and now have Brahmin priests to guide them in the sacramental rituals performed by Rajputs proper.

These Kolis, Shah and Shroff observe, are "fast Sanskritizing as well as Rajputizing themselves." One of their genealogists commented that they still pay less than do Rajputs and do not know the niceties of Rajput hospitality, "but they have great reverence for us." This reverence has declined or vanished among many of their former clients, notably Patidars. As is true elsewhere, the Kolis are adopting practices from a group whose members are discarding the same practices for others that they deem more estimable (Shah and Shroff 1958, pp. 264–268).

An example of these tendencies comes from two villages in central Gujarat, which are only a few miles apart. In both places Patidars are dominant and set the cultural style for other jatis, particularly for the Baria (formerly Kolis). The Patidars of one village have become wealthier than those in the other, they belong to a much higher hypergamous section of their jati, and they have departed more widely from the former Patidar devotion to Kshatriya symbols. The Barias of each village take their cues from their own Patidar neighbors, modeling themselves in the one after the more traditional Kshatriya pattern and in the other after the ways of the newer elite (Pocock 1957b, pp. 25–27).

The cultural influence of socially dominant groups was strikingly demonstrated among Hindus in what was the North-West Frontier Province. Hindus were a small minority among Muslims there; the tradition of Muslim rule and prestige remained strong even under the British. Brahmin priests were not much used among Hindus; they commanded little reverence and less learning. A Hindu of "twice-born" varna would eat meat and eggs "even in the bazar, generally put on the sacred thread only at the time of marriage, recited no *mantra* (save Rama-Nama), knew no Sanskrit and sent his children to the local madrassa run by a Maulvi." Hindu children taught by a Muslim teacher in an Islamic school grew up to be deeply influenced by Islam. But with a shift in political tides these Hindus turned to greater interest in Hindu scripture and acquired it chiefly through the non-Brahmanical Arya Samaj movement (Chanana 1961b, pp. 409–411).

Though the attraction to the life style of the dominant group is strong, it is far from total. The Hindus of the northwest frontier remained Hindus, observing some scriptural ritual even if in attenuated form and maintaining jati differentiation. Where the Rajputs were the overlords, not all the lower jatis emulated them. As we have seen in Ramkheri, some chose the ascetic rather than the warrior model.

The Kshatriya model in all regions includes the broad characteristics of devotion to honor, rule, and martial valor. The Rajpur version of that model adds certain traits, such as hypergamous clan organization. That version itself is observed in different regional varieties; Rajputs of Gujarat differ in certain ways from those of Rajasthan or Uttar Pradesh (Baines 1912, pp. 29–33; cf. Steed 1955; Carstairs 1957; Minturn and Hitchcock 1966). So the men of a rising group who chose the ruler-warrior road of mobility adopted Kshatriya principles for conduct, oriented themselves to, say, Rajput standards, and actually guided their conduct according to the example of those Rajputs whose behavior they could see. The example of the visible reference group is usually much more influential than are abstract principles of scripture or indirect examples in legend and literature.

Modernization as Reference Category

Such cultural adaptations were part of recurrent changes. The overall system of society remained relatively constant even though (and partly because) there was continuous struggle for higher rank. The pervasiveness of these struggles within local systems and across the land, helped to reinforce a villager's conviction that higher rank was attainable and was eminently worth the struggle for it.

In the nineteenth century, European influences began to reach strongly into village society. Villagers were confronted with new conditions, of police and government, for example, with which they had to cope and which had somehow to be fitted into their social organization. There was some adjustment of the system. When the new temporal rulers would not intervene in caste ranking as indigenous rulers might, the ritual criteria came to be more rigidly applied and litigation became a main instrument of caste manipulation. Yet the structure of the villagers' social order was not drastically altered, the mobility efforts observed in the mid-twentieth century are similar in process and phases to those reported in the eighteenth century (cf. Raghuvanshi 1966, pp. 167–169).

Modern influences, however, especially those that came with political independence, are cumulatively bringing about long-range changes, which we will discuss later. Village society was not static under the colonial regime; there were some systemic adjustments, but generally villagers tended to assimilate the main innovations in government, technology, and communications into the established pattern of jati relations. British culture was too alien from the village world to provide a new reference category and British society in India was far too isolated and aloof from village life to yield a new reference group for mobility.

A few quite exceptional Indian groups did adapt their ways to an English model, as some Coorg landowners did to the example of the English planters, but this was far from common and even the Coorg adaptation was limited to selected outer traits, as the club, plantation management, and men's recreational pursuits; it did not pervade religion or family relations (Srinivas 1966, p. 57).

Villagers of middle or low jati who gained assets in modern ways typically used them to acquire the accouterments of high status in the traditional ways. As they did so, those of the higher jatis who had also benefited from modern accretions began to revise their status symbols and standards. Hence ambitious people of lower jatis, as has been noted above, tend to take on traditional symbols of high status that are being relinquished by the higher jatis. The latter are adopting new symbols that are not only indicative of their modern sophistication but also serve as new indicators of their superiority. This is illustrated in Sherurpur village of Faizabad district of U.P. where one man of low jati has become wealthy as a contractor. "He has symbolized his new-found opulence not by becoming a 'modern man' but by building a residence in the village which outdoes the high castes in its traditional architectural style." He has also built a grand rest house for pilgrims, a gift traditionally made by benefactors of high jati rank. The local Brahmins and Rajputs "have little choice left to them than to turn to westernization as a means of maintaining the social distance between themselves and the lower castes which is no longer possible within the old order in the face of the latter's current ability to Sanskritize themselves" (Gould 1961b, p. 947).

The Brahmins and Rajputs here and people of traditionally high rank in other villages do not relinquish their respective varna standards, but add modern standards of education and occupation to them. They are no less eager for substantive privileges of high status; they have taken a new view of the proper symbols and content of that status. Nor do prospering people of low jati ignore the new standards. Many have taken to whatever modern ways they could assume (cf. Srinivas 1966, pp. 66–67). Some of the lowest jatis have struck directly for better status through modern political processes. Most aspiring groups now combine the older and the newer means of raising themselves in the social order.

The Yadava example with which we began this chapter shows the eclectic approach. Those who call themselves Yadavas are urged toward such traditional ways as the wearing of the sacred thread and abstinence from liquor and meat. Yadavas are also advised to abolish child marriage and high dowry payments, practices formerly honored but countered by modern influences. Intermarriage among all jatis now known as Yadavas is endorsed, even though such vast expansion of endogamy is quite contrary to former rules for marriage. The older preference is overridden by the prospect of united political strength which broader marriage ties may bring (Rao 1964, p. 1440).

To take one other example, the Telis of Orissa were notified through the 1959 constitution of their association that all the separate jatis calling themselves Telis should allow complete freedom of intermarriage among them, that high dowries and child marriages should be stopped, and that the children should be given more education (Patnaik and Ray 1960, pp. 73–76).

Some of these resolutions are more readily put into practice than others. Determination to wear the sacred thread in the face of opposition from higher jatis is usually much more appealing (especially when there is a good chance of overcoming the opposition) than is the advice to arrange marriages more broadly. While resolutions against lavish dowries and expensive weddings get resounding votes as tokens of devotion to social progress, it is quite another thing when a member, even a leader of the organization, has to marry off his own daughter and must then demonstrate his own family's status in the jati. Such contradictions between ideal and real practice, between scriptural standards and modern notions, are generally glossed over without much difficulty. The goal is clear. The purpose is to get more respect and esteem from others in the society. A rising group uses all its resources from both the traditional and modern repertoire in order to accomplish that purpose, and combines them in whatever way seems best suited to reach the goal.

The term "Westernization" has been used to refer to the modern repertoire, to those adopted practices and ideas that originated outside Indian civilization (cf. Srinivas 1966, pp. 50–56). But though these traits were originally introduced from European sources, this is not often relevant to villagers. Most of the patterns of government, technology, and communication that were first brought in by Europeans are now firmly part of the village world. Some of them have been so for generations. As far as the villager is concerned they are indigenous and long established. He certainly recognizes the difference between scriptural edict and modern law, between traditional ritual and national ceremonies, but no opposition among them is necessarily assumed.

Secular education, railway and bus lines, newspapers and postal service, introduced food and cash crops, are no longer seen as alien by villagers. Moreover, most innovations are soon adapted to the Indian milieu and take on characteristics notably different from those of the prototypes. Perhaps the term "modernization" avoids the unwarranted implications of "Westernization" provided it is not taken as a slogan of invariably good and desirable progress.

Villagers, in sum, are altering modern patterns, such as those proffered by government agencies or presented through the mass media, to suit village conditions. They are also rephrasing the still powerful reference models of tradition to accord with modern conditions.

CHAPTER 25

Mobility Tactics: Overcoming
External Opposition

CULTURAL models induce social actions. Ambitious men usually have a clear idea of what they want to attain for their jati; getting it demands long, steady social maneuver. They face two tactical necessities. One is to press steadily against the external opposition, against those who feel that their own jati position is threatened by the rise of a lower group and so fight it. The other is to maintain sufficient internal unity to be able to overcome. External opposition may be circumvented through passing and percolation, or it may be dealt with by undertaking a straightforward jati campaign.

The individual villager, as we have seen, commonly engages in different mobility drives for his several social groups, pushing one more than another at a particular juncture, usually giving priority to jati defense over lineage or family aggrandizement. To a villager, his several affiliations are not neatly packaged, discrete entities. He tends to take them together as part of his general position in society. In North India, a man's view of his general position is called his *izzat*, his personal honor. Izzat has to do with a man's obligations and rights through all his social roles; it is the sum of his social credit; it includes all the values and attainments that others give him credit for—as he perceives that credit. Getting a prestigious groom for his daughter or a fine bride for his son is part of maintaining his izzat, as is the daughter's proper conduct and the son's manly behavior. Upholding the tradition of his jati is also part of personal izzat, as is the defense of jati rights against usurpers of lower rank. Thus an individual's izzat is linked to his view of his jati's proper place, power, and prestige.

Contingency and Individual Influence

Mobility tactics follow characteristic patterns, but the contestants themselves are more concerned with the contingency, with the unpredictability of the struggle rather than with its patterned regularities. The observer must focus on the regularities, but he must also recognize that it is the indeterminancy of a contest rather than its general predictability that impels the contestants to keep striving. In particular cases the will and determination of a few men are critical factors no less than are the social and cultural factors.

This has been true in one mobility contest I have observed over a number of years, waged by the Kotas of the Nilgiri Hills of South India. This contest was pressed most vigorously by one man, Sulli, whose life story I have sketched elsewhere (1941, 1960). For decades he had to fight a running two-front battle, with the opponents of Kota ambitions and with his opponents among the Kotas. He eventually won on both fronts; his long, tenacious fight certainly affected the status of Kotas during his life and has probably had long-run effects as well.

The Kotas are a very small group, one of the four aboriginal peoples of the formerly isolated Nilgiri plateau. When the isolation ended, the Badagas, the most numerous group of the four, grew prosperous as potato farmers and their leaders became zealous to reform Badaga ways. Many of them rejected the traditional interdependence between Badaga cultivators and Kota artisans; they began to treat Kotas more like complete untouchables than they had before. Kotas resented this, but only Sulli propounded a program of Kota reform that would counter the Badaga aspersions. The program he concocted for his small group was in essentials quite like the reform programs of the great caste associations. It entailed dissociation from degrading customs and association with elevating practices, of both scriptural and modern origin. Some younger Kotas took his side but many Kotas opposed him bitterly as a wanton violator of precious tradition. Badagas of both the reform and the conservative parties fought his proposals for greater rights for Kotas; both saw him as a threat to proper social order.

The opposition was formidable but Sulli was formidably determined. He divided his enemies and marshaled his strength against each in turn. When Badagas beat up Kotas he stood as champion of the Kotas. Sulli was the only Kota of his generation who knew some English, and so he could write petitions to authorities, use suitable persuasion to bring in the police, and initiate litigation to punish the Badagas' strong-arm men. When he asked for official protection, he portrayed his small, beleaguered, disadvantaged people as standing in desperate defense against the numerous and wealthy Badagas. Government officials, whether of the British regime or the independent state, could scarcely spurn his plea. Nor could Sulli's bitter enemies among the Kota try to undermine him at the very moment when he was defending the honor of them all.

When, on other occasions, the opposing faction barred Sulli from the Kota temples or when a Kota council decided to sever social relations with him, he brought litigation against them, effectively imported police into the village at times convenient for his plans, and appealed to officials as a progressive citizen oppressed by his reactionary brethren.

Sulli was a school teacher for many years, and since his income did not depend on his fellow Kotas he was not so bound by their council edict as an ordinary Kota would have been. As a school teacher he carried the fight for Kota respectability into Badaga villages. When he was appointed as a teacher in a Badaga school all the parents withdrew their children and the school had to be closed. But he tried again, and eventually, because he had the sympathy of some school officials, he succeeded in acting as a teacher to Badaga pupils.

Before the end of his life Sulli was able to see a number of his reforms accepted, his Kota opposition almost gone, and his own place among Kotas secure. If Kotas have not risen much in their local social order, neither are they as lowly as some Badagas would have had them be nor as impoverished as they might have become. An observer can see in retrospect that Sulli's success was likely because he was riding a favoring tide of national history and world events. This wide trend made for propitious official attitudes toward the disadvantaged. But at any one time the internal Kota quarrels and their external contests were touch-and-go affairs with the outcome almost always uncertain. Sulli suffered setbacks as well as victories, and had his determination flagged, his ambitions and reforms might have been frustrated.

Sulli's ambitions were always couched as ambitions for his people. He conceived of no future for himself apart from the fate of the Kotas. Though he disliked many of them and despised more than a few, he felt part of the same social body as all, and agitated in behalf of the whole group.

Individual Passing and Percolation

Leaving one's group and passing as a member of some other jati is a possible mobility tactic but, insofar as can be known, it is not often done successfully. For one thing, it is difficult to bring off; an imposter may be unmasked at any time. This happened to one man in Sripuram village of Tanjore district. He came into the village as a mason by trade and claimed to be by birth a Padayachi, one of the middle jatis. He worked in the village for three or four years, had access to Brahmin houses in the course of his work, and was accepted by men of other middle jatis at his claimed identity. Then one day a visitor saw him sharing betel with such men and expressed surprise. The mason, it turned out, was a Palla, an untouchable, and a jati fellow of the newcomer. The pretender was forthwith beaten and fled from the village (Béteille 1965, p. 81).

Even if those who try to pass move far enough away so that there is slight chance of being recognized, there are still great difficulties in settling into a different village (cf. Mayer 1960, pp. 27–28). The new neighbors want to know who the newcomer's relatives are and what his jati is. Since he cannot produce them readily or substitute convincingly, who will give him a daughter as wife? If he comes with a wife, whom will his children be able to marry? These questions arise in the city as well. A study of educated city people who are of untouchable origin (Isaacs calls them "ex-untouchables") shows that, although they are generally able to gloss over their jati origin in their professional or business practice, their family life and intimate relations are with similarly educated people of like jati birth (Isaacs 1965, pp. 143–149, 157–160). They have a way of passing in public while not passing in private. Isaacs quotes one such informant, who told him that educated people cannot separate themselves from their jati community because without such a community all a man's relationships are awkward. The quotation concludes with the italicized sentence *"In India you have got to be connected"* (Isaacs 1965, p. 147).

There are undoubtedly some who do manage to pass but there is no way of telling how many do so. Occasionally an instance of successful passing is reliably reported, for example, the case of a man from the Jatavs of Agra. Jatavs were formerly leatherworkers, and, as noted again below, they have succeeded in raising their rank considerably. This Jatav claimed to be a Brahmin, apparently with some success, because in 1962 he married a Brahmin girl from Rajasthan (Srinivas 1966, p. 73).

One Harijan, who had passed but later returned to become a political leader among Harijans, explained to me that his father had been a village boy who obtained an education at a mission school. After reaching manhood, he married, had children, and moved to a city, where he took a new name, and gave out that the family belonged to a middle jati. He did well in his profession, severed all ties with his kin, and even succeeded, through astute and costly devices, in marrying his daughters into the jati whose name he had adopted. His son, however, could not forget the family's origins. After he was educated and became a lawyer, he decided to drop the camouflage (with what results for his married sisters I did not find out). He abandoned the assumed name and worked for the Harijan cause.

Another kind of individual and family mobility is through the marriage of girls into a higher group. In large jatis that have ranked hypergamous sections, the more favored girls of the lowest sections are taken by higher ranking men. The young men of these low sections compete for the few girls of their own level who remain available or take a bride from the next lower jati. Thus the lower Rajputs of central Gujarat take wives from the higher lineages among Kolis; as was noted above, men of the lowest sections of the Patidars of this region are sometimes compelled to marry girls of a lower jati because of a lack of eligible brides in their own section.

Percolation also occurs when a girl of a lower jati in a jati-cluster is married to a man of a higher jati in the jati-cluster. Such matches are not approved but can be tolerated. There are two jatis of genealogists in central Gujarat, one using written records, the other relying on oral tales and ballads. When a young man of the latter group learns to read and write he may be hired as a clerk in a family of literate genealogists. In time he may be fully incorporated into their jati (Shah and Shrof 1958, pp. 252, 265–267; Pocock 1957a, p. 19).[1]

Through such channels of percolation, a family may become affiliated with a close but higher jati and may gradually become assimilated into it. No strong claims to high rank are announced and no strong countermeasures are aroused. Infiltration into higher rank rather than capture of it has probably been brought off by many aspirants. Percolation is a quieter procedure that has not yet been well described, partly because it draws less fire and notice, partly because those who take this path have been diligent in covering over all traces of their route to the higher niche.

The Jati Campaign

The mobility tactics of greatest social importance are those undertaken for the jati. Claims to higher rank are common; those who make good their claims must move from substantial secular gains to insistent symbolic assertions. Wealth alone, we note again, is no automatic guarantee of higher rank. Jati members must use it properly so that the jati's rank may be elevated for their children.

Secular gains are primarily the results of family efforts. A profitable transaction is brought off, another field is purchased, a good harvest enables the family to expand its operations. A jati's power

[1] The Coorgs of South India formerly permitted a kind of percolation into their jati that is not common among dominant landowners. In the nineteenth century whole families of non-Coorgs, some of quite high jati, were received as jati members. These were families who had settled in the then isolated Coorg territory and wanted to become assimilated to the dominant group. Apparently the Coorgs also took in some who had been excommunicated by their jati. Very low groups like the Nimar Balahis may do this, but the Coorgs were exceptional among landowners in extending such hospitality (Srinivas 1952a, p. 37; Fuchs 1950, pp. 18–20).

The more common pattern of percolation seems to be illustrated in Gandhi's family. His biographer, Pyarelal, writes that Gandhiji once said that when his father was to be married for the fourth time, there was some difficulty in finding him a bride of his own group probably because Kaba Gandhi was then nearly forty and because his third wife was still living. "As a result, he was married into a family considered to be inferior in the hierarchy of caste" (Pyarelal 1965, p. 186).

increases almost imperceptibly, through prospering family units. An enlargement of economic opportunity in its occupation may enable a number of its families to become richer. As these families prosper, they are apt to favor jati fellows and so they accelerate the general prosperity of the jati.

Gains in ritual rank, however, are typically made by a group for the group. There is little point to wearing the sacred thread unless it is done as a matter of jati right. This is not to say that jati leaders wait patiently until their jati fellows have accumulated a given quantity of wealth and power. Low jatis may make high claims even though the power they have falls far short of that needed to press the claims successfully. Some try any possible opening: witness the untouchables who tried to get themselves inscribed in the Census under Brahmin or Kshatriya titles.

Others have set up confrontations prematurely and have been beaten down (cf. Cohn 1955, pp. 65–74). However, those who are defeated do not necessarily lose very much as a group. Some of the challengers (especially if they are untouchables) may be beaten up, a few possibly murdered. Some of their leaders may expend much of their wealth in the effort. Neighbors of higher rank may squeeze them a little more economically and scorn them a bit more socially. But for the group as a whole not much will change because of the failure of their attempt. If they are Harijans they cannot well be further degraded; their economic services will still be needed. If they are Shudras, they will still be treated as a jati of that category. There are limits to punitive conflict among jatis as there are limits within a jati.

In contrast, such limits are not observed in the status competition among the Swat Pathans of northern Pakistan and among similar peoples on the northwestern borders of the sub-continent. Among them, the competition is just as continuous but it is much more on an individual basis. There is little supervening framework as in a jati order, nor is there much corporate sharing of victory and failure. Hence the results of failure are much more serious; if a Swat Pathan loses the main criterion of rank, the ownership of land, he may sink to the depths of the social scale. Conversely, the rewards of victory are not translated to any long-term group prestige, so that a victory is valid only so long as it can be successfully and individually defended. Rife as is status competition in Indian village society, it seems not so sharp nor so much a matter of life and death as it is in the more atomistic society and more individualized competition of the Swat Pathans (cf. Barth 1959).

How much increase in wealth is required before an advance in ritual rank becomes feasible depends on such variables as the relative size of the jati-group in the village population. A large jati-group is likely to secure status gains more readily than one with few people on the local ground. Srinivas gives the example of one Mysore village in which fishermen are rated so low that they are not allowed to take their processions into the streets of the higher jatis, while in villages where fishermen are in the majority, they suffer no such disabilities (1959, p. 4). Numerical strength in many villages of a close vicinity gives added strength to the jati's cause in each of them.

Another factor is the position from which a jati starts its rise. An already respectable jati may need relatively little secular gain to win a higher ranking while a low group may gain considerably in wealth and still be judged low. In Gaon village of Poona district the jati whose members were temple servants, musicians, and beggars was ranked quite low in an account of 1868, but by 1954 they had given up music and begging and were ranked by their neighbors as being just below the local Brahmins. Their temple service and vegetarian diet enabled them to win higher place with relatively little increase in wealth or power. On the other hand, the leatherworkers have become markedly better off than they were and have reformed their practices considerably, but they have not yet made great gains in rank. Most people in Gaon consider them to be transmitters of touch pollution like the other Harijans.

The leatherworkers have succeeded, however, in getting some local Brahmins to conduct their weddings, though the Brahmin officiants avoid touch contact with the members of the wedding (Orenstein 1965a, pp. 146–148). Securing the services of Brahmins is, as we have noted, an important step in legitimizing a jati's status claims. A beginning is usually made by engaging some of the poorest and not too meticulous Brahmins; more effective legitimation comes when the more respectable Brahmins of the locality provide full sacerdotal services to the jati's members (cf. Srinivas 1966, pp. 24–28).

The small ritual advance of the leatherworkers contrasts with the rise, mentioned in the preceding chapter, of the dominant jati-group in Gaon, which has risen within a century from quite low shepherds to high "Rajputs" firmly entrenched as Kshatriyas. Some of their neighbors in Gaon are annoyed by this, especially so the Marathas who are dominant in the region though not in this village, but who dare not openly challenge the quondam shepherds. Others support their achievement and "their claim was respected to the extent that everyone referred to them by the Rajput title, whether they were present or not" (Srinivas 1966, pp. 145–146). These "Rajputs" have achieved for their jati what many a villager aspires to for his—legitimation of the higher rank by Brahmins, affirmation of it in the daily acts of their neighbors, and confirmation in formal panchayat.

Steps toward higher rank

Such success is achieved gradually, beginning with a series of steps to which others cannot well object, perhaps reform of the jati's marriage practices (how can others protest if the jati's widows are prohibited from remarrying?) or enlarging sources of income which others do not care to have (what harm if earthworkers take a government contract to dig a canal?). Later the ambitious jati members make more open assertions, which are more objectionable to higher jatis. The lowly earthworkers may decide to wear the sacred thread. It is at such a point that escalating aspirations and growing hostility come to a head; there is a confrontation, often followed by other physical, legal, and societal encounters.

In Ramkheri village, for example, the weavers and Bhilalas have taken the preliminary unobjectionable steps, while the oil-pressers have made more overt assertions. As Mayer describes the situation, the weavers (Balai) are untouchables who are quietly preparing to move out of that category. They have stopped eating beef and have dropped former demeaning practices. By occupation they are now laborers rather than weavers. "No explicit demand has yet been made for adjustment of their status, but many Balais maintain privately that they are now no different from other castes, and it is therefore unjust for them to be discriminated against as Harijans." Those of higher jatis are aware of this notion and "there is an undercurrent of feeling against those Harijans who try to assert themselves" (Mayer 1956, p. 139).

The Bhilalas (the name implies descent from Bhil tribesmen) are ranked in the Shudra category but they want to be accepted as Kshatriyas along with the local Rajputs. They proclaim their Rajput origins and play down their tribal associations. As one preliminary gesture, they decided to build a caste temple on the banks of the sacred river Sipra as higher jatis have done; their claim to be known as "Bhilala Rajputs" verges on overt assertion.

The oil-pressers (Telis) have shifted from covert preparation to overt demands. Although they are ranked with Rajputs for some purposes, they are not fully accepted in the Kshatriya category. When they asked to sit in the same line at a feast with the Rajputs they were refused. In reprisal for this assertion the Rajputs refused to smoke in their company, a privilege the Telis had previously enjoyed. But, as Mayer indicates, the oil-pressers will not readily be discouraged; some of them own land, some are educated and have urban contacts. The weavers and Bhilalas, on the other hand, have little land or education and so, like other ambitious but insufficiently strong groups, they must concentrate on bettering their ritual observances rather than on making overt demands (Mayer 1956, pp. 139–141; 1960, pp. 48–49).

At some point a mobile group is likely to perform an overt act that others will take as a clear challenge. Where no untouchable was permitted to own land, the mere purchase of land by a Harijan might be taken as an intolerable disruption of the social order (cf. Harper 1968, p. 46). In the example from Gopalpur village mentioned previously, the low-ranking stoneworkers were allowed to own inferior land but when some of them bought good rice-growing land and one of their young men began to plow it, he was severely beaten by men of higher jatis (Beals 1962, p. 39). Opposition to the ownership of land by lower jatis is passing in most places, but there are many other grounds for confrontations. Village festivals often occasion quarrels among jatis, as weddings may among families within a jati. Some village festivals have been abandoned mainly because they precipitated insoluble quarrels about jati rank.

The symbols themselves become differently interpreted in time. The Noniyas, the earthworkers, of Senapur village and vicinity decided at a meeting in 1936 to put on the sacred thread to show that they were really Chauhans by caste and Kshatriyas in varna. When some of them did so, the dominant landowners beat them, tore off the sacred threads, and imposed a collective fine on the whole jati-group. Subsequently, after their position in the village was stronger, Noniyas individually began to wear the sacred thread without any fanfare. This aroused no violent countermeasures. In recent years, Noniya young men have lost interest in wearing the sacred thread; a number of them have worked in cities and learned that other insignia, a wristwatch for example, are more prestigious than the traditional insignia of the "twice-born." When William Rowe studied the Noniyas, their oldest men did not wear the sacred thread because they were of a generation that had not been strong enough to do so. A considerable number of the middle generation wore it, but the younger men showed decreasing interest in doing so (Rowe 1968, p. 76). Noniyas now are accorded higher status than they were given formerly, and in that sense they have defeated the adversaries who once tore off their badges of higher rank. However, the adversaries themselves have become less concerned with these badges and more interested in other ways of symbolizing and maintaining their dominance.

Whatever issue may precipitate open conflict about rank, the men of a dominant jati are commonly among the main adversaries. They tend to see any alteration in the social order as a potential threat to their dominance and take themselves to be the guardians of that order. "The elders of the dominant caste in a village were the watchdogs of a pluralistic culture and value system," Srinivas writes, and he adds that when a low caste "refused to perform the services, economic or ritual, which it traditionally performed, or when it appropriated an important high-caste symbol, then punishment followed swiftly" (1966, p. 15). Other high jatis may be equally uneasy lest the lifting of a lower group mean the lowering of their own status. Lower jatis may also resent the rise, feeling that they are further demeaned if another jati is added to the number of their superiors. Where no single jati is dominant, the thrust of a lowly group may bring about a coalition of high jatis for the purpose of putting down the challenge (cf. Roy 1963).

To overcome such opposition, the aspirants commonly gather allies of their own. Just as an alliance leader within a jati secures the support of one man by lending him money, of another through the lease of land, of still another by giving him a patron's protection, so the prospering men of a jati secure allies for their jati's advance in the course of their workaday affairs. They attract and bind supporters through the redistribution of their wealth on ceremonial occasions. Their families invite many guests of other jatis to their weddings and, in turn, are munificent about weddings in other jatis. They will give handsomely to the rites for the special deity of a low jati, contribute generously to the temple of a high god, and will liberally support village festivals and other enterprises for the common good. Thus they gather strength for a test of rank. There may be a dramatic confrontation, like the temporary debacle of the Senapur Noniyas in 1936. More likely there are a number of successive encounters, the aspirants gaining in some and losing in others, their hopes only gradually becoming fulfilled and being securely established only after the passage of a generation or more.

The gradualness of this process is brought out in F. G. Bailey's account of the rise of the Boad distillers (Sundi) of Bisipara village in Orissa (1957, pp. 186–198). In the late nineteenth century, this jati was placed among the "Low Hindus" of the village, just above the line of untouchable pollution. By mid-twentieth century it held a firm place near the top of the "High Hindus," ranking just below the dominant "Warriors" (Sudo). The springboard for this advance was a sudden enlargement of economic opportunities when this jati was given a near monopoly of liquor manufacture in the area. This monopoly lasted from about 1870 to 1910 and in those forty years the jati members came to have more average wealth per capita than any other jati-group in Bisipara. They bought land, farmed it with the aid of laborers, and became economically equal to the dominant landowners.

As they accumulated wealth, they sloughed off demeaning traits. Their women cast off a knee-length garment in favor of the long sari worn by Brahmin women of the village. They dropped the traditional occupation of distilling; most of them have stopped drinking liquor. They no longer keep chickens, as low folk do, and they wear the sacred thread as do the high-born. Like other newly arrived they exaggerate their ritual purity. They refuse to take water and food from certain jatis from whose hands even the local Brahmins accept water and food. Their neighbors of other jatis sometimes sneer at their pretensions, but at the same time they agree that the distillers are in the top part of the local order.

This ascent, Bailey emphasizes, probably was accomplished through a long sequence of steps, each a partial rather than a total bid for better position. For example, if you are a distiller (or of any other ambitious jati) and distillers rank below washermen, the first step is to persuade a washerman to wash your family's clothes. This will be for cash payment at first; perhaps later it may develop into the kind of jajmani arrangement that washermen have with high families. The aspiring men also get some untouchables to work for them, again on a contractual arrangement at first and gradually developing into a more permanent patron-client tie. Similar arrangements are established with families of barbers, herdsmen, and Brahmins. Should any of these village specialists refuse to provide their services, others of their occupation from a different village may be hired or may even be permanently imported for the purpose. But a washerman heavily in debt to a distiller would not spurn the distiller's request for a cash arrangement nor long defer jajmani exchange.

The success of the distillers has not altered the structure of the local order even though the specific order of jatis has been shifted. While they are now higher in ritual rank, they uphold the traditional standards of that higher rank. They have come to be about as powerful in village affairs as the "Warriors," and they comport themselves in the manner of the traditional landowners.

Different Routes of Advance

The distillers have followed the traditional upward path; they have emulated a standard reference category and a strong reference group to achieve a higher place in their village. But this is not the only route of social ascent; two others are exemplified in the same village of Bisipara. There is another jati-group of distillers there who have followed a Vaishya rather than a Kshatriya model and, most importantly, have taken as the social stage for their rise a wider area than the village vicinity. They have drawn power from the wider area and have won higher place in it. A third instance is that of the untouchable Pans. The members of this jati seek to rise not only in the village but in the political arena of their state and they have drawn power for their struggle in the village from the political sphere.

The two separate jatis of distillers migrated to Bisipara village from different places. The Boad distillers whom we have been discussing came from the Boad kingdom to the north. The Ganjam distillers came from the Ganjam plains to the south. There were five households of Ganjam distillers in the village in the 1950s, forming only 2 percent of the population as compared with 6.7 percent for the Boad distillers. These five households not only shared in the forty years of lucrative liquor monopoly but also engaged in very profitable general trade. As merchants they kept up their kin and trade connections with the Ganjam plains, unlike the Boad distillers whose interests were concentrated within the village.

The Ganjam distillers have also reformed their jati practices but they have entered very little into Bisipara village affairs, holding themselves politely aloof from the other villagers' pastimes, disputes, and concerns. They were able to do so because they dealt with their fellow villagers as customers more than as neighbors; they were not economically dependent on them because they had little competition as merchants and drew customers from a number of settlements. At the same time they took care not to offend villagers' sensibilities. The villagers in turn were reluctant to offend them because they were rich men with governmental and economic connections outside the village. Their status aspirations have been directed toward a wider sphere and toward a different arena than the village locale in which the Boad distillers won success (Bailey 1957, pp. 199–210).

The other rising group, the Pans, comprise about one-fifth of the village population and some of them have prospered despite their position as untouchables (Bailey 1957, pp. 211–227). British officials gave them advantages in schooling, farming, and government employment as part of a program of uplift, and after independence such aid was increased. As a result, some have become schoolteachers; others are in government service; still others have made money by trading cattle. A number of them own land, and several are as rich as the richest traditional landowners.

With this base the prospering Pans began to reform their jati practices as the Boad distillers had done. They too gave up defiling occupations, changed their diet, dress, and name. But they were not as successful as were the distillers in using their new wealth to secure allies and dependents. Part of the difficulty was that not enough of them were rich. To secure the services of others, from washermen to Brahmins, untouchables need much more wealth, time, and manipulation than do other jatis.

When Pans tried to enter a village temple they were rudely turned away and the higher jatis united solidly to repel them. There were other confrontations in which the Pans were rebuffed. They then turned to outside sources of aid—police officials, government agents, even to a Minister of Orissa State, who happened to be in the vicinity when a confrontation was being staged. Educated Pans, especially those who have been in government service, are much more adept at appealing to officials than are villagers of higher jati rank but with limited social and political experience. The latter were thoroughly intimidated, Bailey comments, by the long and impressive list of people whom the Pans were able to interest in their troubles; they said that the outside world in general and the Congress Raj in particular were on the side of the Pans. Although they were not by any means ready to grant ritual respectability to the Pans, they were far less prepared to oppose them openly. Instead, the higher jatis seemed to be withdrawing from events and circumstances in which a test might be made. This new challenge and the response may well presage a shift away from the traditional processes of recurrent change.

Low-ranking jatis in many other places have drawn on wider political forces to hasten their rise. The Jatavs (ex-Chamars) of Agra City, for example, have done this in a much larger, better organized way than have the Pans of the remote hill village. They have forged modern political instruments of their own, including a political party that has exerted considerable influence on the Agra scene (Lynch 1968).

Dominant jatis as well have taken to maneuvering through political parties in order to maintain and enhance their status (cf. Srinivas 1966, pp. 111–113). This shift to a wider arena of power is not a totally new procedure; able and highly ambitious men have long done so, though the method has become much more common in recent decades.

A historical example of the mobilization of wider resources for social rise is that of the Tagores of Bengal whose efforts to expunge a group blemish were mentioned in Chapter 23 above. Their example also illustrates the strength of opposition to a rise. Despite their great secular achievements, it was well into the twentieth century before they overcame the ritual stigma that orthodox Brahmins of Bengal had attached to their name since the seventeenth century. The Tagores are descended from Brahmins called Pirali who were a separate and beclouded jati of the Rahriya division of Bengal Brahmins (Risley 1892, vol. 2, p. 176). An eminent Tagore wrote out the tale told about their degradation, that their ancestor was tricked into a defiling act by a Muslim official, one Pirali Khan, whom he had offended. This story is convincingly impugned by J. N. Bhattacharya on the basis of internal evidence (1896, p. 123). He conjectures that the ancestor in question was probably a surveyor in the service of Pirali and, as sometimes happened, made himself unpopular by attempting to usurp titles to lands of other Brahmins. Presumably the landowners banded together to ostracize him, perhaps on the pretext given in the account.

Whatever the reason may have been, the Piralis were treated as outcastes by other Brahmins of Bengal in the seventeenth century. In the last decade of that century, one of them moved to the place where the East India Company had established a factory and which was to become the city of Calcutta. Few Brahmins lived in Calcutta during its early decades, most of the prospering residents were weavers by jati origin with a few from the trading jatis. In this frontier town, as we noted, they accepted the Tagores as Brahmins. The family prospered greatly, grew into a proliferating and influential lineage, and became so prominent that they even stimulated a leading Brahmin personage to "form a party for degrading them" (Bhattacharya 1896, p. 123). But the Tagores, as by then they were known (from the anglicization of the honorific term Thakur), were not to be denied and continued to grow in prosperity, fame, and numbers.

By the end of the nineteenth century, members of the Tagore lineages had greatly distinguished themselves in government service, in traditional religious piety, in reform sects, in scholarship, in the indigenous arts, as well as in commerce and industry (cf. Kripalani 1962, pp. 14–32). Their most illustrious son, Rabindranath Tagore (born in 1861) was launched on his career of immense productivity. But their origins as Piralis were not forgotten in spite of the unsurpassed brilliance of Tagore accomplishments. When his family sought a bride for Rabindranath in 1883, their choice was mainly limited to the daughters of a few Pirali families in the small town of Jessore (Kripalani 1962, p. 112).

One commentator who extolled their contributions was moved to write, "If they are denounced as outcasts, such outcasts are the ornaments of the country" (S. C. Bose 1881, p. 175). And in 1896 Bhattacharya wrote, "From a long time the Tagores have been struggling hard to be restored to caste." He observed that they are very orthodox Hindus—with the exception of one family, headed by Rabindranath's father, that belonged to the reform sect of Brahmo Samaj. They could sometimes marry their girls expensively, to Brahmins of the Rahdiya division, but the groom "is himself reduced to the rank of a Pirali, and always demands a heavy premium as a *sine qua non*." Bhattacharya summarized their rank as of 1896: "But the Tagores are now fast rising in the scale of caste. Poor Brahmins now more or less openly accept their gifts, and sometimes even their hospitality; and Sir J. M. Tagore is on the way towards acquiring an influence on the Pandits which may one day enable him to re-establish his family completely in caste" (1896, pp. 119, 124). Their caste disabilities were later overlooked, if not totally forgotten. Perhaps one reason it took some eight generations for the Tagores to achieve respectable rank among orthodox Brahmins was the very magnitude of their accomplishments, which drew envy and enmity as well as fame and fortune.

In all three of these cases, a status rise was accomplished by drawing on resources far beyond the village and its land. The Ganjam distillers followed a more traditional, Vaishya, route in doing so. The untouchable Pans in their backwoods home and the illustrious Tagores in the metropolis both have drawn upon modern political and educational resources.

Jati Leaders and Leading Groups

Those who now lead a jati to higher rank have typically had some modern education and some experience with a greater world than than that of the village and its vicinity. To take the case of Sulli again, as a schoolteacher he had seen much more of towns, of different kinds of people, and of non-Kota standards than had his Kota contemporaries. He understood, for example, that the traditional Kota man's chignon was a token of social inferiority in the eyes of others and not, as most Kotas saw it, the ancient symbol of being a proper Kota man. He realized also that their traditional diet and occupations doomed them to invidious treatment by outsiders. At that time other Kotas were little involved with the Hindus who had come into the Nilgiri area.

Such leaders transmit to their jati fellows the values of the wider Indian civilization, both Sanskritic and modern. The traditional mobility tactics are carried out on a wider scale than before. "The drama of Sanskritization is played on many a village stage, but the script may be written elsewhere, the star performers are often a travelling company, and the critics represent a greater and growing public" (Marriott 1959b, p. 105). A few men rise above the mobility strivings of their jati. A man who attains state or national office cannot keep his jati affiliations in the center of his attention. One who becomes an industrial magnate finds more engrossing pursuits than the uplift of his jati, though jati considerations usually remain paramount in his family life. Such men typically stand ready to help in jati causes, but they are often remote from them.

Their personal achievements are nevertheless of great interest to their jati fellows. The most successful within a jati are held up as demonstrators of the true worth and level of all the jati members. Thus Yadava publications proudly cite not only their mythical progenitors and their historical Rajas, but also contemporaries who have become learned scholars, rich industrialists, and high civil servants (Rao 1964; Khedkar 1959).

Similarly, the example of those sections of the jati that have won higher place in their localities gives heart to others in the jati who are still battling for such place. "Members of minority castes in Rampura occasionally told me with pride that in a particular village their castefolk were numerous and wealthy" (Srinivas 1959a, p. 4). They were trying to identify themselves with jati fellows whom they regarded as having a higher position than themselves. And on a wider scale, the clear success of a low group in raising their social position has a "demonstration effect" on all the lowest peoples in their region. "It was as though they suddenly woke up to the fact that they were no longer inhabiting a prison" (Srinivas 1966, p. 91).

At each step of a jati campaign, in any route of advance, strains are likely to develop within the jati. All jati members do not improve their resources and local standing at the same rate. Some families and lineages, some jati-groups are much more successful than others, but their victories also bring on new problems for them. Marked success attracts notice and tends to unify opposing forces. Thus with success the problems of maintaining internal unity are apt to be intensified. The most advanced groups may have reformed their practices so much that they can hardly bear to be considered as jati equals of those sections who still carry on the demeaning customs. Moreover, the success of one group tends to arouse challenges from within. We have noted that an alliance may be disrupted by the same forces that once helped cement it, namely the desire to challenge those next higher. So is it also within a jati when one group has advanced much more rapidly than others. Overcoming external opposition, as has been noted, is only one part of mobility tactics; maintaining internal unity is the other.

CHAPTER 26

Maintaining Internal Cohesion:
Fission and Fusion

To RAISE their rank, the people of a jati have
to act in unison. They must coordinate their acts of association and
dissociation and mobilize against opposition. They must also display enough uniformity in ritual matters to establish a suitable
rationale for their claims. So the leaders of a rising jati try to keep
all their jati fellows up to the ritual mark; they exhort the laggard
to reform, cajole the powerful to be patient, threaten to punish
recusants. The ritual homogeneity they actually achieve does not
need to be complete, but they cannot afford flagrant disunity. If
some in a jati persist in eating meat and performing servile work
while others proclaim their vegetarianism and occupational respectability, the mobility campaign will be undermined. Any claim by
the reformed to higher rank is likely to be hooted down so long as
their relatives and ritual compeers are so patently low.

This holds true for the maintenance as well as for the advancement of jati rank. The members of a jati, as we have seen, cannot
tolerate a flagrant transgression of their ritual standards by anyone
in the group. If such a violation becomes publicly known, the transgressor must be penalized; if he is not willing to take his punishment and recant, he must be made outcaste. Outcasting is a means
of restoring the jati as a proper unit by redefining the membership
of the group.

Redefinition of boundaries is also used to help raise jati rank. In
the following chapters four kinds of regrouping are discussed. Two
of them, fission and fusion, are usually direct efforts toward mobility. The other two, regrouping on religious grounds and the accretion of tribal peoples, often involve considerations of mobility.

Fission commonly comes about when the more prosperous and
ritually meticulous families within a jati stop intermarrying with the

less advanced families and declare themselves to be a separate jati. Fusion occurs when people of previously separate jatis begin to interdine, intermarry, and merge their mobility efforts, their main purpose being to increase their secular strength. Religious regrouping has occurred when converts to a religious movement have become a new jati. Personal salvation may be the original impetus for conversion but as the individual converts gather together, they tend to develop into a jati. The quest for spiritual improvement has often led to the usual quest for higher rank. The fourth kind of redefinition involves the flow of tribal peoples into caste society. There are still many millions in India who maintain tribal forms of society, but there has been a continual transformation of tribal groups into jatis. Once a new jati is formed, through any of these processes of redefinition and regrouping, it is maintained in the same way as are other jatis of the same loaclity and of similar social level.

Fission

There are several reasons for jati fission. A common one is that some families have taken to a different occupation, have prospered beyond the others, and have gained a better means of acquiring power and education. Migration of part of a jati has often led to eventual fission. The outcasting of a whole section of a jati has sometimes occurred, as has the establishment of a new jati as a result of clandestine unions. Occasionally a jati has split because some have taken on a different reference model from that held by others of their jati.

Jati division because of occupational separation was noted by British observers of the eighteenth century (cf. Raghuvanshi 1966, pp. 169–171), and continued to be mentioned in later ethnographic reports. In the Punjab report of the 1883 census, Ibbetson wrote that it was common for some members of a low group to change their occupation (as from scavenging to weaving) to separate from their former fellows, and thereby to gain in rank; "each caste throws out off-shoots into the grade above that which is occupied by the greater number of its members" (1916, p. 267). From Rajasthan, Baines cited the example of a jati of watchmen-raiders, some of whom became farmers and split away from the main group. Those who remained watchmen held themselves to be the superior at first, "Now, however, the cultivator has advanced in prosperity and refuses to recognize the older section as its superior or even as its equal" (1912, p. 82).

From Uttar Pradesh (then called United Provinces), Blunt listed a number of "relatively new instances of fission, having been reported for the first time at the Census of 1911." One new case was of tailors who took the name scribe-tailors (Kayastha-Darzi) "and have published a monograph on their ethnology" of the kind usually produced by groups trying to rise in the social scale (1931, pp. 54–55, 216). In an instance from Madras, O'Malley cited a report that among some Harijans "there is growing up a special superior caste known as Quinsap, namely those who have served and are descended from those who have served in the Queen's Own Sappers and Miners" (O'Malley 1934, p. 9).

Risley noted in Bengal a stage of partial separation among the Pods, a group of fishermen and cultivators of the districts near Calcutta. He reported that those Pods who were educated would no longer give their daughters in marriage to the noneducated although they would still take brides from them, perhaps because there were not enough marriageable girls among the families of the educated. "But this will right itself in the course of time," Risley was sure, "and they will follow the classic precedent of the twice-born classes and will marry only within their own group" (1915, pp. 164–165, also pp. 118–119, 157–158).

Although such hypergamous distinctions are known in Bengal, the complete break predicted by Risley in the case of the Pods had not occurred a half century after he made the forecast. The educated among the Pods did mount a mobility campaign of the usual type, as Jaya Datta Gupta reports (1959). They succeeded in changing the name Pod to a more mellifluous term, an end they had special reason to desire. As their leaders noted in a 1956 appeal addressed to the President of India, the Bengali term "Pod" is synonymous with "rectum" in English. "Even in this age of marked progress," their appeal stated, "wherever members of this community move in bazars or in public places, in villages or on farms, in every sphere of activities, they are purposely called and insulted directly or indirectly by this word 'Pod' " (Datta Gupta 1959, p. 126). They have been justifiably successful in changing this name, at least officially; their other mobility goals seem not yet to have been fully achieved.

Migration has also been a main cause of jati fission. A number of families move to a new locale, drawn by opportunities for land or work—sometimes driven by wars and famines—and gradually their ties with their original group become attenuated. They find it difficult to arrange marriages and keep up affinal relations over a long distance. If they have moved into a different language area, they may cling tenaciously to their original speech and customs through many generations, but even so they will adapt in some degree to the practices of their new region. Their cultural drift adds to the schism and they eventually become a wholly separate jati.

Although only a very small percentage of the population has migrated in any one period (except at the time of national partition), there has nevertheless been some migration throughout recent centuries.[1] Many tracts of land were brought under plow cultivation after the advent of the British regime. Migration to them was motivated more by a search for food and material security than by a quest for rank and ritual respectability, but if the migrants prospered in the new territory, they sometimes established a new jati that ranked higher in its local order than did the parent jati in the old homeland. A modern instance, mentioned previously, is that of the settlers on the reclaimed lands of the Bengal delta.

Families may migrate because of population pressure. There may be too many barbers or carpenters or laborers for a given locality to support; many a cultivator has found his land too small and has struck out for emptier spaces. A migrant jati usually maintains its separate social identity in the new locale, even though jatis of similar occupation and rank are also there. We have noted two jatis of immigrant distillers in Bisipara village. In Ramkheri the indigenous Malwa carpenters are separate from the carpenters who came into the village from Mewar, although the Mewari's genealogical records indicate that the immigration took place many

---

[1] In medieval South India, families could raise their rank within a short time by moving to a new location. "A section which moved out became a separate endogamous *jāti* after the lapse of several years, and true to caste tradition, each such *jāti* claimed to be superior to the others" (Srinivas 1966, p. 44).

centuries ago. The Mewari carpenters are themselves split into two endogamous bodies, of older and newer migrants (Mayer 1960, pp. 157–158).

Another kind of jati fission, exemplified in the villages around Ramkheri, is the creation of an "outcaste" jati. Whole jati-groups or lineages may be excommunicated quite as an individual or a family may be. In this locality the Rajputs of twelve villages were ostracized for reasons that were not divulged to outsiders. They became a separate endogamous and commensal group (1960, pp. 154–155).

The villages of this vicinity provide an example of jati separation, if not exactly of fission, that has resulted from clandestine unions between members of different jatis. There is a jati called Rajgeria Khati (farmers) whose members do not openly intermarry with the other Khati of the locality. The Rajgeria Khati are said to be descended from offspring of Rajput landowners and their farmer servant girls. Liaisons between masters and servant girls have long gone on; the men may acknowledge their children and provide for them although they cannot take them into their jati. The children of such unions were presumably raised by their Khati mothers and so became a kind of Khati even though they could not be admitted as a member of that jati either. There is some percolation of the Rajgeria Khati into the main Khati group by the girls who may quietly be taken in marriage by men of poor families among the Khati proper (Mayer 1960, p. 155).

A similar group came into being among the Jews of Cochin in Kerala, as we shall note again in discussing religion-based jatis. They formed a third jati of Cochin Jews, called Brown Jews, separate from the White and the Black Jews. The Brown Jews were descendants of unions between White Jews and servant girls who lived in the Jewish households and followed Jewish practices. Hence their children grew up in the Jewish streets, attended the synagogue and the Hebrew school, although they were relegated to an outer annex in each (Mandelbaum 1939). Unlike the Rajgeria Khati, their main affiliation was with the jati and customs of their fathers.[2]

[2] During their existence, the Brown Jews were a very small group and finding marriage partners for their children was always difficult. By the 1960s the group was virtually extinct as a jati. Most of them had been quite

Jati separation has also come about when one part of a jati has taken a reference model different from that held by the rest of the group. This occurred among the Coorgs of South India. In November 1834, some Coorgs severed their ties with the others in a thread-taking ritual on the banks of the Kaveri River and took the name Amma Coorgs. The main branch of the Coorgs were then land-owning cultivators of warrior tradition. The Amma Coorgs chose to adopt Brahmin rather than Kshatriya ways; those who partic-ipated in the rite became lay disciples of a Brahmin monastery. The Amma Coorgs have an origin story telling of their common descent from a Coorg father and a Brahmin mother; whatever the genealogical facts may have been, the jati was founded to follow a more Brahminized mode of life than that led by the other Coorgs. The Amma Coorgs, Srinivas comments, "exemplify a tendency which has always been present in the caste system: a small group of people break off from a larger whole of which they are part, Sanskritize their customs and ritual, and achieve a higher status than their parent-body in the course of a few decades" (1952a, pp. 34-35, 165-166).

The act of jati secession may be dramatically announced, as it was with the Amma Coorgs, although more usually it is quietly and tacitly effected; in either case, however, the split typically comes at the end of a series of strained relations and after a critical threshold for tolerance has been passed. There are countervailing pressures to remain as one jati, just as among a set of quarreling brothers, there are reasons to remain together. Not every jati splits whose families have taken to different callings and have very differ-ent fortunes. In earlier centuries families of highly disparate for-tune remained in one jati and all in a jati did not follow the jati's ascribed occupation. So is it also in modern times. To take some examples from the account of Ramkheri village, there is no ritual separation there between the Nai who remain barbers and those who have become landowners, or between the Nath who seek alms

---

well educated, one or two had married into the White Jews, the others had married spouses of similar education or profession from other Kerala reli-gions and jatis. Although mixed offspring were traditionally ranked lower than either parent in Kerala (Aiyappan 1937, p. 14), the modern education acquired by most members of this group enabled them to transcend the tra-ditional barriers.

and those who have become farmers. Some of the village Chamars are farmers only but they maintain their connections with those who continue to work with hides and leather (Mayer 1956, p. 132). Studies have not yet been made as to why some jatis have split while others, under similar strain, have not. But some indication of the reasons are found in Pocock's comments on the history of the Patidar jatis.

The several jatis of Patidars in central Gujarat have not fragmented further, although in the census reports of the nineteenth century only a few of those who are now known as Patidars had taken that name and there was a wide gulf in manners and wealth between them and their jati fellows who had not yet changed their name. Pocock writes that a contemporary observer might then have reasonably anticipated more fission, which did not occur. One reason may have been their separation into ranked hypergamous sections through which ritual and secular differences could be marked within a Patidar jati without changing the idea of jati endogamy. Pocock suggests also that the increase in agricultural income throughout the region, especially from tobacco growing, helped all groups of Patidars and narrowed economic differences among them. Even famine and plague conditions at the end of the nineteenth century did not widen economic disparities among Patidars because poorer families were impelled to try their fortunes in East Africa where most of them did well. The earnings they sent back to their kin in the home villages helped to lift the lot of these formerly poor families (1957b, pp. 30–31).[3]

Jati Separation and Political Affiliation: the Jatavs

When cohesive forces do not prevail, those who break away exclude themselves from the previous relations with their former jati fellows, and try to include themselves with some other, higher category. The Jatavs of Agra City, as described by Owen Lynch (1968),

[3] Patidars of central Gujarat were united also in their opposition to the local Rajputs, who had been rulers of the state in earlier centuries and were dominant in many villages. Gradually, Srinivas and Shah comment, they asserted their ritual superiority to Rajputs. "At the present moment, Patidars do not accept water or cooked food from Rajputs" (1960, p. 1377). In Chapter 27 we note how Rajputs have responded to this through the formation of a modern caste federation.

provide an example of fission in the classical manner combined with modern political coalition. The purposes of their jati fission as well as of their political affiliation were the same, namely the status rise and material benefit of the group.

Jatavs number about one-sixth of the city's population and began as Chamars who performed the traditional lowly tasks of this jati-cluster, working in hides and leather, occasionally scavenging, mainly doing hired labor. Toward the end of the nineteenth century some of them managed to get a foothold as contractors for municipal construction in addition to contracting for hides and scavenging. Two brothers even became mill owners. Some few Chamars in Agra City thus lifted themselves out of the dismal poverty that was the usual lot of village Chamars.

In the 1920s there rose in Agra a shoe and leather industry of a modern kind (though it was far from a rationalized, integrated industry) which produced for a national, even an international, market. Chamar entrepreneurs were among the leading figures in this industry; their labor force was Chamar, and factory work became virtually the only occupation of their jati fellows in the city. As workers and owners they not only prospered but they had really shifted to a new occupation, one that was without jajmani implications or village sanctions, even though it still involved working in leather. Moreover, the industrial Chamars became more residentially segregated in the city and so were sharply separated from other Chamars both in occupation and residence.

They were now able to send their children to school. The sons of the earlier Chamar entrepreneurs had either attended schools run by missionaries or by the Arya Samaj reform sect, or government schools. The Arya Samaj was an important influence because it offered access to Sanskritic scriptures and practices. The educated young men seized on the ritual symbols and practices thus offered though they were not as enthusiastic about Arya Samaj advocacy of a casteless society. These educated men did not want to abolish caste society but rather to gain a higher place in it. They successfully founded organizations for their jati's advancement in 1917, 1924, and 1930. By 1924 they had also produced a book to prove that they were really Jatavs by name, of ancient Kshatriya heritage. They dissociated themselves from all who were Chamars and even rejected the claim of another rising Chamar group, called Guliya, that they too were Jatavs. When a Swami came to Agra and preached to them about the abolition of caste and endogamy, he was driven out of the city by the leaders of the Jatav movement.

They pressed vigorously in the 1930s to be listed as Jatavs in government publications and to be completely separated from Chamars in official procedures, and they eventually succeeded in this. At the same time, they insisted on being listed with the "Scheduled Castes," the government roster of disadvantaged groups, largely untouchables, who are eligible for special governmental grants and preferments. Many another low jati has been involved in a similar contradiction that is more apparent than real. To men of such jatis it is not an embarrassing contradiction at all; one naturally takes advantage of all that can be had from government, certainly under the British regime, and securing such benefits has little to do with the real sphere of jati relationships. The more serious contradiction for the Jatavs lay in the fact that they were still leatherworkers and while they might carry off a new name and improved ritual practices, they still were weighted down, in the traditional perspective, by the burden of a demeaning occupation. This may have made other means of social improvement, through modern political moves, all the more attractive to them.

The Jatavs began political participation in the 1920s when they petitioned government officials to appoint Jatav representatives to legislative councils and administrative boards. Such appointments were in the gift of the officials, mainly British, who thought it proper that qualified members of lowly groups should have a representative voice in these advisory and administrative bodies. As the nationalist political movement grew, the Agra Jatav organization took political stands and affiliated with similar groups. By 1944–45 the Jatav organization had joined politically with the Agra Scheduled Castes Federation, which was part of the national federation led by the great Harijan leader, Dr. Ambedkar.

In the sphere of party politics the Jatavs were thus allying themselves with some of the same untouchable people from whom they were strenuously trying to dissociate in the sphere of traditional ritual relations. Again the anomaly was more apparent to outside observers than real to the participants. The real issue to them was the material and social improvement of the jati and its members. With the growing postindependence realization of the power of the vote and of elected officials, the educated Jatavs became increasingly concerned with gains in governmental politics rather than with ritual symbols. Some of them followed Dr. Ambedkar's lead in calling themselves Buddhists, as a means of opting out of any system of caste, but this move has been discouraged by the fact that governmental grants to the disadvantaged are specifically for low-ranking Hindus, and they do not want to define themselves out of that category.

Agra Jatavs were prominent in the formation of a new political party, the Republican Party, which was based mainly on lower jatis and on those estranged from the dominant party. It included a diversity of groups—Muslims, Harijans of various kinds, as well as Jatavs; one of the principal leaders was of Vaishya origin. The Jatav coalition with these groups resembles the alignment of a jati-group in a contest between village alliances; it is short term, limited to purposes of political gain, and involves no redefinition of Jatav identity.

Jatav endogamy is not breached nor is Jatav solidarity replaced by allegiance to the Republican or any other party. If some of the symbols of higher jati rank are no longer as prized as they were, the jati as a main identity and focus of loyalty is by no means jettisoned. A rising group like the Jatavs seizes on modern mobility resources, particularly through higher education and political stratagems, but its members continue to hold themselves apart from, indeed to obliterate the memory of, any former associations that might impede their rise.

Forces for Fusion

As the advantages of consolidation became clear, *sabhas* (caste associations; literally, assemblies or leagues) were organized at every social level in all parts of the country. The great impetus to sabha organization came with the Census of 1901 (as was noted in Chapter 25) when the idea spread that the Census could be used as an arena for mobility efforts (Srinivas 1966, pp. 94–100). Jatis in the same cluster joined forces to change the name of their cluster and to press together for governmental advantages. Such associations usually aim for a permanent merging of group identities, unlike the temporary political coalitions of the Jatav case.

While modern democratic conditions have favored fusion, an example of the amalgamation of jatis was noted in the nineteenth century. The goldsmiths of northern India were consolidating their highly fragmented groups, which were "subdivided to an astonishing extent" (Baines 1912, p. 60). They were thinly dispersed, since even a large village could support only a few goldsmith families. When roads were poor and communications uncertain, only a small number of these families could join within a single compass of endogamy. As communications improved, they began to enlarge the area of their marriage alliances and so to enlarge the jati beyond an uncomfortably small number of families.

Caste associations are now established to advance the material welfare and the social status of all members. Their leaders commonly urge intermarriage among all jatis in the association as the main way to guarantee continuing unity and the benefits of unity. But such intermarriages usually come after other beneficial functions are well established. In the next chapter, some characteristic forms and functions of caste associations are discussed; it is useful here to note some tendencies toward fusion apart from the context of a formal association.

To take examples again from Ramkheri village in Dewas district of Madhya Pradesh, two jati-groups of oil-pressers (Telis) there have almost completely merged. Those who immigrated from the Mewar area and those indigenous to Malwa began to interdine and intermarry about 1915; during the 1950s they sat in the same jati panchayat and shared in other jati functions, but still kept different names. Both were then adopting the same new name, however, and were on the verge of becoming one jati. The reason these two jati-groups have united, while two jatis of carpenters and two of goatherds in the village remain separate, may possibly be the strong mobility drive, noted earlier, among the Telis of Ramkheri. This kind of expansion of jati boundaries is comparable to the expansion of a kinship circle by an ambitious and prospering man who turns kinsmen of recognition into kinsmen of cooperation. Similarly he and his jati-fellows may take some who are recognizably close in ritual status into full jati relations.

Fusion also occurs at the top of a local order, for reasons relevant to family rather than jati mobility. Among the twelve Brahmin jatis in Sripuram in Tanjore district, two pairs are beginning to intermarry. Each merging jati is already close to the other in sectarian orientation, language and ceremonial practice. Béteille points out that the "general trend towards the contraction of structural distance between proximate segments" stems from secular and Western influences. The style of life of the different Brahmin jatis has become more similar as it has become more secular and the importance of differences of ritual detail has diminished (1965, pp. 74, 78, 220).

Moreover, an urbanized Brahmin wants to have his daughter marry into a family of comparable education and wealth. If no such match is found in his own jati he will arrange for a suitable groom of a close Brahmin jati, much preferring that his daughter marry an educated boy of a not-too-different jati rather than an uneducated person of his own. He hastens the merging of jatis in order to maintain his family's status and his daughter's welfare.

A man's views of jati fusion are likely to depend on his education and social experience. This was noted in Chapter 14 where Srinivas' comment was cited that an elderly, rural, and illiterate Okkaliga in Mysore may not regard Okkaligas of other districts and divisions as Okkaligas at all. But an Okkaliga lawyer or doctor would regard all the divisions as equally Okkaliga and might give his daughter in marriage to the son of an urbanized and educated Okkaliga who lived in quite a distant part of Mysore, provided the family were educationally and economically of the proper status (Srinivas 1966, p. 115).

The wealthier members of a jati have long had a wider geographic radius of marriage than the poor, and now the more educated, who are generally wealthier also, extend their marriage alliances across jati as well as district boundaries. They rarely marry their children into families of a different varna or jati-cluster from theirs, but rather into a family of comparable modern attainments that shares similar jati status and ritual practices, and speaks the same language.

Resolutions which urge intermarriage among the several jatis of a caste association are commonly adopted at association conventions. These help pave the way for the widening of endogamy, but it is mainly a family's concern for the welfare of its children and the improvement of its status that actually brings about such marriages.

The quest for status impels coordination among close jatis in many other ways besides the ultimate test of endogamy. Resources from far beyond a local social order can now be marshaled to lift a jati in the social hierarchy. To command such resources—of government, education, commerce, and the professions—jati members feel that they need the strength of a broader organization than that of the jati alone. The main trend of jati regrouping, therefore, is toward fusion among close jatis, partly on the level of family unions but particularly through caste associations.

CHAPTER **27** Modern Means for Jati
Improvement: Associations
and Federations

CASTE associations can be much more than just new means for carrying on the recurrent struggles for jati mobility. Some indeed are little more than that, but others have been built up into effective agencies for modern education and for participation in political democracy. As jati members become increasingly educated and involved in state politics, they are likely to alter their views about personal and jati goals. The modern forms of jati organization may have a formidable effect on Indian society. Just how formidable that effect has been and is likely to be remains to be gauged by further studies. It is useful to show here some of the bases on which these associations have been founded and some developing trends in their functions.

These associations have been founded on traditional organizations of various kinds, as is illustrated by the examples discussed in this chapter. The Jats of the districts north of Delhi have revived an old league for military defence. The Iravas (Tiyyas) of Kerala have joined together as followers of a religious teacher. The Telis of Orissa have used their traditional panchayat apparatus. The caste associations in Kanpur City have been organized on several different social bases.

The beginnings of association functions are seen in the case of the potters of western Uttar Pradesh. The Vanniyar and Nadar associations of Tamil Nadu (Madras) show more advanced development, in which association members have had considerable political and organizational experience. Finally, a caste federation is discussed, that of the Kshatriya Sabha of Gujarat; this federation does not seek endogamous merging, as do many associations, but mainly the pooling of political strength.

Whatever the base for a caste association, its leaders generally use parliamentary procedures in their meetings and emulate the organizational style of the main political parties. Each association is intended as an agency for the welfare and uplift of its constituency. Improvement in the education of the children is a constant theme. Reform in both the traditional and the modern modes is urged. Communication is typically fostered by a journal that carries news of association activities and such items as advertisements for potential grooms and brides.

A Jat Confederacy Revived

An old organization that has been revived is that of the Jats in the districts of the Meerut Division of Uttar Pradesh (Pradhan 1965; 1966). These Jats maintained defensive leagues into the nineteenth century, but the leagues lapsed after the uprisings of 1857. After 1947 Jat leaders began to realize that large collective organizations were needed once again, to give strength to political representations and to bolster modern mobility efforts. Jats were still the dominant landowners in their territory, but they sensed the new conditions for power.

In 1950 the first large panchayat since 1857 was assembled, attended by the hereditary leader of all eighteen clan areas of the Meerut Division. This meeting concentrated on the reform of Jat marriage practices and resolved that the amount of wealth expended on weddings should be reduced and that the overweening superiority of groom's family to bride's family should be lessened in a general raising of the status of women. These resolutions, M. C. Pradhan observes, "have had a profound effect upon the people of Meerut Division" (1965, p. 1861). At the next convocation, in 1956, one leader estimated that the Jats and other people of the area had saved 750 million rupees (then the equivalent of some 150 million dollars) in five years. Allowing for forensic rhetoric, it seems quite probable that a considerable amount of wealth was made available for capital investment and other productive uses through compliance with the resolutions. Their enforcement produced additional capital; the fines collected from defaulters were given to existing schools or used to build schools in the clan area. By the third assembly, in 1963, the goals for Jat improvement were enlarged. Better educational facilities were proposed, specifically a girls' college and two military colleges. National defense, increased agricultural productivity, and the removal of "caste distinctions and barriers" were espoused, as was also the protection of cows from slaughter.

One reason for the success of this revived organization is that the component lineages and clans had been kept as viable economic and political units after the military functions of the larger league had been abandoned. The Jats of this area continue to use their traditional panchayats rather than those elected under governmental auspices. The strength of Jat society is further demonstrated by the strong allegiance of educated Jats to their natal communities. Pradhan writes that Jats who have served in the army, in the civil service, or in other modern jobs outside their home area like to return to live in their villages when they retire. "I did not come across even one case where a Jat had sold his property in his native village and had settled down in a city" (Pradhan 1965, p. 1863).

A Religious Foundation; the Iravas of Kerala

Another strong caste association, but one formed at a different social level and cemented by religious appeal, is that of the Iravas of Kerala, who are also known as Ezhavas or Tiyyas and make up more than 40 percent of Kerala Hindus. Their traditional occupation was the making and sale of alcoholic beverage, an occupation that consigned them to low rank in the rigid hierarchy of this region.

In 1854 there was born into one of their families in a village near Trivandrum a child who became the great sage and reformer for all the Iravas. He became known as Sri Narayana Guru and, as Aiyappan writes, his history is the modern history of the Iravas. "Religion has been the greatest of all integrative forces in social life, and Sri Narayana's reforms which welded the Iravas into one powerful community were all through religion" (1944, p. 151). He preached open access to Sanskritic observances by all people and advocated a castless society. His influence did not extend much beyond his fellow Iravas, but among them it had great effect and led to the establishment of a strong association, which has been used for political advance as well as for internal ritual reform.

Intermarriage among the several jatis of the Irava cluster has gone on for decades, in keeping with the appeal of their great sage. The religious appeal also brought about considerable reform of Irava practices. The opposition of higher groups was so strong, however, that their social rise was relatively slow until recent years, when they have been able to benefit from their voting strength and from the new political environment (Aiyappan 1944, pp. 151–162, 188–194; 1965, pp. 147–169; Gough 1963, pp. 192–194; Hardgrave 1964, p. 1847).

A Modernized Panchayat Organization: Telis of Orissa

The association of Telis in Orissa continues with its traditional maintenance functions while pressing for innovative reform measures. In mid-twentieth century Teli leaders were still engrossed in internal tasks and had only begun to take interest in external, political activities.

The Telis are traditionally pressers and sellers of oil, an occupation that is not highly esteemed in the traditional view. They are quite numerous in Puri and adjoining districts of Orissa and have long had an extensive panchayat organization. Their modern association is thoroughly rooted in villages through the old panchayat ties and seems quite well adapted for both the traditional panchayat purposes and for reform (Patnaik and Ray 1960). The traditional pattern includes formal panchayats of higher and of lower jurisdiction. In the 1950s these councils still assessed fines, prescribed purifications, outcast errant offenders.

Patnaik and Ray have analyzed 203 cases, dated between 1942 and 1959, in the records of a panchayat jurisdiction called the "Dominion of Eight-Regions," one of the six in Puri district. Two-thirds of these cases dealt with marriage problems, property and financial disputes, and with the violation of jati standards. Others had to do with sexual crimes, requests for financial assistance, and organizational matters such as the appointment of headmen. In one case the elders of a component jurisdiction were themselves declared outcaste because they had not stopped a woman from giving false testimony in a court case, presumably to the detriment of the jati's larger interests (Patnaik and Ray 1960, pp. 17–20). The council of this Dominion, which covers seventy wards of oilmen, not only assumes judicial jurisdiction over difficult problems but also is prepared to take action to enforce its decisions.

A central concern of council meetings and especially of larger assemblies is the program for Teli improvement and uplift. The preamble to the regulations adopted by one Dominion states that many evils have crept into their society, and so the officeholders are authorized to frame and implement rules to free the society from its present blemishes. The explanatory myth is then given, that Telis were formerly respectable, prospering merchants engaged in overseas trade, who, when the main Orissa ports were closed (through no fault of theirs), were forced to resort to the less respectable occupation of crushing oilseeds. They lost not only their good livelihood but also their ancient level of education. "Everyone should therefore try to promote education and culture in our caste" (Patnaik and Ray 1960, pp. 25, 31, 44).

Education is vigorously advocated in resolutions adopted at almost every assembly; repeatedly Telis are told "that all boys of the jati must learn to read and that needy school boys should be helped from the Assembly's funds." An all-Orissa convention of Telis in 1959 adopted a resolution on education that opened with the comment that most Telis are very poor. "They feel keenly the need of educating their children. Let us encourage the education of children, and build up funds for the grant of scholarships" (Patnaik and Ray 1960, pp. 40, 74). The repetition of this resolution over the years, without mention of schools that have been built or scholarships granted, may indicate that there has been some lag in setting up educational facilities.

Ritual improvement has also been a constant theme in these resolutions. Divorce and remarriage are deprecated, sale of cattle to butchers condemned, peddling of pan (prepared betel leaf and areca nut) prohibited as a debasing occupation (Patnaik and Ray 1960, pp. 22, 29–36, 42–43). The repeated adoption of such resolutions through the years may also bespeak some failure to enforce them. The traditional name, Teli, with its disparaging overtones is rejected and a new, more respectable name meaning "merchants" is taken.

The general policy of most jati associations, that of combining traditional steps and modern measures, is summarized in a resolution adopted by the Teli association. "It is necessary [for us] to observe the old laws which have been in vogue from ancient times; while, at the same time, new regulations should be adopted in consonance with the times" (Patnaik and Ray 1960, p. 26). The two are not necessarily compatible, however; questions of priority arise. For example, there was heated debate at the all-Orissa meeting in 1959 on a proposed *dharmashala*, a pilgrims' lodge, in the pilgrimage center of Puri. To build such a lodge would be a traditional act of piety that would provide a center where jati fellows from various parts of the state could meet and become imbued, under religious auspices, with a spirit of jati solidarity (cf. Mayer 1960, p. 255). The proposal was opposed by younger delegates who argued "that instead of erecting a mansion which does not particularly serve the interests of the caste, it would be a hundred times better to build a hostel for students belonging to the caste" (Patnaik and Ray 1960, p. 72).

At the same assembly, free intermarriage among the three main jatis of Telis in Orissa was once again espoused. The anthropologist who attended this meeting happened to be sitting next to an elderly delegate as one speaker, a prominent Congress Party worker and a leader in the Sabha, was advocating the merging of the three into one endogamous unit. The old man whispered that it could not happen now, and, pointing to the speaker said, "I am a Haladia Teli by caste. Will he agree to marry my daughter to his son? He will then be outcasted. I will also not dare to give my son in marriage to his daughter from whose hand no one in my family would accept water" (Patnaik and Ray 1960, p. 77). Sabha collaboration for him stopped short of endogamy. But the younger and educated members of that assembly felt no reluctance and were beginning to arrange such marriages. The president of that conference even advocated the "establishment of friendly and marital relationships with oilmen in other parts of India." This association and others in Orissa had, in the 1950s, taken relatively little part in local and state politics as similar associations in Madras and in other states had done for decades.

Caste Associations of Kanpur City

In any caste association, the prime movers toward fusion and modern reform are likely to be those who have a modern education. They are concentrated in the cities, and the headquarters of an association is likely to be in a city. A study of eight caste associations in Kanpur City illustrates both their variety and their similarities.

The organization of the Kanya Kubja Brahmins was the first in the city in 1915. Its purposes were only those of education, and having securely established an Education Trust that maintains secondary schools the association became defunct. Brahmin concern with education was not new, but the push for modern education, which included education for girls and even night classes for women, was a departure (Nandi 1965, pp. 87–88).

The organization of the sweepers was the last to be founded, in 1957. But it began in strength, with aid from the All-India Sweepers' Association in Delhi, and with a government grant. The initial enrollment was 3000 members. It too provides education, especially primary education for children. A main reform purpose is to reduce the drinking and gambling habits of the jati's men. Other reforms are less emphasized, perhaps because they must await educational and economic improvements (Nandi 1965, pp. 94–95).

The other associations in Kanpur spread a wider net for reform. The Omar Vaishya tradesmen, for example, advocate educational and economic cooperation and also reform of marriage practices. Some of their resolutions have apparently been followed, such as the abolition of dancing by prostitutes at weddings. Others, like the reduction of dowries, have been given mainly lip service. The latter is a characteristic reform effort to reduce disparities within the group between the families of bride and groom. It may also be a gesture toward reducing the social disparity between men and women through upgrading the status of a bride and her family in relation to the groom and his family (Nandi 1965, pp. 91–93; Fox 1967, pp. 580–582).

Whatever specific reforms are urged at association conventions, more and better education for their children is almost always part of the improvement program. All agree on this, old and young, wealthy and poor, the better educated as well as the illiterate.

An Incipient Association; Potters of Western U.P.

Potters in the western districts of U.P. and in Delhi State have special difficulties in organizing. Though hundreds of thousands of them live in this territory, they are dispersed and are not numerically strong in any one locality; consequently they cannot hope to marshal decisive voting strength on their own. Moreover, the dominant landowners in many of their villages are Jats who, as we have seen, are quite effective in keeping control of the land.

These potters have little opportunity to obtain an economic base for jati mobility and they are, to boot, increasingly threatened by technological displacement. Blocked from economic opportunities, knowing little about the "twice-born" models and not much interested in them, their aspirations are focused on modern education. Very few of them have yet had much education, but it is the one glittering avenue of promise to better jobs, more prestige, and a higher standard of life for the individual and the group. Even with few educated people in their number, the strains between educated and uneducated leaders, which were noted among Telis and other groups, are already apparent.

Their incipient organization has been studied by Veena Monga (1967), who stayed in the potters' camp during one of the great annual festivals at Gadh Mukhteshwar on the banks of the Ganges. A great market fair takes place at the same time as the religious festival; the potters are especially active in the market for donkeys, mules, and horses, the animals they use to transport their wares. Potters stay in their own encampment during the days of this religious event. With several thousands in camp, they can call panchayat meetings to settle disputes and association assemblies to debate resolutions.

Their association has had a tenuous career since 1924; it lapsed and then was revived. In 1967 there was a Sabha tent in the potter encampment. About twenty men, who were addressed as "Pradhan," heads of their local associations, congregated there. Two of these men had some modern education—one was a librarian and the other a practitioner of indigenous medicine. Several other educated men were present and took part in the association discussions.

The educated are clearly the elite; their dress, speech, and manners are accorded highest prestige and respect. One of the richest potters in the camp lived quite like the poorer ones; none of his family had a single change of clothes nor were their meals any more sumptuous than those of poorer potters. The main difference was that the rich man was educating all his grandsons. So prized is education that in the potters' discussions Harijans are held up as "an ideal example" of how to secure educational benefits from the government.

The more traditional leaders, however, are not very easy about the educated among them. They feel them to be condescending and quite impractical. The educated, for their part, try to show some formal respect for the illiterate leaders, but hold themselves to be much better. Even an educated man must depend on his jati fellows; only with their children can he arrange marriages for his sons and daughters (Monga 1967, p. 1054). Endogamy remains a force, as G. S. Ghurye has noted in many writings, that binds the members of a jati, the educated as well as the illiterate, in all parts of the country (1961, pp. 209–210).

A division of function has begun to appear in the affairs of the potters' association. The older, uneducated leaders continue to settle disputes and maintain the jati's unity, matters at which the educated are not competent because of their lack of relevant experience and interest. The educated men are given the lead in initiating educational measures and reforms, and in relations with officials. At the time of Monga's observations these potters, as a group, had scarcely begun to participate in state politics. But as an association becomes more effective in internal cohesion and improvement, its leaders tend to look to improving its external relations, especially in politics. The political activities of the Yadava and Jatav associations have been noted above. Two other associations illustrate the development of such political functions.

Political Engagement: the Vanniyar Association

The Vanniyar and Nadar associations of Madras State share a similar political history. Both groups were engaged in mobility efforts in the first half of the nineteenth century; both achieved considerable economic gains and internal reforms in the first half of the twentieth century; both overcame strong opposition to their rise; both used their associations to gain political benefits; and both eventually withdrew their associations from party affiliation. These case histories illustrate a significant new social factor, the effect of the caste association in bringing its members into the processes of political democracy.

The Vanniyar number nearly 10 percent of the Madras State population, and in the four northern districts where they are concentrated they comprise about one fourth the population. Some are still landless laborers but many have become landowners, modern artisans, and tradesmen. The former jati divisions among them have been modified in recent times.

A record of 1833 shows that Vanniyars petitioned even then for an official decree that they were not "of low caste." They were among the first to use the Census for mobility claims, petitioning in 1871 to be listed as Kshatriyas. Their association was founded in 1888. By 1891 one of their educated men had produced the usual book to assert and document their merit, and by 1931 their former name no longer appeared in official records (Thurston 1909, Vol. 6, pp. 1–28; Rudolph and Rudolph 1960, pp. 13–15; 1967, pp. 49–63).

After national independence opened new opportunities for improvement, the Vanniyar association became politically active. Lloyd and Susanne Rudolph have traced the history and shown the results of their activities. The association pressed the Congress Party for jobs and preferment for Vanniyars. When that party did not respond to their satisfaction, they contested elections as independents. They were most interested in elections to the district boards, not only because they could muster decisive voting strength in certain districts but also—and this is generally true of the political efforts of caste associations—"because the subjects falling under the competence of district boards, especially educational and medical facilities and road building, were of the greatest local and political interest" (1960, pp. 16–17).

Vanniyars generally did well as independent candidates; in 1951 a Vanniyar political party was formed which soon split into two parties. Their candidates nevertheless could mobilize Vanniyar voters, using the traditional panchayat network. In the 1952 elections they won 13 percent of the seats in the Madras legislature. Vanniyars naturally voted for candidates of their name and grouping, who presumably understood their needs and shared their aspirations. In this traditional mode of alignment in a partisan context, they were repeating the initial, and often continuing, trend wherever democratic elections are established.

The two Vanniyar parties were later dissolved, their leaders joining other parties. But the Vanniyar association has flourished and has steadily pressed for political benefits. It has worked for educational gains, schools for the children, scholarships and academic support for the youth. It has sought civil service jobs and political appointments for Vanniyars. It has urged general development projects, hydroelectric schemes, roads, and land reform, which benefit all in the localities where Vanniyars live.

The Vanniyar secured some governmental advantage by having themselves officially classified as a "Backward Class" and so entitled to certain preferments. As was noted before, this formal classification as a disadvantaged, and presumably low-ranking, group is not seen as hampering the group's claims to higher status in the real ranking of village life. Vanniyars have markedly improved their ranking as well as their general political and economic position. A notable part of this rise has been accomplished through their caste association (Rudolph and Rudolph 1960, pp. 18–22). And even though Vanniyars have not voted solidly for any one political party, they have benefited from their general political participation. Thus in the elections of 1962 in the South Arcot district, all three major parties chose Vanniyar leaders (L. I. Rudolph 1965, p. 984).

Political Engagement: the Nadar Association

The Nadars have also waged a long, hard, and successful mobility campaign. Their traditional occupation was the same as that of the Iravas of Kerala, the making and sale of alcoholic liquor, the fermented product of sap ("toddy") tapped from a palm tree. The Iravas became unified under a religious leader and his doctrine; the Nadar achievement has been through secular, reformist, and political means. Some Nadars, as will be noted again in the discussion of religion-based jatis, did become converts to Christianity, but they number only about 150,000; the Hindu Nadars now number between one and a half to two million in Madras State.

In the early nineteenth century Nadars were ranked, in some localities, with those jatis whose women were not allowed to clothe themselves above the waist as women of the higher jatis did. First the Christian converts among them breached this rule and then some of the Hindu women among them followed suit. The higher jatis were outraged that these women should put on airs and blouses; they threatened violence and riots erupted. The Governor of Madras intervened in 1858 to grant permission to women "of the lower castes" to wear a cloth over the breasts and shoulders. The Maharaja of Travancore also felt moved to issue a proclamation on the matter, but he temporized a bit. He allowed their wearing an upper cloth in the manner of fisherwomen or "their covering their bosoms in any manner whatever, but not like women of high castes" (Thurston 1909, Vol. 6, p. 365).

In the latter part of the nineteenth century a good many became prosperous merchants. In 1874 these Nadars led an attempt to secure the right to enter the great temple at Madurai. They lost that round, but continued the struggle for temple entry, bringing a suit to the High Court in Madras and then to the Privy Council in London. They lost that case also; the judge was sympathetic and commended them for their "education, industry, and frugality," but he felt forced to rule that they should have separate but equal religious facilities (Raj 1959, pp. 87, 222, 261; L. I. Rudolph 1965, pp. 978–981; Rudolph and Rudolph 1967, pp. 36–49).

The Nadars' bitter opponents were Maravars, the jati just above them in most of their localities. The Nadars persisted in their claims to Kshatriya status, and the wealthier, merchant families called themselves Nadars rather than Shanars, the term for toddy-tappers. At first these wealthier families tried to separate themselves from their jati fellows who continued as toddy-tappers, but by 1910 many of them had shifted from a fission to a fusion strategy. They founded a caste association and their leaders urged the uplift and reform of all Nadars and intermarriage among the five Nadar jatis.

Their caste association soon became one of the largest and most active in Tamilnad. Its agents toured the villages to establish panchayats, schools, and cooperative banks. By 1921 the Census Commissioner announced that by order of the Government of Madras their former name would no longer be used in official records, all of them would be recorded under their preferred name, Nadar.

In the 1920s and 1930s their district organization began to take active interest in state politics. In one district where the Nadar merchants were predominant they backed the Justice Party as against the Congress, and when a young Congress worker, who was to become the most famed Nadar of all, Kamaraj Nadar, appeared at a meeting in the early 1930s, he "was stoned by the community as a traitor to his caste" (Hardgrave 1966, p. 616). However, Nadars in other localities supported the Congress Party, and by 1947 the great majority of them did so. The Nadar caste association aligned itself with the Congress Party.

Later, the association was taken out of party politics because there were strongly divergent party affiliations among its members. The organization continues to work for the uplift of all Nadars (Raj 1959, pp. 180–199), not all of whom are at the same level. In some localities the traditional occupation is still followed by most; in other places Nadars are mainly merchants. In the large cities many are in the professions and in government service as well as in trade.

Nadar political activities differ in each of these places, as Robert Hardgrave has observed (1966, pp. 618–621). Where Nadars are numerically predominant and are still impoverished tappers, politics are mainly factional, among different alliances of Nadars. Voting behavior there is an extension of traditional village politics within a preponderant jati. In another constituency the Nadars are mainly merchants and are a minority as against the dominance of their old opponents, the Maravars (cf. Baranov 1965). Voting alignments there are like village contests among jatis, with a smaller jati shifting its support about to gain greatest advantage.

In Madurai City, Nadar merchants are concentrated in two wards, and these generally return Nadar candidates to the city council. But in this city there are also Nadar factory workers and students, whose political affiliations hinge on their occupational interests, which are quite different from those of the Nadar merchants. This is all the more so in Madras City. "In Madurai and Madras, caste has by no means ceased to be an important factor in determining political behavior, but it is only one of a multiplicity of variables which affect the individual voter's decision" (Hard-grave 1966, p. 620).

Nadars are predominant among the merchants of Madurai, as Myron Weiner observed when he studied political behavior in that city in 1962. The Nadar merchants contribute a portion of their income to their caste association, which runs schools and a bank and issues a weekly newspaper in the city. Their civic concerns are lodged in their caste associations as much as in political activity; in politics they tend to take a utilitarian rather than ideological approach to the Congress Party. "Thus, although the Nadar merchants have displaced the Brahmins and Saurashtras at many levels of leadership within the party and within the municipality, they lack the party *esprit* which these other communities had" (Weiner 1967, p. 421). However, they are apparently not lacking in devotion to their own association.

The association was used as a direct political instrument when Nadars, as a group, either held power or were acting together against other groups. This use of the association is less feasible among urban and educated Nadars, who do not readily line up in a solid political front. Among them the association is used for a less direct but nonetheless effective purpose, that of bringing economic and educational advantages to its members. With those advantages, they can then acquire political influence according to their own party preferences.

The success of Nadar social mobility is summarized in Lloyd Rudolph's study of their political activities: "The community has breached the pollution barrier, changed its rank within traditional society and now occupies an important place in the modern society of Madras and India" (1965, p. 981). Rudolph gives particular attention to the contribution of caste associations in general to political development in India. His conclusions are reflected in the title of this article, "The modernity of tradition: the democratic incarnation of caste in India." [1]

Rudolph notes that caste associations have become vehicles for internal cultural reform and external social change; they have

---

[1] L. I. Rudolph's book of 1967, written with Susanne Hoeber Rudolph, includes much of the material in this article as well as treatment of other subjects. It bears the title, *The Modernity of Tradition, Political Development in India.*

united jatis and have taught illiterate peasants to participate in modern politics. They have enabled disadvantaged groups to find advantage in their numbers. The result has been to make representative democracy meaningful and effective in the new nation and in caste society (Rudolph 1965, pp. 981–982, 985). All this, Rudolph continues, belies the predictions of Marx and of others that caste society could not adapt to modern conditions and that a totally new social structure would have to be erected.

It may be too early to assess this adaptation; the impact of caste associations is still in the making and relatively little detailed information about them is now available (cf. Bailey 1963b, p. 128). Some have taken a politically adaptive step beyond that of caste association; they have formed federations.

Federation: the Kshatriya Sabha of Gujarat

The advantages of association have induced some to press beyond the ready base of a jati-cluster. The Yadavas, for example, have tried to bring together all in India who were traditionally of pastoral occupation and of broadly similar tradition and status. Within Madras State, the leaders of three sets of jatis have begun to combine their respective caste associations under one name (L. I. Rudolph 1965, p. 984; Gough 1963, p. 193).

This kind of outreach has led to the founding of federations in which there is no emphasis on the merging of the component jatis as there usually is in a caste association. The leaders of a federation stress the mutual benefits that can come out of the united efforts of many jatis.

One of the most active caste federations is the Kshatriya Sabha of Gujarat. It dates from 1946 and includes several jati-clusters of the region, notably Rajputs, Bariyas, and Bhils. The federation tries to upgrade the customary ways of all who affiliate with it and to augment their joint political strength. A study of this organization by Kothari and Maru concludes that "it represents a step beyond caste association in Indian development towards a political community" (1965, pp. 34–35).

This federation of "Kshatriya" jatis in Gujarat had certain organizational assets from the start. Rajputs tend to be more concerned with secular power than with ritual niceties and so they welcome as allies (when they stand in need of them) all jatis who follow the Rajput model and the Rajput lead. In much of Gujarat the Rajputs felt in need of allies since many Rajputs there were poor, some were landless, and most were losing ground to more efficient cultivators, especially the Patidars.

When independence opened new avenues of politics, two Rajput leaders took charge. One was a powerfully persuasive figure, the other a very efficient administrator. The two led the federation for many years. Reforms were urged in the form of an interesting combination of traditional uplift, Rajput militancy and Gandhian nonviolence. Great feasts were staged at which people of all the federated jatis interdined in symbolic reduction of social distances. These distances had traditionally been great, from Rajput nobles to tribal Bhils. The federation even took the initiative in bringing Muslim Rajputs back into the fold.

The President of this Sabha told Myron Weiner, "We have taken all the backward peoples who are martial by nature and called them Kshatriyas." As the Congress Party had taken up the Harijans, he continued, so had his association taken up all the low-ranking groups of Gujarat who display "intense nationalism," who show "spirit and action." The other founder put it more generally by stating that the Kshatriyas are a class not a caste (1967, p. 97–99). Not all blue-blooded Rajputs could agree to this but their opposition was not great. Many of them could swallow a common meal with Bariyas and Bhils, if they could thereby resume the cherished Rajput role of political leader. The Bariyas, for their part, still revering the traditionally esteemed models, felt honored by tokens of equality from Rajputs and foresaw achievement of something like Rajput status through the Kshatriya association. They supported it in great numbers. Another unifying force, particularly in central Gujarat, was Rajput antagonism against Patidars. Many Patidars, through diligence and intelligent management, had prospered as farmers and merchants and had gained considerable local power. In a good many localities they had, in effect, ousted Rajputs from their former dominance, or so it seemed to many Rajputs and their allies (Kothari and Maru 1965, pp. 36, 43; Weiner 1967, p. 93).

For a time, the federation also included Kshatriya jatis in the adjoining region of Saurashtra, but this soon lapsed because the

Rajputs of that region were still the dominant landowners. They were not then interested in the political measures advocated by the poorer Rajputs of Gujarat (Kothari and Maru 1965, pp. 38–39).

Within Gujarat, the federation gained important political influence. Its leaders backed the Congress Party at first but became dissatisfied with the response of Congress leaders to their requests. They expected the political party to give them direct compensation in jobs and political nominations in return for their support. The Congress Party leaders were perfectly willing to make the usual political calculations of ethnic and caste representation but would not consign a definite number of preferments to the keeping of a caste federation (Weiner 1967, pp. 106–109). In 1955, when the Congress Party resolved that its active members could not hold simultaneous membership in any caste or communal organization, the Kshatriya federation dissolved its political allegiance to the Congress Party and later aligned itself with the Swatantra Party. Since then the federation has swung its influence in various party directions. At one time it united with those Patidars who opposed the Congress Party. Then the Congress Party gave more attention to its problems with Kshatriyas and organized its own Kshatriya Sabha. In 1967 the principal founder of the federation was reelected to Parliament for the Congress Party (Weiner 1967, pp. 113–114).

Despite its organizational assets, the leaders of the federation have had difficulty in holding it together because primary loyalties remain with the jatis. A federation's problems of unity are even greater than those of an association (Harrison 1960, pp. 105–109; Rudolph and Rudolph 1960, p. 11).

Yet the Kshatriya Sabha illustrates the adaptability of contemporary men and of their traditional institutions. Many of the Rajputs of Gujarat still take pride in their ancient feudal tradition. Nevertheless they have accepted the modern version of social hierarchy and the revised rules for attaining social eminence. The traditional Rajput goal of being secular rulers may still be cherished, but the Rajputs are willing to fall in with the modern means for reaching that goal.

Wider Ties and Deeper Change

In sum, many villagers now press for higher status through caste associations and federations. Proposals for cooperation among closely similar jatis are usually accepted readily; effective joint action in at least a few matters has often followed. Merging through intermarriage meets more resistance and in any event cannot be consummated overnight. The power base of an association can relatively quickly be built up through mobilizing voting strength. As villagers become aware of the potential rewards of electoral victory, they rally increasingly to groups that lend themselves to political action. Well suited for the purpose is the jati-cluster—formerly a category of attribution, now turned into a group for joint action. The head of the Congress Party organization in Gujarat put the trend succinctly to Myron Weiner: "As soon as people become a little more conscious politically they become more caste-conscious" (Weiner 1967, p. 106).

Occasionally political gains and status advantages are still accomplished through fission. The Jatavs of Agra have split away from their former jati ties, but they are quite unusual in that they had a large concentration within one city. They too are now reaching out for wider alliances.

The Nadar case is more characteristic of contemporary trends. Nadars were waging mobility battles long before they organized an association to aid in their campaign. Some Nadars tried jati fission first, but changed to fusion and association when they realized that under modern conditions their purposes would be better served by uniting than by separating. A smaller group had less chance than a larger group had of building schools, of getting governmental preferments, and, latterly, of electing powerful officials. Moreover the traditional ritual symbols of high rank, which could be won by a smaller, tightly disciplined group, were losing some of their appeal. Once the Nadar association was made into an effective instrument, its leaders engaged the organization in state politics and then, in a subsequent stage, decided that the members' interests were better served by withdrawing the association from politics.

In all stages of association activities, among Nadars and among others, the grand strategy remains the same. The goal is to lift one's group in the social hierarchy. In the course of achieving this the more immediate strategy is switched from fission to fusion. This switch does not require great departures from traditional mobility patterns, as was noted in the case of Yadava adaptation. It entails familiar ways of attracting allies, parallel conditions for successful mobility, and, importantly, the same moral rectitude of striving for one's kin and jati. It does, however, sacrifice homogeneity in ritual symbols and practices in favor of material benefits and modern prestige symbols.

A caste association typically helps advance the traditional conditions for successful mobility. Secular resources can be strengthened by lobbying and through united economic efforts. Customary ways can be reformed, especially through modern education, which also yields economic benefits for the educated. The association leaders press for official recognition of the group's merit. The change of name used to be a main target; more substantive indications of worth are now sought, especially in the form of high positions and prestigious jobs for the group's members.

Government resources can help greatly in achieving social rise in the eyes of one's neighbors—who remain the critical judges of one's real rank. So a rising jati has a heavy stake in political power. Hardgrave writes that "As caste solidarity has increased, caste has been politicized and drawn into the political system as a major actor" (1966, p. 614; also Harrison 1960, pp. 132–136).

Jatis have long been politicized in their localities; what has significantly changed is the widening of political engagement from village and locality to district, state, and nation. Traditional jati panchayats usually tried to keep government out of jati affairs. This is still so in some measure, but caste associations now court government aid. Status advantage remains a motivating force and so competition among caste associations appears, not infrequently in political rivalries.

Competition among political parties is built into the present political order, but parties do not often command the kind of moral allegiance that a jati and even its association can elicit. A man who works for his caste association can be understood by villagers as helping his family and kin, as trying to establish the proper dharma of his whole group. There are, to be sure, dedicated workers for political parties and there are villagers who are imbued with a party ideology of moral justice. But most villagers understand the ideology of jati and varna better than they grasp the ideologies of political parties.

The trend toward fusion follows much of the traditional pattern for jati mobility, but the new elements in the process may eventually alter the process itself. The arena of competition is larger, and government is a principal force in it. Methods of organization are shifting from the relatively loose, implicit organization of the jati to the explicit, formalized, bureaucratic organization of the association. The alternate models for mobility are beginning to be merged into one generalized model of educated, politically influential, and wealthy people. The social hierarchy tends to become much less differentiated in both social distances and cultural differences.

Modern education has become a prime source of both prestigious symbols and substantive power, so most aspiring groups put heavy stress on the education of their children. They need not simultaneously relinquish traditional symbols of high status, but their educated children are more inclined to bypass or modify these symbols. A good many caste associations maintain their own schools, college hostels, and scholarships. The associations allow people of disparate interests and background within a jati-cluster to work together. The educated (who provide the new leadership) and the uneducated cooperate in them, as do urban and rural members, and those of traditionally higher and lower status within the cluster.

The individual villager still tends to see his personal rise and the status of his family as being linked in considerable measure—though not so completely as formerly—to the rise of his jati. Social rank is still a central concern for many in the village. But as the moves for social mobility are modernized, the nature of the hierarchy is being altered. A headline in the *Statesman*, quoted by Lloyd Rudolph, referred to this trend, "Caste hierarchy declines, as casteism rises" (1965, p. 989).

The impetus to form a caste association comes out of the same motives that impel people to strive for their jati's rise. The leaders of an association commonly urge cultural adaptations, hold up models for mobility, combat external opposition, work for internal cohesion in ways similar to those discussed in the previous chapters on jati mobility. But the newer ways also differ from the more traditional maneuvers in being adapted to modern political and social conditions. In altering the traditional mobility moves, jati leaders may also be modifying the fundamental components and processes of the traditional social system.

Srinivas concludes that the trends toward political mobilization by jatis "all suggest that changes of a fundamental kind are occurring" (1966, p. 117). In assessing these changes, in asking whether they are likely to be recurrent or systemic, it is useful to consider them in the perspective of other kinds of major change that have gone on in Indian society for centuries. These are changes through regrouping on religious grounds and changes undergone by tribesmen when they shifted into jati society.

PART **VII** *Recurrent Change*
Through Religious and
Tribal Movements

CHAPTER 28

Social Regrouping through
Indigenous Religions

RELIGION has been, and continues to be, a matter
of absorbing interest for many in India. "Theological discussions,"
Srinivas observes, "are freely entered into by people who meet for
the first time in trains, in buses, in hotel lobbies" (1966, p. 143).
The participants in these discussions do not restrict themselves to
any narrow definition of theology; religious talk readily edges over
into politics or medicine or anything else.

In former centuries no aspect of life was set apart from religion.
Not every person was necessarily pious or god-fearing, but religion
was taken as all-pervasive. All social relations were inevitably and
legitimately suffused with religious ideas and acts. Hence social
movements were couched in religious terms, and personal restive-
ness and social disaffection could best be expressed as religious strivings. As new social ideas were developed, they were offered under
the aegis of religion.

Movements to reorganize society in India were therefore expressed mainly through indigenous sects and through introduced
religions. Equality rather than hierarchy among all believers was a
common theme, and in almost all these movements the devotees
finally came to sort themselves into jatis and to act like other jati
members in their local order.

Recurrent change through religion has typically been sparked by
personal quests for salvation rather than by sheer mobility aspirations, but the social outcome of these personal quests has consist-
ently turned out to be quite like the outcome of the mobility drives
discussed above. Once a new dispensation becomes established as a
sectarian jati, its followers may come to dominate their localities.
Then their ways, including their religion, may be emulated by sub-

ordinate groups just as any dominant jati may be taken as a reference group. This kind of emulation or conversion should be distinguished from the process considered in this chapter through which persons become devotees, devotees form a cult, the cult becomes a sect, and the sect turns into a jati.

Straightforward emulation, as when clients are attracted to the religion of their patrons, servants to that of their masters, or subjects to that of their rulers, does not occur automatically. Many clients, servants, and subjects have steadfastly kept to their own religion through long periods despite (or because of) strong efforts by their superiors to convert them. We cannot here attempt an analysis of the conditions under which a subordinate will or will not be attracted to the religion of the superior, we need only note that such attraction has been effective in some cases and has been resisted in others. To cite one example of effective attraction, the report of the 1931 Census in the Punjab noted that a good many Hindus of lower jatis were becoming Sikhs because they "obviously considered that they gained in status as soon as they ceased to be Hindus and became Sikhs." An account of a Sikh village testifies that such conversions were going on there in the 1950s and for the same reason (Khan 1931, pp. 293–294; I. P. Singh 1961, p. 191; Srinivas 1966, p. 101).

Many were converted to the religion of temporal rulers, as to Islam when Muslims held power and to Christianity during the British regime. Though religious leaders have deplored this motive for conversion, it has long been a potent one. The direct status gain that converts derived was usually not great. Untouchables who became converted to Christianity, to Islam, or to Sikhism were not immediately taken as social equals by their coreligionists, and certainly were not treated more respectfully by neighbors of different faiths (cf. Béteille 1965, pp. 92, 98; I. P. Singh 1958, p. 485).

The original inspiration for much religious change has commonly come from a charismatic teacher who drew disciples to his revelation of the true path to eternal salvation. He characteristically taught some reform of social practice as the earthly counterpart of his fresh vision of eternity. As his words and example fired his followers and their numbers grew, they built a religious movement separate from their former society. Sooner or later that movement was reabsorbed into the system of caste society.

It seems almost to be a property of this social system that such movements well up periodically, develop through the cycle, and then devolve back into the system. This trend has often been remarked by scholars, though detailed comparative studies remain to be done (cf. Karve 1961, p. 109; Srinivas 1966, pp. 75–76; Weber 1958, pp. 19–20). Jawarhalal Nehru wrote ruefully about this process, perhaps with some concern lest his own valiant efforts for social reform be caught up in the same massive drift. He said that it was curious and significant that throughout Indian history great men have given repeated warnings against priestcraft and the rigidity of the caste system. Powerful movements have risen against them, "yet slowly, imperceptibly almost, it seems, as if it were the inevitable course of destiny," caste organization has grown and spread. "Rebels against caste have drawn many followers, and yet in the course of time their group has itself become a caste" (1946, p. 112).

"Inevitable destiny" is not an answer that really satisfied Nehru or suffices for other students of Indian society. We have to clarify, as best we may with the available evidence, how it was that those who held other ideas of a good society were repeatedly absorbed into caste organization and into the caste processes of recurrent change.

Individual Choice and Religious Change

Religious cults still rise in every part of India. A villager today joins a religious movement for reasons probably much like those that influenced earlier generations of devotees. To begin with, a villager finds in religion his (or her) principal opportunity for personal choice. Much in his life career is quite tightly prescribed, but he does have some option about which deity to single out for special devotion, how to express that devotion, and which personal mentor to select. Narrow though this choice may seem to an outside observer, religion does afford the villager a wider range of choice than is easily available elsewhere. Religion is generally seen as a benign field of conduct. So long as a person shows the recognized signs of behaving religiously, others give at least conditional approval to what he does. One member of a family may take a deity or a ritual not shared by others of his family. Some families worship in a different manner from their jati fellows without demur from the others, provided that their worship does not violate jati standards (cf. Karve 1961, p. 121).

Religion also provides alternate roles for those ill-suited to the roles they have inherited. One such person, a Rajput overlord in Gujarat village, has been described by Gittel Steed (1955). As a young man he inherited a position of responsibility and leadership, yet he was not comfortable with the role of martial Rajput. Unusual circumstances had given him an unusual upbringing; he was reared in his mother's natal family, surrounded by strong women. In any event, he is mild-mannered and retiring. After bouts of hysterical symptoms and of opium use, he has turned to intensive religious devotion. This is quite understood by his kinsmen and neighbors, and although he does not conform to usual Rajput conduct, he is not considered particularly deviant. "His recent preoccupation with religious practices was also well within a pattern of alternative choices that was common to the larger Hindu society" (Steed 1955, p. 143). As was noted in Chapter 22, a deviant personality as well as a gifted one can become a sanyassin, a holy person dedicated to a deity.

Religious cults were, and are, among the principal voluntary associations available to individual villagers. Hence they have been used as ways of expressing discontent with the established order, or of seeking political and economic change.

Religion answers many personal needs. A youth can gather with his agemates to sing sacred hymns; women can publicly express their inner feelings through special religious rites. A main religious search is that of finding a particular holy person in whom one can discover the real truth. To this person a man or woman can give unalloyed allegiance and from him he can receive inner strength.

The sheltering canopy of religion is best held over a man by his own mentor, his guru. Voluntary personal dependency is not invidious; dependence on a true guru is a great good. In his guru a man seeks, and often finds, a figure whose spiritual superiority is unquestioned, who is nurturant and noncompetitive, who can lift his disciple out of the abrasive tussles of everyday social relations. Very many village men seek out such a mentor. Dumont estimates that "A majority of Indian heads of families, of all castes, even Muslims, have chosen a *guru* who has initiated them while whispering a mantra in their ears, and who, in principle, visits them once a year"

(1960, p. 60; cf. Ferguson 1963). A man may shift from one guru to another and his relationship with any one may be brief and tangential, yet he characteristically does not give up the search. Many a man finds a guru with whom he can forge a close bond and whose words are taken as guides to life. The guru himself is commonly the disciple of yet another holy man, often one who has departed the present life and who was one link in a generational chain of disciples preaching the word of some great soul of the past. The guru inducts his pupil into the way shown by the founder.

A modern example is the cult of Saibaba, a Muslim saint whose tomb and main shrine are in Maharashtra. Saibaba's teachings have many Hindu adherents in South India, including Western-educated people, and Srinivas reports that there are Saibaba prayer groups in several South Indian cities (1966, pp. 132, 143).[1] If these groups establish some regular communication, agree on a new ceremonial agenda, codify the teachings, and support professional religionists, they will then have developed into something more than a zealous set of cult adherents. The fact that Hindus are prominent among the devotees of a Muslim saint reflects the belief that a holy man's earthly background and affiliations are of far less importance than his spiritual achievements.

A sanyassin is expected to cut off his secular attachments, to abandon all considerations of kinship, jati, and village. Hence when a sanyassin acts as guru he is likely to pass lightly over such matters or to brush them aside entirely as inconsequential and positively harmful to the spirit. The circle of his devotees characteristically tries to ignore social distinctions in the context of worship. Joining with dedicated worshippers answers the personal needs of a man (or a woman) in ways acceptable to his kin and neighbors. It gives welcome scope for personal choice. It offers new or expanded roles, perhaps especially attractive because they are different from those thrust on him by others. Submission to a new religious discipline can enhance his sense of power and relieve his feelings of helplessness. Moreover, many in India find great personal reward in being the disciple of a guru and in gathering with fellow disciples.

[1] In 1968 I visited an old friend in a Badaga village in the Nilgiris. I noticed a new picture in the display of religious pictures in his home. My friend told me that it was a picture of Saibaba, whom he had seen, so he said, when the holy man had visited the Nilgiris a few years before.

Such groups are legion, most have brief existence and little social consequence. But some endure, coalesce with others, and regularize their religious activities; their participants become known as members of a cult. Occasionally a cult gathers strong momentum, perhaps because of favoring social or economic conditions (cf. Bendix 1960, pp. 202–205).

The devotees, inspired by success and fired with zeal, make the cult a pervasive force in their lives. They use it as their primary social identification and try to widen the influence of their guru. This requires organized effort; as their organization becomes established and their new identity becomes known and accepted, the band of devotees develops into a sect. Members of the sect tend to form an endogamous unit, which functions socially as another jati. In this way devotees from diverse social backgrounds come to redefine their jati identity so that it is one with their religious allegiance.[2]

A Modern Religious Movement in Madras City

Three historic religious movements are discussed later in this chapter, but first a contemporary example of religious movement in the making is examined. It entails both traditional and modern elements and may not develop into anything much more than it was in the 1960s. It is not yet an established sect, still less has it produced new jatis. But it may become an important influence in revising former groupings among the educated, wealthier people of Madras. The account of it by Milton Singer (1963) shows how traditional forces of religion are being channeled in modern Madras City.

This movement arises from an old form of worship called *bhajan*. The word means "prayer" or "devotional song" and also carries the meaning of a gathering of devotees to sing and worship. The traditional emphasis is on spontaneous meetings in which worshippers can communicate with the beloved deity, and with each other, in a free outpouring of songs, words, and acts. In Madras City five types of bhajans are held, ranging from informal weekly meetings in a private home to annual ten-day festivals with crowded agenda

[2] English observers reported the rise of a number of new sect-based jatis in the eighteenth century (Raghuvanshi 1966, pp. 169–170); most of these jatis are now forgotten.

culminating in a marriage ceremony of the gods Krishna and Radha. Although such festivals resemble traditional performances, they are now elaborated in ways different from the older, traditional ceremonies.

Three gurus are credited with giving the ritual and philosophy of this Radha-Krishna bhajan its canonical form. All lived near Kumbakonam in Tanjore district in the seventeenth century. Their teachings were introduced into Madras City about 1900 through disciples from the Kumbakonam locality—one a former schoolteacher, another a government accountant, a third an official. They initiated others as followers of the Kumbakonam Gurus in the traditional manner by imparting a secret verse and a set of religious instuctions. One of the present leaders of the bhajan cult is a retired film actor who was so initiated.

Though the relation between guru and disciple is an intensely personal one, Singer notes that among the devotees whom he studied it can have important social consequences. "This evidence suggests that, far from being an independent mode of transmission which transcends the social structure and the culture, the guru-disciple relationship operates as the very lifeline of the culture and social structure" (Singer 1963, p. 207). It is a voluntary relationship, but it does not exist in a social vacuum. A disciple puts himself under a guru's guidance because he already shares many of the values that the guru teaches. There is room for innovation as well, and a guru can bring about certain adaptations in religious practice.

Some gurus and devotees in Madras City have promoted bhajans so successfully that from small, informal hymn sessions there have developed complex organizations. One of them stages a variety of religious performances, "elects officers, solicits donations, prints announcements and invitations, and issues an annual report with an audited account of its revenues and expenditures" (Singer 1963, p. 195). In 1958 the officers of this group called a conference of all leading bhajan devotees of the city. A federation of some forty-five bhajan groups was set up; it now holds conferences annually, conducts special festivals, and plans to include affiliates from the whole of the state of Madras. Other Radha-Krishna devotees will have nothing to do with this elaborate organization, holding that gatherings of devotees should be informal and unscheduled in order to maintain the spontaneous feelings of love and equality that should prevail in such sessions. But the majority of the bhajan devotees in the city find advantage in organization.

They are mainly professional men—government officials, business executives, doctors, university professors, accountants, and musicians—and are predominantly Brahmins. In one list of financial contributors only some 20 percent were non-Brahmins and about 55 percent were Smarta Brahmins, from the jatis following the intellectual philosophy propounded in the eighth century by the sage Shankara. Singer comments that it may seem strange that so many adherents of the emotional, personal, bhajan worship should come from an intellectual and scholastic tradition. But, as he points out, Smarta Brahmins have long been the most civic-minded among Tamil Brahmins, more concerned with the general polity of religion than with narrower sectarian interests. Their founder, Shankara, led the Hindu restoration against Buddhists and sought "to build an all-India Hinduism that could rise above the doctrines and practices of any particular group or region" (Singer 1963, p. 210). Shankara's modern followers in Madras City may also be building a bulwark against challengers, especially their contemporary political assailants who take an anti-Brahmin line.

The *bhajan* groups bring together Brahmins and non-Brahmins. They dramatize aspects of the Brahmin tradition; they provide social nuclei for the new elite. They follow the ancient devotional pattern in ways that are adapted to the realities of modern city life. Professional colleagues, work groups, neighborhood associations have a new importance in the city. The basic bhajan group is a neighborhood group. The participants come together weekly in a private home; they also invite colleagues from their work or relatives who may live in another neighborhood. The host derives some prestige from the meeting; guests take this way of making friends in the big city. The participants find benefit in regular religious sessions even though these sessions are quite different from the intricate, time-consuming daily rituals practiced by their forebears. A monthly bhajan brings people of various neighborhoods together; the annual festival attracts crowds from all parts of the city.

The ritual stresses the equality of the devotees. There are mutual embraces and prostrations of each to all; people of different jatis mingle in an informal, friendly way. Singer points out that the equality shown in this religious context is not meant to be extended literally to other contexts. The devotees interpret the prostrations as expressions of humility and tokens of an ideal, not as indicative of habitual daily conduct.

The contemporary bhajans, like the caste associations, are adaptations of traditional patterns to modern circumstances. As village Brahmins in Tamilnad did not have strong jati organization, so their educated descendants in the city do not develop strong caste associations. Yet even though the bhajan movement is intended for the benefit of the individual soul and many adherents bear witness to the spiritual grace they derive from it, participation in it also has social consequences. Educated people of diverse jatis and geographic origins are brought together and establish friendly relations.

Although there is talk of a "casteless, sectless, ecumenical form of Hinduism," Singer observes that "already tendencies have appeared toward new forms of ritualization, intellectualization, and sectarianism which render such an outcome unlikely" (1963, p. 226). It may be that this bhajan cult or something like it will lead to structural revisions of caste and sect among its adherents. Systemic changes are in train in India, as they are throughout the world, and the ecumenical vision held by Indian sages may yet come to pass. However, the historical record attests that in the past such visions, in India as elsewhere, have become translated socially into a more parochial *oikumene* than the visionaries sought. If it does nothing more socially, the cult is likely to revise the divisions among Tamil Brahmins in terms of modern realities rather than of ancient doctrines.

From Casteless Cult to Sectarian Jati

The growth of this bhajan cult illustrates only part of the historical cycle of religious regrouping. The cycle begins with people who are restive in their faith and restless in their social order. They take the open option of religion to change their personal circumstances. It is an option available even to untouchables, who have produced many sectarian movements and some renowned saints. It is true that those who were most severely pinioned by poverty did not have enough leeway to take even the religious option. But some untouchables did, and many more of higher jati have changed their social identity through accepting a new religious dispensation.

A person makes this choice by placing himself under the guidance of a guru and within the tradition of a line of gurus. In a devotional tradition each soul is taken, in the ideal if not in practice, as an equal manifestation of divine grace and each person as an equal sharer in its beneficence. The fervor of surrender to guru induces a fever to gather with companions in devotion and to convert the as-yet unenlightened. These inclinations lead to concerted acts for social purposes.

In due time the cohort of devotees requires hierarchical leadership; the role of personal guru is developed into the office of guru for the sect (cf. Bendix 1960, pp. 202–205). This institutionalized guru may attract personal disciples but he is more likely to be a kind of religious headman who periodically makes a stately tour about the circuit of his faithful. He regulates their conduct, adjudicates their disputes, refreshes their sectarian allegiance. The faithful in their localities marry within their group, hold panchayats for the group, keep social distance between themselves and lower jatis, observe certain standards of pollution and purity, and in general fit into the local caste order. They have then come full circle, from being a member of one jati to being a member of another jati, this one based on sect.

Sectarian jatis are typically open to certain kinds of converts. In Ramkheri village, for example, there are three sect-based jatis. One centers on Shiva and is ranked with the Rajput bloc; another focuses on Vishnu and is allied with the vegetarian jatis in the village. Both accept converts, but only those of equal or higher jati rank. The third sectarian jati is classed with the Harijans; its members revere the teachings of Kabir, a saint of the fifteenth century (Mayer 1960, p. 28; 1956, pp. 118–119).

The local ranking of a sectarian jati, like that of any jati, depends on both ritual and secular factors. Lingayats in western Mysore are rated quite high because of their general ritual purity and secular strength, despite their deliberate transgression of certain standards, as in their refusal to have their women observe menstrual seclusion. In Bengal, the jati of Vishnu devotees is also treated as one of the higher, even though its members accept recruits from most other jatis, even from those of very low rank.

Only a few sectarian jatis have been studied closely and those mainly in their theological rather than in their social aspects (e.g.

Allison 1935; Deming 1928; Kennedy 1925; Orr 1947). We do not yet have detailed analyses of the forces that have brought about this kind of recurrent change, but we do know the social outcome of the major religious regroupings in Indian history. The process is illustrated in the histories of three existing indigenous religions of India—Jainism which dates from the 6th century B.C., Lingayatism which began in the twelfth century A.D., and Sikhism, dating from the fifteenth century.

Indigenous Religions

Each of these three indigenous religions began with a founder who preached a new way of faith which his devotees took as a new way of life. In fulfilling the new precepts they separated themselves from established groups. All three founders emphasized the way of devotion over scriptural knowledge and ritual diligence, two other traditional avenues to salvation. Renou comments that in Hinduism "there is no sect without some element of *bhakti*" (1953, p. 93). But a founding guru could scarcely stress anything but devotion. If he is to open a new way, there is as yet no new scriptural learning or uniquely relevant rites developed for it. These follow later, but in the founding period it is devotion that must necessarily spark the movement. Devotion, moreover, can be given by any person, whatever his social degree. Each of the three founders accepted all devotees as equal; each proclaimed an ingathering of all regardless of status; each wanted no invidious social distinctions to be recognized among any of his faithful.

All three movements rose out of Hinduism and bore a social message that modified the Hinduism of the time. Each founding sage preached that caste distinctions did not exist in the sight of God and should not exist among his followers. His devotees deviated from the ways of their neighbors, opposed them and were opposed by them; but they had to operate within the same general society and had to use similar standards in doing so. So much did each of the three movements become social establishments that in time anti-establishment groups splintered from them, led by zealous reformers seeking to revive the pure principles of the founding guru.

The founder's social doctrine has not been abandoned in any of these three sects; it is embedded in the sacred writings and repeated in ritual prayer. But it is held as an ideal that must be tempered by the realities of society. This is not to say that this social ideology makes no social difference. Sectarian jatis do differ in being open, usually, to some recruitment by conversion. Their members interdine and generally interact more freely with others of the same faith. They feel themselves part of the same band of believers when they confront nonbelievers; their solidarity is based on their scriptures and sometimes is riveted by a tight organization. Nevertheless, the members of these sects also uphold the characteristic principles of caste organization. They maintain separate endogamous groups within the sect. They observe standards of pollution and purity that are in the main (though not in all specifics) like the standards observed by others of their region. They keep untouchables at a social distance, even those untouchables who have become committed devotees of the same sect. The system has triumphed over the revelation in that the devotees do indeed act as jati fellows in a caste order, but each sect also upholds its distinctive ideals in particular ways that distinguish its adherents from all other religions.

Jains

Jainism was one of the first of the indigenous religious movements. The great sage of the Jain religion, Mahavira, lived from about 540 B.C. to 468 B.C. and so was a contemporary of the founder of Buddhism (ca. 563 B.C.–483 B.C.). The two teachers had broadly similar life histories and their respective teachings have had great consequence to the present day. Buddhism is a vast force in Asia, but it was almost extinct in India until taken up in recent years by the backward-classes movement. Jain devotees have practiced their faith for more than twenty-five centuries and have created a large scriptural literature. (Modern scholars have particular appreciation for Jain monks who held that it was a deed of religious merit to copy and preserve any manuscript.) However, Jainism did not spread beyond the Indian subcontinent and eventually came to be centered mainly in the regions of Gujarat and of Mysore.

Mahavira's teachings concerned the relation of one's soul to the timeless cosmos. Only indirectly did he discuss the social order, less rigidly demarcated in his time than it later came to be. He and other Jain sages stressed that personal acts, not ascribed status, determined all that was important for the soul. "The doors of Jainism," Sangave writes, "were thrown open to all and equal opportunity was given to everybody to practice religion according to his capacity." This modern Jain scholar further comments that the ancient teachers of Jainism envisaged "a society wherein classes were not watertight compartments and complete freedom was granted to people to change to the class of their own aptitude" (Sangave 1959, pp. 67–70).

That social vision has yet to be realized among modern Jains. More than any other sect they have divided themselves into numerous jatis, some so small that they are en route to extinction. A 1914 directory of one branch of Jains listed 87 castes of which 41 had a population of less than 500. Sangave mentions "nearly sixty" endogamous groups, each with a population of less than one hundred (1959, p. 73).

Many Jains are tradesmen. A common explanation of this is that an orthodox Jain cannot be a farmer because Jainism places strict prohibitions on violence and on the taking of life, and ploughing crushes the life of worms. Although trade is a common calling for Jains, there are Jain jatis of diverse rank and occupation. Some are cultivators. Jains in South India rank themselves in four divisions, headed by those who are temple priests. The priestly jati acts in the manner of a Brahmin jati among Hindus, with the main exception that even these highest among Jains will interdine with all other Jains of their region.

Jains reflect the characteristics of their region of residence. In Gujarat they maintain hypergamous sections, as do other Gujarat jatis of similar social level. In South India, they have high priests who are like the chief gurus among other South Indian sects. Each high priest presides over a territory and is elected by representatives from the villages. One such high priest "has supreme authority over all Jainas south of Madras, but not over those of Mysore or South Kanara with whom the former have no relations." He periodically tours his territory, "settles caste disputes and fines and excommunicates the erring" (Sangave 1959, p. 111).

Perhaps because so many Jains were competitive, independent merchants, they have been inclined to split into very small exclusive groups. Thus one dogmatic difference separating two groups was whether their ascetics should use peacock feathers or cow hair to brush off insects. Territorial bounds also can be quite narrow; Jains in Ahmedabad City did not marry their daughters outside the city (Sangave 1959, pp. 62, 157).

Many reform movements have arisen in the long history of Jainism. Renou describes the annual assembly of one such group that was founded in 1760. Their ninth pontiff presided, "like a Mahavira redivivus," exemplifying the founder's severely ascetic rule. "It is not unusual to see one of them (as I have) freely choose to die in the way characteristic of the Jainas, ending a life of austerities by abstaining from food altogether" (Renou 1953, p. 124). Such sects within a sect tend to repeat the social cycle of the larger movement. Another such splinter group within Jainism numbers about 10,000. Sangave says of it, "Even though at present there are six castes among the Taranapanthis, they were really against the caste distinctions" (1959, p. 55).

The modern trend toward fusion is beginning to reverse the Jain predilection for fission. Some Jains have long intermarried with counterpart Hindu jatis. The counterpart jati bears the same name, follows the same occupations, and has the same characteristics save for the worship of Hindu deities. A woman generally takes on the religion of her husband in such marriages. When regional and national associations of Jains were formed, their leaders urged that intermarriage be arranged among Jain jatis rather than with Hindus (Sangave 1959, pp. 77, 86, 156). Jains, too, are beginning to consolidate into larger units and so the modern adherents of this ancient reform sect may be entering a new cycle of reform.

From a distance of nearly two and a half millennia, we cannot say much about the social origins of early Jainism. However, from the somewhat more ample data of recent years, we see that Jains have operated as a set of jatis, separate in identity but similar in form and function to other jatis of their level and locality. Their special characteristics include their propensity for asceticism, their inclination toward trade, their proclivity to extreme fission. These traits are now being modified, especially in the trend toward fusion.

Lingayats

Lingayats began as forthright reformers. They call their religion *Virashaivism* (that is, strong, stalwart devotion to Shiva). The term

Lingayat comes from their rule that members must always wear Shiva's emblem, the lingam. A principal statement of their belief is the *baswa purana*, the teachings of the sage Baswa (or Basava), who may have been the main founder of the sect and certainly has been a central figure in it. These teachings tell that when Baswa was to be invested with the sacred thread when he was eight years old, he refused and said, "I am a worshipper of Shiva and do not belong to the generation of Brahma. I am the axe laid to the tree of caste" (McCormack 1956, p. 2). Lingayat reform was aimed at Jainism as well as at Hinduism. Since Jains were powerful at the time of the great rise of Lingayatism, Jain temples and Jain merchants became special targets of attack for zealous Lingayat converts (Renou 1953, p. 121).

Lingayats carried their egalitarian beliefs so far that they treated women as religious equals. They abolished some fundamental pollution observances of Hinduism, especially those of birth, death, and menstruation. Hindus who want to keep free of such pollution must keep their distance from Lingayats because they cannot be sure how virulently polluted a Lingayat might be at any time. In other ways, however, Lingayats uphold purity practices more stringently than do many Hindus. They are strict vegetarians, do not use alcoholic liquor, and are meticulous about personal ritual cleansing.

In the Lingayat heartland of northern Mysore, their jatis are of about the same variety as among the Hindus of the region. Despite the explicit rejection of caste-ordering in Lingayat scripture, Lingayats group themselves into ranked jatis. The highest are the Jangamas, hereditary priests and teachers. Those among the Jangamas who dedicate themselves entirely to the religious life as celibates and ascetics are the principal religious mentors. This is a feature of a number of sects. Some of the devotees choose to become living exemplars of the true faith and in doing so become active preservers of the sect as a social entity. Lingayat ascetics are particularly influential because reverence to one's guru is a central article of the faith. As one modern Lingayat scholar puts it, reverence to the guru has no limit. He is superior to father and mother since he is the cause of spiritual birth, which is far more important than physical birth. "He is considered to be worthy of more reverence than is due to Siva, the Supreme, because it is he who leads the soul to unity with

Siva" (Nandimath 1942, p. 54). These priests-preceptors minister
to all Lingayat jatis; they interdine with all save with those untouchables who profess to be Lingayats but are kept apart, because
of their jati pollution, by others of the sect (Farquhar 1920, pp.
262–263; Thurston 1909, 4:251–252).

Lingayat jatis receive converts, but these must adhere to the
puritan rule of the sect, including abstinence from meat and liquor.
Hence there were few converts from the lower jatis when the Abbé
Dubois observed the sect in the early nineteenth century (1928, pp.
118–119). There are also initiation ceremonies by which a Lingayat
can rise from a lower to higher status within the rank order of the
sect (Thurston 1909, 4:251).

Their organization links each Lingayat to a guru in his village
and to a greater figure in a religious supercenter. Each family is
hereditarily associated with a particular lineage of priests, Jangamas,
from whom it takes its gurus. Each Jangama lineage, in turn, is associated with one of the five main Lingayat *maths*, monastic establishments, which are located in the five great centers of Shiva pilgrimage in India. When a Jangama boy is initiated, a representative
of that center must be present. Each center has a *jagadguru swami*,
a "world-master" who tours about visiting the Lingayats associated
with his math. A visit from the great guru strengthens Lingayat
solidarity in several ways. The deep reverence he commands enables him to settle disputes promptly and effectively; his visit provides status validation within the Lingayat groups; and the great
pomp and ceremony mustered for the visit demonstrate to all, not
least to the Lingayats themselves, the power of their sect (McCormack 1963, pp. 62–64).

Although they have flouted certain precepts, Lingayats have been
the carriers of the basic Sanskritic principles to others, as to the
Coorgs. In their evangelical vigor, they spread out and sought to
affect others. Their emphasis on vegetarianism, on reverence for
guru and scripture, and their general puritanism demonstrated to
tribal and lower groups some of the main elements of the twice-
born" as reference category, even as the Lingayat missionaries de-
cried the "twice-born" jatis as reference groups (Srinivas 1952, p.
225).

Despite their ritual separatism, Lingayats are as concerned with
their rank in a local order as are those of other jatis. Lingayats have

also tried to use the Census operations as a means of raising their social status. In 1891 and 1901 they presented petitions to census officials and to the Maharaja of Mysore asking to be recognized officially under a high-sounding title and as a high group. By 1904 a Lingayat association was formed and grew rapidly. After independence, Lingayats came to be one of the two main political forces in the state of Mysore and they now maintain vigorous political as well as religious organizations. After eight centuries of development in one cycle of recurrent change, the members of this sect, too, are embarking on the new fusion-political process.

Lingayat history illustrates the cycle of sectarian development. Lingayats began as fierce opponents of the establishment. The principal members of that establishment were the inheritors of an earlier reform movement. The Lingayats vehemently opposed some parts of the Sanskritic tradition yet were instrumental in disseminating other essential elements of the tradition. They were, at the time of their beginnings, extremely egalitarian in certain respects and they built a particularly sinewy sect organization that bound Lingayats together over wide areas. Nevertheless, they were as sensitive to local ranking as were any others in their villages and they tried to improve and defend their rank just as did the others.

Sikhs

Sikhism is a relatively modern movement which was founded by Guru Nanak (1469–1539), the first of a succession of ten great Sikh religious leaders. Its roots lie in the Bhakti tradition of Hinduism and in the *Sufi* inspiration of Islam. Nanak started with the watchword "There is no Hindu, there is no Mussalman" and rejected all social distinctions among his followers. He is remembered by Punjabi villagers of all religions by such sayings as this: *Guru Nanak Shah Fakir, Hindu ka Guru, Mussalman ka Pir*. Guru Nanak, the king of religions, to the Hindu a guru, to the Muslim a saint (K. Singh 1953, pp. 25, 41–42; 1963, pp. 17–98).

Guru Nanak censured those who would condemn fellow men to untouchability. He himself chose as a close companion in religion a Muslim musician, who would have been regarded as an untouchable by Nanak's kinsmen and jati fellows. Nanak was probably of a Khatri jati, traditionally tradesmen and government officials in the

Punjab, though the name Khatri is from the word Kshtriya. The nine Sikh Gurus who came after him were certainly Khatris.

Guru Nanak adopted a practical means of proclaiming his social doctrine by setting up free community kitchens at which all his believers ate together, whatever their caste origins. The tenth Guru, Gobind Singh, established the principal Sikh institutions. He dramatically and publicly initiated five of his followers, of different jatis, into the new fraternity which he named the Khalsa, "the pure." They drank together out of the same bowl and were given new names with the suffix "Singh" attached. This common surname later exasperated bibliographers and payroll accountants, but, with the abolition of distinctive jati names, all Sikhs were further made equal (K. Singh 1953, p. 30).

The faith spread in the Punjab (though scarcely beyond it) making mass conversions especially among the clans of Jats. As the believers increased in number and influence, they roused fears in the temporal rulers and were persecuted. They resisted, organized, and developed from a fellowship of reconciliation into a militant sect. A great military leader, Ranjit Singh (1780–1839) led the Sikh warriors to the conquest of the Punjab and beyond. After his death the state he had consolidated fell apart, the British took control over the Punjab, and Sikhism again became more a religious than a secular force.

The Sikhs, like the other sects, did not fully realize the egalitarian doctrines preached by the founding Gurus. In surveying Sikh history, Khushwant Singh writes, "If intermarriage is considered the test of equality, at no time was there much inter-caste marriage between Sikhs converted from different castes. The untouchable converted to Sikhism remained an outcaste for purposes of matrimonial alliance" (1953, p. 45). He was kept apart for other purposes also; Sikhs were recruited into the Indian Army by the British and, as Sir Athelstane Baines noted, a recruit from the lowest of Sikh jatis "makes a capital soldier, but has to be brigaded in separate regiments, as the other Sikhs, with their eye on the traditional calling, refuse to associate with the convert, even in religious ceremonies" (Baines 1912, p. 83). Whatever may have been the case in the old British Indian Army, jati differences among Sikhs are suspended in the village practice of religion; even the lowest sit in the temple.

Studies of Sikh villages document both jati separation and religious integration. In Daleke, Amritsar district, there are ten Sikh jatis, one Christian jati, and several Hindu jatis. Jat Sikhs are dominant, other Sikh jatis are those of agriculturist-merchants, artisans, potters, water carriers, washermen, laborers, sweepers, even barbers. Since orthodox Sikhs must not cut their hair, a jati of Sikh barbers might seem superfluous. But they mainly perform the extrabarbering duties done by traditional barbers; they are cooks, workers, and managers at all ceremonial occasions and they also serve as messengers and matchmakers (I. P. Singh 1958, pp. 480–482).

The main cleavage among Sikhs in Daleke is between the lowest, the Mazhbis, and all others. The Mazhbis live in a separate hamlet and have a separate well. Yet no miasma of touch pollution is attributed to them; they sit among others in the temple (though the more finicky women of the other jatis take care to sit away from them); they contribute grain to the temple kitchen and partake of the consecrated food prepared there. In the village they are not addressed as are other Sikhs by the honorific title Sardar (captain or military leader), but out of the village their beards and turbans mark them as Sikhs and they are addressed as Sardar (I. P. Singh 1961, p. 219). All other Sikh jatis in Daleke interdine, attend each others' domestic ceremonies and share in communal rites. The cultivator jatis hold themselves to be of higher rank than the artisan and serving jatis. Though marriage is generally within the jati, women may be brought in from lower jatis; there were fifteen women in the village whose jati was "not known." They face little disadvantage on that account and their children suffer none.

Complete abolition of jati divisions among Sikhs is still urged by itinerant preachers. One such reformer spoke in the Daleke village temple while I. P. Singh was there. A Mazhbi rose to ask whether any in the audience would receive his daughters into their families in marriage. "Practically everybody in the audience, consisting of all castes, raised his hand." But when he asked who would give girls in marriage to his sons, no one volunteered. Even under the eye of the preacher, no one of higher jati would make that gesture (1958, p. 487). But in ritual performance, even Mazhbis are equals. One of the *granthis*, the religious functionaries, of the village is a Mazhbi. He is given the same respected position as is given to the other granthis in Daleke, one of whom is of the washerman jati, another a carpenter, and one a Jat (I. P. Singh 1958, pp. 483, 487).

In another Sikh village, Nalli in Ludhiana District, there are seven Sikh jatis. Here also there is quite free interdining and interchange except with Harijan Sikhs. Only one couple had married across jati lines; a Jat Sikh had a wife of the water-carrier Sikhs. One of his clansmen suggested that because he was mentally defective and poor he had been unable to get a Jat Sikh bride (Izmirlian 1964, pp. 23–28). In both these villages, alliance divisions and factional conflicts are not crystalized along jati lines.

Each Sikh jati accepts Hindu or Muslim converts who are from a social level similar to its own. Among some Punjabi Hindus one of the sons in a family may be reared as a Sikh. Until recent decades, Brahmin priests were regularly brought in by Sikh families for their domestic rites. This is done much less often now; Sikhs are now inclined to stress the autonomy of their religion and the independence of the sect. In Daleke village the complete break with Brahmin priests came when a Jat Sikh married a Muslim woman who had been converted to Sikhism. The Brahmins could not tolerate this confusion of faith and threatened to break off all ritual services to their Sikh clients. Nothing daunted, the Sikhs publicly celebrated the conversion and marriage (I. P. Singh 1958, p. 484).

In this village as in others, Sikhs observe a vigorous round of ceremonial activities which help bolster their faith and serve to solidify the sect. The temple is the scene of many activities—discourses, teaching, scriptural readings, informal storytelling—as well as being the setting for the round of rites in which all Sikhs participate (I. P. Singh 1958, pp. 496–497).

As Sikh institutions became established, separatist groups split off, each under a leader who rallied followers to what he believed to be the true, pure precepts of the founding Gurus as against the current practices of the Sikh establishment. One such sect within Sikhism is called Kukas. The sect rose in the mid-nineteenth century under a founding seer who was succeeded by a gifted executive leader. Kukas are an austere group, more rigorously puritanical than are other Sikhs. They give themselves over to a euphoric kind of worship in which they voice loud *kuks* (shrieks). Most Kukas were converted from the lower jatis; they feel that they are the elect, the true, saintly fraternity, as against the other, impaired Sikhs. They number more than half a million and, though they admit converts, they do not marry outside the fold of Kuka believers (K. Singh, 1966, pp. 127–135).

This fissive trend of the nineteenth century was reversed in the twentieth, among Sikhs as among others, by the attractions of fusion. A main stimulus toward unity arose from resentment about the mismanagement of Sikh temples. The hereditary priests of the great shrines, some of them Hindus, asserted proprietary rights in the temples and in temple endowments. In 1920 a number of Sikh leaders organized and, after several years of lobbying, succeeded in having the temples placed legally under the trust of an elected committee, known as S.G.P.C. This committee became a kind of Sikh government within the national and state governments. Income from the temple endowments sustained it; the more militant adherents formed a pressure group, even a striking force (K. Singh 1966, pp. 193–216). Through this organization Sikhs exerted political influence, and in 1966 they were able to bring about the division of the Punjab into two new states of India, Punjab Subha and Haryana. Sikhs now form a majority in Punjab Subha, they were a minority in the undivided state. They are well embarked on the fusion-political process, though internal rivalries keep boiling up among alliances in the state capital as in the villages.

Sikhism began as a way of cultural fusion. The founder's ecumenical vision was directed toward bringing together Hinduism and Islam, Hindus and Muslims. Along that way, however, Sikh converts separated from their former jati affiliations and split again after Sikhism became an established religion. The modern fusion organization among Sikhs has gained notable strength, though it also has suffered the usual fragmentation pangs that come in the aftermath of power.

Personal Conversion and Systemic Stability

Religious movements offered the principal means by which people in this social system could regroup themselves in far-reaching ways. People in all complex societies sooner or later rearrange their social groupings in order to adapt to external change and internal development. Jati mobility has been one adaptive process in this social system, the rise of sectarian groups has been another. Once a sectarian rise had been accomplished, the new group continued in the common pattern of jati mobility.

Incipient sects had the advantage of being voluntary associations of like-minded, like-motivated people. A family, even an individual, could independently join such an association because of the favorable attitude toward a person's dedication to almost any religion, provided that the religion did not carry sinister social overtones. A religion that threatened jati standards and jati integrity was to be shunned. Within that provision, devotional differences were and are readily tolerated.

No wonder, then, that cults have mushroomed in the past and continue to appear. Most of them eventually die out. Some persist, grow until they reach a critical mass for firm establishment, and develop into organized religions. They can reach the later stages because of a combination of inspired leadership, self-sacrificing followers, and other fortunate circumstances—"blessed" circumstances, the true believers firmly hold.

As a cult becomes an organized sect, its people have to operate as a unit in the larger society. In India, villagers knew of no other way to participate in the larger society than as members of a jati. And so the regrouped devotees became members of a jati. What typically began as a deeply stirring religious experience felt by many, sometimes did stir the social system as well, but in ways that helped to preserve the fundamental structure of the social system. This is not to say that these indigenous movements had no effect in the society. Some have considerably affected the culture of their region; some have shaped the trend of political events; a few have influenced the civilization. But none has altered the basic system of jati relations.

In the twentieth century a change in the redistribution process seems to becoming about. The bhajan movement in Madras apparently is not developing quite in the traditional cycle, nor have such wider reform movements as the Arya Samaj done so. Other means for social redistribution and adjustment are becoming available; political and educational agencies are being put to these uses.

The sects discussed so far are indigenous. World religions were brought into India, attracted converts, and became established there. These, too, provided avenues for social regrouping, and converts to them also continued to maintain jati organization and mobility drives.

FOUR scriptural religions, Islam, Christianity, Zoroastrianism, and Judaism were brought into India and became established there. The origins of each in the land are historically obscure though mythologically elaborated. Merchants seem to have been instrumental in each introduction. They came into India from abroad, settled there in small colonies, prospered and attracted converts, perhaps as much by the inspiration of their thriving example as by their proselytizing zeal. Zoroastrianism and Judaism continued in that way, carried by relatively small, localized groups.

Islam and Christianity, however, became more widely accepted in India, apart from the original settlements, after rulers of these religions conquered large territories. Emulation of the temporal rulers and the persuasive power of their resources had something to do with this acceptance though some became converts for essentially spiritual reasons and others were converted because of a desire for social regrouping.

The foreign merchants and rulers were too few or too aloof to induct converts into a new way of life as well as into a new mode of worship. They offered a reference category rather than a reference group. Converts lacked any new social base to go with their new scripture and had little alternative but to continue in the pervasive caste system. They became jatified (linguistic structure too can assimilate foreign elements) and reentered the typical struggle for social mobility. The Parsis, however, did not divide into separate jatis. There were some attempts among these Zoroastrians toward jati separation, but the attempts were overridden. Their rejection of jati division may help explain why they later took so successfully to modern social models.

The adherents of the introduced religions have responded to modern influences with search for wider alliances and identities. Their ways of doing so vary greatly. Large groups of Muslims have become more purely Islamic in their religious practices. Some Jews have emigrated to Israel. Many Christians look to modern education as the best avenue to wider affiliation, to the careers and broader associations open to the educated.

Islam and Christianity have had important influence in India, but village Muslims and Christians carry on their social relations in ways that are generally similar to those followed by their neighbors of other religions. Muslims and Christians participate in their local social orders as jati groups; their mobility drives are in the characteristic patterns and fall into the systemic process of recurrent change. However, religious affiliation does make for certain social differences as well as broad similarities.

Religious Differences and Social Similarities

Muslims in India are about one-ninth the national population; only Indonesia and Pakistan among modern nations have more Muslim citizens. Historically, the Muslims of the subcontinent have contributed notably to Islamic thought as well as to Indian civilization (cf. Smith 1957, pp. 256–291).

Muslim villagers are generally aware of the special career of Islam in India and of the distinctiveness of their religion among others in India. They believe that their social organization is different from that of Hindus. "Orthodox Muslims," Zarina Ahmad points out, "resent the word caste being used for the Muslim religious groups" (1962, p. 329). Though their doctrine and their popular theory assert that all Muslims are equal, the actual social practices of Muslim villagers usually parallel those of their Hindu neighbors. The differences between them can be of vast consequence in certain contexts—the partition into two nations is witness to that—but the differences do not necessarily lie where popular theory holds them to be.

Muslims in all regions of India class themselves into endogamous, hereditary groups which are ranked in relation to each other (cf. Ansari 1960; S. C. Misra 1964; Imtiaz Ahmad 1965; Kudryavtsev 1965). Hereditary occupations are usually attributed to each group;

members of each traditionally participate in jajmani relations with families of other jatis in their locality. Where Muslim untouchables exist, they are so treated by both Hindus and Muslims. Muslims usually differ from Hindus in certain family practices, as in permitting parallel-cousin marriage or in allotting greater inheritance rights and stricter seclusion to women; but in other family relations they are usually like the Hindus of their place and social level. A Muslim group in a village maintains its internal cohesion much as does a similar Hindu group. In some regions the same term is used for a Muslim as for a Hindu jati (cf. Eglar 1960, p. 29; Misra 1964, p. 139). In all, it is not misleading for our present purposes of social analysis, to speak of Muslim jatis.

Yet the social differences must be recognized. Muslims of all groups in a village interdine freely (except possibly the local Muslim untouchables), they worship in the same mosques, they participate in ceremonies together. Village Muslims are strongly on guard against individual pollution, as in menstruation and childbirth, but their views of corporate, permanent pollution are more diffuse and are officially disclaimed.

Endogamy is relatively looser. There is apt to be greater latitude for hypergamous marriages; social percolation is easier. Secular power is brought to bear more quickly and forcefully in gaining higher rank. The ritual criteria include exalted ancestry, zeal for Islamic practice, scriptural learning, and freedom from defiling occupations and demeaning customs. These are important but are not as weighty in the Muslim ranking as are the ritual criteria in ranking among Hindus. Hence mobility into a higher rank tends to be more common and is achieved more readily by separate families. Prospering families still must take on pure and genteel practices in the usual mobility pattern, but there is less resistance to their rise in the local Muslim hierarchy, provided they have wealth and use it with proper discretion. Muslim villagers agree that certain Muslim groups are high and others are low, but they show perhaps even less agreement than do Hindu villagers about the precise order of ranking in the middle ranges. This is partly because the order of rank has little place in religion and lacks supporting ideology.

Other doctrinal differences between Islam and Hinduism are well known, even by villagers (cf. Mandelbaum 1947). Islamic doctrine, for one matter, is monotheistic, Hindu doctrine is more eclectic.

But for pragmatic purposes of religion, Muslims and Hindus of a locality often use the same shrines and practitioners. This is noted in an account of a village near Hyderabad in Andhra Pradesh, where Muslims are about one-tenth the village population. These Muslims take only a nominal part in Hindu festivals but they "are active and enthusiastic in planning measures to ward off evil spirits, ghosts, and epidemics in cooperation with their Hindu and tribal neighbors" (Dube 1955a, pp. 189–190). Such cooperation is not uncommon. Hindus and Muslims in a village are usually willing to participate in each other's pragmatic rites, even though neither would ever worship in the mosque or temple of the other religion. Both use shamans of either religion, depending on the priest's reputation for effective practice rather than on his formal faith (Mandelbaum 1966, p. 1178).

In their social strivings Muslims may vie with other Muslims of a locality in the same ways in which Hindu families and jatis carry on their rivalries. Riots between Muslim factions have long been reported (cf. Martin 1838, Vol. 1, p. 144). Muslim and Hindu neighbors cooperate in some contexts and not in others. The differing contexts have not yet been studied closely although it is clear that whenever religious differences become salient social markers, the followers of each religion tend to see themselves as upholders of the one true faith, a tendency not restricted to Indian villages.

Indian Muslims share some of the basic social characteristics of the civilization, in their jati arrangements for example. They also share in the characteristics of the region in which they live and the social-economic level to which they belong. They see themselves as being distinctive religiously and they give a special phrasing to the traits they share with non-Muslims. Yet in many respects their social relations are quite like those of their non-Muslim neighbors. A vivid example is that of those Muslims in Kerala who were matrilineal in the Nayar manner, utterly unlike the patrilineal emphasis of Islamic scripture and of other Indian Muslims (Gough 1961, pp. 415–442; Yalman 1967, pp. 372–374).

In all regions, Muslims carry on their social relations in ways characteristic of their locality. Thus one account of a village in West Bengal reports that the three levels of Muslim jatis there "are very much akin to those of the parallel Hindu castes of the village." Here the Shaikhs are the highest and are completely endogamous.

Cultivators make up the middle bloc and fishermen the lowest. The Muslim fishermen may not take water from the tanks used by the higher Muslims nor are they allowed to enter the village mosque (Guha 1965, pp. 168–169).

A review of village studies in East Pakistan concludes, "In summary, the Muslim caste-like groups are much like their Hindu counterparts, especially among the specialists and menials. Nevertheless, if the Muslim group are to be called castes, it must be recognized that they are part of a considerably more flexible system of social stratification" (Beech, et al., 1966, p. 11).[1]

Some of the best studies of Muslim groups have been done in Uttar Pradesh and in West Pakistan. These studies further indicate that Muslims share in the social characteristics of their region, participate in the patterns of mobility, and enter into the processes of recurrent change.

Muslims of Uttar Pradesh

Muslim social organization in the state of Uttar Pradesh, with nearly eleven million Muslims in the 1961 Census, has been sketched by Ghaus Ansari (1960). He reports that U. P. Muslims group their jatis in several blocs, not unlike the varna categories. A main distinction is between the Ashraf, the "honorable," and all other Muslims, the Ajlaf. The division has been compared to the Hindu dichotomy between the "twice-born" varnas and other Hindus, but Imtiaz Ahmad (1967) stresses that the term Ashraf refers more to the esteemed style of life than to any specific jatis or blocs.

Those who are called Ashraf are usually held to be descendants of distinguished foreign, non-Indian, ancestors. They are traditionally the landowners, the civic and religious leaders, the wealthier and more purely Islamic among the Muslims of their locality. According to Ansari, four "classes" (i.e., jati-clusters) of Ashraf are found in Uttar Pradesh, of whom the highest are the Sayyad, "princes." This line is believed to come from the daughter of the Prophet and her husband, the fourth Caliph of Islam. Sayyads are

---

[1] Bengali Muslims are said by Karim to take particular pride in foreign ancestry. Distinguished forebears from anywhere outside of Bengal seem to validate Ashraf rank; if they were from outside India, "it is the better" (1956, p. 134).

further divided into some twenty sections; endogamy is common within each section but is not mandatory. Next are the *Shaikh*, "chiefs," believed to be descended from Arab ancestors who were among the first followers of the Prophet. Marriages may be contracted between families of their sections and Sayyads, but rarely with families of the two other high groups, the *Mughals* and *Pathans*. These two are reputedly descended from Mongol and Afghani conquerors in India (Ansari 1960, pp. 35–38; Z. Ahmad 1962, pp. 326–328).

At the bottom of the Muslim ranking are those Muslims who do scavenging, sweeping, and other menial tasks. In Uttar Pradesh they are commonly descended from converts who retained their former jati name, occupation, poverty, and disabilities. Muslims of higher status do not ordinarily take food from them. Sometimes they are not allowed to worship inside the village mosque but must stand and pray outside (Ansari 1960, pp. 50, 58). They are treated in much the same way as their Hindu counterparts. However, a high Muslim may choose to take food from them or worship with them without incurring the kind of penalties that a high-ranking Hindu might suffer for such transgression.

The middle ranks among Muslims of U. P. include Muslim Rajputs and the "clean occupational castes." The social distance between them and the highest Muslims is illustrated by Zarina Ahmad's observation that in the villages she studied no member of an Ashraf group will marry a non-Ashraf or even take food with one (1962, p. 327). There is broader interdining among Muslims elsewhere in U. P. Muslims of the Shi'ah sect are reported to be more stringent about food than are Sunnis. Shi'ahs are supposed to refuse prepared food from any non-Muslims but Sunnis will take such food from "clean Hindu castes" (Ansari 1960, pp. 40–41, 54–55, 58).

Village studies from U. P. show that Muslims operate in their local social order much as do Hindus of similar status. In one village of Saharanpur district about half the land is owned and cultivated by the Hindu jati of Tyagis and the rest by Muslim Tyagis. They are descendants of a common ancestor and together they dominate village affairs (Gupta 1956, p. 31).

A study of kinship among Ashraf Muslims in several parts of U. P. concludes that their kinship terminology and inheritance rules are essentially similar to those of the higher Hindu jatis of the same localities (Vreede–de Stuers 1963). Muslim artisans provide services under the same conditions as do their Hindu counterparts and manage their jati affairs quite like a comparable jati of Hindu artisans (Ansari 1960, p. 56; Misra 1964, pp. 139–149).

An incident from a village of Lucknow district illustrates Muslim sensitivity to rank. One of the guests at a wedding in an Ashraf family was a woman of the *manihar*, bangle-seller jati who had just returned to the village after a long absence. Her husband had prospered; she wore expensive clothes, and, not being recognized as she came in, she was seated at a table with Ashraf ladies. In the middle of the meal, one of the Ashraf women recognized her; the other women "at once stood up and refused to sit at the same table with the *manihar* woman. It caused a lot of embarrassment, but the *manihar* lady had to sit and eat on the floor" (Z. Ahmad 1962, p. 331). In their precipitous, upright act these Muslim ladies were doing what Hindu ladies of high jati would also do in like circumstance. This is not to say that Hindus and Muslims in Uttar Pradesh have identical social views or that the views of either Hindus or Muslims remain unchallenged. Differences as well as similarities exist and must be taken into account; social changes are impending among Muslims as among Hindus.

Villages of West Pakistan

The establishment of Pakistan has had important consequences in the lives of its citizens. Yet studies of Pakistan villages since independence show a considerable continuity in the traditional social groupings. Thus Zekiye Eglar has described a Punjabi Muslim village in which "A child learns the caste it belongs to from the time it begins to speak and tells it when he gives his personal name. Very early, the child also learns that it can marry only within its own caste" (1960, p. 29). These villagers consider caste practices as having been borrowed from the Hindus and as referring primarily to inherited occupation, but they hold strongly to these practices nevertheless.

In this village of Gujrat district, West Pakistan, jajmani relations are like those among Hindu Punjabis, but high rank is more closely and immediately bound to the ownership of land. Very few

artisans or servants own any land at all; status within the landowning group depends on the amount of land each family possesses.
Eglar emphasizes the importance of gift exchange, called *vartan
bhanji*, at all social levels and in all important contexts. These exchanges pivot around the daughters of a family, who are therefore
central to social relations among families, jatis, and villages. Since
the daughter is the central figure "one may say that a daughter is
as crucial to *vartan bhanji* as *vartan bhanji* is to the whole of the
traditional culture" (Eglar 1960, p. 101). Similar analyses of gift
exchange in other villages have yet to be made. It may be as
dominant a concern of women elsewhere in the land as it is in this
Muslim village in the Punjab. Certainly women talk a good deal
about this in other places.

An account of another Punjabi village illustrates the way in
which Muslim villagers continue the life style of their ancestral
Hindu group. In this case they are Jats, who are dominant landowners in a village of Gujranwala district, West Pakistan. Jats,
whether Hindu, Sikh, or Muslim, pride themselves on their un-
varnished manner, their straightforward response, their taste for a
fight. The Muslim Jats here are in the same mold, believing that a
person who has no enemy, whom nobody fears and whom nobody
obeys, is worthless. Inayat Ullah, who has studied this village,
reports that "The first question to be asked from a visitor is about
his caste, as this information decides whether he is to be given a cot
to sit on or is to seat himself on the ground; and whether a special
meal is to be cooked for him, or whether ordinary food would be
sufficient."

There are some thirteen artisan and laborer jatis among the village Muslims. They are mainly endogamous, though landowners
occasionally take specially favored brides from them. Pride in one's
jati is strong at all levels; brave deeds by a jati fellow are a source
of pride; misdeeds, especially sexual lapses by women, disgrace all
in the jati. "Usually, every member of the caste feels it his duty to
defend his caste against every sort of accusation and to live up to
the tradition of his caste" (Inayat Ullah 1958, pp. 170–174). Conversion to Islam has not dampened pride in jati traditions.

Pride in one's group is also strong in a Muslim village of Dadu
district in Sindh, West Pakistan. There are some twenty-seven

ranked groups in this village, the groups are called *zat*.[2] The four highest have produced an unusual number of scholars, teachers, and government officials; they have given the village considerable renown. Their motivation toward modern achievement, Honigmann believes, stems from their pride of rank and their drive to maintain it. As among other Muslims, wealth is requisite for such rank but does not necessarily command it. Observance of certain standards, as the seclusion of women, endogamy for girls, limited hypergamy for boys, are still relevant for high rank. A main attribute is noble ancestry, which means that the men of the group have long been wealthy, respected, learned, and free from any need to do manual labor.

Yet noble ancestry alone is not sufficient; there are four Sayyid families in the village who are not counted among the village leaders. Though presumably descendants of the Prophet, they are given respect "from the religious, not the social point of view." They are lacking in the kind of education and government service that are now important criteria for high rank (Honigmann 1960a, pp. 8–12; 1960b, pp. 833–839).

In these villages of West Pakistan, social relations are hierarchically arranged in the general pattern followed by most people on the subcontinent. Mobility drives, both in the traditional and modernized modes, are also broadly similar among Muslims and others of each region.

Social Mobility Among Muslims

Prospering Muslims pass upward in the familiar pattern. Low-ranking families who become rich disappear from their former social niche and reappear in a higher Muslim stratum. Single families can do this over a few years; the rise of whole groups takes longer but

---

[2] The author notes that Muslims do not employ the term "caste" with the meaning it possesses for Hindus. But his explanation of the terms used in this Sindhi village, called Pat, points up the parallel usages. "The leading families of Pat refer to themselves as constituting four or five 'castes' (English-speaking villagers and public records used the words 'tribe', *zat*, and 'community' interchangeably with 'caste'). . . . Such castes are ideally endogamous, marriage into a *known* family bearing the same surname being preferred" (Honigmann 1960b, p. 833).

the sequence of steps is broadly the same. "As soon as a lower class Muslim makes money, he puts his women in *purdah* (a practice observed only by the Ashrafs), starts going to the communal prayers in the mosque and goes to Mecca for pilgrimage" (Zarina Ahmad 1962, p. 329). Such families cast off inferior occupations, whether as weavers or barbers or butchers, become landowners and assume the manners of landowners. They give more assiduous attention to religion in ways that are beyond the means of those who work with their hands. They secure the services of a reputable ritual leader, a *Maulvi*, to conduct their life-cycle and domestic rites. Once they acquire some aura of respectable rank, they negotiate for prestigious marriages for their children. As they succeed in this, they place themselves in a higher bracket of rank among the local Muslims (Ansari 1960, pp. 38–39; Misra 1964, p. 169). Having done so among Muslims, they presumably acquire like respectability in the eyes of the non-Muslim villagers, though there have been few descriptions of the mutual ranking of Muslims and Hindus in a locality.

The case history of a rising Muslim family in eastern Uttar Pradesh is told by Zarina Ahmad. A new Muslim family came in to a village of Barabanki district, built a big house, and set up a large brick-making works. Their sons were being educated in town; their women were in strict *purdah;* their elders were constantly at prayers in the mosque. The family called itself Shaikh, but it soon became known in the village that they had been Julahas, weavers, in their former home. Most of the landowning Ashraf families of the village kept aloof from the newcomers, refusing to attend their social occasions. After a time a few of the Ashraf did accept their invitations.

With this small encouragement, the family "took a very daring step," and sent a proposal for their son's marriage to an Ashraf girl. The boy was well educated, the parents rich, the match attractive— save for the groom's origins. After a year of negotiation, the alliance was settled and the marriage celebrated with lavish pomp. The other Ashraf families of the village were much annoyed, not only at the fact of the alliance but also at its pretentious display. The new couple felt this animus and moved out of the village permanently, though the family remains and maintains its claims. "But, within a generation or two, these facts will be forgotten and they will become genuine Shaikhs" (Z. Ahmad 1962, pp. 331–332).

To repeat, in another version, the popular saying about mobility that was quoted earlier, "We used to be butchers and now we are Shaikhs. Next year if the harvest prices are good for us, we shall be Sayyads" (cf. Ansari 1960, p. 37; Blunt 1931, p. 184; Misra 1964, p. 170). Some aspiring Muslims change their jati names as other ambitious villagers have done. The 1931 Census report for U. P. lists three Muslim jatis with fresh claims to being Shaikh; formerly one was a weaver, one a musician, and one a butcher group (Ansari 1960, p. 38). Not all such Muslim groups seek to change their names, however. The Sunni Vohras of Gujarat were mainly farmers at the beginning of the twentieth century. They have since become predominantly traders and have much improved their jati practices as well as their occupation, but they keep the same name (Misra 1964, pp. 169–170).

Gujarati Muslims seem to have been particularly prone to fission. There are at least six jatis of Memons, tradesmen, and four of Vohras, cultivators. These are further subdivided by allegiance to different holy men. The families of one part of a jati may become adherents of a particular saint while others in the jati give allegiance to a different holy man; the two sides will have little to do with each other (Misra 1964, pp. 138–142).

New jatis have arisen from indigenous Muslim sects much as they did from indigenous sects of Hinduism. The two major sects of Islam, Sunni and Shi'a, were brought in with Islam itself. In India each of these major denominations was further divided. One of the offshoots of the Shi'ah are the Isma'ili, some of whom acknowledge the Aga Khan as their head. There are several Isma'ili jatis, the Bohras and Khojas of Gujarat being the major groups among them. Some of the Muslim sects indigenous to India developed quite eclectic doctrines. Khoja doctrine, for example, held at one time that the Aga Khan was an incarnation of the "glorious Tenth Avatar," the future manifestation of Vishnu (Khadduri and Liebesny 1955, pp. 117–119). One Muslim cult was founded by a Syrian of Jewish origin and included Jewish and Christian as well as Hindu rites; other Muslim sects gave honor to Hindu deities (Aziz Ahmad 1964, pp. 155–163).

A modern sect, the Ahmadiyas, was founded in the late nineteenth century by a powerful sage in a small town of the Punjab. His followers have become more than a sectarian jati, they form a close-knit community engaged in economic activities as well as in vigorous missionary work. Their center has been described as a combination of modern enterprise and fundamentalist theology; their very activism has drawn attacks from other Muslims. Like the more vigorous Hindu sects, the Isma'illis and the Ahmadiyas have developed a particularly effective internal organization. This helps bring them prosperity which in turn eventually yields respectable status in their localities (Smith 1957, pp. 230–231; Spate 1954, pp. 189–192; Misra 1964, pp. 15–68).

Aspiring Muslims emulate their local elite as Hindus emulate theirs. One observer has described the Muslim process under the term "Ashrafization" (Vreede–de Stuers 1962). Such emulation is much more than just a way of social climbing; it is seen as a means to moral, transcendental personal improvement. Those who shift to a more devout Islamic way of life, who attend to prayers and rituals more assiduously, who give hours to reading or listening to the Koran, who school their sons to the beauties of Islamic literature, do so not only because they can afford to and because it is the path to higher status, but also because they want to be better men, finer servants of God. A Muslim who intensifies his devotions, like a Hindu who deepens his piety, is not only following the main chance in the game of social elevation, he is also pursuing the revealed direction toward the good of his eternal soul.

The spiritual gain does not lessen one's need for proper social maneuver. A rising family must take on other Ashraf ways, such as having the women observe strict seclusion. This is a sure sign of prosperity, since women so secluded cannot work out of the house and must be able to afford servants. Outer symbols must also be changed. The poorest usually wear the same dress as do the poor among non-Muslims of their locality. But among the wealthier and higher villagers, a distinctive Muslim costume is worn nowadays and rising families tend to adopt the distinguishing dress (cf. Misra 1964, p. 167). At a still higher social level, modern educated Muslims generally adopt Western-style dress and revise their domestic practices quite as do their Hindu counterparts. They may wear traditional Muslim dress on symbolic occasions and give some deference to Ashraf ways, but they have added new elite standards that combine Islamic precepts, Ashraf manners, and modern mores.

These elite standards are beyond an ordinary Muslim villager's knowledge and certainly beyond his reach. If he has status ambitions, he is intent on dropping debasing customs and on assuming respectable ones. He is likely nowadays to drop specifically Hindu customs, such as in the form of marriage or the *rakhi-bandhan* ritual between brother and sister. In modern times Muslims of higher rank frown on the use of specifically Hindu practices.

It was not always so, at least not in the Punjab. In the 1883 Census report for the Punjab, Ibbetson wrote that in the eastern part of that region, "conversion has absolutely no effect upon the caste of the convert. His social customs are unaltered, his tribal restrictions are unrelaxed, his rules of marriage and inheritance unchanged; and about the only difference is that he shaves his scalplock and the upper edge of his moustache, repeats the Mahomedan creed in a mosque, and adds the Musalman to the Hindu wedding ceremony" (1916, pp. 13–14). Ibbetson did say that since the 1850s there had been a Muslim revival in the Punjab and that the adherence of Muslims to Islamic law and custom was growing stronger. But it was not only Muslims in the eastern Punjab who neglected their scripture, the Hindus of the region did not set great store by the local Brahmins or by Sanskritic scripture. In the twentieth century, however, Punjabis of all religions came to be less blithely eclectic and more observant of their respective doctrines.

The primary goal of ambitious Muslim villagers in all regions is to gain better status among the Muslim groups of their locality. If they achieve that they also rise in the general status system of the village and its locality. The bracket of Muslim jatis is articulated into the local system of rank. As we have noted, untouchables are treated as such by all in a village, whether they are Hindu or Muslim. A wealthy Muslim landowner of distinguished bearing and esteemed ancestry is generally given respect by all in his locality.

Islamization and Modern Adaptation

Relations between Muslims and non-Muslims were severely jolted throughout the subcontinent and completely severed in many places during the political developments of the 1940s. Then, as commonly occurs in times of general tension, the usual village rivalries were consolidated into larger oppositions. Status rivalries among particular jatis or alliances were relinquished for more massive encounters. The years before independence saw a steady increase, spurred by national forces, in mass confrontations between Hindu and Muslim villagers. In earlier periods, such antagonisms might flare when one side publicly celebrated its festivals. The adherents of the other religion were then particularly sensitive to any gestures or status claims made in the celebration that might disparage their own position, but once the day of struggle was past, villagers usually reverted to the daily round of interchange among jatis and families of all religions. National events exacerbated this antagonism and made it a continuous affair, even in villages, until it resulted in the climactic separation of nations (Mandelbaum 1947).

After independence, massive demonstrations of rivalry within each nation were elicited by various issues; one such issue has been the claims of linguistic regions for proper rank and recognition. Tensions between Muslims and Hindus have erupted in violence in certain places and times, but these tensions were not the paramount reasons for internal strife in either nation, nor have they become a dominant issue of internal politics.

Muslims in India soon resumed their efforts for group improvement and social mobility, as did non-Muslims. Many of the Muslim jatis have followed the general trend toward federation, reform, and political participation. Reform, as for Hindu jatis, entails a combination of traditional high practices and prestigeful modern ways. Reform among Muslim villagers particularly, means greater observance of their religious traditions and so there has been a marked turning toward Islamic practices and symbols.

This intensified Islamization is shown by the Meos, the dominant jati in some two thousand villages on the borderlands of Rajasthan and Punjab. They tilled a poor land and in earlier centuries often resorted to raiding. They became Muslims about the fifteenth century, perhaps in the hope that the Muslim rulers might then deal more leniently with them. After their conversion they continued as bearers of Rajput values and kept their Rajput customs, adding such Muslim practices as circumcision and burial of the dead. They maintained jajmani relations with Hindu artisans and with the Brahmins who conducted some of their rites.

After 1947, however, the Meos found the old relationships to be unworkable.[3] Their former clients and servants began to break away and to demand more money and independence. Meos realized that they needed better cooperation within their own group and with others beyond their territory in order to be effective in modern ways, especially as participants in state politics. They had been singled out as Muslims by others in their region, subjected to hostile gestures and even to clumsy attempts at reconversion. Proud of their identity as Meos, they received a most cordial reception from other Muslims while the non-Muslims around them were decidedly cool. Some of the Meos, perhaps a fourth, migrated to Pakistan but the rest remained in India. They have now become far more dedicated to Islam than they had ever been before. They are determinedly giving up Hindu practices and are diligently trying to take on Islamic ways, though they are not always sure what these ways may be. They have built new mosques; they wear a new style of dress; they have begun to eat meat, even buffalo meat. "It is not at all an exaggeration to say that the Meos have adopted more of Muslim practices in the last 17 years than they had in the previous 450 years" (Aggarwal 1966, pp. 159–160).

Their original conversion required no profound turn to scriptural Islam; they kept their former ways quite intact and only added an overlay of Muslim features. But if they are now to be as effective politically as are other organized groups, they need stronger internal unity than before and wider alliances. They look for both in the context of Islam, and so they have become stauncher Muslims, partly for reasons of religion, but partly also in order to become better participants in the democratic processes of the Indian nation.

Muslim groups in other parts of India have been forming political alliance with fellow Muslims much as caste associations and federations have been formed (cf. Wright 1966; Srinivas 1966, pp. 73–74). In the present trend Muslim leaders in India tend to emphasize the distinctive symbols of their religious heritage while striving to integrate their people into the national spheres of politics, education, and economics, and to gain a good place for them in these spheres.

[3] An account of recent Meo history as seen by one of their political activists is by Chowdhry Abdul Haye (1966).

CHAPTER **30** Social Aspects of Introduced
Religions: Jews, Parsis,
Christians

JUDAISM, Zoroastrianism, and Christianity have been
rooted in India for more than a millennium. The followers of
each religion have participated in their local social systems as jati
members. The historical evidence on Jews and Christians in India
is particularly useful in showing how the social themes of these
religions came to be adapted to the prevailing mode of Indian society. Hence our discussion of Jews and Christians gives particular
attention to their historical development.

Jews: Two Settlements, Five Jatis

The ancient Indian settlements of Jews are in Cochin (in the state
of Kerala) and in Maharashtra. Although both settlements were always numerically small, they were divided into jatis. The Jews of
Cochin have been more extensively described than have those of
Maharashtra.

The three jatis of Cochin Jews numbered about twenty-two hundred persons in the seventeenth century and there were fewer still in
later times. Yet they have firmly maintained their religious identity
for at least a millennium (Mandelbaum 1939). Their earliest docu-
mentary record is found in a set of copper plates of about the elev-
enth century. Inscribed on these plates are grants conferred in per-
petuity by the reigning Raja to a Jew named Joseph Rabban. He
and his posterity were granted a principality and all its revenue.
They were also given such prerogatives as the right to ride an elephant, to be carried in a litter, to parade with a state umbrella, to
be preceded by drums and trumpets, to have criers call out before

their approach so that the lowly might withdraw from the streets. The date inscribed is not certain but has been interpreted as 1020 A.D. It is clear that a Jewish community must have existed in the Raja's domain for some time before the date of the grant. Such boons would not have been bestowed on a recent arrival (cf. Fischel 1967).

There is a Jewish tombstone in Cochin bearing a date equivalent to 1269 A.D. and there are historical records of the Cochin Jews from every century thereafter. A traveler's report of 1570 gives the first mention of their social organization as including "a Sephardi community and other congregations of the black Jews." The Sephardic families were almost all descendants of immigrants from Europe, North Africa, and the Middle East who had come in after the Portuguese opened the sea route from Europe to India in the early sixteenth century. But two families of the Sephardis, or the White Jews as they came to be called, were descended from Jews who had been in the region long before the first Portuguese arrived.

After the Dutch ousted the Portuguese from India, a delegation was sent by the Amsterdam Jewish congregation to conduct an enquiry into the condition of their coreligionists in Cochin (cf. Fischel 1962). The account of their researches, published in 1687, shows that there were then two jatis of Cochin Jews and that their relations were like those of a higher and a lower jati elsewhere in this region. The White Jews were generally lighter in skin color than the Black Jews, though some of the White were as dark as any of the Blacks.

The White Jews would not intermarry or interdine with the Black Jews and would not even count a Black Jew as one of the *minyan*, the minimum member of ten required for congregational worship. The Black Jews repeatedly challenged the assumed jati superiority of the White Jews. In the sixteenth century they sent petitions to rabbinical authorities in Egypt, asking that their claims to equal status with the White Jews be confirmed. There is a record of another petition for equality in the year 1723, this one addressed to the Raja of Cochin, specifically asking that women of the White Jews be made to wear the same headdress as women of the Black Jews. The Raja in his wisdom decreed that the women could wear what they pleased.

For a time there was a splinter group within the Black Jews

reminiscent of those among the indigenous sects. One of their seven synagogues lacked its own ritual butcher and its members arranged with the White Jews to certify a member of that congregation for the office. Previously, candidates for this post were ordained only by Black Jews; the other congregations of Black Jews gathered in council and outcast all in the errant synagogue. For generations they were not allowed to worship with the others. Marriage to one of their girls meant that the groom could no longer participate in his former synagogue. But a single congregation was scarcely enough to form a separate jati, so the quarrel gradually lapsed and in the mid-twentieth century was almost forgotten.

A third jati did rise from converts made by the White Jews from among their servants. They were called by the Hebrew term *meshuhararim*, "the manumitted," and called "Brown Jews" in English. Conversions were still being made when I made a brief study of the Cochin Jews in 1937. One of them explained the process in this way. "The servant feels more secure in his master's house if he becomes a coreligionist of the employer." He went on to tell that many of the servants had spent all their lives in Jewish homes and had participated in the ceremonial cycle and daily practices of Judaism. "They feel associated with Judaism in every way, and want to become Jews in name also. And the servants who are born in Jewish houses sometimes have Jewish blood in their veins." He concluded that in the Passover ceremony, the convert sits at his master's table as an equal, in accordance with scriptural rule, "and so achieves a prestige which the non-Jews among the servants cannot attain."

In the twentieth century, the Jews of Cochin have shown the characteristic reach for wider affiliations. A good many of them have found it in Zionism and have emigrated to Israel.

The other ancient settlement of Jews in India is larger, with some 14,000 people, but it is still a tiny enclave in the Marathi-speaking region. These Jews now are known by the Hebrew term, Bene Israel, sons of Israel, but prior to the eighteenth century they knew almost no Hebrew and apparently had no knowledge of or contacts with other Jewish groups. They lived in several Konkani villages as oil-pressers. This is not a prestigious occupation and they did not rank high in their villages. They were distinguished by certain religious traits that were unlike those of any of their neighbors.

For one thing, they were known as Shanwar Telis, Saturday oilmen, because they would not work on Saturday. They knew nothing of Judaic scriptural law, but they did observe certain Jewish festivals. They maintained some of the Judaic dietary regulations and practiced circumcision. Their one Hebraic formula was the Shema, the brief confession of faith, which they recited as an incantation at every ritual occasion (Strizower 1959, pp. 45–47).

Like oil-pressers in other regions, they attempted to improve their local status by such reforms as purifying their diet and prohibiting the remarriage of widows. After Cochin Jews established contact with them in the eighteenth century and after they came to know of other, foreign, Jews in Bombay City in the nineteenth century, the reference model of Judaism was opened for them. They took to it but did not relinquish their jati divisions.

Like the Cochin Jews but independently of them, the Bene Israel were separated into two jatis, the higher being called the Gora, the fair ones, and the lower the Kala, the dark ones. They too did not interdine or intermarry, though they did worship in the same synagogues. Those of the higher jati claimed purer Jewish ancestry; the lower, they alleged, was of mixed origins.

The separation continued into recent times, even in the city of Bombay. One woman of the Gora jati recalled, "My mother used to get furious when Kala came near her cooking utensils and would push them away. She would not allow Kala to touch any utensils which she used for food" (Strizower 1959, p. 49). Most of the Bene Israel now live in Bombay City; a good many of them have migrated to Israel. The barriers between the two jatis are far less rigid in the city than they had been in the Konkan villages, but even in the 1950s a betrothal across the two jatis raised family objections as well as some disapproval among the local Jews (Strizower 1959, pp. 48–49, 56).

These Jewish jatis provide further examples of the gravitational attraction of the Indian system of caste. Similar influence is exerted by the social order of any civilization on the smaller, culturally divergent groups who live within it.

Parsis

The Parsis have not split into separate jatis. Their religion, Zoroastrianism, was introduced to India from Persia in about the 8th century A.D. Parsis were a small, little known mercantile community in the western part of India until recent centuries, when a number of their families became successful industrial entrepreneurs and merchant tycoons. Parsis as a group then acquired cultural and financial influence far beyond their modest number of about 115,000 people. Much of their culture, apart from religious rites, was like that of other trading communities of Maharashtra and Gujrat. Their internal councils resembled the panchayats of trading jatis, though perhaps they were more effective than most of these. In their localities, they constituted another jati, mainly of traders.

Though Parsi families strive for status as do families of other jatis, there has been little formal separation among Parsis. One short-lived separatist move occurred in the eighteenth century when families of hereditary priests decided to set up hypergamous relationships with lay Parsis, to take daughters from the laity as brides but not to give their own daughters into lay families. The incensed laity passed a resolution in 1777 that reversed this order; the quarrel grew until a government commission of three "English gentlemen" arbitrated the matter in 1786 and smoothed over the rift (Karaka 1884, pp. 219–233). Since the mid-nineteenth century Parsis have been among the leaders in the Indian trend toward modernization; their example has been emulated by other modernizing groups in their region and elsewhere in the country.

Christians of the Earlier and of the Later Foundation

Christianity was brought to India in two main movements separated by more than a millennium. The first movement occurred in the early centuries after Christ when Christian travelers, following the trade routes from the Levant, settled along the coast of Kerala, made converts, and established permanent groups of Christians there. The second wave began in the sixteenth century when Europeans seized political control over trade centers and eventually over the entire subcontinent. This second introduction of Christianity into India was different from the other religious introductions in that it was carried forward by missionaries, who were professionally dedicated to making converts. Their efforts, moreover, were bolstered by the powers of the state and by the obvious material advantages of their European culture.

The first advent of Christianity produced social results like those caused by the first entries of Jews and of Muslims along the west coast of India. The ancient Christian population of Kerala was much larger than that of the Jews but not so large as that of the Muslims. Known as Syrian Christians because their liturgy is mainly in Syriac, they long maintained intermittent contacts with centers of Christianity outside India. Like the Cochin Jews, they too possess ancient copper plates that confer privileges on some of their families; they seem to have been under the protection of Rajas in medieval times, perhaps because they acted, as did the Cochin Jews, as reliable middlemen in trade and as functionaries in government (Anantakrishna Ayyar 1926, pp. 50–57).

As tradesmen and government servants the Syrian Christians were ranked above the artisan and laboring jatis but well below the priestly and warrior groups. Their way of life, except for religious practice, was not notably different from that of their neighbors of similar rank and occupation. They grouped themselves into a number of jatis; the principal differences among them were denominational and territorial (Anantakrishna Ayyar 1926, pp. 60–61). The jatis of Syrian Christians jockeyed for status as other sectarian jatis have done, and like them they became part of the local caste orders.

The second, European, introduction of Christianity posed fresh problems to Indians. The religion was seen as an adjunct of a most powerful culture and society. The culture could yield great material benefits but it was so thoroughly alien that few Indians could imagine themselves as full participants in it. Hence the religion, freely profferred as the one part of that culture they were urged to share, seemed more the property and hallmark of the foreign rulers than the spiritual legacy for all mankind that their missionaries said it was. Some attributes of the rulers were not unattractive, but other attributes would undermine the fundamental ritual basis of high rank.

Moreover, although the Christian missionaries insisted that all believers were equal before God, they and other Europeans kept meticulously aloof—as much so as the haughtiest of indigenous sects—from any token of social equality, whether in everyday dining or in intermarriage. The equality they insisted on seemed confined to the hours of church worship and even then the padre sahib was unquestionably the actual first among putative equals.

The European administrators by and large were content to have it so. From the earliest Portuguese establishment to the high noon of British control, they found it useful to be accepted as a species of especially powerful and socially distant Kshatriyas who would not try to impose their own religion on all their subjects, though they would welcome and even favor converts. But some of the missionaries felt caught in a strong dilemma. Their sacred commitment was to bring as many heathen as possible into the fold, to change their lives religiously. But they soon found that to change lives religiously they also had to change them socially, since ritual and social elements were inseparable in the Indian view. And shifting their converts' social organization was a mighty task. The alternative was to accommodate the missionaries' standards to Indian social values.

One of the first to face this dilemma with courage and ability was Roberto de Nobili, an Italian Jesuit, scion of Tuscan patricians, a prodigy of learning in his youth, related to two Popes and nephew of the distinguished and influential Cardinal Bellarmine (Cronin 1959). De Nobili set foot on Indian soil in Goa in 1605 and died in Mylapore near Madras City in 1656. During the half century of his missionary work he did what no other European missionary had been able to do before and what exceedingly few did after. He set out to conquer Hinduism from within, to convert by colloquy with Brahmins in their sacred language and to convince all Hindus through the example of his ascetic life.

He lived that life as a sadhu, clad in the saffron robes of an ascetic, keeping to high standards of Hindu ritual purity in his diet, in his daily activities, and in his social contacts. Almost all his missionary efforts were carried on where there were few or no Europeans, where no European force could protect him should the local Raja or the populace turn against him. He learned to speak Tamil and other vernacular languages fluently so that he could convince the temporal rulers; he mastered Sanskrit and Sanskritic scripture so that he could sway learned Brahmins on their own theological grounds through the cogency of his arguments for

Christianity. He believed that once he was able to make convinced Christians of those at the top of the social order, all the rest would follow.

He did have successes. He and his associates made a good many converts, 150,000 by the end of the seventeenth century, but there were also great difficulties. Near to his locality in Madurai, a mission of Portuguese priests had established a church among fishermen. Wearing their contaminating shoes, eating their polluted diet, ignorant of the language and the civilization, such priests could still do something for fishermen and others of the lowest jatis; they could do nothing but arouse disgust when they tried to come close to Brahmins and others who valued their own high status.

De Nobili could not associate with such priests and still maintain his reputation as a sadhu worthy of respect. He could not break totally with them lest his religious superiors take offense, as they indeed did from time to time. He tried visiting his fellow Europeans under cover of darkness and eventually had to face hostile formal investigations from both his own Church and from the indigenous authorities.

De Nobili's strategy for the conversion of India was an extension of that propounded earlier by Saint Francis Xavier and it was carried on for several decades after de Nobili's death. A set of instructions for missionaries given in 1659, as quoted by a contemporary Jesuit, offered these recommendations. "Ne vous efforcez pas de détourner les peuples de leur rites et coutumes, pourvu qu'ils ne soient pas ouvertement contraires à la religion et aux bonnes moeurs. Quoi de plus absurde que de vouloir remplacer ces coutumes par celles de la France, de l'Espagne, ou de l'Italie ou de toute autre partie de l'Europe? Ce ne sont pas ces coutumes qu'il faut implanter, mais la Foi, qui ne repousse les usages d'ancien pays, s'ils ne sont pas mauvais, mais veut au contraire qu'on les conserve" (Castets 1931, pp. 564–565).

These sage instructions could not be carried out for long. To keep the customs of this country meant that Christians, both the missionaries and converts, had to keep social distance among the jatis of their converts. For a time those who followed de Nobili's lead actually did this and a Catholic priest who ministered to Brahmins avoided any contact with a fellow Jesuit who worked among untouchables. But this accommodation to jati practices clashed too violently with European notions and it was banned in a papal decree of 1704. The same decree declared that Christianity should be presented to Indians in a form that was not repugnant to them. Catholic missionaries did generally make some attempts to respect purity observances, as in abstaining from beef and even other kinds of meat, but they were far from ritually pure by Indian standards (O'Malley 1941, pp. 50–53; Neill 1934, pp. 60–62).

After Protestant missionaries arrived in considerable numbers in the nineteenth century, their denominational conferences regularly discussed caste divisions among converts and passed resolutions condemning jati practices among Christians (Raj 1959, pp. 64–77). Some of the missionaries, both Catholic and Protestant, recognized how impossibly difficult was the rootless position of any convert who faithfully tried to follow their social as well as spiritual advice.

The Indologist Max Müller recognized this clearly, even though he himself never visited India. Indian converts were not admitted to what they saw as English caste, he noted, so a potential convert dreaded the prospect of an isolated position. Müller recommended that measures should be adopted to give converts something in place of the caste position that they would lose. "In a certain sense no man ought to be without caste, without friends who take care of him, without companions who watch him, without associates whose good opinion he values, without companions with whom he can work for a common cause." He added that the healthy life of a political body, meaning a modern political body, can only be supported by means of associations, circles, leagues, guilds, clans, clubs, or parties; ". . . and in a country where caste takes the place of all this, the abolition of caste would be tantamount to a complete social disorganization" (Müller 1868, p. 358).

Converts might have adapted the religion to the social system more smoothly, as indeed the Syrian Christians did, had it not been for the overseeing presence of the resident missionaries. These men were generally against the Indian social order yet were unable to provide feasible alternatives. As a result, converts were mainly made from very low jatis, from those who had nothing to lose and perhaps could gain something in status and livelihood. In the Punjab, as Khushwant Singh comments, Christian came to be synonymous with sweeper despite some conversions from the Sikh elite (1966, p. 138).

The Abbé Dubois sadly wrote about the low state of Christianity in India at the beginning of the nineteenth century, attributing the decline of Christians in number and in the quality of their devotion to the "immoral and disorderly conduct of the Europeans," who overran the country and provided horrid examples of Christianity. "A Hindu who embraces Christianity nowadays must make up his mind to lose everything that makes life pleasant. . . . He is abandoned and shunned by everyone" (1928, p. 301).

The Abbé was condemning the conduct of European soldiers and officials, but he implied that the missionaries too, in their disregard of Indian ritual sensibilities, made it hard for villagers to accept the religion. In spite of this, many did become Christians, though they were a small fraction of the population in most areas. The total Christian population in India in 1961 stood at some eight million. Some who were not untouchables were converted for reasons of factional advantage, others for the connection they might make with secular power and especially for educational opportunities, and some for essentially religious reasons.

One who became a Christian as a result of his spiritual quest was Narayan Vamen Tilak (1862–1919), a learned Chitpavan Brahmin. He became renowned among Christians in Maharashtra and wrote notable poetry in Marathi as well as numerous tracts, articles, and sermons. He did much to transpose Christian concepts into a language of poetry and prose that could appeal to the literati of Maharashtra. But by his day, the tide of Indian intellectual opinion was already firmly set against the proffered religion of the rulers (cf. Winslow 1923; L. Tilak 1950).

A Christian Jati: Nadars of Tamil Nadu (Madras)

In spite of the difficulties inherent in conversion to Christianity, functioning jatis of converts did take form and were articulated into their local social hierarchies. An example is the jati of Christian Nadars in Madras, who were noted above in the discussion of caste associations. From their traditional occupation of brewing and selling alcoholic drink, a good many came to prosper in more lucrative and respectable occupations, mainly as traders and money lenders. They became known for their industry and zeal for education. Contemporary Nadars, both Christian and Hindu, share the view that Nadars are hardworking, enterprising, thrifty, and reliable (Raj 1959, pp. 87, 222, 261).

Perhaps it was because a good many Nadars were enterprising and were very restive about their low status that some of them took the avenue of conversion as a way to better rank despite the outcasting and all the other difficulties besetting that road. One of the earliest Protestant converts among Nadars had previously been a leader in *Shaktipuja*, the cult in which caste barriers were formally broken in a ceremony of eating and drinking together by people of different jatis. He was the leader among the fifteen families in his village who, in the words of a contemporary account, "are attached to this kind of worship, and they esteem it a great honour to have renounced caste . . . but having heard the word of God, he has become a Christian and abandoned Saktipuja" (quoted in Raj 1959, p. 123). It may be that he found in Christianity a better instrument than *Shaktipuja* to accomplish the same mobility goals.

In any event, the number of Nadar converts grew steadily well into the twentieth century. Though the missionaries urged them to become one united body in the fellowship of Christianity, it was not possible for Nadars and other converts, especially in South India, to do so. Hilda Raj points out that the converts "were sorely in need of belonging somewhere socially and culturally." They could not possibly belong with Europeans in either respect and other converts "who had higher social status than the Nadars would not join with them, those from a lower social status would not be socially acceptable to the Nadars" (1959, p. 215).

Hence they had no alternative but to form a new jati once they had been received into the new religion and were consequently thrown out of their natal jati. The new jati became almost as rigorous an endogamous unit as their original jati. The Christian Nadars have much the same marriage preferences and affinal relations as do the Hindu Nadars; they use similar kinship terms and roles; they observe similar practices of ritual seclusion and purification (H. Raj 1959, pp. 183, 199, 207–212).

Splinter groups separated from the Christian Nadars as they did from other religion-based jatis. One schismatic sect developed briefly under a leader who preached that the European elements in Christianity perverted the true belief, that the New Testament was the chief purveyor of this taint and so true believers should revere only the laws and commandments of the Old Testament. The founder of this revelation accordingly called himself Rabbi and sought correspondence with Rabbis elsewhere. When Hilda Raj searched for this sect in 1956 it had disappeared without trace in the villages where once it had attracted followers (1959, pp. 131–135).

In the end, Nadars who became Christians did not gain status advantage in the villages over those who remained Hindus. But they did have easier access to education. A relatively larger proportion of them have qualified for professional positions and prestigeful employment; a good many have migrated to the cities.

The need for wider alliances also touched the Christian Nadars, and one effort at fusion has been the federation of Protestant denominations in the Church of South India. Another is the Nadar caste association, which we have discussed in an earlier chapter. Any Nadar, whether Hindu or Christian, may belong to it and Christian Nadars do participate in its activities.

Among the Christian Nadars, as among other Christian converts, the missionaries' exhortations that they change their social system could scarcely succeed (cf. Risley 1951, pp. 80–82). The exhorters had little appreciation of the nature of such change or the drastic personal consequences of attempting it. The missionary approach of de Nobili and his followers, that of accommodating to the caste system and working for religious change within it, was also not feasible because it conflicted at too many points with the standard of the European social system, especially in its colonial version. The second movement of Christianity into India seems to have had the greatest impact on Indian society through its efforts in modern education.

Religious Conversion and Recurrent Change

In sum, the introduced religions produced social results like those of the indigenous sects and for similar reasons. Converts were redistributed into new groups or revised the forms of worship of existing groups, but the groups functioned as component parts of the general social system and their members acted socially as jati members. In certain respects Muslims and Christians made special contributions to Indian civilization. They maintained links with coreligionists of other civilizations and were instrumental in the reciprocal influence between civilizations. The Muslims' contribution in this manner was greater in earlier centuries, the Christians' contribution greater in more recent times.

Those who adopted a new faith, whether the faith was an indigenous sect or an introduced religion, eventually reconciled their new doctrine to the traditional system. In doing so they completed the pattern of recurrent change through religion and also reentered the cycles of recurrent change through jati mobility.

In addition to these types of recurrent change within local systems and within the general system of Indian society, there has been another kind of repetitive process. It has involved the inflow of tribal peoples into caste society, a movement that required them to shift from tribal principles of social action to those of caste society.

CHAPTER 31   The Accretion of
Tribal Peoples

THE shift of tribal peoples into jati society has
been going on for many centuries and it is still an ongoing, indeed
an accelerating, process. More than thirty million people were
counted as tribals in the 1961 Census of India. Many of them are
taking on jati practices and are becoming integrated into local
hierarchies in ways followed by other tribesmen long before them.
Those ways form another process of recurrent change in jati society, not by internal regrouping as in religious movements, but by
the gradual transfer of individuals and groups from a tribal kind of
social system into local caste systems. Once a tribal group becomes
a jati, its members are likely to enter the usual mobility drives as
do members of sectarian and other jatis.

Tribesmen who adopt jati customs are, often unwittingly, changing some of their primordial principles of conduct. They are moving
themselves and their groups into a different systemic level of
culture and society, in which fresh potentials for further development become possible. Difficult choices and personal dilemmas are
involved in that move, complicated by the new avenues to potential power and the newer models of the educated elite.

The discussion of tribal changes, in this chapter and in the
next, deals with the nature of tribal social systems and the recurrent
transfers from them into jati systems. This analysis also provides a
contrastive perspective in which to view the whole system of caste
society in India. That view in turn suggests some general differences between tribal social systems and those of civilizations.

Tribe: Official Designation and Actual Characteristics

The shift into jati society is usually gradual and undramatic. There is no absolute cultural or social distinction between all tribal and all caste peoples, but rather a range of variation between tribal and caste traits. At the middle of the range there may be very little difference between a group that considers itself a tribe and one that claims to be a jati.

The requirements of law and administration, however, demand a sharp definition of who is to be counted as a tribesman. Article 46 of the Indian Constitution directs that "The State shall promote with special care the educational and economic interests of the weaker sections of the people, and, in particular, of the Scheduled Castes and Scheduled Tribes and shall protect them from social injustice and all forms of exploitation." Other articles of the Constitution confirm this directive and much legislation has been enacted to implement it. Special grants, scholarships, government preferments, have been made available to members of a scheduled group.

That schedule was initially promulgated by Presidential order and can now be modified only by an Act of Parliament. So the administrative definition of who is a tribesman was set by presidential or parliamentary decision without much social analysis. The courts have had to clarify some of the criteria in order to judge, for example, whether a man of the Moka Dora tribe whose family had, since 1928, claimed to be Kshatriyas should be allowed to take a seat in Parliament that was reserved for a member of a Scheduled Tribe (Galanter 1966b, pp. 631–635). But the court decisions have not materially altered the method of defining who is a tribesman by Presidential order.

The official schedule of tribes was used in the 1961 Census of India as similar designations had been used in earlier Censuses. Census officials have complained at regular decennial intervals that it is sometimes scarcely possible to draw a clear line between a tribal and a caste group (Ghurye 1959, pp. 1–9). The official listing, however, does cover the bulk of those whose culture can be placed within the tribal side of the scale by anthropological criteria. The spectrum of Indian groups called tribal, by official notification or popular usage, ranges from hunters and gatherers who are clearly outside of caste society, to settled village groups that function as jatis.

Some such groups are quite small; the Kotas discussed below are little over 1000 in population. Other tribal names are applied to millions; for example, the term "Santal" includes over three million. The larger tribal groupings are not organized entities; their tribal name refers to an array of groups who speak the same language and share certain cultural characteristics. They usually have little acquaintance with others of their name beyond their own locality. Within their villages and localities, however, most tribals have a strong sense of their distinctiveness and hold themselves to be quite separate from jati villagers. Language is a distinguishing trait for many tribal groups. The five million speakers of languages of the Munda stock are mainly tribesmen. But other tribal people do not have a distinctive language, and speak a dialect of the regional language.

Omitted from the present discussion are the tribal groups in the extreme eastern and western salients of the subcontinent. They were too different and too distant from jati society to have been much affected by it. The eastern groups, in what is now the North East Frontier Area, Nagaland, and adjacent sections, have ancient affinities with Southeast Asia in language and culture, though their more recent ties are with Indian culture and government (cf. Burling 1960). The Muslim tribesmen of the northwest are culturally closer to tribal peoples of the Afghan and Iranian highlands than to villagers of the Indo-Gangetic plains, though they too are now closer to their national government and society than they formerly were.

Most tribal peoples of India live in hilly or forested terrain where population is sparse and communication difficult. They are found from high valleys near the spine of the Himalayas to the hills of southernmost India. The main tribal territories are in the broad central belt of hill country from West Bengal, Bihar, and Orissa on the east, through Central India, to the upland parts of Rajasthan, Gujrat, and Maharashtra on the west. Although there are great cultural and social differences among the tribal peoples dispersed across India, some preliminary generalizations can be made about them.

Among none of these peoples is there the complete dichotomy between tribal culture and civilization which appeared when Europeans first confronted native peoples in the Americas, Africa, and Oceania. Even the most remote and isolated of tribal groups in India has certain cultural traits in common with jati people, as for example in the nature of ritual purity and pollution, in the worship of local spirits, and in kinship practices[1] (cf. Jay 1959, pp. 81–83, MS. 1961a, pp. 32–34).

Yet there are some broad distinctions between tribe and jati. Five aspects of these distinctions—social, political, economic, religious, and psychological—are discussed here, though it must be recognized that in actual behavior there are many nuances and gradations. Some tribals are closer to the jati side of the scale than are other tribal groups and, conversely, some jatis are closer to tribal characteristics than are other jatis (cf. Majumdar 1958b, pp. 355–361; Atal 1963; Dube 1960; Roy Burman 1960; Risley 1915, pp. 72–76; Vidyarthi 1967; Weber 1958, pp. 30–33).

Tribal and Jati Characteristics Compared

One difference between tribal and jati society is in the quality of interpersonal relations. In tribal life the principal links for the whole society are based on kinship. Individual equality as kinsman is assumed; dependency and subordination among men are minimized. Agnatic bonds form the fundamental web, affinal ties are of lesser significance. Lineages or clans tend to be the chief corporate units; they are often the principal units for land ownership, for defense, for economic production and consumption. Each man considers himself entitled to equal rights with every other. Although there is some subordination by age and sex, age dependency is relatively short and women's dependency relatively shallow.

An extreme example of individual autonomy in the tribal mode

[1] I became vividly aware of this at the start of my first field work in India when I reached a group of Urali who lived so deep in the Travancore jungle that they used tree houses to keep out of the way of the elephants and other wild animals with whom they shared their habitat. Yet these Urali, I soon discovered, would regularly pack their cooking utensils and set off for a day-long trip to market. They took their pots with them because, they said, they would not accept food cooked by anyone but an Urali (Mandelbaum 1939a).

are the Paliyans, food gatherers in the hills of western Madras. Social cooperation among them is limited to nuclear families and even the families are not very cohesive. They live in small settlements, but there is little cooperation among the families of a settlement. Marriage is an arrangement among equal families; marriages commonly founder because of suspected infringements of personal independence (Gardner 1966, pp. 393–397). There are very few tribal groups as starkly individualistic and atomistic as are these Paliyan. Most tribesmen have larger corporate groups than the family and wider social cooperation. Some even tolerate dependent groups in their villages; the tribal Konds of Baderi village in Orissa have a resident group of untouchables serving them. The great difference is that tribal people consider such dependent groups to be useful but dispensable adjuncts to their own society and not integral, necessary parts of it.

Jati members, especially of the higher ranks, hold quite different assumptions about kinship and society. The Brahmins of Kumbapettai village, for example, are not very far in miles from the jungle Paliyan but are at the other end of the tribe-jati scale. Kinship for them cannot possibly pervade all their society; they could not be Brahmins without subordinate jatis of laborers, artisans, sweepers. Far from assuming equality, they assume inequality in society; rather than minimizing dependency, they stress and try to prolong dependency in their families.

But the contrast is less sharp in other social matters and at other jati levels. In Kumbapettai, individual equality is asserted more within a low jati than among Brahmins, and personal dependency is slighted. Women of the lower jatis are less dependent and children are subordinate for shorter periods than they are among the Brahmins (Gough 1956, pp. 844–849). And even among Brahmins, equality among the senior men is strongly defended. A Brahmin householder considers himself equal to any other Brahmin head of family. He does not readily subordinate himself socially to any of them, and he is most jealous of his equal rights among the men of the jati.

Jati and tribe are similar units in that each is considered by its members to be an endogamous entity composed of ritual equals. The crucial difference is that jati members, on the one hand, believe they must have nonkinship relations with others in their society and that these relations must be arranged in an order of dominance and deference. Tribesmen, on the other hand, tend to see their society as held together by kinship bonds and do not insist on hierarchical ordering. Further, jati people expect their village society to be culturally heterogeneous, each jati following a unique combination of customary practices; tribesmen expect their society to be homogeneous or, at least, not necessarily heterogeneous.

In political organization, tribal people do not usually maintain strong, complex formations. These require specialized roles and dominant-subordinate relations, neither of which is congenial in the tribal view. Kingdoms were established among some of the more populous tribes, but most of them had only precarious support and the rulers often made use of specialists imported from caste society. Although tribesmen have often been under the nominal control of rajas, few have acted the part of faithful, steadfast, and subservient subjects (cf. Weber 1958, pp. 30–32).

Tribal lands tend to be vested in clans; the kinsmen of a clan together share a productive territory. This land-clan nexus is singled out as the main differentiating feature between tribe and jati in Bailey's analysis of the tribal Konds and their caste neighbors. The Konds have localized clans, "Membership of the clan is, under this system, a condition of holding and exploiting land in the clan territory. A right to land is not achieved by subordination to anyone else, but by equality as a kinsman" (1961, pp. 11–12).

Direct access to land, according to Bailey, is the prime test of tribal organization. The larger the proportion of a given group in India that has direct access to land, the closer that group is to a tribal kind of organization. Conversely, the author concludes, the larger the proportion of those in a group whose right to land is achieved through a dependent relationship, the more does that group maintain a jati organization (Bailey 1961, pp. 11–14; also Bailey 1958, 1960).

This test has been criticized by Louis Dumont (1962) as being too narrow and by Surajit Sinha as not corresponding closely enough with other criteria of tribal organization. Sinha would rather take the land tenure criterion as one among other distinguishing features (1965, p. 60). In general, tribal people believe that a productive territory should be shared by relatives of a clan or lineage and that every such relative has some rights to that territory. Most jati members hold no such assumption, though some in North India, as the Jats of Meerut division, share this basic concept (Pradhan 1965, p. 1823; Kudryavtsev 1964).

Another difference between tribe and jati in political organization lies in the mode of incorporating new groups, whether migrants or allies. The tribal Konds incorporated new groups haltingly, occasionally by making them into fictive kinsmen; they could cooperate effectively with agnates and affines but could not readily deal with nonkinsmen. The Oriya villagers had no such difficulties; they could have economic, political, even religious collaboration with others without disturbing the kinship spheres of their jatis.

Tribal societies are more "segmentary." Tribesmen see the component groups of their society as more autonomous, viewing each group as similar in function and status to any other segment of the tribal society. Jati societies are more "organic" in that each jati is part of an organic whole; its members provide necessary, specialized functions for the whole. Each unit is not taken to be autonomous or necessarily equal to any other (Bailey 1960b, pp. 243–248; 1961, pp. 12, 15).

In subsistence economy very few tribal groups still are hunters and gatherers, but some continue to practice shifting agriculture. This, as was noted in Chapter 22, is variously called slash-and-burn, swidden, or axe cultivation. A patch of jungle or forest is cut down, burned over, planted for several seasons until soil fertility declines. It is then abandoned as the cultivators move on to repeat the process on another nearby tract. There is a certain congruence between shifting agriculture and tribal organization. A swidden economy cannot support so many in a given locality as can be maintained by plough agriculture. A relatively low population density per acre can be supported by swidden methods, but added input of labor does not yield enough to feed added people. Accordingly, there was little need for incorporative social mechanisms under swidden agriculture. The constraints of the technology precluded the possibility of much incorporation (cf. Geertz 1963, pp. 1–37; Elwin 1964, pp. 48–56).

The greater social potentials of plough agriculture were demonstrated to the Konds when some of them switched from swidden cultivation. Many then came down from the hills into the valleys and concentrated in larger groups. Rice fields, being productive capital investments, were worth fighting for as swidden lands were not, and therefore political alliances were developed and strengthened (Bailey 1960b, pp. 63–68). A swidden economy does not provide a sufficient base for strong political leadership or enough surplus to support the specialists in crafts and religion necessary for a jati society. A plough economy does provide these and also fosters political grouping and action. However, the congruence of social and economic organization is not absolute; some people who are clearly tribal in social organization nevertheless practice plough agriculture (Fernandez 1965). Conversely, there are jati villages where population is sparse and agricultural productivity low, but where jati standards are observed. Plough agriculture was probably essential for the original development of the civilization, producing a surplus that could be used to support technical specialists, state government, and full-time religionists. The main economic differences between tribal and jati societies in recent centuries, however, have been more related to economic values than to agricultural technology.

Tribesmen place little value on surplus accumulation, on the uses of capital, and on market trading (S. Sinha 1958b, pp. 509–510; 1963). To cite an extreme example again, the Jungle Chenchus are gatherers and hunters whom Fürer-Haimendorf studied in their remote jungle area of what is now Andhra Pradesh (1943, pp. 57–83; 1967a, pp. 17–24). Their main subsistence at the time of the study (1940–1949) was from the day-to-day collecting of food from the jungle. They did not store food against an emergency and lived from hand to mouth in a nearly literal sense of the cliché. There was little economic cooperation among their families, each being an autonomous economic unit, though they did aid each other in illness or accident. A few of them cultivated small plots and kept cattle, but in general there was quick consumption of all that was produced. Any surplus or windfall was rapidly distributed and consumed.

They knew about settled village life and indeed some Chenchus of this Mahbubnagar district migrated to jati villages. But the others remained in the jungle because they preferred the life there even though they knew about the boons of the more foresighted, controlled village life. There are very few tribal peoples who take so little interest in tomorrow as do these jungle Chenchus, but in general, tribesmen are much more given to quick consumption and generous distribution than are caste villagers. Those of the lowest jatis in a caste village are sometimes accused of similar inclinations by their wealthier and higher neighbors. The high label the low as feckless and improvident, as caste superiors are apt to do elsewhere in the world. This is a convenient rationale for the superiority of the high and they may try to see to it that the low have little opportunity to be provident and purposeful.

It is generally true that the values of a tribal group, in the aspects here noted, are more like those of the low jatis in a locality than of the high. But though Harijans and tribesmen may be similarly disinterested in long-term planning, there is a main difference between them in the pursuit of wealth. The aspiring Harijan who accumulates wealth is acting in a way that is respected in his society, though he himself may face the most bitter opposition, but a tribesman who works hard beyond the call of tribal custom and who is closefisted goes counter to the values and opinions of his society. Tribesmen are not averse to accumulating food stores, to deferring consumption, to maximizing productivity, but they characteristically feel that these worthy pursuits should not be pressed so hard as to interfere with the prompt prospect of pleasure.

Tribesmen do not usually take to trading or to making financial transactions. The trader's role is counter to their preference for openhanded relations. Thus, as Martin Orans tells, some of the Santal tribesmen try trading, but "It is difficult to square the basic reciprocity of relations in a kin society like that of the Santal with the impersonal and contractual relations of the market." Fledgling entrepreneurs usually fail in business because they are overgenerous in extending credit and underinsistent in collecting debts. Most know something about the ways of the market and the common swindling manipulations. "But the traditional Santal, once at the market, is too eager a buyer, too poor a haggler, and too readily drawn into pleasant social intercourse to hold his own" (Orans 1965, pp. 40–41).

Government officials have long deplored the fact that traders from the plains almost always exploit the tribesmen with whom they deal. The tribal seller often gets absurdly low prices for what he has to offer and pays immoderately high prices, often forfeiting his land when it is worth taking. This happens because a tribesman usually prefers to act as a generous kinsman rather than as a self-seeking trader intent only on personal profit. Coupled with this is the priority tribesmen give to immediate enjoyment over deferred gratification.

Most tribal people can and do work diligently when necessary, but typically they do not find much pleasure in the sweat of labor, in the righteousness of abnegation, or in visions of future power. Perhaps, a tribesman may agree, the deferred rewards might be greater in the end, but who can tell when the end will come and what unforeseen difficulties may intervene?

In religion also there are differences between the tribal and the jati sides of the cultural scale. Tribals tend to stress the short-term, pragmatic functions of religion as well as long-term transcendental functions, and they do not differentiate these two aspects as sharply as do caste villagers. As was noted before, the transcendental functions have to do with the long-term welfare of society, with the explanation and maintenance of institutions, with the continuity of society by the proper passage of individuals through the life cycle from impending birth to departure of the soul. The pragmatic functions are for personal benefits, for immediate needs, for individual welfare. Jati people tend to maintain different forms, practitioners, and behavior patterns for each of these two aspects of religion. The transcendental complex is mainly in the keeping of the higher jatis and the pragmatic in the charge of the lower, though both complexes can be used by villagers of all jatis. Tribal peoples do not maintain two distinct complexes; they tend to use similar forms, practitioners, and patterns for both functions of religion.

In jati villages the priest, who serves the universal gods of Sanskrit scripture, is a religious technician quite separate from the shaman, who has direct, personal contact with local deities. The priest, often a Brahmin, holds hereditary office and high jati rank while the shaman is usually from the lower jatis and gains prestige through his personal achievements. The priest is supposed to be an examplar of ritual purity while the shaman is mainly expected to demonstrate the immediacy of supernatural forces. Tribesmen do not usually make such distinctions between shaman and priest, who may serve the same gods or who may be combined in the same person. Both help chiefly to deliver supernatural boons rather than to demonstrate the sacrosanct life (Mandelbaum 1966; 1964, pp. 8–11).

A tribal religion typically combines features of the tribal culture of the region with some from Hindu worship. Tribal peoples do not have direct access to the rich resources of scripture, and so their religions tend to be less systematized, less specialized and elaborated than is the Hinduism of the higher jatis. The lower jatis in a village may have as little direct knowledge of scripture as tribal people but their beliefs and practices are more directly influenced by scriptural Hinduism.

Asceticism is usually respected by tribesmen as a powerful way of exerting pressure on certain gods, but it is not elevated as the supreme path to the good life or to any blessed afterlife. Nor do tribesmen commonly set great value on puritanical modes of conduct in this life for the sake of a happier hereafter (cf. S. Sinha 1958b, p. 512).

This is well documented in Fürer-Haimendorf's comparison of moral concepts among the South Asian peoples whom he has studied. The results of his remarkably extensive fieldwork have been published in three of the major works on peninsular Indian tribes as well as in several books on the tribes of northeast India and of Nepal. He has also studied a Hindu jati, the Chetris of Nepal. The Chetris believe that supernal merit can be gained from "morally positive conduct"; most tribesmen have little or no such idea. "For although some of the tribes also believe in a sequence of lives, and others set great store on the acquisition of *social* merit which raises a person's status in this life, in none of the tribal societies did we encounter the idea that moral choices affect a person's fate in a future existence" (Fürer-Haimendorf 1967a, p. 168). The moral outlook under a tribal system of society is much more concentrated on this world; such a society has very little interest in any other.

Finally, there is a psychological factor that underlies the other differences. Tribal people generally take direct, unalloyed satisfaction in pleasures of the senses, whether in food, alcoholic drink, sex, song, or dance. The "twice-born" tend to be ambivalent about such pleasures; they are inclined to defer them or to refine them or to surround them with elaborate ritual. Kshatriya men (though not their women) are allowed more latitude for pleasures of the senses, but still in a more restricted way than tribesmen enjoy.

This contrast is well described by G. M. Carstairs, who studied it from his dual vantage as psychiatrist and anthropologist. He tells how his understanding of the higher jatis was sharpened when a band of Bhil tribesmen appeared in the Rajasthan town where he was working. They performed a three-day religious dance, and in the process provided Carstairs with the contrastive perspective he needed. "Here was clearly a people whose values were strikingly different to those cherished by my Hindu informants, as the latter indeed insisted" (1957, p. 126). The Bhils were boisterously demonstrative; they shouted, sang, laughed aloud, and were unashamedly drunk in public. Shocking to the townsmen was the open display of affection between a Bhil man and his wife.

When Carstairs later stayed in a Bhil village, his medical patients included many with venereal diseases. Not one, however, mentioned the complaint he had so often heard from other men, that they had suffered loss of strength through sexual relations. The Bhils have no use for celibacy or asceticism. They enjoy life zestfully, accepting pleasure and dangers as they come (they are a violent people), and in their homeland "they regard themselves as inferior to none, carry themselves proudly and look strangers squarely in the eye" (Carstairs 1957, pp. 132–136).

The capacities of tribal peoples for direct, spontaneous emotion and personal independence captivated a good many Westerners who came to know them. British officials were apt to feel protective about tribals—after they had crushed all traces of armed rebellion (cf. Hutton 1941). Special legislation was enacted to safeguard tribal interests and such legislation increased after independence. One eloquent student and defender of tribal peoples in India, Verrier Elwin, tells in his autobiography how greatly he was influenced by their style of life. The youth dormitories of the Muria tribe conveyed to him a message which, he wrote, is typically Indian. It is that human love and its physical expression is "beautiful, clean and precious" (1964, pp. 168–169). This is scarcely typical of the Indian ascetic tradition, but it is known to tribal people in India.

Tribesmen are drawn together by their bent for enjoyment.

Martin Orans tells that when a Santal meets a fellow tribesman from a distant place, one of the first questions he asks, in the traditional custom, is "How is pleasure in your region?" He thinks of "pleasure" as preeminently a social experience—the festive atmosphere at ceremonies, the dancing, drinking, and comradeship that are enjoyed then. "Pleasure, as the Santal understand the term, is a shared understanding which creates immediate bonds with cotribals wherever they may be from." (1965, pp. 8–9).

This happy solidarity is one reason why some have resisted jati relations. There were other reasons as well. Until the nineteenth century most tribal groups had very little contact with jati villagers and civilizational centers. Many were additionally insulated because they spoke languages different from those used by the nearest jati people. However, some who have had long and near acquaintance with jati people have still remained tribesmen. The Konds of Baderi village have lived within two miles of an Oriya caste village for perhaps as many as eight centuries and have remained tribal Konds. There is a jati of Kond potters in the Oriya village, so not all resisted the pull of jati life. Many did resist, however, until recent decades when the movement toward the jati end of the continuum accelerated. Like any continuum, this one involves both differentiating features and common properties. The most remote of tribal groups carries culture elements of the civilization; the most sophisticated of jatis is also a putative kin group like a tribe.

The Shift Toward Jati Values

As a tribal people begin to take on jati traits, perhaps restricting their diet, they become involved in other jati values as well, as in restricting their social contacts (cf. Sinha 1958b, pp. 515–517; 1965, pp. 61–64). When members of a low jati alter their conduct in order to rise socially, they already have such values as asceticism or hierarchy embedded in their culture. They know about them; they are not reluctant to acknowledge and to enact them when they can. But in tribal life, little esteem is given to ascetic ways, to pervasive hierarchy, to other values of the "twice-born" model. There is apt to be, therefore, more internal struggle within a tribe about adopting a caste trait because it may be taken to symbolize, and rightly so, a shift away from tribal values. Among the Kotas, a change in men's hair style became a grave issue of factional conflict (Mandelbaum 1941 and 1960).

When a tribal group does become drawn into a jati order, its members, too, try to cast off demeaning customs and to adopt prestigious ones. At first they need not discard much, perhaps only such gross matters as cow sacrifice, but as they become more actively engaged in the competition among jatis, they feel pressed to alter more of their culture. Their tribal values become changed at different rates but in the same general direction.

In social relations, they shift from relative equality among kinsmen toward the hierarchy in which dependence is incumbent on everyone. Even those at the very top of a jati order must depend on those inferior to them. Role specialization does increase productivity, and social stratification does provide incentive for aspiration, but both require greater dependency than does the tribal norm.

In political affairs, tribesmen usually feel small obligation as subjects of a ruler or as citizens of a state. But with involvement in jati society they become more open to political influence from outside their communities, and their own village affairs tend to become more politicized. Factions and feuds are not absent from tribal society, but alliance politics seem to be more prevalent in jati society. Few jatis feel so securely entrenched that they can be oblivious of challenge from others; in a tribal society there are fewer positions of power to be challenged.

In economic relations, tribesmen shift from sharing liberally with all in a small community to more selective and directed sharing with those of a larger society. From dealing quite openhandedly with kinsmen, they engage in more limited transactions with jajmani associates and in the guarded games of commerce with customers and merchants.

The transition in religious outlook shifts a tribesman from a close and knowable cosmos to a vast universe that is unknowable in all its reaches. Much of the knowledge in the more complex religion is vested in scriptures that are in the keeping of specialist jatis. The daily discipline of one's own body and mind becomes a main arena of religious observance. In the course of the shift some elements of the tribal religion are incorporated into the pragmatic complex and others are merged with Sanskritic deities and rites. The pragmatic functions of religion are relegated from primary position to an important but secondary place. The local tribal godling may be transformed from an autonomous power to a subservient specialist. As tribesmen become drawn into the race for respectability, more of their tribal ways must be given up. Dancing at ceremonies, libations of alcoholic liquor, and youth dormitories are among the customs disapproved by religious arbiters, who teach that some acts are good or bad morally, quite apart from their immediate consequences.

Another kind of change is in self-view. A tribesman is inclined to see himself as an independent agent who prizes the sense pleasures through all his life. As a jati member a man must defer some pleasures, he must deny others for the sake of his jati's status in the village and of his personal fate through eternity. These constraints are supposed to yield future rewards, though tribesmen have often been dubious about that.

The assimilation of tribal groups has gone on for a very long time. The tribes of the Gangetic plain, according to D. D. Kosambi, were conquered by and assimilated into the kingdoms of Kosala and Magadha beginning in the sixth century B.C. (1965, pp. 120–132). From the third century B.C. there are references to tribes in the edicts of Ashoka, as in this passage about Ashoka's benevolence: "The Beloved of the Gods even reasons with the forest tribes in his empire, and seeks to reform them. But the Beloved of the Gods is not only compassionate, he is also powerful, and he tells them to repent, lest they be slain" (Basham 1954, pp. 53–54). Tribal peoples in later eras were similarly warned that if they were to be the beloved of the Beloved of (other) Gods, they had best stop raiding the king's subjects and change their savage ways.

During the British regime, the raiding was largely quelled, but officials were not so enthusiastic about changes in other tribal customs. They frequently deplored the assimilation of tribal groups into jati society. Sir Herbert H. Risley noted the process in his report as Commissioner of the 1901 Census, having observed it since 1873. He wrote "All over India at the present moment tribes are gradually and insensibly being transformed into castes." He hoped that future studies would "throw some light upon the singular course of evolution by which large masses of people surrender a condition of comparative freedom and take in exchange a condition which becomes more burdensome in proportion as its status is higher" (1915, p. 72). This movement is generally irreversible. Tribes have often become jatis, only rarely and under exceptional circumstances have jati members turned to tribal practices.[2]

Attractions and Repulsions of Jati Society

To illustrate some of the ways by which tribesmen become drawn into jati society, examples from three tribal peoples can be considered. The first is from the tribal Reddi (not to be confused with jatis of the same name) of the Bison Hills in Andhra Pradesh; the others are the Raj Gonds and the Hill Maria Gonds.

The Reddi example centers on the activities of a single family, that of a headman. Reddi chieftains were appointed as headmen (called *muttadar*) by the British and given responsibilities for the collection of revenue. They received an income for their duties and had more contact with outsiders than did their fellow tribesmen. By 1941–1943, when Fürer-Haimendorf studied the group, some of these headmen had added plough cultivation to shifting agriculture and had taken Lingayat religious mentors. They were wealthier and held themselves to be superior to ordinary Reddis.

One such headman had gone further and had declared, as had his father before him, that he was not a tribesman at all. He asserted that he did not belong to any Reddi clan, that he was a "Raj Reddi" of Kshatriya ancestry. It was known that his mother had been a tribal girl, though a Brahmin had been hired to perform a special ceremony at her wedding that purportedly enabled her to eat with her husband.

This headman had married a girl "of his own caste" from a distant place, again with the benefit of Brahmin clergy. Other headmen sneered at his pretensions but "locally his claims to higher caste are generally recognized and his aloofness from the social and ritual affairs of other Reddis places him outside and above tribal life and distinguishes his status vis-à-vis his subjects from that of

---

[2] One possible case is that of the Badagas of the Nilgiri Hills, who came from the plains of Mysore into the isolated Nilgiri area some time after the twelfth century. They presumably were a jati people at the time of their migration and adopted some tribal characteristics (Hockings 1965, pp. 12–13).

other muttadar, who live within the fold of Reddi tribal custom."
The other Reddi headmen had begun to bridge the cultural distance between tribe and jati; this one had, apparently successfully, crossed over through the unusual expedient of establishing his own family jati (Fürer-Haimendorf 1945, pp. 167–173).

Contrasting examples of the movement from tribal to jati society are from two divisions of the Gond peoples. The Raj Gonds have moved directly into high jati rank; the Hill Maria Gonds have tried to reject jati entanglements yet have become involved in them. There are more than four million Gonds in all; their language is of the Dravidian stock and their main locale is in Andhra Pradesh and adjoining states. The Raj Gond case was briefly mentioned above.

There were Raj Gond kingdoms in earlier centuries, though their Rajas did not alter the tribal character of the Gonds (S. Sinha 1962, pp. 61–65; Fuchs 1960). Raj Gonds are now the dominant jati in certain villages of Andhra Pradesh, one of them being Dewara in Adilabad district. When S. C. Dube studied this village in 1950, all the villagers acknowledged that leadership in local affairs was largely in the hands of the Raj Gonds. This was so in spite of the highly unusual fact that these Raj Gonds were still sacrificing cows and eating beef. Yet men of the other jati-groups, except Brahmins and some weavers, accepted water from them. The lower Hindu jatis also accepted food from them.

One reason for this exceptional latitude was that the Raj Gonds wielded strong power in their locality and long had done so. Another reason was that the district had been part of the dominions of the Muslim prince, the Nizam of Hyderabad, whose government, not unlike the British, was inclined to take the side of the tribals in any conflict with jati people. At the time of Dube's study, the princely rule had been deposed but the new governmental influence had not yet taken full effect (1955a, pp. 189–190). These Raj Gonds had entered into jati relations practically on their own terms. Other jatis were immigrants into their territory who had accepted their suzerainty, and their dominance had been further buttressed by the state.

The Hill Maria Gonds, by contrast, have kept themselves isolated from jati relations and have resisted Hindu influences. They show the kind of distaste for jati ways which has slowed the assimilation of some tribal groups. The Hill Maria Gonds are among the most isolated of the Gond tribesmen. They number about ten thousand people in the forested hills of Bastar, the largest district of Andhra Pradesh and one with exceptionally poor communications (Jay MS. 1961a; Grigson 1949). Hill Marias know about commensal taboos and about other jati restraints even though there are only a few families of jati people in their territory. They know that they may take food from some but not from others, and that there are jatis whose members will not accept food from them. That knowledge is useful mainly when Hill Marias attend a regional fair or market.

Their deep disinclination to change toward jati ways is shown in one village where good land for growing rice by plough cultivation is available. The staple of Hill Maria diet is millet, grown by slash-and-burn tillage. Though rice cultivation is vastly more productive, it is not feasible on the dry, steep slopes of most of the Hill Maria territory. But even in this village where rice growing is feasible and profitable, only a fourth of the families have given up axe cultivation. Most cultivate by axe as well as plough; they are reluctant to abandon shifting cultivation because it symbolizes for them the tribal way of life.

They suspect that if they go over to rice cultivation entirely they will also be going over to a different way of life, one in which they may lose much that they now cherish. Shifting cultivation "at once provides them with their daily sustenance and sets them apart as a people, separate from all others" (Jay 1961b, p. 1371). They want to be separate; the alternative they fear is to become a dependent, inferior, disoriented jati. They dislike jati people and think of themselves as being outside jati relations. Nevertheless, they are taking up some Hindu religious practices to complement their tribal religion and they are accepting other jati features. While they reject the religion of Hindus they are adopting important parts of it. "Thus we might say," Edward Jay concludes, "that Marias are becoming Hindus in spite of themselves" (1961a MS. p. 39).

The attractions of jati society for tribesmen are manifold. Tribal leaders sense the promise of more secure power and eminence within their group. Hindu religious practices appear to be useful ways of invoking supernatural help. Some tribesmen attach themselves to jati villages because they can get food and work there (cf.

Bose 1953b; Sachchidananda 1964; 1965). The changeover may take generations, but after it has been accomplished, those whose forefathers lived under a tribal system of society have shifted to a different system, that of jati. It is a different system not only because it is operated on different principles but also because it has different capacities. The tribal assumption that kinship ought to pervade all one's society (those who cannot possibly be kinsmen can scarcely be fully men) is replaced by the concept that kinship is compartmentalized within a hierarchy of specialized, organically related jatis, with regular ways of relating to nonkinsmen.

The carrying capacity of the tribal system is limited just as the production capacity of swidden agriculture is limited. A tribal system cannot accommodate as many people acting cooperatively as can a system of jatis. Jati society can include a far more diverse and productive array of specialties and specialists. It can therefore include a far greater content of knowledge, because specialists can amass specialized skills and information and make them available for social use. Moreover, tribal social systems have much more limited capacities for adaptation; as tribal peoples the world over take on new technologies and ideas they find it difficult to adapt tribal systems to them, and many have to make quite abrupt social changes. Jati societies have been more adaptable to modern circumstances, as our discussion of recurrent change has indicated.

Tribesmen in India use various tactics to alter their former social relations, as the Reddi and Gond examples illustrate and as the case examples given in the next chapter show. These examples also show that all the varied tactics press in the same general direction, toward civilizational characteristics. What is to be rejected is frequently more apparent, to tribesmen as to aspiring jati villagers, than just what should be adopted. Tribesmen have been given special incentive to take to political means for mobility because government law and agencies have provided legislative seats and other advantages for them.

These provisions came before there was mass pressure from tribal peoples themselves for special political treatment. The benefits were established by the founders and leaders of the new nation because of their political beliefs. They were, and are, intent on reducing the more gaping social disparities within the nation. Designating tribes and low-ranking jatis as disadvantaged and as in need of government aid is a means of redressing the balance of Indian society, or rather of hastening a new kind of social calibration. There has been considerable criticism of the manner in which the proffered advantages have been administered and of the way in which they give a scheduled group a vested interest in continuing to be declared "backward." Nevertheless these redressive measures have had effect. This new kind of political counterchange has quickened the absorption of tribal people into the mainstream of national life.

CHAPTER 32

Direction of Tribal Change

THE direction of tribal change in India is clear and expectable. Virtually all tribes are now shifting toward jati characteristics, a movement which has greatly accelerated as communications have improved and external forces have impinged more closely. Seen from afar and in the large, when tribals are viewed as a culture type, it is quite certain that this shift toward jati society will continue apace. However, when we examine the change at close range, in particular tribes, villages, and families, we find much conflict about which cultural direction to take, considerable uncertainty about which values to cherish, frequent personal oscillation between the requirements of differing social structures.

Tactical Problems and Long-range Trends

The direction seems clear in the grand sweep of the observer's eye. But the outcome of a struggle is typically far from certain to those engaged in it on the ground. There are many possible ways of adapting. The advent of political democracy has opened new possibilities for tribal people as well as for other villagers; tribal leaders, too, have seen the advantages in acting as voters and lobbyists.

Government authority used to sit lightly with tribal people. Foreign Rajas might claim territories inhabited by tribal groups but usually they were not strong enough to impose firm controls over them, nor were most tribal lands worth great conquering effort. British administrators quelled the more extravagant tribal customs, such as human sacrifice or the elimination of tax collectors, but for the most part they did not tamper directly with a tribal way of life save to try sporadically to preserve it. After political independence, however, the hand of government became more ubiquitous than it was before, and the arm of government stronger in the tribal villages. The opportunities to share in the body politic became apparent, especially at election time.

These changes have altered the choices before tribesmen and have sometimes added to their perplexities as well as to their advantages (cf. Bose 1964; Fürer-Haimendorf 1967b). Jati members face similar conflicts and uncertainties, but tribal peoples must cope, in addition, with the special problems of adapting tribal characteristics to modern requirements. To illustrate the choices and conflicts that tribal people now face, examples from five widely separated groups are given.

The first, from a Kond village in the highlands of Orissa, shows how tribal leaders now have to switch from one mode of conduct to another if they are to be effective. Effective adaptation may be hindered, as the example from the Kotas of the Nilgiri Hills shows, by a self-image that is no longer appropriate to their contemporary social scene.

Tribesmen are also switching their reference models; the Bhumij of West Bengal had gone far toward accepting the Kshatriya model when some of their leaders urged a turn toward the newly advantageous posture of a culturally deprived people. As such, they can obtain political and material advantages to attain more rapid social rise. This shift to a new model may be spurred by external circumstances, as is shown in the example of the Bhotia who were sped toward a modern model by the borderlands inroads of Communist China. The fifth case example is that of the Santals, particularly those Santals who live in the steel city of Jamshedpur and its vicinity. Their ancient antipathy toward jati people and jati practices has been bolstered by their industrial contacts. The reference model that their leaders ardently advocate is one that seems to entail a reversion to traditional tribal customs. The reversion is only in appearance; in actuality it provides a means by which Santals can adapt to modern political participation and social advance.

The agents of change in these examples include indigenous Rajas, religious mentors, secular teachers, government officials, tribal association leaders, Christian missionaries, and Hindu social service workers. Each kind of agent has tried to direct change in his special mode. Often enough, one kind of agent is violently opposed to those of another kind. Nevertheless, despite their diversity and antagonisms, all have wanted tribesmen to adopt similar, civilizational principles of conduct.

Konds of Baderi Village, Orissa

The dilemma faced by Konds is exemplified by a quarrel in which the headman of Baderi was the central figure (Bailey 1960b, pp. 197–237). One day the headman was an infuriated, unfettered tribesman who shouted abuse and threatened violence against the despoilers of his people from the jati village; the next day he listened meekly to advice from a Hindu guru and pledged to give up drinking. One purpose of his having a guru was to learn how to behave like a "Hindu gentleman" so that he could better deal with officials.

Baderi village is in the Phulbani district of central Orissa in the hill area called the Kondmals. There are well over half a million tribals who speak Kui, the Dravidian language of the Konds; most jati people in Orissa speak Oriya, a language of the Indo-European stock.

On the day of the quarrel at Baderi, the headman had been drinking when a man from the nearby jati village of Oriya-speakers came to see him about buying some turmeric roots. This visitor was the same Nrusingh whose several roles were discussed in an earlier chapter. Though a Harijan, he is one of the better educated in the locality and has become relatively affluent through his trading activities. He also holds a minor official post as assistant to the Oriya revenue headman.

On catching sight of Nrusingh the headman exploded with rage and abuse. A few days before, it had been discovered that Nrusingh had cheated one of the Konds by pocketing part of the tax payment that the Kond had turned over to him. Incensed by this incident and inspirited with alcohol, the headman aggressively made for Nrusingh who promptly fled out of reach. The headman's anger was then vented in a tirade against three men from the Oriya village who happened to be about, two traders and the local school teacher. That evening, still enraged, the headman vented his anger on his son and daughter-in-law. The couple appealed to the headman's Oriya preceptor. The next morning this preceptor visited the now sober headman, gave him advice, and got from him a promise to stop drinking.

This last act illustrates in miniature what seems to be a major contradiction in Kond behavior. On the day of his anger at Nrusingh the headman railed against Oriya evil; on the day of his sobriety he solemnly promised an Oriya that he would keep Oriya high-caste values.

Several impulses were compounded in his wrath. As headman he had the contradictory responsibilities of representing outside authority in the village and of championing his people against outsiders. The former obligation he ignored in this episode, the latter was demonstrated in great amplitude and emotion. His immediate target was an Oriya Harijan, but he reviled Oriyas of all kinds and jatis "with a coarse invective as liars and thieves who live only to make money by cheating others." Further, he charged, they use their better education and political power to extort money from the poor Kond tribesmen. These are two facets of the same grievance; Oriyas cheat Konds in trade and cheat them also through abuse of their political power. "It is their [the Konds'] standard complaint and it is in this area of social relations, rather than in culture that they see themselves different from and opposed to the Oriyas" (Bailey 1960b, p. 232).

Konds dislike trading while a good many in the Oriya village thrive by it. Konds consider trade to be "at once beneath their dignity and beyond their capacity." The proud Kond relegates business dealings with his produce to the untouchables in his village. Moreover, most Konds believe that they are not clever or wily enough to engage in trade successfully.

Trading was involved in the episode at Baderi village in that Nrusingh had come to buy some turmeric, the main cash crop raised by the Konds. But neither then nor subsequently did this specific relationship enter into the headman's attack. Trading and commerce, Bailey notes, are taken to be outside the other kinds of social relations. This is probably why the Konds, with their inclination to wrap all social relations in a kinship bundle, despise trade. Yet when they do engage in it, as in selling turmeric to Oriyas, they follow the logic of the marketplace and do not mix trade considerations into other social interests (Bailey 1960b, pp. 132, 185, 205,

226–228). They decry the isolating of trade from other social relations, yet they do isolate their business relations when they buy or sell.

The newer influences on Kond life are reflected in the headman's oscillation from one day to the next. His spiritual adviser is an Oriya who has a large clientele; this mentor's task with Konds is to teach the Konds the Hindu way of life. The headman listens to and pays for the guru's counsel not only for religious reasons, but also for reasons that have to do with the struggle for control of modern forms of political power. "It is an advantage in this struggle to be a Hindu gentleman and not an uncouth aboriginal." The headman functions at the grass-roots level of this struggle, but he is aware that unless he can take on certain manners and refinements, he and his people cannot have ready access to the fountain of political benefits (Bailey 1960b, pp. 235–237).

For centuries ambitious tribal chieftains have taken Hindu mentors in order to gain more durable power by learning to be proper Kshatriyas. This older tutelage was mainly intended to enhance the rule of a tribal chieftain over his own people; now, however, even a village headman seeks guidance from a Hindu preceptor, not only to solidify his own power but also to exploit the power newly available through political democracy. The headman of Baderi, who is a loud defender of tribal tradition, maintains his prestige and authority by "being at the same time both a traditionalist and a progressive" (Bailey 1960b, p. 237).

The Konds of Baderi have been situated within two miles of an Oriya village for perhaps eight centuries and so they share some elements of Oriya culture. The concept of pollution is held in both places, certain ritual traits are common to both, inheritance rules and such personal values as the immense need to have a son are similar (Bailey 1960b, pp. 91, 93, 133, 175). The Kond village even harbors four specialized groups, Kond smiths, herdsmen, and menials, and some families of Oriya herdsmen. The dominant clan of Konds deals with them in the manner of a dominant jati in a caste village. The Kond landowners, however, seem less concerned about their dependents than Oriya landowners are about the work and the deference they expect from theirs (Bailey 1960b, pp. 121–156).

These similarities have not blurred the strong sense of social distinction that the Konds feel, nor have they eroded the tribal features in Kond culture. The Konds are well aware of the contrast between their customs and those of Oriyas or of "Hindus" in general. They differ in visible, immediately apparent ways, as in language, in traditional dress, and house form. They differ also in the symbolism of their rites and ceremonies. In agriculture, Konds and Oriyas use the same techniques for growing rice but Konds also cultivate swidden fields on the mountainsides and the Oriya villagers do not. Bailey comments that the Konds say that they are Hindus like everyone else, but they make a sharp distinction between themselves and the Oriyas (Bailey 1960b, pp. 3–4).

Though Oriya rulers had anciently settled military colonies among the Konds and had tried to control them, the Konds would not become acculturated and remained very largely their own masters. They refused to be dutiful subjects, dependable allies, or dependent auxiliaries. They maintained the kinship base for their society, kept its religious autonomy, preserved its economic values and its psychological stamp. They gave limited homage to Rajas and tolerated specialized jatis in their villages, but they considered none of them essential to their way of life.

In the twentieth century this accommodation did not work so well as it had before. The Kond territory became much less isolated and much more open to influences from outside the Kondmals. Konds began to want some of the things Oriyas possessed and they began to form an association, as jatis have done throughout India. They organized an uplift association, called the Kui Samaj, which tries to do for the Kond tribe what the headman's guru was supposed to do for the headman of Baderi village. It is a self-preceptorial effort to enable Konds to gain advantages in the larger society with which they are now engaged. It is also intended to preserve Kond identity, to solidify Kond unity, and to deliver votes (Bailey 1960b, pp. 186–193). Konds are numerous enough so that they have much more to gain by remaining a distinctive group than by assimilating with some jati bloc or merging into a political coalition.

The new trend was still much in the making at mid-century. The Kui Samaj was not yet a mass organization and representative democracy was only sketchily understood by most Konds. However, Bailey tells us that an ambitious Kond does not now aim to rise only among his clansmen and villagers nor does he aspire, as his predecessors would, to be headman for a set of villages. Rather, he tries to get into the inner circle of the Kui Samaj, to work in a political party, "and eventually to reach the top by becoming a member of the Legislative Assembly" (Bailey 1960b, p. 186). In making his way toward the new top, he must appear to be both a tribal traditionalist and a political progressive, an appearance not easily maintained.

Konds now operate in three social-political arenas: they carry on some of the features of the tribal way of life, they are acting increasingly as a jati, and they are beginning to bid for place in the democratic polity (Bailey 1960b, pp. 269–272). Different rules are appropirate to each arena and Konds now find themselves in situations in which they are not clear about which mode of behavior is appropriate. This, to be sure, is part of every man's dilemma in any society. The uncertainties are greater for some personalities and at particular stages of each person's life cycle. But the personal choices are not made any easier when a man's society is in transition and a headman may act like a direct, unbridled tribesman one day, and then take the part of a dutiful disciple the next, in order to command power in an evolving political order on still another day.

Kotas of the Nilgiri Hills, Tamil Nadu (Madras)

The choices that are actually made are guided by a people's perception of themselves. Often these perceptions are legacies from an earlier period and do not serve the group well in adapting to contemporary realities, a lag sometimes found in great nations as well as among tribesmen in India. Thus the Kotas of the Nilgiri Hills generally hold a view of themselves as proud aborigines, entitled to special considerations because of their seniority on the land and the artisan skills they can provide. They are, in fact, a minute part of the present population of the district, unknown to many in the area. There are only seven small villages of Kotas, about 1100 people in all, yet they maintain their own language, religion, social organization, and lively sense of distinctiveness. The general processes of change noted in larger tribal societies go on as well within this little enclave. Their case illustrates how the self-image of a people can impede their adaptation to a current situation.

In my study of the Kotas, I have seen men vacillate between

tribal and jati modes of behavior. In funeral ceremonies, for example, many buffaloes used to be sacrificed to speed the departed soul and to demonstrate the solidarity of the bereaved kinsmen. As the influence of jati practices grew, funeral sacrifices came to be deprecated. In the village of Kolmel all agreed to limit themselves to one buffalo for all mourners at the annual memorial rites. However, when this ceremony was next held a conflict arose. The mourners did not want to be so restricted. Each of them had been in favor of the limitation in the council meeting, but in his role as mourner he wanted to follow the old tribal practice and to sacrifice as many buffalo as he could afford for the honor of his family (Mandelbaum 1954b, pp. 82–84).

The factional rift between Kota traditionalists and the reformers led by the schoolteacher, Sulli was discussed previously (cf. Mandelbaum 1960, pp. 221–255). Kotas of both factions bitterly blamed their neighbors, the Badagas, for Kota disabilities. They still saw the Badagas as an integral part of the old order of the four Nilgiri tribes and not as the Badagas are today—an enterprising people, many of whom are seizing the new economic and political opportunities, and most of whom are uninterested in the former tribal relationships.

That old order of the Nilgiri tribes was, in effect, a caste order that was carried on in isolation from the centers and carriers of Indian civilization (Mandelbaum 1956, pp. 33–45). There was no knowledge of scripture to bolster it, no Brahmins to legitimate it, no Kshatriyas to rule over it. Yet the social order functioned well for centuries. Before the British came into the Nilgiri Hills in 1819 and opened up some roads to the plateau, the people of the region had few contacts with the villagers of the plains below their homeland. Each of the four Nilgiri groups was a tribal society in the main, yet each was specialized in some degree and dependent on the others for certain economic and ritual services.

The Kotas still think of themselves as an important element in that order. They were the artisans and musicians for the Badaga cultivators, for the Toda pastoralists, and for the Kurumba sorcerers. Families of each tribe carried on jajmanilike relations with families of the other three tribes. Badagas and Todas considered Kotas to be defiling inferiors because they provided music for funerals, handled carcasses, worked in leather, and ate the flesh of cows and buffaloes. Kota musicians at a Badaga ceremony were fed separately, used separate utensils, and were not allowed into the inner parts of a Badaga house or close to the sacred things. When a Kota met a Badaga or a Toda he used to make formal gestures of respect as from a subordinate to a superior.

Yet this deference did not, in earlier times, seem onerous to Kotas. Although they gave the gestures of deference, they did not feel totally subordinate. They had their own lands, did some farming, and kept some cattle and thus were not completely dependent on the Badaga farmers for grain or on the Todas for dairy products. They lived in their own villages, governed themselves, and were not under any daily rule by overlords. Moreover, they knew that unless they provided tools for the other groups the others could not carry on their work, and unless they provided music some of the main ceremonies of the Badagas could not be completed. When there was a falling out between Kotas and Badagas, the Kotas would withhold their services. The Badagas would feel the pinch enough to compromise and arbitrate.

The Badagas were and are the most numerous of the four indigenous peoples. In the first Census of 1871 there were 19,476 Badagas, 1,112 Kotas, 693 Todas, and 613 Kurumbas. By the Census of 1961 there were 85,463 Badagas while the other three groups were about as large as they had been ninety years before. In spite of these population figures, Kotas do not consider Badagas to be overwhelmingly more important than are Todas and Kurumbas. Their origin story tells that Kotas, Todas, and Kurumbas are descended from brothers who were put on the Nilgiri land by a creator father who assigned them their special tasks and mutual obligations. Badagas were latecomers (historical evidence corroborates Kota folklore in this) who fled to the hills from the Mysore region some centuries ago and were allowed to settle there by the permission of the ancient inhabitants.

As for all others who live in the Nilgiri district now and make up the bulk of the population, they do not figure much in Kota legend or historical reference. Thousands of migrants from Madras and Kerala have settled in the Nilgiris, attracted by the salubrious climate, fertile lands and opportunities for employment. In the Kota view, they are in the Nilgiris but not really of that area. In mid-twentieth century the older Kotas still perceived the Nilgiris as the vouchsafed homeland of the four tribes and saw themselves as a pivotal people among the four.

The facts have become far different. The Nilgiri district now holds some 400,000 people. Of the four indigenous groups only the Badagas have kept pace in numbers and prosperity. As they increased in wealth and education, many of them found that their traditional associations with the Kotas hampered their jati ambitions. They realized, for example, that people of respectable rank did not dance at funerals to Kota music as had been Badaga custom. When tools and utensils became readily available in markets, most Badagas found the traditional association with Kota families to be unnecessary and irksome. They had no further need to rely on Kotas, who were supposed to be inferior dependents but who acted more like independent claimants.

A main factional split in Badaga society came about 1930 on the issue of Kota music (cf. Hockings 1965, pp. 111–113, 134–138). The reform faction was against using Kota music at funerals; the conservatives were just as determined to keep it. At funerals of the promusic faction, antimusic zealots interfered. In 1936 there was a riot at one such funeral; police fired on the crowd and two Badagas were killed. By the 1960s the reformist Badagas had largely prevailed, only a few conservative Badagas used Kota services, and even they did not keep up the full traditional relationship. For a time Badaga reform leaders held a special animus against Kotas. To those Badagas who were anxious to shed all traces of their former, quasi-tribal state, the Kotas posed a threatening presence; they reminded the Badagas of what they wanted to forget, that not so long ago Badagas had followed customs unsuitable for a jati of respectable and educated people.

Badagas, conversely, appear as the main adversaries in the Kotas' view. The conservative Kotas resent the Badaga withdrawal from the old relationship which, as they understand it, was formed in the beginning of time and should not be unbound in the present mid-course of time. Though they would like to have the payments they used to get, they do have land and are not in dire need of Badaga patronage. Their resentment is mainly because the old harmonious Nilgiri order, as they nostalgically recall it, has been abolished, because the Badagas have reneged their ancient obligations, and because the Kotas now see no satisfactory place for themselves in the new situation. Moreover, some Badagas actively denigrate the Kotas, and, even worse, many Badagas ignore them.

The progressives among the Kotas resent Badaga opposition to their efforts to improve their social standing. Sulli fought against Badagas for decades, first to secure the right of a Kota to be a schoolteacher, later for the right to be served in eating places in town and for similar acceptance as a citizen with equal rights. In the main, Sulli succeeded in his struggles, but the next generation of Kotas, especially those who have had some education, seek a still better status for Kotas.

Eleven hundred people might be enough for a viable tribe or jati, but it is far too few to count for anything in the modern political arena. The Kotas feel the need for wider affiliations but as yet do not know with whom to form them. A few are beginning to realize that both Kotas and Badagas are caught up in the same current of great affairs, and that somehow Kotas have to revise their ancient images and adapt to the requirements of their present world.

Bhumij of Barabhum, West Bengal

Those tribals who choose to reform face difficult decisions about how best to change. The Bhumij, a people who number about half a million in Bihar and West Bengal, exemplify such problems of choice. In a series of writings, Surajit Sinha has described how most of them had gone far toward becoming jati folk and had convinced themselves that they were Kshatriyas, when some of their leaders realized that the traditional Kshatriya way was no longer the best means for social advance. These men decided that there was more to be gained if Bhumij declared themselves to be tribesmen.

Such a reversal is not easy because the Bhumij had committed themselves so strongly to the Kshatriya goal. The dilemma is illustrated in an account of a 1954 meeting of Bhumij leaders. The majority supported the drive for Kshatriya status, which had been led by the large landowners for some forty years. But at this meeting contrary opinions were heard. One Bhumij, who had been an M.L.A. (a member of the state legislative assembly) said, "The programme for labelling our caste as Bhumij-Kshatriya should be abandoned. I know from my experience as an M.L.A. that if we claim to be Kshatriyas, then we shall get no facilities from the Government as *Adibasis*" (S. Sinha 1959, p. 24). Another speaker also urged that Bhumij proclaim themselves as *Adibasis*, members of an aboriginal tribe, and be officially listed as such. He pointed out that if they insisted on being Kshatriyas, they would logically have to give up doing their own ploughing, they should stop widow remarriage and shun rice beer. Despite decades of reform exhortation, many Bhumij still followed tribal practice in these matters. He ended with the question, "What shall we gain following the examples of our Zemindar class?" (S. Sinha 1959, p. 25).

Some Bhumij zemindars, the large landowners, had become accepted as Kshatriyas and had separated themselves completely from Bhumij society to form a new jati (S. Sinha 1959, p. 11; 1962, pp. 52–58, 72–75). The masses of Bhumij, however, were not wealthy enough to take that step—they could not afford the cost of Brahmins, genealogists, and special Sanskritic rites—nor did they want to foreswear all the pleasures of tribal custom.

The Bhumij speak Bengali and live in multijati villages in which they are often the dominant group. Their territories were not particularly isolated, so jati people have lived in their villages for centuries. One such village is Madhupur in Barabhum pargana near the Bihar–West Bengal border.[1] Of the six jati-groups in the village the Bhumij are the wealthiest, with about four-fifths of the land, but there are also some Bhumij in the village who are landless laborers. Even the poorest among them share the Bhumij self-view that they are the ancient inhabitants and present lords of their homeland. The wealthier families uphold more elegant standards of diet, drink and ritual, and they tend to marry into other well-off families. The poorest form yet another marriage class whose families have lower sumptuary standards (S. Sinha 1959, pp. 12–13; 1962, pp. 48–52). None consider themselves to be separate from the other Bhumij, however.

The Bhumij of Madhupur carry on jajmani relations with a half dozen or more specialist jatis; they meet people of some thirty jatis at the weekly market. They are so far assimilated to jati standards as to require services of Brahmins, barbers, and washermen.

[1] Barabhum pargana was in the Manbhum district of Bihar. In November 1956 the bulk of this district was reapportioned to the Purulia district of West Bengal.

They regard themselves as a Hindu jati and are so regarded by most others (S. Sinha 1959, p. 10). But there are vast disparities of opinion among their neighbors as to where the Bhumij are to be placed. The people of the three other tribal groups in the locality consider the Bhumij to be among the highest of jatis, equal to or higher than the Brahmins. But the more prestigious of the local Brahmins rank the Bhumij far below Rajputs and traders, about at a level with washermen, weavers, and distillers (S. Sinha 1965, p. 74; 1959, pp. 10–11). These Brahmins will not officiate for Bhumij; even the wealthier Bhumij can persuade only hard-up, "degraded" Brahmins to minister for them. This may explain why some Bhumij leaders are quite ready to cast their political lot with tribal peoples among whom they are held in high esteem.

Bhumij are rated low by these Brahmins because, for all their aspirations, few of them have completely renounced tribal traits concerning diet, women, and death. Many still drink liquor and eat chicken; their women are free to remarry and even to dance at ceremonies; their dead are buried rather than burned, and the bones later reinterred in a custom common to many Indian tribal cultures (S. Sinha 1959, p. 11; 1965, pp. 75–77). Though Bhumij are the dominant group in many of the villages in which they live, they are still not wealthy and powerful enough to persuade the authentic "twice-born" to turn a blind eye to their tribal failings. The higher jatis see them as a tribal lot who follow debased customs. Their tribal neighbors, however, see them as dominant landowners who uphold both Kshatriya and indigenous standards, so they place Bhumij high among the superiors in the region.

The reform movement has had some effect. Sinha writes that their gay sensuality has been slightly toned down in order to make a good impression on the higher Hindus (1965, p. 79). But the toning down has not been so great as to curtail their overriding bias toward a good time. Bhumij are generally diligent farmers, but they believe that the reward for work should be pleasure rather than the accumulation of capital.

Migrants into their villages, especially cultivators of the Mahato jati, are more inclined than the Bhumij toward cool calculations of future profit and less to the hot pursuit of pleasure. A number of these Mahato are thrifty and capital-oriented, and despite legal safeguards against the loss of land by Bhumij, some of the Bhumij lands have been passing to immigrants imbued with the ethic of hard work and capital gain (S. Sinha 1963). Following this ethic yields greater income, which is commonly redistributed to attain lasting symbols of rank. As an aspiring jati, the Mahatos in this area have organized an association that urges reforms quite like those proposed for the Bhumij (Das Gupta 1962).

Unlike the Mahato, a good many Bhumij seem less attracted by the future benefits of higher rank than by the immediate pleasures of festive celebration in jovial company.

The attraction of these pleasures has proved quite durable; Bhumij have known of the other standards for a long time. Jati models were introduced when Bhumij chieftains, probably between the thirteenth and sixteenth centuries, granted lands and privileges to Hindus of high jatis and induced them to settle close to the ruler. The Brahmins taught the chiefs how to be proper Kshatriyas and invested them with the panoply of that status complete with initiation, sacred thread, and noble pedigree.

Thus equipped, the Bhumij chiefs convinced themselves that their powers and legitimacy had been destined from above. Some did extend their power beyond the limited scope ordinarily feasible in a tribal society. These rulers also established transcendental rites in Bhumij culture. Tribal deities were elevated to world (and state) guardians; tribal rites became state ceremonies. Not much of the tribal culture was disrupted and new elements only gradually seeped into Bhumij villages. The Hinduization of the ruler and of his backwoods court helped him maintain a center of power even if his subjects continued to see him as a temporary first among permanent equals. As a Raja's rule became firm, tribesmen could travel farther from their home village, could witness the ceremonies at the court, and could meet new people at the weekly markets that were established as part of the civilized regime.

Village headmen usually led the rest in acculturation since they had wider contacts and greater income. A headman might perform the Durga Puja (a main Bengali ceremony); he would avoid doing manual labor and would keep his women restricted to the bounds of the village. Even the ordinary Bhumij cultivators were half-seriously called *Raja Lok*, "royal people," by others in their villages. They felt themselves connected with the rulers but they were too remote from the Raja's court to do much about transforming their tribal ways (S. Sinha 1957a, p. 31; 1962, pp. 38–55; Navalakha 1959).

This, then, was the condition of Bhumij culture when British administrators came into their territories. In 1833 one official visited the locality that includes Madhupur village; he described the Bhumij there as professing to be Hindus but without any respectable Brahmin to officiate for them. Fifty years later, in 1883–1884, H. H. Risley reported that the Bhumij of this area worshipped Hindu as well as tribal gods and that the "more advanced" among them employed Brahmins as family priests, though these were probably not "respectable" Brahmins. They were beginning, Risley noted, to forget their totemic clan divisions and he speculated that they would soon abandon the tribal groupings in favor of more aristocratic designations. "The tribe will then have become a caste in the full sense of the word and will go on stripping itself of all customs likely to betray its true descent" (Risley 1915, p. 75; S. Sinha 1959, p. 9).

The Bhumij did try to do this but the pace was not fast. It began to quicken in later decades; the history of Madhupur village illustrates the trend (S. Sinha 1959, pp. 12–30). In 1897 a holy man of a Vaishnava sect was induced to live in the village. The villagers had previously known that such holy men would initiate Bhumij devotees into a state of religious grace and would act as their preceptors. It was not until the widowed mother of the village headman decided that she needed spiritual initiation that they procured a holy man of their own. He preached the ascetic ideal, led in frequent hymn sessions, and conducted recitations at which the lessons of the Sanskritic texts were told in the vernacular. The villagers thus gained a resident tutor in Sanskritic lore. Some of the villagers rejected the guru's precepts and only a few were devoted enough to adopt all of his doctrine, particularly his central message that "The discharge of semen is the root of all evil."

This holy man moved to a nearby village in 1910, and in 1914 another was brought in. The replacement was thought to be even more learned in scripture than the first, but he preached a hedonistic doctrine. With relief the families that had stopped drinking liquor and eating fowl now took up such practices again and joined with the new preceptor in merry song and dance. The new guru continued to tutor the villagers in stories from scripture even though he stressed a different aspect of scripture than did the ascetic guru.

Then, about 1921, the villagers heard rumors that a new divine being had appeared on earth and preached the ascetic vegetarian way. So influential were these rumors that some in Madhupur forthwith disposed of their chickens and goats. Then came the news that the name of the heaven-sent Raja was Gandhi. In 1923 townsmen who were followers of Gandhi appeared in the locality and set the record straight. Mahatma Gandhi, it transpired, wanted the people to give up liquor and to wear homespun, but he did not ask them to give up meat or fish, so they said.

In the following years there were a number of meetings in this vicinity at which Congress Party volunteers lectured on political independence, on the use of nonviolent methods, and on how to live a clean life based on moderation. These lectures, moreover, revealed that people could formally organize for reform. The principal Bhumij leader of the locality was stimulated to convene a meeting in 1935 at which the association of "Bhumij-Kshatriya" of the district was founded. At the meeting resolutions were passed about reform of diet and about the proper conduct of women. In the next year officers of the new association toured the villages and levied heavy fines on violators. There was a great slaughter of chickens and a diminution of tribal rites, but after the first flush of zeal, chickens reappeared and liquor was brewed again. Still, there were certain tribal practices, such as group dancing by women, that were really abolished. In this way, the movement for national independence gave added impetus to the shift toward jati standards.

A great turn came with independence in 1947. Rumors of clashes with Muslims spread and Bhumij leaders were called together to hear an orator of the pantribal party, the Jharkhand Party. He urged them to take up their bows, arrows, and spears against the rumored danger. But the Bhumij were not much attracted to close alliance with other tribal groups; they thought of themselves as true Kshatriyas, perhaps only a bit manqué. When elections came to be held, the Bhumij association was used as a means of mobilizing votes. As government officers and political candidates came to their villages bearing gifts actual and promised, the Bhumij began to take a greater interest in political participation than in the refining of their ritual purity or of their women's deportment in dance. Sinha tells of a meeting of Bhumij he attended in 1958 in which only lip service was given to Kshatriya status and in which the emerging leaders were literate, educated commoners rather than the landed chiefs. At this meeting it was resolved to insert the term Adibasi, aboriginal, in the name of the association so that it became, rather paradoxically, the Bhumij Adibasi Kshatriya association.

Since the 1950s, Bhumij interest in being known as Rajputs has progressively waned, yet many Bhumij are loath to declare themselves as tribesmen because they and their forefathers insisted so long that they were Kshatriyas. Sinha points out that the Bhumij find it more difficult to adapt to the new situation than do others, less Hinduized, tribal groups. "With the unfulfilled craze for Rajput recognition still lurking in their hearts and a residue of the broken landed aristocracy yet remaining in their midst the Bhumij and the Raj Gonds find it hard to adjust to the current secular demands made upon them" (S. Sinha 1962, pp. 78–79).

They have not become "a caste in the full sense of the word" as Risley predicted, though in the first half of the twentieth century they shifted appreciably in that direction. The Bhumij Rajas had some acculturative effect, but important change began in the late nineteenth century when sectarian holy men came to live in villages like Madhupur. The influence of these holy men accelerated the shift toward jati standards, though they ostensibly preached a casteless creed, and this trend gained momentum when a Bhumij leader adopted some of the organizational techniques of the nationalist workers who came to the locality. Before many years had passed, however, the success of the nationalist movement brought about new conditions that made the Kshatriya campaign seem, if not irrelevant, then certainly insufficient to gain more assured power and better status for Bhumij.

The new men in power were opposed to some parts of the "Bhumij-Kshatriya" reform (the greater seclusion of women, for example); they were indifferent to other parts of it, such as the taboo on eating chicken; and they placed much greater emphasis on such matters as education and political organization. The stride of the old reform leaders thus faltered as their chosen road became obscured and new, swifter ways to social advance seemed available. Hence the conflicts and waverings that have appeared in recent Bhumij meetings.

The new political ways nevertheless have a good deal in common with the program of ritual reform. Both assume a desire to rise higher in a wider society than just that of Bhumij. Both require moderation, discipline, postponement of immediate gratification. The nationalist dispensation demands quite as much discipline as do the "twice-born" standards, but this discipline is directed more to acquiring education than to regulating diet and to developing political roles rather than to separating sexual roles. Both movements require that salient tribal values be dropped in favor of more constrained behavior and wider social relations.

The Bhumij who now want the group to be classified as a tribe do not aim to revert to a previous state of tribal isolation and cultural separation, but rather to push zealously ahead toward secular gain and wider social advancement. These goals were introduced through the Bhumij Rajas and were later reinforced by sectarian gurus. The holy men, who thought they were lifting the immortal souls of their followers, also sharpened their material ambitions by opening a wider world for them. These ambitions were further heightened among those who received some modern education, who are urging the tactical shift to tribal classification within the same strategy of social mobility.

Bhotias of Johar Valley, Uttar Pradesh

The Johari Bhotias had little hesitancy about declaring themselves, in the 1950s, to be tribals entitled to special governmental protection, although they too had previously claimed Kshatriya rank and had done so quite successfully. There are special circumstances in their case, as Ram Srivastava has cogently shown (1962). First, these Bhotias live in the Johar Valley high in the Himalayas; their villages lie between 11,000 and 13,000 feet above sea level in the Almora district of U.P. Secondly, they are traders who traditionally have carried goods, mainly salt, between Tibet and India. Finally, any conflict they may have had about their status was vastly overshadowed by the greater conflicts that ensued after the armies of the People's Republic of China took over Tibet (Srivastava 1962).

There are both jati and tribal villages in the lofty valleys on the

Himalayan edge of the subcontinent. The jati folk carry on an attenuated jati order, as was previously noted. The tribals in these regions differ from the jati people in the ways noted in the previous chapter, though the cultural distance between jati and tribe is usually not great. The perceived social distance, however, can be very great. In the four valleys in which Bhotia predominate, there are Brahmins and Rajputs of ancient residence and also "immigrant" Brahmins and Rajputs (the forebears of these immigrants have lived in the region for "anything between twenty to fifty generations"). Both kinds of Hindus look down on the Bhotia as tribesmen who will eat beef.

The term Bhotia in the Himalayan borderlands is used for any kind of trader who plies between Tibet and India, but the Bhotia proper are those (some 22,000 in 1961) who live mainly in the four valleys northeast of Almora town and speak a distinctive language of the Tibeto-Burmese stock. The Bhotias of Johar Valley are nearest to the towns and have had closer contacts with Hindus and Hinduism than have the Bhotia of the three eastern valleys. They have also prospered in trade, have become much more like a Hindu jati, and have claimed Rajput status.

Unlike the Johar Bhotia, the eastern Bhotia show only traces of Hindu rites. They continue to have "a nightly gathering of unmarried men and women who dance, drink, and sleep together" (Srivastava 1962, p. 66). This custom and their other tribal ways violate the sensitivities of pious Hindus who know them. When a zealous Hindu missionary came to one of the valleys (which is on a pilgrimage route), built a temple and schools, and organized a society for service to them, they did at first promise him that they would give up drinking, smoking, and the insouciant commingling of sexes. But after a few months the holier but drabber life suddenly palled and they burst into drink, dance, and pleasure again (Srivastava 1962, pp. 7-72).

Johari Bhotias, as befits a more acculturated group, carefully dissociated themselves from the eastern Bhotia. Their trading successes have made them the wealthiest among the 10,000 residents of the Johar Valley. They have secured the services of Brahmin priests and pride themselves on being stricter in their Rajput deportment than are the old Rajputs of the valley. But these Rajputs hold that their Bhotia neighbors must be low; if they are not actually beef-eaters themselves, they deal and possibly eat with Tibetans who are certainly beef-eaters (Srivastava 1962, p. 54). The Johari Bhotias responded to such slurs as other disparaged aspirants have done. They organized an association for reform; one of their leaders started a journal and compiled a genealogy which showed them to be true-blooded Rajputs (Srivastava 1962, pp. 68–69).

Their competence in trade is not as anomalous as it would be for other tribals. Tribesmen, as we have noted, prefer to couch all friendly social relations in the idiom of kinship. Since a trader can scarcely treat customers and suppliers as kinsmen, tribesmen do not usually make good traders. Moreover there is the inclination to share one's stock in trade freely when one sees an occasion for joyous celebration, which in the tribal view is often. The Johari Bhotia, however, carry on a trade that involves arduous travel across some of the highest passes in the world; it is not at all like a casual jaunt to the weekly bazaar. Their main stock in trade, salt, is not a commodity to be consumed in one festive burst. Moreover, the trade is not with fellow tribesmen, but with outlanders of different religion and manner. Hence this trade is more like a foray into alien territory than like a business deal in the grain or cloth bazaar.

An enterprising, traveled people, the Johari Bhotias sent their children to modern schools so that by the time of independence there were educated men and women among them who followed national developments and soon recognized the advantages of voting strength. They formed a "Kumaon Bhotia People's Federation," made overtures to the previously deprecated eastern Bhotias, and presented petitions to Government asking that regulations be enacted to protect all the Bhotias.

Then came the events that prompted them to look more anxiously to government protection. When the Chinese took over Tibet, they insisted that Tibetans deal with China rather than with India. This quickly stifled the Bhotias' trade. With this loss, the Johari Bhotias became all the more eager to share in any benefits their government might give. They began a campaign to be counted as a scheduled tribe even though the Uttar Pradesh government had decided that none in the state should be so listed. Johari Bhotias are not concerned about any opprobrium in this official designation. Their need for aid is all the greater because their own social campaign has been undermined by battles between great nations.

Santals of the Jamshedpur Vicinity, Bihar

Santal mobility efforts are aimed directly toward the new political power and status, passing over the traditional varna models. Santal leaders do advocate new standards for conduct but they present them as Santal virtues, sanctioned by Santal tradition and deities, rather than as a return to ancient Kshatriya or Brahmin models. This movement insists on preserving the ancient Santal identity and gods and deliberately rejects some of the most sacred elements—the sacredness of the cow for one—in scriptural Hinduism. The special quality of Santal mobility is illustrated in Martin Orans' comment that "Once I saw a young party activist who had grown up in the Jharkhand movement persuading an older Santal with a few years of education that he must take up beef eating again if he wished to preserve the Santal caste" (1965, p. 108).

The Santals are one of the largest of tribal groupings in India. There are well over three million who speak Santali, a language of the Munda stock, and who live in parts of Orissa, Bihar, and West Bengal. There was very little political cohesion among them but there was and is considerable cultural similarity and very strong feelings among all Santals that they are utterly different from Hindus (Culshaw 1949, pp. 15–24). This powerful sentiment was reinforced by the great event of their history, the Santal rebellion of 1855–1857, an uprising that is still commemorated in their songs and tales and holds a central place in their memory.

The rebellion was a convulsive attempt to wipe out the steady loss of land and livelihood to nontribal immigrants into their territories. Like other tribal peoples, Santals could not cope with the financial and legal procedures that the newcomers manipulated nor could they resist the blandishments that led them into debt and to legal loss of their lands. After years of fruitless complaints they united to rise in arms. With arrows, spears, and axes they slaughtered many of the immigrants, routed the police forces sent against them, and even held off an army unit (O'Malley 1941, pp. 421–430). But they were finally defeated in a series of bloody debacles and their leaders were imprisoned or executed. The rebellion has become a glorious memory of courage and unity against insufferable wrongs and has deepened Santal feelings of separatism.

Santal detachment is social rather than cultural. The Santal have kinship usages similar to those of Hindus of the region, they depend on artisan jatis for most manufactured goods, they bring in Harijan midwives to assist at births. Some even establish bonds of fictive relationship with jati people, though close ties with particular friends do not erase their opinion of jati people in general. Orans writes, "that portion of Santal culture shared by all Santal is so marked with Hindu traits that it would be a monumental task to indicate all of them" (1965, pp. 42–43; see also Datta-Majumder 1956, pp. 98–129; Kochar 1963, pp. 176–178).

Some of the wealthier, landed families took on "twice-born" practices; beef eating and cow sacrifice were abandoned, dress and marriage customs were changed. The significant fact is that almost none tried to become Hindu or to be known as a jati. Christian missionaries made some Santal converts, particularly the mission supported by Scandinavian and American efforts, which included over 25,000 Santal Christians in 1941. Among the Santals as elsewhere in India, a major contribution of the missionaries was to open educational opportunities for many who would not otherwise have had any schooling at all (Orans 1965, pp. 87–90; Culshaw 1949, pp. 161–174).

In 1908 the steel mill and the company city at Jamshedpur in southern Santal country were built. These establishments had important bearing on Santal adaptation. Both educated and illiterate Santals found suitable work there; in the industrial setting they saw no reason to try for higher ritual rank or to emulate the traditional models of high status. The outlook of the Jamshedpur workers became known to other Santals. "The aspiring Santal who was well acquainted with Jamshedpur might adopt Western clothes, an automobile or motorcycle, and a *pukha* house (one with modern facilities) rather than vegetarianism, teetotalism, and a sacred thread. . . ." (Orans 1965, p. 101). Not many rural Santals are educated and wealthy enough to aspire to such heights, but they follow the lead set by educated Santals. One of the educated became a founder of a popular new religious cult and others are the chief supporters of the mass political party.

The cult was established partly in anticipation of the 1951 Census, to show Santal strength. Many Santals had previously been enumerated as Hindus by the census takers. The cult is called *Sarna*

Dharam Semlet, Sacred Grove Religious Organization, after the main locale of the tribal deities and the site of religious ceremonies. A Santal high-school graduate was one of the chief creators of this religion and has been given the title of Esteemed Guru. He has written a long epic-heroic play that is a parable about the proper duty of the Santals, the iniquity of jati people, and the noble virtues of the Santal heroes. It indicates to Santals that they too are worthy of having a scriptural epic. Another educated Santal has adduced archeological evidence in support of the story; less sophisticated Santals say that the epic play was written as the result of a revelation. The Guru has invented a script for writing Santali and there are plans for an authoritative text of Santal tradition written in the new script (Orans 1965, pp. 113–119). The new rites emphasize the main features of tribal worship, not only worship in the sacred grove, but also offerings of beer, dancing at ceremonies, and even the sacrifice of cows. In these matters, they make no concession to Hindu sensitivities, indeed they stress such distinguishing features as ways of differentiating themselves from Hindus.

In a larger respect, however, this revitalization movement has made a fundamental concession.

Its proponents implicitly tell the Santal that the traditional tribal religion, which lacked scripture, preceptors, epics, and large-scale coordinated ceremonies, needs to be remodeled. It is being recast in a transcendental mold fashioned after the examples of Christianity and Islam as well as of Hinduism. This implicit acknowledgment is part of what Orans calls the "rank concession syndrome," the acceptance by tribal peoples of their social and cultural inferiority to jati society and their consequent attempts to raise their social level in their own terms and by their own means (Orans 1965, pp. 123–146).

One of the means to advancement is the Jharkhand Party founded by Jai Pal Singh, an Oxford-educated Christian of the Munda tribe. A proclaimed aim of the party was to carve out a new state of the Indian union in the Chotanagpur area in which tribal peoples would be numerically dominant. Although it was organized as a pantribal movement, it also helped unify the Santals within their localities. It gave them a contrajati cause and a program on which all Santals, educated and noneducated, landed elite and ordinary villagers, could agree. It reinforced their ancient separatism from jati people while it mitigated cleavages within their own Santal society. The area headquarters of the party were located just outside Jamshedpur and served as a rallying place for Santals as well as for other tribals in the city and surrounding villages.

For the Santals in Jamshedpur the party offers an important new basis for social interaction and solidarity. Their industrial jobs do not provide for their social needs; the traditional solidarity rites cannot well be carried on in the city. Marriages tend to be contracted between individual families and weddings are no longer great dramatic declarations of alliances formed between two large groups of kin. Although the old Santal ceremonies cannot be staged as they were in the villages, political rallies serve some of the same social functions. Plays are performed, traditional dances are arranged, songs and conviviality prevail. The rallies are pleasure occasions similar to the festive occasions so important in traditional Santal life (Orans 1965, pp. 93–104). And yet the pleasure is not really the same; the occasions are more scheduled and limited, and the leaders guide the celebrations through a tempered, sober program.

Although educated Santals set no great store by the high insignia of Hinduism, they have been disciplined by their schooling to accept certain of its scriptural values, such as the emphasis on deferment of gratification. They have been indoctrinated with the idea of the advantages of thrift, moderation, and hard work, or at least of a regular stint of work. This acculturation is increasing now that Santal children in the vicinity of Jamshedpur attend school. The changes Orans noted, particularly among Santal industrial workers, are likely to continue and to accelerate. One of the fundamental changes is an increased emphasis on work, study, and rank attainment and a concomitant discouragement of "pleasure" (Orans 1965, p. 109). Thus many Santals are finally taking on the attitudes and values of contemporary Indian civilization even as they are vigorously rejecting the traditional symbols of Hinduism.

Social Transitions and Systemic Stages

These case examples illustrate the general trend of change among most tribal peoples in India. Like the Kond headman of Baderi village, they are making a dual transition, shifting to traditional jati standards and, in midcourse, adding changes toward modern, especially political, conduct. Among the five groups we have discussed, the Kotas are handicapped in this effort by their small number and by their lack of a wider jati-cluster, of ready-made allies. This may be why some Kotas cling to the nostalgic and obsolete view of what their wider society was like. Tribal associations have been formed among each of the other four tribes discussed. To be sure, the mere existence of an association does not guarantee that it will have social impact; some remain empty forms, others quietly become defunct. Nevertheless, an association does indicate that some leaders have become aware of the need for a new kind of social organization to grapple with the new conditions of social hierarchy.

The Bhumij have had some difficulty in making the new adaptation because many of them find it hard to forget what they claimed to be. They had nearly nailed down their claim to be Kshatriyas when they were directed toward a different model and organization by the movement for national independence.

The Bhotias had few difficulties in turning about, but they had the added push of the modern expansion of China, which sent them rapidly toward the shelter of their government. Santal leaders, too, have not been reluctant to try modern political organization, although they have done so on their own terms. They developed their own sect and supported a tribal political party. Under the banner of tribal cultural revival, they are trying to alter their basic tribal characteristics to accord with those of Indian civilization.

Konds have been more typical of the present trend among tribal peoples. Their tribal association attempts to do for all the Konds what the headman's guru was trying to do for his disciple. In teaching the headman to be a devout Hindu and a "Hindu gentleman" the guru enables him to participate more effectively in the new mode of local politics. The tribal association, quite like a caste association, is trying to reform Kond customs, to improve Kond education, and to pave the way for political weight in state politics.

In certain ways modern standards resemble the old tribal characteristics. Educated people are usually in favor of a greater degree of personal equality, of individual independence, of marital choice, of dietary latitude than is traditionally proper for those of high jati rank. These modern values are closer to tribal than to "twice-born" standards. In many other ways, however, the modern values impose requirements that any civilization, including the traditional Indian civilization, imposes on elite classes. The requirement for self-discipline, for greater specialization of function, for differentiation of roles, and for the maintenance of widespread relations beyond those of kinship.

The several civilizational styles that have been pressed on tribesmen are alike in fundamental respects even though they differ vastly in content. Tribesmen have been exhorted by modern-day Hindu preachers to turn to the purer practices of the high varnas; Christian missionaries have advocated Christian values; welfare workers have explained the advantages of modern conduct and education. The protagonists of each give them similar advice; they urge them to defer immediate gratification for the sake of some greater, long-range good, to mask expressions of sensuality, to prize sobriety and hard work, to revere the written word and the learned code. Now their own association leaders urge them to show these values in their personal conduct for the greater good of their ancient tribe.

In the long view of human change, we see that the development from tribe to jati began in India several millennia ago when technological innovations, especially that of plough agriculture, made possible the social-cultural invention of civilization. The Indian version of civilization developed caste organization. Improved technology opened the possibility for civilization development, but civilization and civilized peoples did not overwhelm all tribal societies.

In recent centuries the intellectual revolution of science and the great technological revolutions have similarly opened many new possibilities for human development. Worldwide changes have been set in motion and the movement is influencing the lives of Indian villagers, whether they are organized in jatis or in tribes. Both jatis and tribes are far less isolated than they were, both are much more affected by world forces, both are much more closely bound into their wider, national society.

The closer social involvement brings cultural changes. Some tribesmen, like the Hill Maria Gonds, make the changes unwillingly because they feel disadvantaged by them. Like many other tribesmen of earlier times they feel that any gain in material benefits and social resources is offset by losses of firm identity, close solidarity, religious satisfaction, and emotional security. They do not want to slip from a proud tribe to an inferior jati. Such ideas have long influenced tribesmen to hold off encroachments of jati people and customs.

Now, however, the encroaching pressures are greater and the advantages of change seem larger. Tribesmen and jati villagers are being influenced in the same tidal direction of change. That tide does not wash away or wipe out difference among groups nor the considerable difference in the pace of their change. It does steadily press them toward a new kind of social organization and a revised set of cultural standards.

In the long view of caste society, the absorption of tribal peoples into jati structure is part of recurrent change. New recruits are incorporated; the overall social system and the component systems remain unaltered. But from the view of tribal society, the same events entail systemic change. Former tribesmen enter into a different kind of social system when they act fully as jati members. They then take on more differentiated roles and more specialized functions than they typically have under tribal organization. In comparison with tribal organization, jati organization makes it possible for a society to have a much greater carrying capacity in numbers of people and in productive content.

Jati organization, as we have seen, is being changed. Status advance can now be played out on larger social scenes than before, those of region, state, and nation. In the wider scenes, there is more differentiation, specialization, and carrying capacity than there usually is within a parochial jati hierarchy. This suggests that caste society may be undergoing systemic change to a new level of social organization. The systemic change in jati organization may perhaps be understood as recurrent change toward modern, global organization, just as systemic change in a tribal society can be seen as recurrent change into caste society.

PART **VIII** *Continuities and Trends*

CHAPTER 33

Psychological Forces, Social
Processes, and Systemic
Shift

THE people who together engage in a social sys-
tem must share certain critical psychological characteristics if the
system is to work. The following summary of our social analysis
therefore begins with a discussion of two psychological factors
that are particularly important in this system. One is a cognitive
assumption, the other is a personal motivation. The two are used
as generative principles in the grammar of social action. Both are
applied in much of a person's social interaction. These themes of
personal behavior underlie the social competition that is carried on
at all levels. The very acts of waging competitive conflict help to
confirm the contestants' conviction that status is worth the struggle.

Contests for status are part of the adaptive capacity of the
whole social system. Groups that came to be materially successful
(whether through their abilities, or fortunate opportunities, or
both) could rise in their local social orders and did not feel impelled
to disrupt the general system. Also, a local order could be adapted
to accommodate new groups and institutions. The people of a
locality could set up relations with alien groups without feeling
that their own social integrity and status were necessarily endan-
gered by such relations. The groups that were absorbed socially
generally became assimilated culturally to the precepts of caste
society.

These processes resulted in recurrent change in local social orders
and in the long-term stability of the fundamental system. The
parameters of that system are now being altered and with them
some of the systemic principles appear to be changing. The shifts
may possibly affect the psychological modes of perception and

motivation that have supported the traditional social concepts and structure. The psychological features of cognitive assumption and personal motivation have been mentioned in earlier chapters; it is useful to examine them together here.

Themes of Personal Behavior

The cognitive assumption is that most interaction occurs between a superior and a subordinate, or between representatives of a dominant and of a dependent group. One's society is therefore seen as a hierarchical order; that order defines the relative positions of the actors in a social situation in advance of their interaction. Dominance and subordination are fundamental dimensions in all societies, not only in India, and advance definition of social position is a requisite condition in all social systems.

In Indian village society the hierarchical assumption is applied particularly widely, stringently, and intensively. It is constantly reinforced by being linked to a person's bodily experience as well as to his religious beliefs. Each person's biological functions, especially his acts of ingestion, are in some measure the concern of all in his jati. If he falls below the jati's standards of ritual purity and pollution, then all may be in peril of sinking to a lower social position. His body thus becomes an arena in which weighty issues of group status are at stake. Each child learns that he himself becomes more defiled or more pure according to his daily acts and experiences. The criteria of ritual purity and pollution that mark off these different states of an individual's being are also used to demarcate the social strata of his society.

Some important exemptions from the hierarchical perspective have been noted above. Within the family, relations between brother and sister and between mother and child are construed with a different emphasis. A self-dedicated holy man, a sadhu, has presumably removed himself from the social frame. There are situations in which hierarchy is not a primary assumption, as among those who are struggling together against a common opponent, whether they are persecuted sectarians or college classmates. These and other exceptions are not few, but they are nonetheless exceptions to the prevailing assumption of hierarchy.

In relations among people of different jatis, the hierarchical assumption has been linked with postulated differences in ritual pollution and purity. One outcome of holding these linked assumptions is that the ritual superiority of Brahmins has been acknowledged by most of those who held secular power. Brahmins could legitimate power and sometimes made skillful use of this prerogative. Another reason Brahmins possessed such durable influence was that the dominant jatis (and the Rajas in earlier times), in acknowledging the ritual superiority of Brahmins, were also affirming the validity of the hierarchical principles central to their own conduct. For this reason also there has been considerable inertia about untouchables rising and Brahmins falling in a local order. In maintaining clear extremes of their social order, the people of a locality were also maintaining clear exemplars of the assumptions by which they regulated their lives.

Those assumptions are translated into a social map by the varna categories, to which have lately been added the overlapping categories involving modern conduct. Muslims, Christians, and Jews set up analogous divisions of their own. Ambitious villagers model their conduct according to the reference category of a high varna and, more particularly, after the living examples of the reference groups whose behavior they can see. In their emulations and mobility struggles, villagers demonstrate to themselves and to all their society, in the characteristic circular way, that their hierarchical assumption is indeed true.

Coupled with this image of hierarchical society is a characteristic image of one's self as worthy of being a superior within a close bracket of rank. A man does not typically feel impelled to challenge the superiority of those high above him in any hierarchy; dependency on such superiors is not deprecated, whether the superior is a revered guru or a powerful official. Subordination to someone in a proximal rank, however, is often felt to be uncomfortable and something to be changed as soon as possible. This personal motivation is the other source of the perennial press toward recurrent change.

How this motivation and confident self-image have been inculcated are matters about which we can only speculate, since detailed studies are not yet available. Certainly these ideas are absorbed early in childhood from family experience. Perhaps one factor is the great importance to a mother, at almost all social levels, of the birth of her child. The child, particularly the first son, becomes a kind of social savior for her; each of her other children, in turn, can be the subject of her open emotional expression in a milieu that provides few other approved emotional outlets for a young woman. It may be that this focusing of maternal attention and affection gives a child an especially strong sense of his own worth. Whatever the causal factors in Indian family life may turn out to be, it is clear that these motifs of personality have been widely shared by men and women of the various regions and social strata on the subcontinent. This same personal motivation bestirs untouchables at the bottom of a local order (provided that they are not utterly crushed by poverty) as well as the elite of the upper ranks.

The response to acts rising from this motivation is defensive. The same man who gathers his strength to challenge a superior knows that some of those subordinate to him are probably preparing to challenge him. This makes him very sensitive about the prerogatives and symbols of any superior status he may hold. It leads to a style of personal relations that I have elsewhere termed "aggressive defense" (Mandelbaum 1955, pp. 235–239).

As against the instability of proximal relations there is the relative stability of distal relations. Villagers not only agree that there is a hierarchical frame to society but also that certain parts and figures are outside the arena of open competition.

Within a family a man's father has the more distal role, his brother the more proximal role. Solidarity among brothers is apt to weaken once the authority of the father is gone. One brother challenges another, eventually the family separates, with added bitterness because each tends to blame the other for rupturing the ideal. Both also blame the women, partly to gloss over fraternal hostility, partly because the women of the family are also competitors among themselves. The young bride must be subservient to her mother-in-law, but as she becomes a mother and a matron she can begin to challenge her mother-in-law and to contend with any other of the sons' wives in the family. Although certain aspects of family relations do indeed differ by social level and by region, these family processes are shared across regions and jatis. When a low-ranking family begins to rise, its members tend to take on the family patterns of the higher jatis.

Beyond the family, one lineage of a jati may challenge another; the people of one village, under some circumstances, try to outstrip another village. The principal group for challenge and confrontation, however, has been the jati. It is, as we have seen, a main unit of a man's identification, a principal agency for individual and group power, the chief vessel of status. A villager's aggressive defense of his honor—the term izzat, as previously noted, expresses the concept for many in North India—combines defense of personal and family status with defense of the integrity, standards, and prestige of his jati.

Competition and Conflict as Systemic Processes

Competition among jatis is common and is better understood as an outcome of the basic motivation than as the root cause of village conflict. The importance of this motivation is shown when a jati or a jati-group is so firmly entrenched that its members fear no challenge from others. Challenge and conflict are then likely to come up *within* that group. Some of its members will feel subordinate to other members and will sooner or later dispute their superiority. The personal motivation toward challenge of immediate superiors is constant, and so is social competition.

It is a competition without end, not only because every superior feels that some of his subordinates will eventually defy him, but also because a man who is a superior in certain contexts generally feels himself to be a subordinate in others. He may be impelled to try to improve his position in those contexts while being warily defensive in others. The competition can yield enlivening rewards as well as nagging anxieties. A man may get considerable personal satisfaction from the results of his status strivings, as he does when he brings off an advantageous marriage in his family, or gains a precious ritual symbol for his jati, or helps put a kinsman into a position of power and prestige.

Competition is pervasive in many life situations, but there is also much in a villager's life that it does not pervade. As we have noted, there are exempt relations and situations. Relations between fully acknowledged superiors and reciprocally valued subordinates tend to be secure and assured (cf. Carstairs 1957, p. 106). The subordinate then prizes rather than resents his dependency. For some people religion is a secure resource against the abrasions of competition. In the scriptural ideal a man who has fulfilled his family duties opts out of the social competition and into religious devotion. There are also some individuals and groups who prefer to be neutral and who try to remain on the sidelines of any competitive arena. Often they succeed in doing so for a time, but they are apt to be nudged periodically into competition by forces of the social system.

Failure in mobility efforts is allayed by the very assumption of social hierarchy. A defeated group is not obliterated or condemned to complete helplessness. Some of its members may be beaten, a few even killed, a number of its wealthier families may lose much of their wealth, but the group is generally not much worse off than it was before. The victors are usually satisfied to have the defeated resume their subordinate positions. The superiors need their goods and services, and they also need inferiors below them to shore up their position as superiors.

The ideology of noncompetitive varnas is firmly believed while competitive social action among jatis is zealously waged. At any given time and place, some groups may be rising and others may be losing ground in their local order. This fluctuation is one reason for differing opinions about just where a particular group is to be placed.

Conflict within families is also disapproved in the villagers' ideology yet is inherent in their actual relations. In a family the stress point at which conflict is likely to erupt occurs when grown brothers, bereft of parental regulation, must reach some important decision about their domestic economy.

Among jatis, village ceremonies have often been occasions for outbreaks of conflict when each jati at the feast must be seated in order of relative rank. Such conflicts may consolidate each contesting group and reinforce the idea that higher rank is highly important. So quarrels about rank result from and also buttress the psychological themes.

Adaptive Capacities

The traditional social system was putatively closed and immutable but actually provided openings, if difficult and limited ones, for the rise of ambitious groups. The *Manu* version of fixed varnas was rarely denied, but the real possibility of status rise promised success to those who could best adapt. Adaptive success for a group within the society could be initiated by skillful development of economic resources, by military conquests, by settling new lands, by adroit trading or political acumen, or through any other fortunate exploitation of the environment. Military prowess has not been a means for jati rise for some time, but the other avenues to status gain are still in use. Few can achieve much ritual advance in their own lifetime, but they may raise their material base enough to glimpse the self-promised niche that may be occupied by their descendants.

A main adaptive feature of jati society as a whole is the capacity to absorb alien groups who then become contestants for rank and thus supporters of the whole system. Such groups could readily be absorbed because jati villagers did not feel threatened by cultural differences among their neighbors. They could carry on restricted relations with those of different customs without loss to their own standards or status. Tribesmen have been continually absorbed socially and then assimilated culturally; jati folk could accept them as low-ranking dependents or, if circumstances so dictated, as dominant landowners, without impairing their own caste society. Immigrants from another region of India or from outside the subcontinent were similarly accommodated. The early Christian, Jewish, and Muslim traders were absorbed into jati society and retained their religious identity. Foreign raiders who settled down to found dynastic kingdoms made their peace with the jati system. The British tried to keep aloof from the system of caste relations, but as wielders of paramount political power they did affect the system. Yet for all their influence on it they did not change the fundamentals or the pervasiveness of caste relations.

Jati people could cope with introduced institutions as well as with introduced groups. The British brought in new kinds of bureaucracy, law, learning, and technology; all were promptly utilized for jati as well as personal purposes. When the colonial bureaucracy was established, for example, there was not much question as to whether taking part in it was good for one's family and jati. Those who understood that they could get a respectable place in that hierarchy were usually far more concerned about how to get the highest possible place than whether it was good to participate at all. They took to the new institutions as providing auxiliary criteria of high status, new opportunities for attaining higher rank and additional channels for mobility.

Long before the impact of European influences, villagers dealt with strong outside influences—economic, governmental, and religious—without changing the bases of their social structure. The economic effects of irrigation, for example, were anciently felt in villages of the Tanjore area and the jati structure was fully maintained. It was maintained in Totegadde in Mysore where a cash crop has been grown for centuries. Such economic forces have had important consequences. They have affected the order of the jatis in a locality but they have not disrupted the jati order.

In governmental matters, villagers had ways of giving a Raja his minimal due while actually managing their local affairs through their own devices. British institutions of government were potentially inimical to the traditional system, but as we have seen, villagers quite successfully subsumed British law and police order within their own political code and jati order.

The introduced religions of temporal rulers, Islam and Christianity, attracted millions of converts and influenced the whole civilization. Their influence did not undermine the traditional social system. Moreover, the internal tendency toward religious revolt against the system created social groups that were regularly incorporated back into that system.

Social Mobility and System Maintenance

The system was used so adaptively because people applied the thematic principles both steadfastly and flexibly. They applied the hierarchical perspective steadfastly to new as well as to habitual situations; they applied it flexibly, not insisting on any single or completely calibrated hierarchy for all occasions. There is a certain flexibility even at the extremes of a local jati order. Most in a locality agree that certain jatis are lowest, but members of each of these low jatis typically insist that at least one of the others should be ranked below their own group. In this sense there is usually no absolute bottom to a local ladder of rank and in a parallel sense there is no absolute top.

Those who occupy the topmost rung are apt to compete among themselves for the best place along that rung, or they may look to a grander struggle in a wider arena. During the British regime, for example, a Maharaja might be the unchallenged suzerain within his state, with only a very few and broad constraints imposed on his conduct by the paramount British authority. Yet many such princes constantly tried to improve on the honors officially allotted to them at ceremonial occasions from, say, a ceremonial salute of nine guns to the eleven-gun class.

The drives toward social advance are quite constant, but the tactics for advance are varied. Different routes are possible; the traditional alternatives are in the three "twice-born" varnas. Though these reference categories are very different in certain respects, all three stipulate certain broadly similar kinds of behavior, as in the relations between men and women and in the discipline of conduct. Those who attempt to move up into any one of these higher echelons must conform to the broad standards required of all leading groups in Indian civilization. A convert to Islam or Christianity from a low jati is urged to discipline himself in ways that are similar in general, though different in details, from those he would follow in seeking high varna status as a Hindu.

Whatever route may be chosen, effective rise begins with the prospering of individual families. Hopes for higher rank are futile unless steeled with secular strength. Individual families can achieve real advance only as part of a larger group and so prospering families deploy their secular resources to achieve ritual gains for their group. To succeed, their leaders must simultaneously cope with external opposition and maintain internal strength.

Success against opposing jatis is usually achieved gradually, in a series of steps beginning with changes to which others cannot well object. As the aspiring villagers build a base of wealth and purity, they begin to make more open assertions that are more objectionable to those who rank above them. In Senapur village, the Earthworkers decided to wear the sacred thread. It is at such points that escalating aspirations and growing hostility to them come to a head and there is a confrontation, commonly a whole series of physical, legal, and societal encounters. The confrontation may be delayed if the higher groups have taken to modern standards and therefore set less store by the traditional symbols that the aspirants are trying to attain. The confrontation may be postponed but it is not annulled.

To overcome in such confrontations, an aspiring group must mobilize united effort. Unity is usually a difficult problem. All sections of a jati do not improve their resources and local standing at the same rate. The most advanced sections may have reformed their practices so greatly that they can scarcely admit to being jati partners with those who have not reformed. Moreover the success of some tends to arouse challenges from others within the jati.

If the more successful members find that they cannot muster enough cultural and social unity for their purpose, they may redefine the boundaries of the group. In the traditional process the more advanced or dissatisfied families split off and declared themselves to be a separate jati. Occasionally such sections joined with similarly mobile sections of other jatis in an action that entailed fusion as well as fission. With fresh unity, they then proceeded to battle for higher rank.

Individuals identify with different kinds of groups as different situations require and may compete for higher rank in each context. A vigorous villager strives mightily to advance and defend his family's rank among the families of his jati, but when he participates in a village panchayat on an issue affecting his jati, he is apt to be a firm proponent of the jati more than of his family. Should the repute of his village be at stake on some occasion, he is likely to identify with the village and to challenge those of other villages.

In some contexts he may fight to advance the status of his religion, or his region, or his language group. To be sure, he may not always know where to put the greater effort. He does not always switch identification smoothly; a village leader may sometimes be torn between advancing the interests of his village or that of his jati.

Moreover, an ambitious leader must be task-oriented as well as rank-oriented. He must focus on what is to be done for the village as well as on who gains rank advantage by what is done. The two interests are usually not completely separate; the one impinges on the other, but neither should be scanted if the leader is to be successful in an enterprise. Balancing off each consideration is a constant problem for leaders at all levels. This is indeed true in all complex societies; it is a particularly potent problem for village leaders in India.

Those who strive for social mobility do not challenge the hierarchical frame but believe rather that they are only trying to restore their proper place within it. Those who oppose them believe that the climbers are trying to alter the ordained order of society.

From the wider view of our analysis, the challengers are right, though not for the reasons they give. They are right because their efforts are part of the grand counterchange within the general social system through which secular power and ritual rank are kept in a broad parity. That parity, however, is not without exceptions. There are poor and ineffectual Brahmins, even whole jatis of them. Conversely, an occasional village Harijan may be rich and influential. Yet by and large, the higher jatis of a locality are the wealthier and more powerful, the poorest are also lowest in ritual rank. So, as we have noted, acts that are intended to disturb an existing, static local order of rank, simultaneously serve to maintain the dynamic, adaptive general system of jati relations.

Recurrent and Systemic Change

The system of society in India was changed in the ancient past; the earliest Vedic scriptures reflect a social order of relatively open classes rather than of bounded jatis. After the classic system of caste became established, perhaps a millennium ago, temporal rulers sometimes intervened in the ranking but did not alter the systemic principles. A freebooter who seized state power could enhance the rank of his own jati and could manipulate the village ranking of other jatis through grants of land and of privilege.

During the period of British rule, ranking seems to have become more rigid. Greater emphasis was apparently given to the ritual criteria for rank, and greater power apparently accrued to jatis whose men were already high and dominant. These were not really systemic changes. The major social units remained the same; the assumptions about high and low status were unchanged; relations among jatis were carried on in the same way; and mobility campaigns continued, though with some shift in mobility tactics.

Political independence has set in train a series of social and economic changes that are still very much in the making. In some ways the trend seems to be a return to the precolonial condition when state power could directly impinge on jati ranking. Modern political power is based, not on military conquest, patents of nobility, and grants of land, but on voting influence, official positions, and such boons as tube wells, roads, and import licenses. Changes in the avenues to wealth and power have brought about changes in mobility procedures. Some low-ranking groups, obstructed in their villages, have appealed to higher political authorities, have organized for voting purposes, and have acquired offices, grants, and local influence. They have detoured the traditional step-by-step procedure and have struck directly for respectable status through political action.

With the increasing success of such actions, there has come a consequent decline in the attractions of the traditional symbols of high rank. Thus those Noniyas who succeeded after long and bitter struggle in wearing the sacred thread now find that their sons are quite uninterested in doing so. Men of the higher jatis are no longer so concerned as they were about who wears this ritual badge because many of them, like the younger Noniya, are more concerned with badges of higher modern education than with badges of higher varna status.

Ambitious men now find the fusion of jatis for political strength more effective than the fission of jatis for ritual purity. Hence many jati leaders urge the enlargement of their endogamous group by encouraging marriages among previously separate, though similar, jatis. The trend is toward fewer, wider, better organized jatis. Villagers continue to assume that endogamy is a central factor for social solidarity, that social groups are ranked, and that one's own group must constantly try to advance or to defend its social position. The systemic changes that are in view do not point directly toward an unstratified society but toward fewer and more homogeneous social groups. These changes will not necessarily be rapid; much hinges on the rate of economic improvement.

The major changes in Indian society are in the same direction as that taken by broad changes in other contemporary societies. The general trend is toward the narrowing in cultural disparities and in social distances between groups in a society, though scarcely toward any total elimination of stratification. There is a general shift away from traditional status symbols to modern political and technological symbols. Disadvantaged groups at every level of society are entering the political arena as they had not been able to do before.

The common trends come out of the broadly similar influences of modern technology, industry, education, and communication. These forces set the parameters for the evolving social systems, though they do not determine the precise nature of any of them. But the parameters do frame a new type of social system, to which most of the former systems are being changed. This brings us back to the suggestion raised at the end of the previous chapter. It seems that the systemic changes within one major society, as in India, do appear as incipient recurrent change when viewed in the perspective of modern world civilization.

CHAPTER **34** Trends

INDIAN society is being changed in some major ways. These shifts are still in the process of being worked out and their full importance cannot yet be assessed. However, certain directions of social development are clearly apparent. We discuss these trends in this chapter, focusing on changes in family relations as illustrative of the general direction of social change and of a particular paradigm of change.

Drives and Hindrances to Social Change

Many in India now take government to be a principal engine of social change. Even those who are politically conservative agree that a good part of social change must be stimulated and directed by governmental agencies. Main responsibility for these innovative, reformist functions of government rests with the new elite, as M. N. Srinivas terms the growing class of educated people in India from whose ranks come those who manage the affairs of state (1966, pp. 69–82). Though members of this class vary greatly in their political views and social identifications, they share certain basic concepts about the desirability of social change and about desirable kinds of change.

The successes of new elite since independence are sometimes overlooked or underrated. A glance at the condition of other peoples who achieved new nationhood at about the same time shows that those of India might have fared a good deal worse if their national leaders had been less astute, dedicated, and able. Yet there are few, whether villagers or urban elite, who are satisfied with the achievements thus far or with the current rate of change toward the material and social goals that many in India want to reach.

The nation's potential for achieving these goals is handicapped by several sets of circumstances. One is the sheer magnitude of the problem of changing the ways of so large a population with so many living in deep poverty. There are, in addition, the inherent contradictions and inevitable conflicts that confront any people whose leaders seek rapid development—contradictions made less tractable in India by the size of the population and the extent of the poverty. Some observers have said that national plans have been hampered by misconceptions concerning the nature of Indian society—a hindrance that is of particular interest for our present study.

The magnitude of the effort required to direct fundamental social changes in a nation that includes about one seventh of the human race has been amply noted by many writers. Only a few of the main facts and conclusions need be cited here. Although economic output has been rising steadily, the gross national product is still relatively low. Within the nation, a large part of the population is abysmally poor.[1] Families that are so perilously poor— and there are many millions of them—can scarcely do much about raising their productivity or changing their social standards.

The problem of population growth illustrates one of the many contradictory situations that planners and legislators must face. Allocating substantial resources to improve health and lengthen life may well increase the pressure of population on the nation's economy and so diminish the sparse resources available for development purposes. Other contrary pressures arise between the drive for social equality and that for productive efficiency. Wider distribution of land ownership may, in the initial stages, lower production because of the disruption in agricultural management. A most important difficulty is that major development projects are long-term enterprises which take many years before they can pay off, yet political leaders come under public pressures to produce tangible benefits quickly.

Added to the popular pressures for swift material results are the

[1] For example, a 1962 sample survey of 8,655 rural households showed that the poorer 50 percent of these households held about 7 percent of the total reproducible wealth, and accounted for about 22 percent of the total income. The households in the poorer half of the sample owned very little of the total land; 62 percent of them had incomes of less than $250 per year (Lokanathan 1965a, pp. vii, 112–121; 1965b, p. 3).

ideological pressures for quick social results. The major political parties have held forth the promise of greater social justice as well as greater prosperity for the nation. National leaders have frequently depicted the caste system as the great obstacle in the way of achieving both justice and prosperity (e.g. Nehru 1946, pp. 112–113; Narayan 1958, p. 87). Such leaders feel that they must use strong rhetoric if they are to jolt the strongly entrenched social system, but the rhetoric tends to becloud the social perceptions of planners and legislators. If policy makers view much of the existing village society as absolutely inimical to national welfare and as a system that must be eliminated before long, they are not intellectually prepared to deal with that society in suitably constructive ways. They cannot quickly eradicate the social patterns they condemn and they are not likely to search for those forces in the existing society that can be channeled toward the constructive goals they desire.

Misconceptions about Social Change

Misconceptions about the nature of Indian society have been cultivated by some scholars. A volume of essays by an economist, K. William Kapp, entitled *Hindu Culture, Economic Development, and Economic Planning in India* (1963), is a case in point. One of Kapp's principal conclusions is that ". . . Hindu culture and Hindu social organization are determining factors in India's low rate of development" (p. 64). Kapp's views parallel those of Max Weber whose work of 1915 on the religion of India has influenced a good many of the later sociological and economic writings (cf. Weber 1958; Bendix 1960, pp. 158–211; Singer MS. 1969).

In a rebuttal to Kapp's arguments and to the Weber thesis, Milton Singer has pointed out that adequate empirical evidence for such conclusions is not given in the works proclaiming this thesis and that there is considerable evidence to indicate that Hindu culture and caste society have not had any great dampening effect on economic development. Moreover, Kapp's conclusions are largely speculative extrapolations from misunderstood scriptural concepts. These speculations, Singer says, are presented as if they were "a collection of proven generalizations from which far-reaching policy decisions should be drawn" (1966, p. 505). Singer notes that some policy-makers in India share these unproven and misleading ideas about the relation of Indian society to economic development. "In that case, these ideological commitments of a relatively small group of political and intellectual leaders may become as important a limitation on economic growth as any feature of the traditional value and belief system or of the social structure" (Singer, 1966, p. 502).

The common clichés about caste society and economic development appear in Gunnar Myrdal's comprehensive, and in some respects, most illuminating *Asian Drama*. Myrdal begins by stressing his commitment to "a broad institutional approach" (p. ix) but despite the cogency of his institutional analysis in economic terms, he underestimates the force of the institutions of Indian society. Thus Myrdal writes (p. 1081) that in the main there are no institutional spurs driving Indian people to work and work hard. Quite to the contrary, as the village studies show, the prevalent quest for status is a constant spur to hard work, though the fruits of diligent labor may be spent in expensive confrontations, in litigation, in conspicuous consumption, and in other ways that an economist might describe as uneconomic. These may well be disadvantageous in the economist's perception, not necessarily so in the villagers'.

When Myrdal states (p. 1692) that the masses in South Asia do not calculate rationally in terms of costs, returns, and maximum profit, he is neglecting their own social calculations which are as rational in their village milieu as the economist's calculations are in his milieu. In the same passage, Myrdal writes that the masses in countries like those of South Asia are not interested in raising their living standards and he adds that this is "confirmed by anthropological studies all over the world." Anthropological studies confirm no such conclusion.

Some of Myrdal's comments are cogent, some even startling. For example he notes that on the basis of all his information he believes that the masses on the Indian subcontinent live in worse poverty than did those in the Western European countries during the several centuries before the industrial revolution (1968, p. 688). He also concludes that the growth of population is the single most important social change that has taken place in South Asia since

World War II. "It has been far more important than any reform or development efforts and it has done a great deal to thwart these efforts" (1968, p. 1530).

Yet some of his statements about Indian society and character are very wide of the mark (cf. Madan 1968). He says, for example, that to a Western observer the main source of India's weakness (presumably economic weakness) lies in the human factor. It is not, Myrdal continues, a lack of innate abilities or technical skills, but rather a lack of initiative, of interest in improving their economic status, of respect for labor—"the imprint of the caste system on their character" (p. 1148).

While some "Western observers" hold such opinions, as does Myrdal, other observers both Western and non-Western, have vigorously (and in my view, correctly) challenged these views (cf. A. K. Singh 1967; Morris 1967; Singer 1966; 1969). Moreover, studies of actual village life in India show little lack of initiative or absence of desire for improvement but rather reveal impediments to entrepreneurial efforts from the economic situation, the political environment, and the social apparatus. Pinning the blame on the "human factor" falls in with the common exhortations to villagers and townspeople that they work hard, reform their customs, eschew temptations, and rise above human fallibilities. There is an abundance of such moralizing; there is, however, a lack of clear understanding of the social forces involved, of the real nature of caste systems, and of the actual potentials for institutional change. Those concerned with economic and social development in India gain little by being told that India's greatest problem is the imprint of the (misunderstood) caste system on the people's (undefined) character.

Such notions, like the varna concept, provide an oversimple explanation of a complex situation. But unlike the varna theory, these ideas are more likely to undermine than to bolster the social purposes of those who hold them. To advance these purposes, the main problem is not how to kill caste relations most quickly but how best to channel the dynamic forces in village society so as to construct a new system of relations with greater advantages for all in the society. Radical extirpation is urged by some ideologists and commends itself to some activists as the only road to their goals. That road has well-known disadvantages as well as obvious attractions. When a political-social upheaval does occur in a society, the people have to develop any new relations and institutions largely on the basis of those they already know. A clear understanding of that social basis can surely benefit those—of whatever political persuasion—who are trying to direct change. The difficulties of Indian development can only be compounded if misleading notions about the nature of Indian society hold sway.

Particularly misguided is the notion that there must be inherent contradictions between established customs and modern innovations. As we have noted in previous chapters, there has been considerable cultural continuity along with modern social change. Villagers have generally extended their previous ways more than they have taken up totally new roles and institutions. They could do so because the people of India have maintained a complex society for many centuries; they had long possessed the capacities for maintaining a civilization when they met the ideas, artifacts, and representatives of modern Western civilization.

This is illustrated in an 1819 account of the village of Lony (now Lonikand) twelve miles from Poona. It was written by Thomas Coats, a surgeon who lived in Poona for seventeen years and had traveled extensively about the countryside. Coats's account was the basis for a restudy done in 1954–58 by G. S. Ghurye and his associates (Coats 1823; Ghurye 1960).

When Coats wrote his account of Lony, the village had been under British control for less than two years and had been little altered by that control. The villagers were thoroughly engaged in a monetary economy and in market exchange. There was a school for children of the higher jatis. Coats observed that even though the ordinary cultivators were not literate, they were minutely informed about everything that related to their calling and many of them had a "tolerable knowledge" of the leading events of their country's history. "On the whole, they are better informed than the lower classes of our own countrymen, and certainly far surpass them in propriety and orderliness of demeanour" (Coats 1823, p. 192).

In 1819, the year when these observations were written (the year also of Queen Victoria's birth), the villagers of Lony had recently been incorporated into the largest political domain that had ever existed. Yet some twenty centuries earlier, this locality had been part of another empire, that of Ashoka, which was then one of the largest political domains that had ever existed. Although the Lony villagers did change their ways during the one hundred and thirty years when they were under British cultural influence and political rule, and although the pace of change has quickened since independence, yet much of the ground plan of their culture, as described by Coats in 1819, is still evident in Ghurye's book of 1960.

Recognition of such continuities diminishes the supposed antithesis between "traditional" and "modern" ways. So-called traditional patterns have not been held static and modern kinds of behavior are commonly fitted into long-standing patterns of action. To be sure, the continuities do not avert conflicts, contradictions, and dilemmas. Any major shift in emphasis inevitably discomforts some who have social and personal investment in the previous state of affairs.

To illustrate the trends of modern social change we next examine changes in family roles and relations. A social system tends to be stronger than any of its component groups and as weak as any of its fundamental principles. Particular groups—jatis, dynasties, sects, colonial powers—have come and gone in India without drastic impairment of the general social system. Certain units of society, the clan for one, have waxed and waned in importance at particular times and places, and the general system has remained quite the same. If, however, many in a society change their fundamental ideas about what their social order is and should be, then major change is likely to impend. Our discussion of family change is therefore particularly concerned with possible change in the integrating ideas about the family.

Family Changes and Continuities

The "breakdown" of the joint family in India has often been forecast on the grounds that joint families were suited to the old agricultural societies but are dysfunctional under present conditions. Hence a sharp break between the "traditional" joint family and the "modern" nuclear family is supposed to occur. This view has been challenged by studies showing that the form of the family is not so closely linked to the type of economic organization (cf. Kapadia 1966, pp. 273–308, 329–331; Singer 1968, pp. 423–424).

Most students of the family do recognize that there is a general tendency in modern societies toward placing greater importance on the conjugal bond between husband and wife and toward decreasing the demands of the consanguine ties, especially those among siblings, but this is a long-term trend rather than a cause for abrupt revision of family relations. Because so many studies of family trends in India have been focused on the supposed passing of the joint family, there has been more counting of heads clustered in households than examination of continuities in family functions and values. A. M. Shah is one of the scholars who has sharply questioned the approach to family studies that assumes "an inevitable trend from large and complex (or joint) to small and simple households." He points out that the normal, cyclical development of an Indian family must be distinguished from basic changes in family organization (1968, pp. 133–134).

In that cyclical development, as we noted in the chapters of Part II, a nuclear family typically becomes a joint family when the sons marry and continue to live in the parental home with their wives and later with their children. That joint family eventually splits into smaller families, usually after the death of the father. The period of joint family living tends to be longer among owner-cultivators and among the wealthier and higher ranking families in general. It is shorter among the poor and also among those who receive a cash income, whether from the practice of modern irrigation agriculture or from the practice of modern professions. There are other variations, as among families in different regions of the country, but underlying all the variations are certain widely shared ideas. These ideas hold that the security and safety of the family group depend on cooperative relations among the men, between a father and his sons, and among brothers. The mutual loyalties among the men of a family should not be weakened by the loyalty of a son to his wife. The men of the family are expected to provide the durable continuity, the women are recruited into it from other families and are expected to pose a potentially disruptive force. Yet through the women of his family, especially from his mother's brothers, a man often gets great support and affection, given to him as a person rather than as the bearer of an agnatic role.

The family ideals have not always been carried out in full, but they typically have been strong influences on each person's family experience. In assessing the present power of these ideas, two studies provide useful information. One is by M. S. Gore (1968) on Aggarwal families, traders and merchants by traditional occupation, living in and around Delhi. The other is by Milton Singer (1968) on the families of the leading industrial magnates in Madras City.

Gore's study is based on the responses to an extensive questionnaire which was answered by members of 399 families, including urban and rural residents and some from "fringe" villages near the city. Responses were also obtained from 100 additional families of professional men and office workers who did not follow the jati's traditional occupations. Their educational level was much higher than the average of the main sample in which the family heads had received relatively little formal education (Gore 1968, pp. 77–91).

The study, completed in 1961, presents two main conclusions. "One is that the sample as a whole still largely conforms to the pattern of joint family living in behavior, role perception and attitudes." The other is that urban residence and education "do seem to introduce a certain measure of variation." But the variation is more in the attitudes given in questionnaire responses than in actual conduct. Education through high school or college was a main influence in a respondent's readiness for family change; urban residence, by itself, was not. In fact, among families of traditional occupation and limited education, "the rural-urban differences were not apparent" (Gore 1968, pp. 151, 232). The answers on living arrangements and on the position of the women of the family showed that the great majority of families in the sample kept the traditional patterns in these respects. More than half of the families were nuclear at the time of the response (263 of 499), but 86 percent of the heads of nuclear families had previously lived in joint families. The members of nuclear families did not reject the ideal of joint family living, although they interpreted the ideal to mean filial rather than fraternal solidarity (Gore 1968, pp. 109, 235).

Similar findings have been reported from other jatis and from other parts of the country. The ideals of family life are still powerful ideas. The solidary relations are, in considerable degree, honored and maintained. Certain shifts are being made. Fraternal solidarity is not stressed as much as it was formerly. Women's position in family life is being changed. Thus among the Aggarwals there is less rigid separation of the physical space for men and for women. Yet acceptance of changes in family life is much more a matter of word than of deed. The most marked shifts, both in verbal answers and in social behavior, are among those who have had a secondary or higher education.

In his foreword to Dr. Gore's book, W. J. Goode sets the results of this study in the frame of world trends in family relations. Goode points out that the ideology of change may have significant effects before there is any strong impact from modern urbanization and that this ideology can facilitate subsequent urbanization and industrialization. Goode affirms the thesis that family systems throughout the world are generally moving in the direction of the conjugal pattern, but notes that the transformation may not take place swiftly (Goode in Gore 1968, pp. vii–viii).

In the study by Singer, nineteen of the leading industrialists in Madras City and members of their families were interviewed to learn how these men are adapting the old family ideals in the urban setting. These are families of educated, wealthy, and highly successful people. Their present family relations are decidedly different from those which each of these tycoons knew when he was growing up in a village or small town. Family size, the position of women, the daily family routine are different. Yet cultural continuity is also clearly evident, "families living in nuclear households continue to maintain numerous joint family obligations and, for the most part, continue to subscribe to the norms of that system" (Singer 1968, p. 438).

One of the ways of maintaining both persistence and change is through compartmentalization, the traditional mode of separating the standards of the work sphere from those of the domestic sphere. In their household behavior, members of these families tend to observe scriptural standards much more closely than they do in their activities outside the house. These industrialists separate the two spheres of action more sharply than was done in their boyhood homes and the scope of the work sphere is far greater, but the modern practice stems from ancient precedents (Singer 1968, pp. 438–444). This device, it must be noted, is not restricted to the industrial elite. Even the men who pull rickshaws in the streets of Lucknow similarly separate their standards for conduct in the work domain from those followed in their homes (Gould 1965a, p.

31). Another adaptive process is called "vicarious ritualization" by Singer. An industrial executive of this sample cannot faithfully fulfill his domestic ritual duties so he employs professional priests to perform the rituals for him and also encourages his wife and children to ritual devotions. He does not reject the familial aspects of his religion but delegates them to others.

In the management of their firms these industrialists have adapted some of the traditional patterns of family management. Control and ownership are separated in both business and family; the family head controls the business, the shareholders or coparceners defer to his authority. Singer comments that the practices used in the joint family "offer some distinct advantages for organizing an industrial enterprise (1968, p. 445).[2]

Whether the family practices of these first-generation magnates will be maintained in the following generations is an open question but it seems clear that joint family ideals and practices do not necessarily undermine economic development as some writers used to assert (cf. Goode 1963, p. 205). Villagers and townspeople are neither summarily rejecting the ideals of joint family living, nor turning headlong to the conjugal family. The proportion of nuclear households has increased among many groups, more because of economic factors than because of any spurning of joint family obligations (cf. Kapadia 1958, p. 260; Desai 1964, pp. 145–147; Driver 1963, pp. 41–56). Allegiance to these obligations may be weakened in time but as yet this sense of obligation continues to be strongly upheld by many in India.

Shifts in Family Roles and Obligations

More marked change is becoming apparent in the family roles of women. The women of a household are not so formally dependent on the men and so segregated from them as they used to be. A wife's fate is not quite so totally dependent on her husband's in that widows are now being allowed to remarry in some of the higher jatis in which widow remarriage used to be absolutely pro-

[2] The paternal authority which one of these industrial leaders wielded is reflected in the fact that, as a believer in birth control, he himself had a vasectomy and then persuaded other male members of his family and about 3,000 of his male employees to do the same (Singer 1968, p. 435).

hibited (cf. Goode 1163, p. 365; Gore 1968, p. 216; Kapadia 1966, pp. 174–179; Madan 1965, pp. 26, 122; Pocock, 1954, p. 201). Even divorce, now legally possible, is resorted to by a few from higher jatis (Deshpande 1963; Kapadia 1966, pp. 186–197; Ross 1961, p. 273).

Villagers are well aware of changes in women's roles as is illustrated in a report from Senapur village near Banaras. A team of anthropologists interviewed 29 men and women (all of them over 55) of Senapur in order to record their impressions of the major changes they had witnessed. "Without exception, all the subjects commented, sometimes at great length, about the relaxation of *parda,* or the seclusion of women" (Opler 1960, p. 94). In most jatis in Senapur a young woman had been obliged to demonstrate her subordinate position by strict avoidance of her father-in-law and elder brother-in-law, by demure deference to her mother-in-law, by staying close to the household and by not showing in public any special attachment to her husband. By the 1950s, as all the respondents agreed, the young wives of Senapur were much less careful about avoidance practices, they were going out of their homes more freely, and they were more willing to accompany and assist their husbands publicly. Both husbands and wives were less inclined to make a great secret of their intimate meetings.

The respondents were quite clear about the reasons for the change. It was initiated, they asserted, by the young men and especially by those men who had had experience outside the village and those who had a high school or college education. Men who had worked or studied in cities saw women there going about much more freely than did Senapur women. Some city women worked in offices and shops, some participated in the professions and in politics. The men from Senapur took these women's activities as part of higher and highly desirable social status. So on their return to the village they encouraged their wives to be less constrained and more outgoing. The wives of the educated men usually have some education also and they gain in personal confidence because of their education. Such women do not accept the complete subordination of the young wife as readily as did their uneducated mothers and grandmothers.

This is not to say that joint family ideals are obsolete in Senapur. In the 1950s there were twice as many joint families as there were nuclear families in the village and four-fifths of the people lived in joint families. Nevertheless, as the older people of Senapur are aware, the changes in women's conduct may well have important effects on the nature of family relations (Opler 1960, pp. 96–97).

Similar changes are indicated in a variety of studies. The age of girls at marriage in most parts of India is steadily and significantly rising (Kapadia 1968, pp. 158–159; Ross 1961, pp. 245–250, 282; Goode 1963, pp. 232–236; Kannan 1963, pp. 187–192; Driver 1963, p. 61). The bride who comes to live with her husband in his family's household is not often a youngster just a few weeks or months from her menarche, but is typically more of a young woman with some sense of her own abilities and personal rights (Kapadia 1966, pp. 327–328). Family members who aspire to prestigious status generally try to give their daughters some education. The pick of the potential grooms are educated boys who demand that their brides also have an education, though not usually to a level as high as their own.

The education of girls is increasing with great rapidity in villages whose leaders want to gain a reputation for being progressive. Mrs. Kamla Nath studied the women in one such village, Jitpur in Ludhiana district of the Punjab. In a sample of eighteen households, the 14 women above the age of thirty-five were illiterate. There were 22 women below thirty-five; 12 of them, more than half, had had some education. Of the 18 girls of school age (6–14 years), all were going to school. There were 10 daughters-in-law of these households living outside the village because their husbands were in military service or held white collar jobs. All 10 of these women had been educated, presumably to about the high school level. Mrs. Nath reports that all families in the village are sending their girls to school and the more progressive are sending them to institutions for training to equip them for teaching or other careers. "Girls are being educated because educated men, who are in [government or military] service and who are the prized grooms, want educated wives" (Kamla Nath 1965, p. 815). An incidental result of this development is that young men of the village who are illiterate or barely literate have great difficulty in securing brides.

This switch in two generations within the sample households from totally illiterate women to totally literate girls is one indication of the general change in women's roles in this village. Thus many of the girls now ride to school on bicycles, in a way that "would have been unthinkable a generation earlier, when a girl was not allowed to go out of the village unescorted" (Kamla Nath 1963, p. 815). Jitpur is a particularly prosperous village in a progressive district, and the degree of change there is not typical of Indian villages. But the direction of change in women's activities in Jitpur is entirely typical of the trend that is seen throughout the nation.

One consequence of the increasing number of women who have had a high school or a college education is that an increasing number of them find employment in clerical, administrative, or professional work (Gadgil 1965; Chhibbar 1968, pp. 120–123). Their number is not large in comparison with the number of women who work on the land or in unskilled jobs, but educated working women are now numerous enough in the cities so that the idea of a woman of high status holding a paid job is no longer a startling or repugnant idea.

The family roles of men as well as of women are being changed. Men who earn incomes in their own right, whether as cultivators of cash crops, businessmen, employed workers, or professional men, can become independent of paternal authority at an earlier age than formerly. Even where such independent incomes are not significant factors, as among the Rajput families in Khalapur village, the family relations of men are being altered. A Rajput father there is expected to be a fairly stern and remote figure to his children but this is much less true now than it used to be. He is also supposed to be the disciplinarian of his children and, among the men of the household, his own father and brothers are supposed to be the child's defenders. A man was expected to have cordial relations with his brother's sons rather than with his own. This is still considered to be proper but actually seldom occurs. Now the brothers tend to separate and each man interacts with his own children (Minturn and Hitchcock 1966, pp. 118–119).

In many families across India, family elders seem to be less apprehensive than elders of the previous generation were about a son's relations with his wife; they seem to be less fearful that the conjugal relation may threaten parental authority and fraternal solidarity. More open relations between husband and wife are being tolerated and less drastic separation between the male and female spheres is widely accepted. Not only is there less stringent avoidance between a young husband and wife but there is less also between father and son.

For a man, earlier personal and economic independence should make the strains of family separation less difficult than they formerly were. For a woman, the transition from daughter to daughter-in-law may not be as traumatic as it used to be, though new kinds of personal problems may well arise in the new family situation. For the society, these changes in family roles are portents of systemic changes that may come. Among the bulk of the population they are still only portents. The long-established constellation of family roles is being modified in many families but most villagers follow the family cycle in much the same way as in previous generations, though they do change the duration of particular phases of the cycle.

K. M. Kapadia summarizes his extensive studies of family trends in India by emphasizing that the joint family ideal still has powerful influence on individual behavior. He writes that even a man who has himself broken away from his parental family to start an independent household will typically expect to maintain a joint family when his own sons marry. Married sons usually feel obliged to provide for their elders in case of need and to hold themselves responsible for the education and marriage of their younger siblings. "A person who fails in these duties is talked of as faithless and henpecked, not only by his relatives but also by his neighbours" (Kapadia 1966, pp. 332–333). Few can resist such pressures; characteristically the values of the family ideal are personally internalized as well as socially imposed. Another element of the traditional family pattern, the pressure to have children, especially a goodly number of sons, remain strongly felt by men and women alike.

Urban residence, as was noted in Chapter 3, does not necessarily accelerate changes in family relations; the wider ties of kinship are in some ways strengthened in the city. Villagers who come to work in a city often live close together in kin-based groups, which serve them as a refuge against the anonymity of city life and as a source of protection against urban dangers. In a study of rickshaw-pullers in Lucknow, Gould concludes that "compound kin groups are retained with great frequency in the urban environment regardless of occupation" (1965, p. 46). A similar conclusion is drawn by

William Rowe from his study of 46 men from Senapur village who were working in the city of Bombay. All but one were living in tightly controlled kin groups; the groups were formed either on the basis of actual (though not necessarily close) kinship or through bonds of fictive kinship. The ideal that all men of a village are village brothers, Rowe comments, has greater meaning in the city than almost anywhere else (Rowe 1964, p. 21).

A considerable proportion of city families maintain joint family obligations with parents and siblings in a village. Many an urban household, Srinivas observes, is only the satellite of a kin group in a village or town several hundreds of miles away (1966, p. 138). Among city families, Srinivas adds, those of the new elite are most clearly changing their patterns of family life, in part because they may be separated from their closest kin by large distances and in part because they live in a social and cultural environment that is so greatly different from that of their village or small-town relatives. Such households often lack elders who would care deeply about traditional family customs; the parents' concern is rather with their children's success in the educational and career competition (Srinivas 1966, pp. 138–139). Yet among many families of the new elite, marriage continues to be a test of family status, weddings are still occasions for great expenditures, matches are commonly arranged by parents and kin, and endogamy is still a serious consideration.

Changes in Marriage Patterns

There has been much public concern about large dowry payments and inordinate wedding expenses. Newspapers editorialize on these subjects; political leaders discuss them; legislatures have passed laws aimed to regulate them. The practice of making dowry payments is not new, especially among the higher jatis of North India, and such payments have helped to ensure the stability of a marriage and the good reception of a bride by her husband's family (cf. Goode 1963, pp. 211–212). In recent decades dowry costs are said to have risen sharply in the heightened status competition for educated bridegrooms. The burden of dowry obligations falls heavily on families endowed by the biological lottery with a preponderance of daughters. Their outcry has long been heard (Ross 1961, pp. 260–264; Cormack 1961, pp. 113–114). Writers and reformers of the nineteenth century denounced the practice; more recent comments are no less critical. Thus Kapadia flatly says, "Education, instead of mitigating the evil, has worsened it to scandalous proportions" (1966, p. 137). In 1961 the Indian Parliament passed the Dowry Prohibition Act. "So far," Srinivas writes, "the Act has not had much success in combating the institution" (1966, p. 126). Nor is it likely to have great success unless many more people in India change their ideas about the central importance of family status and about the proper ways to maintain and raise that status.

The costs of wedding celebrations as well as the costs of dowries draw anguished cries from families caught in this kind of nuptial squeeze. Although these costs have regularly been denounced by intellectual and political leaders, heavy wedding expenses continue to burden many families. The wedding remains, as was noted in Chapter 6, a main event in the family cycle and a principal occasion for demonstrating and validating social ties. It may even be relevant to the family's future credit rating as is noted in an account of the merchant jatis of a town in Ambala district, Punjab. "The ceremonies of marriage and the public display of dowry serve as public statements of one's financial position and are meaningful to other members of the local community" (Hazlehurst 1966, p. 116).

Large wedding expenses, at all social levels, are intended to assure the social welfare of the family's children and to enhance the family's reputation. Family elders, especially the women, commonly believe that their economic resources can be expended in no better way than for these purposes. They argue that economic capital is not worth much unless it can be translated into social capital. Economists and planners have deplored these expenditures, vast in their totality, that do not help to increase economic productivity. Members of a family, however, typically feel that no investment deserves higher priority than investment in the social security of their children.

The choice of a spouse remains very largely a matter for negotiation and decision by the family elders. Young people, especially those with a high school or college education, are preponderantly in favor of securing greater freedom for themselves in the choice of a spouse (cf. Goode 1963, pp. 216–217; Ross 1961, pp. 251–260). Many of them have gained the right to see, perhaps to talk with, a prospective marriage partner. A few may veto a proposed match if they actively dislike their parents' choice. The extent to which the young principals participate in marriage arrangements has been variously reported. On the basis of her studies in Bangalore, Aileen Ross concludes that educated young people have few opportunities for such participation (1961, p. 279). B. V. Shah's survey in Gujarat, however, indicates that college students have come to take considerable part in the choice of their marriage partners (1964, pp. 80–104). C. T. Kannan's review of several relevant studies notes that such young people are now "fully consulted" before a decision on a marriage arrangement for them is made (1963, p. 198). In general, however, the initiatives and negotiations for the marriages of educated young people are largely where they traditionally have been, in the hands of the parents and elder kinsmen.

The wording of some of the matrimonial advertisements in newspapers seems to signify bold departures in marriage norms but analyses of such advertisements show that the great majority of them stipulate the traditional criteria (plus education) and the usual procedures for arranging marriages in urban middle-class society (Aiyappan 1955, pp. 121–122; Anand 1965; Gist 1953; Niehoff 1958; Reyes-Hockings 1966).

Although endogamy remains a major consideration in arranging a marriage, the boundaries of the endogamous group, as previously noted, are typically being enlarged, and marriage partners may now come from formerly separate jatis of the same jati-cluster (cf. Kapadia 1962, pp. 85–86). A few marriages do occur between spouses who openly acknowledge that they come from quite disparate jatis and Kannan's study of intercaste marriages indicates that the number of such marriages is increasing, but such unions are still very exceptional even among urban and educated people (Ghurye 1961, pp. 204–205; Gore 1968, pp. 204–207; Goode 1963, pp. 215–217; Kannan 1963, pp. 198–217; Kapadia 1966, pp. 118–119; Newell 1963; Patterson 1958; Ross 1961, pp. 270–273).

Marked changes have been made in the laws that pertain to family relations. K. M. Panikkar summarized the new thrust of legislation when he wrote that the Constitution of India "not only has assumed but has proclaimed in clearest terms its right and duty to legislate for social needs" (1961, p. 81). Among the most pressing of these needs is that for "equality of opportunity for men and women." Legislators have followed the constitutional mandate by enacting the Hindu Code and other acts that attempt to redesign Indian family life as no earlier governmental authorities have tried to do. The former rules for inheritance have been altered, as have such matters as the legal recognition of the varna categories and legal preference for joint families (cf. Galanter 1965, p. 79).

These far-reaching changes in family law have not, as we have seen, quickly brought far-reaching changes in family life. The new laws have removed legal obstacles to family changes but they have not imposed restrictions on maintaining joint-family relations (though some of the tax and land laws are alleged to do so). Derrett's assessment is that "So long as the father and his sons regard themselves as jointly and successively responsible for the maintenance of members of the family, the joint-family will remain, and the MHL [Modern Hindu Law] has not taken away its juridical framework" (Derrett 1962, p. 46).

Fathers and sons (and mothers!) generally hold to this concept of family responsibility whether they are urban professionals or village cultivators. As citizens or as legislators, educated people have generally been more ardent for changing family relations within the nation than for challenging old family values closer to their own homes. Their political ideology on this matter has commonly outpaced their family behavior. Nonetheless, they are generally shifting their family behavior as well as their ideas toward the kind of relations between the sexes, between spouses, and between parents and children that the new conditions of world civilization appear to favor

A Paradigm of Change

At all social levels then, changes in family roles and relations are well under way. The direction of change is toward greater emphasis on the conjugal bond and toward lessening of the formal separation of men and women. The new ways of earning a living, the wider spread of schooling, the modern facilities for transport and communication, the post-independence climate of legislative action have all affected people's ideas about their families.

The degree of change varies not only according to education and jati but also according to the kind of ideas that are being altered. The new family law reflects the great change in the ideas held by educated people about how family relations ought to be carried on. The concepts that govern specific roles are also being changed. As we have noted in the critical matter of women's roles, ideas about the proper conduct of the girls and women of a family are being revised in the villages and these revisions may well affect the whole range of family conduct.

In the matter of the unspoken, pervasive, and deep-lying themes of behavior, however, the degree and direction of change are not so clear. While the more rigid hierarchical gradations within the family are being mitigated, status competition among families seems hardly less than it was in the past century. New symbols of family prestige and new content for family status are sought, but the perspective of ranking and the competition for prestigious standing, as noted in the matter of dowry and wedding expenses, seem undiminished. The new family ideals and the new laws have opened the possibility of systemic changes in family relations, in which the fundamental roles and processes will be redefined. Yet the motifs of behavior that underlie many social relations, including family relations, seem to be little affected. Perhaps these bedrock ideas will continue to underlie future systemic forms and processes.

Ideas about jati and village, about social mobility and political participation, are being revised in ways similar to those we have noted in family relations. People throughout India commonly keep to traditional social patterns while adapting them to modern circumstances. Abstract ideals are most readily revised; fundamental motifs of cognition and motivation seem little altered and are evident in the newer arenas of competition.

The jati continues to be the principal unit of endogamy, a significant attribute of identity, a common locus for interaction, and an important vehicle for social mobility. All these functions, as we have noted, are being reinterpreted. Not only is endogamy more broadly construed than it was before, but also personal identity is not so sweepingly a matter of jati membership as it formerly was. The members of almost every jati are becoming increasingly diversified in occupation, education, income, and residence. Such diversities have long existed within jatis but they are now more consequential than before. Moreover, many more people now work outside their home localities and in activities for which jati considerations are not directly relevant (cf. Gist 1954; Kapadia 1963; Mathur 1959; Sharma 1961).

Villagers continue to see their local social order as being made up of ranked, interdependent jatis, but they are revising the criteria for the ranking and the meaning of the interdependence. The former jajmani relations, as noted above, have lately been much curtailed. Families of different jatis remain dependent on each other economically and frequently also ritually and politically, but the dependence is neither so great nor so mandatory as it was in the past century.

The cultural and social distances among jatis are being reduced. Vast disparities remain everywhere in India but there are now opportunities and new stimuli to better one's position in the local hierarchies. Those of the lowest jatis now have at least potential access to the Sanskritic traditions and to traditions of the modern, educated elite. Very few in a Harijan jati may actually know much about either high tradition but many of them will know of some members of their jati-cluster (or of one like it) who have triumphantly participated in both. The example of those who succeeded in making a great personal rise (Dr. Ambedkar is a prime example) encourages others in striving for jati and political rise.

The decrease in social distances among people of different jatis has been very slight in some places and quite significant in others, but the unmistakable trend is toward greater social rights for people of disadvantaged jatis. As their objective social disabilities are in some degree overcome, their subjective feelings of resentment tend to grow and to be more forcibly and openly expressed. As their social hopes rise, their acceptance of demeaning status falls. Some, following Dr. Ambedkar's lead, have tried to eject themselves from the system of ranked jatis by becoming converts to Buddhism.

Many in the lowest jatis remain abysmally poor and their poverty shackles their efforts to rise. The benefits of the general increase in national productivity tend to accrue to families of middle and high income, so the economic gap between the poor and the wealthy may have increased in many localities. Yet opportunities for economic betterment are now more open to people of the lowest echelons than they were before independence; as Harijan families manage to pull themselves up economically, they commonly expend some of their added income on their children's education as well as on the older tokens and ceremonials of higher status.

Land continues to be the major economic resource for most villagers and where the families of one jati own much of the village land they still tend to dominate village affairs. That dominance, however, is now subject to a new means of challenge through the power of the vote. Voters in India can be as misled and manipulated as those in other countries, yet the votes of a numerous jati cannot be ignored by those who want to manage public affairs, whether in a village or in a larger constituency.

In this way, a person's role as citizen and voter has become attached to his role as jati member. The realities of jati membership have been affected by modern ideals of social justice propounded mainly by educated people. Affirming these ideals, leaders of the new elite have brought about legal and political changes that have modified the previous potentials of jati roles. Jati membership has become an important factor in wide political arenas; in these arenas the contestants often display the kinds of perception and motiva tion that have characterized village contests.

The village typically continues to be the chief scene of the villager's activities and the main nexus of his social relations. While many villagers have had more experience outside the village than did their forefathers and know a good deal more about the world beyond their locality, their chief concerns are still centered within their village and locality. Many are aware that their village is changing. Because national leaders have recognized that the welfare of the country rests on democratic development in the villages, governmental activities in villages have been greatly increased. Elected village panchayats have been established as the local agencies for economic development and social betterment. The acts that set up these statutory panchayats were the expression of an ideal of village democracy held by the educated. As with other legislation based on such ideals, there have been considerable difficulties and delays in realizing the purposes of the legislation. Nevertheless, the statutory panchayats are beginning to work well in some places, though not many of them have achieved the high purposes for which they were established. These elected bodies have augmented the functions of government in the village; they have not usually augmented village solidarity. In some ways the added functions of government—as in providing water, schools, special grants—have introduced new reasons for conflict as well as for cooperation. The new village panchayats are developing modern means of cooperation but they also reflect the older struggles for status.

Contests about social mobility have long been at the heart of village politics. Mobility efforts have now become increasingly related to political participation in district, state and even national politics. The resemblance of political behavior at these higher levels to the style of village politics is not because state and national leaders are only village elders transposed, but because both villagers and the new elite stem from the same civilizational roots and share in the perceptions, motivations, and values that characterize the civilization (cf. Morris-Jones 1967).

A new phase of social development may well follow the rise of industry and the great improvements in agricultural technology. Both are still in beginning stages and only a few studies of their social impact have yet been made. The available studies of factory workers indicate that they may be changing their social patterns more rapidly than is generally true for villagers, but that jati considerations remain of importance to them, not only in domestic activities but also in the recruitment and management of industrial workers (cf. Lambert 1963).

As the people of India attain new levels of technological and economic advance they also meet fresh problems of social and cultural adaptation. A potential resource in coping with such problems is the intelligence that can be provided by students of society. That intelligence is more than knowledge of statistics, patterns, institutions; it also entails the process of acquiring knowledge about people, of testing ideas and expanding understanding through asking productive questions. Such questions are apt to be concerned more with social adaptation than with the supposed demise of tradition. The questions are likely to be more useful if they are based on the concept of people acting in social systems rather than focused on presumed failures in moral rectitude. Political and religious leaders have to speak out on moral issues but planners and policy makers must know that systemic relations as well as moral principles govern the behavior of men and women.

Each social system is more amenable to certain kinds of change than it is to others. The paradigm suggested in this chapter indicates one aspect of this differential: generalized ideals have been more readily shifted than have the concepts about specific roles and relations. These, in turn, have been altered more than have the implicit, but powerful, psychological motifs. It is the social scientists' task to test this suggestion and all other theoretical formulations in a wide variety of social contexts so as to expand and refine man's knowledge of human behavior. It is the task of those concerned with the welfare of people to use the current state of that knowledge toward the best advantage of the people.

Appendix

THE CONCEPTS OF SYSTEM AND
OF STRATIFICATION

Uses of the Concepts

The use of the concept of system has the merit of eliminating some misleading dichotomies and of including crucial social factors in one model. Structure and process, concord and conflict are viewed in the same general perspective. Stability and change, norm and deviance can be examined together. There need be no treatment of social control apart from social conformity. The system is the social control; the feedback of counterchange is as integral as is the expected interchange. A people's main values are expressed in the kind of systemic order they seek and maintain.

Social structure is here taken as one aspect of social system. The concept of structure focuses on the component groups and their interrelations at a particular time. The concept of system adds the processes of counterchange among the groups and the systemic changes that they produce over time.

A social system is kept constantly in motion and can be adaptively changed. As an adaptive means, people use their systems, not merely to cope with their world, but also to elaborate their lives and to create new ways of life. The concept of system guides us to see a society as more than the sum of its parts, to try to understand it—in Redfield's rather paradoxical phrase—as an "analyzed whole." My own use of the concept has been informed by the writings of Homans (1950), Nadel (1951), Redfield (1955), Vogt (1960), Parsons (1961), and by the more recent syntheses by Buckley (1967).

Yet any concept that purports to embrace so much can explain correspondingly little specifically. It is a potent means of departure, not of arrival. Moreover, its use entails some lingering questions.

Whose concept is it? Is it only in the eye and mind of the professional beholder or is it a verity of human life, part of the people's
truth? As we use the concept here, it is both. The people whose
society we study have quite lively ideas (not necessarily accurate
ones) about the systemic nature of their society, which influence,
if they do not determine, their social relations. Their ideas are important elements in our analysis.

Another question is about the boundaries of a system. A family,
as we have noted in Chapter 1, is a component of a larger system
of kinship. But kinship is also one of the subsystems of the larger
society. If we focus on family relations, each family should be
viewed as part of a general system of family relations. Similarly,
religious, economic, and political activities can be considered as
separate systems for certain purposes and as subsystems in other
contexts of analysis. On this question, too, we are guided by how
the people whom we study perceive various contexts of action and
how they differentiate among them, though we must separate their
notions of ideal conduct from that which they expect and that
which is actually realized.

Finally, there is always some question about the application of
any guiding concept, no matter how cogent or sound it may be. We
tend to focus on the evidence that fits more neatly into the system
concept and look past that which does not fit so well. Because we
postulate counterchange, we produce the real evidence of counterchange. Because we postulate that there are systemic social relations,
we do not test the utility of the concept at every step of the exposi-
tion. Because we postulate a general human preference for orderly
relations and for a return to order, we may slight disorder and dis-
array in social relations, or interpret them as a means of attaining
some new and more satisfactory order—which they may or may
not be. However, the general test of the usefulness of a concept is
whether it helps to clarify, explain, and assess probabilities, not
whether its use surmounts all questions about it and gaps in it.

The subject of social stratification is more in the background than
in the foreground of this enquiry. We are dealing with *the* classic
instance of stratification as frame and focus for a civilization, yet
we must also recognize that ideas about stratification are being
changed in India in ways similar to those in which other peoples
throughout the world are shifting ideas about social divisions. These

grand changes are close to the nerve and bone of most modern nations. Hence intellectuals and political activists everywhere are apt to be absorbed with one or another aspect of the subject of social strata and the proper rights and rewards pertaining to each grouping. Stratification is considered to be the main distributive arrangement of a society accounting for who gets what, how, and why (Gould 1960a; Tumin 1967, p. 12; Lenski 1966, pp. 1–23). So it is no wonder, as Melvin Tumin comments in his survey of the subject, that the study of stratification has come to assume a central place in modern sociology. He notes that it has become a "dominant pursuit" of sociologists and is likely to continue to be, so long as inequalities are critical for the life-chances and life-patterns of people in different strata of a society (1967, pp. 10–11). Anthropologists have not been so heavily engrossed with this subject as have sociologists, but they well recognize its importance.

Some of the writings on stratification stress the objective criteria and the material forces that impel social divisions. Others emphasize the subjective views that the participants hold. Karl Marx set off great consequences with his testament of the technological causes and the objective criteria for social classes and his analysis of the inevitable conflict between classes. More recent sociological writers, Lloyd Warner and Talcott Parsons among them, have noted that a major factor is how people understand the nature of their society and how they consequently class themselves. Parsons points out that social relations inevitably involve value choices and moral judgments, and the way in which stratification is carried out depends on the moral evaluations made by the people (1953; 1961, pp. 42–44).

A much debated issue is between those who emphasize that stratification supports stability and those who view stratification as an inherent source of conflict. The former tend to dwell on order, rewards, interdependence, subjective satisfactions, the latter on power, exploitation, strain, objective causes for dissatisfaction (cf. Lenski 1966, pp. 22–23, 441–443; Dahrendorf 1966, pp. 714–718). The manner in which this issue has been debated seems less apposite for an understanding of Indian society than for other societies. Social divisions in India most clearly follow both objective and subjective criteria; they involve both stability and strain, both co-operation and conflict. The problem is not whether the one kind or the other kind of influence prevails but how much of each exists and under what circumstances.

Another debated issue is whether highly stratified societies outside of South Asia can usefully be labeled caste societies, with the implication that they share important characteristics with the Indian systems. This idea has been explored by Barth (1960), by Bailey (1963a), and especially by Gerald Berreman, who has strongly maintained that they do, drawing his evidence mainly from a comparison of India and the American South in the mid-twentieth century.

What Kind of System is a "Caste System"?

A caste system, as Berreman discusses the concept, is one that is composed of ranked groups. Membership in a group is only through birth. The groups are exhaustive, exclusive, and discrete; that is, every person is a member of such a group and of only one; he is clearly recognized by others as a member of his separate group. Membership in his group influences most of his roles and activities; there is a high degree of "role summation." No one should try to change his inherited membership and any attempts by individuals to shift themselves to a higher group are strongly disapproved (Berreman 1966, pp. 275, 285; 1967a, p. 48; 1967b, p. 355).

Relative rank affects almost all social relations. Most interaction among people of different groups involves considerations of superiority and inferiority, and superiority means greater privileges, precedence, and a larger share of the good things in life. Each group is a firm entity, named, bounded, self-aware, culturally homogeneous. Because interaction between people of different groups is limited and that within a group is more intense, the members of a group tend to share distinctive cultural characteristics. A caste system is therefore one of cultural pluralism (Berreman 1967a, pp. 46, 55; 1967b, p. 354).

The groups are interdependent; each needs the services or goods provided by others. But they are held together less by agreement about mutual needs and purposes than by the coercive power wielded by the superior groups. (Other students of caste systems recognize the importance of coercive power but do not consider it to be the sole cement of such a system.) The inferior groups conform in their actions, not necessarily in their ideas about the reasons for subservient behavior (Berreman 1966, p. 289; 1967b, pp. 352–357).

A general concomitant of such a system, Berreman notes, is that the higher groups explain their superiority in terms of a moral evaluation that shows why they are intrinsically more worthy. They take a paternalistic attitude toward the lower people, considering them to be childlike, irresponsible, incapable of finer feelings or higher achievements. The lower do not share these views but adjust to the superior power by avoiding conflict, by apathy and psychic withdrawal, or by overcompliance. Other concomitants are the restrictions on relations between people of different groups. Eating and sitting together, marriage and sex relations are rigidly controlled or are forbidden (Berreman 1966, p. 308; 1967a, pp. 59, 64).

The higher, privileged groups hold that the social order is static; the lower strive to improve their status. Any system of marked stratification is itself a source of mobility motivation as Veblen, Bendix and Lipset, and others have noted. Such mobility striving is a constant dynamic force in a caste system. Berreman discerns a difference between India and the U.S. South in that a lower group in India is usually more interested in achieving superiority for the group rather than equality in the society, whereas Southern Negroes, because the society of the deep South has two main divisions rather than multiple groups, have objected to the system as well as to their position in it. In this way there is more consensus about the proper nature of the social system in India than in the South, though Berreman stresses that in neither place do the lower groups accept the concept of their inferiority (1966, pp. 298, 308, 318; 1967a, p. 66).

The principal functions of a caste system, as Berreman sees them, are to perpetuate social and cultural diversities, and to enforce and articulate them. Privilege is protected through power. These functions, his discussion notes, are highly disfunctional in the modern world, irrelevant to human welfare and sources of unnecessary conflict and suffering (1967b, pp. 352, 356–366).

The critics of such definitions of "caste system" question whether the category is a useful one. Certain groups, such as the low-ranking groups in Japan, do not fit readily into the general definition (cf. DeVos 1967). These critics point out, moreover, that specialization is essential in all modern societies and leads to some degree of stratification and ranking. Social and cultural diversities have to be articulated in all societies; each separate group tends to seek some privileges and power for its members. These processes are inherent in a complex society and, as processes, can scarcely be called disfunctional. The trend in most contemporary societies is certainly away from the inclusive, invidious distinctions of caste divisions but also it is away from cultural pluralism and toward a cultural conformity, which some deplore. Those critics add that the discussions of caste systems in general have done little to advance an understanding of caste organization in Indian civilization (Leach 1960, 1967; Dumont 1967; S. Sinha 1967; Cohn 1968, p. 196).

But at least these discussions of what is meant by a "caste system" help us to understand the systems of Indian society as part of the human continuum, as special phrasings and configurations of social processes common among much of mankind. It is especially important to understand the dynamic nature of the Indian systems, because they have so often been depicted as static in Hindu scripture and in villagers' concepts, as well as in much of the writing on the subject.

Bibliography

AGARWALA, B. R.
  1955   In a mobile commercial community. *In* Symposium: caste and joint family. Sociological Bulletin 4:138–146.
AGGARWAL, PARTAP C.
  1966   A Muslim sub-caste of North India: problems of cultural integration. Economic and Political Weekly 1:159–167.
AHMAD, AZIZ
  1964   Studies in Islamic culture in the Indian environment. Oxford: Clarendon Press.
AHMAD, IMTIAZ
  1965   Social stratification among Muslims. The Economic Weekly 10: 1093–1096.
AHMAD, ZARINA . .
  1962   Muslim caste in Uttar Pradesh. The Economic Weekly 14:325–336.
AIYAPPAN, A.
  1937   Social and physical anthropology of the Nayadis of Malabar. Bulletin of the Madras Government Museum, n.s., Volume 2, No. 4.
  1944   Iravas and culture change. Bulletin of the Madras Government Museum, n.s., Volume 5, No. 1.
  1955   In Tamilnad. Sociological Bulletin 4:117–122.
  1965   Social revolution in a Kerala village: a study in cultural change. Bombay: Asia Publishing House.
ALLISON, W. L.
  1935   The Sadhs. London and Calcutta: Oxford University Press.
AMBEDKAR, B. R.
  1948   Remarks on draft constitution. Constituent Assembly Debates, Official Reports, Volume 7, No. 1, pp. 38–39.
ANAND, K.
  1965   An analysis of matrimonial advertisements. Sociological Bulletin 14:59–71.
ANANTAKRISHNA AYYAR, L. K.
  1926   Anthropology of the Syrian Christians. Eranakulam: Cochin Government Press.
ANSARI, GHAUS
  1955   Muslim marriage in India. Wiener Völkerkundliche Mitteilungen 3:191–206.
  1960   Muslim caste in Uttar Pradesh: a study of culture contact. The Eastern Anthropologist (special number) 13:5–80.

ATAL, YOGESH

1963   Short-lived alliances as an aspect of factionalism in an Indian village. The Journal of Social Sciences (Agra) 3:65–75.

n.d.   Trends of change in village politics: a case study. Mussoorie: Cultural Institute of Study and Research in Community Development. Mimeographed, 7 pp.

BACHENHEIMER, R.

1956   Theology, economy and demography: a study of caste in an Indian village. MS., 11 pp.

BACON, ELIZABETH E. (editor)

1956   India sociological background: an area handbook. New Haven: The Human Relations Area Files.

BADEN-POWELL, B. H.

1896   The Indian village community. London: Longmans, Green and Co. (Reprinted by HRAF Press: New Haven, 1957.)

BAILEY, FREDERICK G.

1957   Caste and the economic frontier: a village in highland Orissa. Manchester: Manchester University Press.

1958   Political change in the Kondmals. The Eastern Anthropologist 11: 88–106.

1960a   The joint-family in India: a framework for discussion. The Economic Weekly 12:345–352.

1960b   Tribe, caste and nation: a study of political activity and political change in highland Orissa. Manchester: Manchester University Press.

1961   "Tribe" and "caste" in India. Contributions to Indian Sociology 5:7–19.

1963a   Closed social stratification in India. European Journal of Sociology 4:107–124.

1963b   Politics and social change: Orissa in 1959. Berkeley: University of California Press.

1964   Two villages in Orissa (India). In Closed systems and open minds: the limits of naïvety in social anthropology, Max Gluckman, editor, pp. 52–82. Chicago: Aldine Publishing Co.

1965   Decisions by concensus in councils and committees. In Political systems and the distribution of power, F. Eggan and M. Gluckman, editors, pp. 1–20. London: Tavistock Publications; New York: Frederick A. Praeger.

BAINES, ATHELSTANE

1912   Ethnography (castes and tribes). Strassburg: Trübner Verlag.

BANNERJEE, HEMENDRA NATH

1960   Community structure in an artisan village of Pargannah Barabhum. Journal of Social Research (Ranchi) 3:68–79.

BANTON, MICHAEL

1965   Roles: an introduction to the study of social relations. London: Tavistock Publications.

BARANOV, I. L.

1965   "Kastovyi bunt" v Ramnade ("The caste revolt" in Ramnad) In Kasty v Indii (Caste in India), G. G. Kotovshii, editor, pp. 262–273. Moscow: Akademiia Nauk SSSR. Institut Narodov Azii.

BARNABAS, A. P.
  1961   Sanskritization. The Economic Weekly 13:613–618.
BARTH, FREDRIK
  1959   Political leadership among Swat Pathans. London School of Economics. Monographs in Social Anthropology, No. 19. London.
  1960   The system of social stratification in Swat, North Pakistan. *In* Aspects of caste in South India, Ceylon and Northwest Pakistan, E. R. Leach, editor, pp. 113–146. Cambridge Papers in Social Anthropology, No. 2. Cambridge: Cambridge University Press.
BASHAM, A. L.
  1954   The wonder that was India. London: Sidgwick and Jackson.
BASU, N. B.
  1957   Gango (an instance of Hindu method of tribal absorption). Bulletin of the Tribal Research Institute (Chhindwara) 1:40–47.
BASU, TARA KRISHNA
  1962   The Bengal peasant from time to time. London and Bombay: Asia Publishing House.
BEALS, ALAN R.
  1955   Change in the leadership of a Mysore village. *In* India's villages, pp. 132–143. Calcutta: West Bengal Government Press.
  1959   Leadership in a Mysore village. *In* Leadership and political institutions in India, R. L. Park and Irene Tinker, editors, pp. 427–437. Princeton: Princeton University Press.
  1962   Gopalpur. New York: Holt, Rinehart, and Winston.
  1964   Conflict and interlocal festivals in a South Indian region. The Journal of Asian Studies 23:95–113.
  1965   Crime and conflict in some South Indian villages. Mimeographed, 23 pp.
        Dravidian Kinship and Marriage. Unpublished paper.
BEALS, ALAN R. AND BERNARD J. SIEGEL
  1966   Divisiveness and social conflict: an anthropological approach. Stanford: Stanford University Press.
BEBARTA, PRAFULLA C.
  1966   Family type and fertility. Economic and Political Weekly 1:633–634.
BEECH, MARY JANE, O. J. BERTOCCI AND L. A. CORWIN
  1966   Introducing the East Bengal village. *In* Inside the East Pakistan village. (Asian studies papers. Reprint series, 2.) East Lansing: Michigan State University.
BEIDELMAN, THOMAS O.
  1959   A comparative analysis of the jajmani system. Monograph of the Association for Asian Studies, No. 8. Locust Valley, New York: J. J. Augustin.
BENDIX, REINHARD
  1960   Max Weber: an intellectual portrait. New York: Doubleday.
BERREMAN, GERALD D.
  1960a Caste in India and the United States. American Journal of Sociology 66:120–127.
  1960b Cultural variability and drift in the Himalayan hills. American Anthropologist 62:774–794.

1962a Behind many masks. Ithaca: The Society for Applied Anthropology.

1962b Caste and economy in the Himalayas. Economic Development and Cultural Change 10:386–394.

1962c Pahari polyandry: a comparison. American Anthropologist 64: 60–75.

1962d Village exogamy in northernmost India. Southwestern Journal of Anthropology 18:55–58.

1963 Hindus of the Himalayas. Berkeley and Los Angeles: University of California Press.

1965 The study of caste ranking in India. Southwestern Journal of Anthropology 21:115–129.

1966 Caste in cross-cultural perspective: organizational components. *In* Japan's invisible race, George De Vos and Hiroshi Wagatsuma, editors, pp. 275–324. Berkeley and Los Angeles: University of California Press.

1967a Stratification, pluralism and interaction: a comparative analysis of caste. *In* Caste and race, comparative approaches, A. de Reuck and J. Knight, editors, pp. 45–73. London: J. and A. Churchill.

1967b Caste as social process. Southwestern Journal of Anthropology 23: 351–370.

BÉTEILLE, ANDRÉ

1962 Sripuram: a village in Tanjore district. The Economic Weekly 14:141–146.

1964 A note on the referents of caste. European Journal of Sociology 5:130–134.

1965 Caste, class and power. Berkeley and Los Angeles: University of California Press.

BHARATI, AGEHANANDA

1961 The ochre robe. London: Allen and Unwin.

1963 Pilgrimage in the Indian tradition. History of Religions 3:135–167.

1966 The decline of teknonymy: changing patterns of husband-wife appellation in India. MS., 12 pp.

BHATT, G. S.

1958 Occupational structure among the Chamars of Dehra Dun. Sociological Annual 1:32–43. Dehra Dun: Sociology Association, D. A. V. College.

BHATTACHARYA, JOGENDRA NATH

1896 Hindu castes and sects. Calcutta: Thacker, Spink and Co.

BLUNT, E. A. H.

1931 The caste system of northern India. London: Oxford University Press.

BOSE, A. B. AND N. S. JODHA

1965 The jajmani system in a desert village. Man in India 45:105–126.

BOSE, A. B. AND S. P. MALHOTRA

1964 Studies in group dynamics (1): factionalism in a desert village. Man in India 44:311–328.

BOSE, NIRMAL KUMAR

1951 Caste in India. Man in India 31:107–123.

1953a Cultural anthropology and other essays. Second edition. Calcutta: Indian Associated Publishing Company.

1953b The Hindu method of tribal absorption. *In his* Cultural anthropology and other essays, pp. 156–170. Calcutta: Indian Associated Publishing Co.

1954 Who are the backward classes? Man in India 34:89–98.

1956 Culture zones of India. Geographical Review of India 18:1–12.

1957 The effect of urbanization on work and leisure. Man in India 37: 1–9.

1958a East and west in Bengal. Man in India 38:157–175.

1958b Some aspects of caste in Bengal. Man in India 38:73–97.

1958c Types of villages in West Bengal: a study in social change. The Economic Weekly 10:149–152.

1960 The use of proceedings of caste panchayats. Journal of Social Research (Meerut) 1:98–100.

1964 Change in tribal cultures before and after independence. Man in India 44:1–10.

BOSE, N. K. AND SURAJIT SINHA

1961 Peasant life in India: a study in unity and diversity. Anthropological Survey of India. Memoir No. 8.

BOSE, SHIB CHUNDER

1881 The Hindoos as they are. London, Calcutta: Edward Stanford, W. Newman and Co.

BOUGLÉ, CÉLESTIN

1908 Essais sur le régime des castes. Paris: Felix Alcan.

BRASS, PAUL

1967 Regions, regionalism, and research in modern Indian society and politics. *In* Regions and regionalism in South Asian studies: an exploratory study, R. I. Crane, editor, pp. 258–270. Duke University Program in Comparative Studies on South Asia. Monograph No. 5.

BRIGHT, WILLIAM

1960 Linguistic change in some Indian caste dialects. International Journal of American Linguistics 26:19–26.

BROWN, W. NORMAN

1957 The sanctity of the cow in Hinduism. Journal of the Madras University 28:29–49.

1961 The content of cultural continuity in India. The Journal of Asian Studies 20:427–434.

BUCKLEY, WALTER

1967 Sociology and modern systems theory. Englewood Cliffs, New Jersey: Prentice Hall.

BURLING, ROBBINS

1960 An incipient caste organization in the Garo Hills. Man in India 40:283–299.

CARSTAIRS, G. MORRIS

1953 The case of Thakur Khuman Singh: a culture-conditioned crime. British Journal of Delinquency 4:14–25.

1955 Attitudes to death and suicide in an Indian cultural setting. International Journal of Social Psychiatry 1:33–41.

1957   The twice born: a study of a community of high caste Hindus. London: The Hogarth Press.

1961   Patterns of religious observance in three villages of Rajasthan. Journal of Social Research (Ranchi) 4:59–113.

CASTETS, J.

1931   L'église et le problème de la caste au XVIᵉ siècle. Revue d'Histoire des Missions 8:547–565.

CHANANA, DEV RAJ

1961a   Caste and mobility. The Economic Weekly 13:1561–1562.

1961b   Sanskritisation, westernisation and India's Northwest. The Economic Weekly 13:409–414.

CHAUHAN, BRIJ RAJ

1960   An Indian village: some questions. Man in India 40:116–127.

CHHIBBAR, Y. P.

1968   From caste to class, a study of the Indian middle classes. New Delhi: Associated Publishing House.

COHN, BERNARD S.

1955   The changing status of a depressed caste. In Village India, M. Marriott, editor, pp. 53–77. Chicago: University of Chicago Press.

1957   India as a racial, linguistic and cultural area. In Introducing India in liberal education, Milton Singer, editor, pp. 51–68. Chicago: University of Chicago Press.

1959a   Some notes on law and change in North India. Economic Development and Cultural Change 8:79–93.

1959b   Madhopur revisited. The Economic Weekly 11:963–966.

1960   The initial British impact on India: a case study of the Benares region. The Journal of Asian Studies 19:418–431.

1961a   Chamar family in a North Indian village. The Economic Weekly 13:1051–1055.

1961b   The development and impact of British administration in India. New Delhi: Indian Institute of Public Administration.

1961c   From Indian status to British contract. Journal of Economic History 21:613–628.

1961d   The pasts of an Indian village. Comparative Studies in Society and History 3:241–249.

1962   Review of M. Marriott, caste ranking and community structure in five regions of India and Pakistan. Journal of the American Oriental Society 82:425–430.

1965   Anthropological notes on disputes and law in India. American Anthropologist 67:82–122.

1967   Regions, subjective and objective: their relation to the study of modern Indian history and society. In Regions and regionalism in South Asian studies: an exploratory study, R. I. Crane, editor, pp. 5–37. Duke University Program in Comparative Studies in Southern Asia. Monograph No. 5.

COHN, BERNARD S. AND McKIM MARRIOTT

1958   Networks and centres in the integration of Indian civilisation. Journal of Social Research (Ranchi) 1:1–9.

COLE, B. L.

1932   The Rajput clans of Rajputana. Census of India, 1931, 27:134–141.

COLLVER, ANDREW
1963   The family cycle in India and the United States. American Socio-
        logical Review 28:86–96.
CORMACK, MARGARET L.
1961   She who rides a peacock. New York: Frederick A. Praeger.
CRONIN, VINCENT
1959   A pearl to India. New York: E. P. Dutton.
CULSHAW, W. J.
1949   Tribal heritage: a study of the Santals. London: Lutterworth
        Press.
DAHRENDORF, RALF
1966   Review of G. Lenski, power and privilege. American Sociological
        Review 31:714–718.
DAMES, MANSEL LONGWORTH (editor)
1918   The book of Duarte Barbosa, Volume 1 (Volume 2, 1921).
        London: The Hakluyt Society.
DAMLE, Y. B.
1963   Reference group theory with regard to mobility in caste. Social
        Action, April 1963.
DANDEKAR, V. M. AND KUMUDINI DANDEKAR
1953   Survey of fertility and mortality in Poona District. Poona: Gok-
        hale Institute of Politics and Economics.
DARLING, MALCOLM LYALL
1934   Wisdom and waste in the Punjab village. London: Oxford Uni-
        versity Press.
DAS GUPTA, BIWAN KUMAR
1962   Caste mobility among the Mahato of South Manbhum. Man in
        India 42:228–236.
DATTA GUPTA, JAYA
1959   A study on the Paundra Kshatriya of West Bengal. Bulletin of
        the Department of Anthropology, Government of India 8:109–
        130.
DATTA-MAJUMDER, NABENDU
1956   The Santal: a study in culture change. Department of Anthropol-
        ogy, Government of India. Memoir No. 2.
DAVIS, KINGSLEY
1951   The population of India and Pakistan. Princeton: Princeton Uni-
        versity Press.
DE, BARUN
1967   A historical perspective on theories of regionalism in India. In Re-
        gions and regionalism in South Asian studies: an exploratory study,
        R. I. Crane, editor, pp. 48–88. Duke University Program in Com-
        parative Studies in Southern Asia. Monograph No. 5.
DEMING, WILBUR S.
1928   Rāmdās and the Rāmdāsis. London, Calcutta: Oxford University
        Press.
DERRETT, J. DUNCAN M.
1960   Law and the predicament of the Hindu joint family. The Eco-
        nomic Weekly 12:305–311.

1961   Illegitimates: a test for modern Hindu family law. Journal of the American Oriental Society 81:251–261.

1962   The history of the juridical framework of the joint Hindu family. Contributions to Indian Sociology 6:17–47.

1963   Introduction to modern Hindu law. Bombay: Oxford University Press.

DESAI, I. P.

1955   An analysis. *In* Symposium: caste and joint family. Sociological Bulletin 4:97–117.

1956   The joint family in India: an analysis. Sociological Bulletin 5:144–156.

1964   Some aspects of family in Mahuva. New York: Asia Publishing House.

DESHPANDE, KAMALABAI

1963   Divorce cases in the court of Poona, an analysis. The Economic Weekly 15:1179–1183.

DEVA, INDRA

1958   The sociology of Bhojpuri folk-literature. Doctoral thesis, Lucknow University.

DEVONS, ELY AND MAX GLUCKMAN

1964   Conclusion: modes and consequences of limiting a field of study. *In* Closed systems and open minds: the limits of naïvety in social anthropology, Max Gluckman, editor, pp. 158–261. Chicago: Aldine Publishing Co.

DE VOS, GEORGE

1967   Discussion. *In* Caste and race: comparative approaches, A. de Reuck and J. Knight, editors, pp. 74–77. London: J. and A. Churchill.

DE VOS, GEORGE AND H. WAGATSUMA

1966   Japan's invisible race: caste in culture and personality. Berkeley: University of California Press.

DHILLON, HARWANT SINGH

1955   Leadership and groups in a South Indian village. Planning Commission, Programme Evaluation Organisation. New Delhi: Government of India. P. E. O. Publication No. 9.

DIEHL, CARL GUSTAV

1956   Instrument and purpose: studies on rites and rituals in South India. Lund: Gleerup.

DREKMEIER, CHARLES

1962   Kingship and community in early India. Stanford: Stanford University Press.

DRIVER, EDWIN D.

1963   Differential fertility in central India: Princeton: Princeton University Press.

DUBE, S. C.

1955a   A Deccan village. *In* India's villages, pp. 180–192. Calcutta: West Bengal Government Press. (Second edition, 1960, M. N. Srinivas, editor, pp. 202–215. London: Asia Publishing House.)

1955b   Indian village. Ithaca, New York: Cornell University Press.

1955c   Ranking of castes in a Telengana village. The Eastern Anthropologist 8:182–190.

1956   Cultural factors in rural community development. *In* The Indian village: a symposium. The Journal of Asian Studies 16:19–30.

1958   India's changing villages. Ithaca, New York: Cornell University Press.

1960   Approaches to the tribal problem. Journal of Social Research 3: 11–15.

DUBOIS, JEAN ANTOIN, ABBÉ

1928   Hindu manners, customs and ceremonies. (Translated by Henry K. Beauchamp.) Oxford: Clarendon Press.

DUMONT, LOUIS

1951   Kinship and alliance among the Pramalai Kallar. The Eastern Anthropologist 4:3–26.

1953   The Dravidian kinship terminology as an expression of marriage. Man 54:34–39.

1957a   Hierarchy and marriage alliance in South Indian kinship. Occasional Papers of the Royal Anthropological Institute, No. 12. London: Royal Anthropological Institute.

1957b   Une sous caste de l'Inde du sud. Paris: Mouton.

1959   Dowry in Hindu marriage as a social scientist sees it. The Economic Weekly 11:519–520.

1960   World renunciation in Indian religions. Contributions to Indian Sociology 4:33–62.

1961a   Les marriages Nayar comme faits indiens. L'Homme, Revue Francaise d'Anthropologie 1:11–36.

1961b   Marriage in India: the present state of the question. Contributions to Indian Sociology 5:75–95.

1962   "Tribe" and "caste" in India. Contributions to Indian Sociology 6:120–122.

1963   Le mariage secondaire dans l'Inde du nord. Paris: VIth International Congress of Anthropological and Ethnological Sciences 2: 53–55.

1964a   Marriage in India: the present state of the question; postscript to part one. Contributions to Indian Sociology 7:77–98.

1964b   A note on locality in relation to descent. Contributions to Indian Sociology 7:71–76.

1966   Homo hierarchicus. Essai sur le système des castes. Paris: Gallimard.

1967   Caste: a phenomenon of social structure or an aspect of Indian culture? *In* Caste and race, comparative approaches, A. de Reuck and J. Knight, editors, pp. 28–38. London: J. and A. Churchill.

DUMONT, LOUIS AND D. POCOCK

1957a   For a sociology of India. Contributions to Indian Sociology 1:7–22.

1957b   Village studies. Contributions to Indian Sociology 1:23–42.

1957c   Kinship. Contributions to Indian Sociology 1:43–64.

1960   For a sociology of India: a rejoinder to Dr. Bailey. Contributions to Indian Sociology 4:82–89.

DUTT, NRIPENDRA KUMAR

1931   Origin and growth of caste in India. London: Kegan Paul, Trench, Trübner.

EDGERTON, FRANKLIN

1952   The Bhagavad Gītā. Part 2: Interpretation and Arnold's translation. Cambridge: Harvard University Press.

EGLAR, ZEKIYE

1960   A Punjabi village in Pakistan. New York: Columbia University Press.

ELWIN, VERRIER

1964   The tribal world of Verrier Elwin. New York and Bombay: Oxford University Press.

EMENEAU, MURRAY B.

1956   India as a linguistic area. Language 32:3–16.

EPSTEIN, T. SCARLETT

1959   A sociological analysis of witch beliefs in a Mysore village. The Eastern Anthropologist 12:234–251.

1960   Economic development and peasant marriage in South India. Man in India 40:192–232.

1962   Economic development and social change in South India. Manchester University Press; New York: The Humanities Press.

FARQUHAR, J. N.

1920   An outline of the religious literature of India. London: Oxford University Press.

FERGUSON, FRANCES N.

1963   The master-disciple relationship in India. Research Reviews (University of North Carolina) 10:22–26.

FERNANDEZ, FRANK

1965   Indian tribal societies: tribal or peasant? MS., 13 pp. (Mimeo.)

FISCHEL, WALTER J.

1962   Cochin in Jewish history. American Academy for Jewish Research, Proceedings 30:37–59.

1967   The exploration of the Jewish antiquities of Cochin on the Malabar Coast: a historical-critical survey. Journal of the American Oriental Society 87:30–51.

FORTES, MEYER

1958   Introduction. In The developmental cycle in domestic groups, pp. 1–14. Cambridge Papers in Social Anthropology, No. 1. Cambridge: University Press.

FOSTER, GEORGE M.

1965   Peasant society and the image of limited good. American Anthropologist 67:293–315.

1966   Foster's reply to Kaplan, Saler and Bennett. American Anthropologist 68:210–214.

FOX, RICHARD G.

1967   Resiliency and culture in the Indian caste system: the Umar of U. P. The Journal of Asian Studies 26:575–587.

FREED, STANLEY A.

1963a   Fictive leadership in a North Indian village. Ethnology 2:86–103.

1963b   An objective method for determining the collective caste hierarchy of an Indian village. American Anthropologist 65:879–891.

FREED, RUTH A. AND STANLEY A. FREED
1964   Spirit possession as illness in a North Indian village. Ethnology 3:152–171.
1966   Unity in diversity in the celebration of cattle-curing rites in a North Indian village: a study in the resolution of conflict. American Anthropologist 68:673–692.

FREEDMAN, MAURICE
1962   The family in China: past and present. Pacific Affairs 34:323–336.

FRYKENBERG, ROBERT ERIC
1963   Traditional processes of power in South India: an historical analysis of local influence. Indian Economic and Social History Review 1:1–21.

FUCHS, STEPHEN
1950   The children of Hari: a study of the Nimar Balahis in the Central Provinces of India. Vienna: Verlag Herold.
1960   The Gond and the Bhumia of Eastern Mandla. New York, Bombay: Asia Publishing House.

FUKUTAKE, TADASHI, TSUTOMU OUCHI, AND CHIE NAKANE
1964   The socio-economic structure of the Indian village. Tokyo: Institute of Asian Economic Affairs.

FÜRER-HAIMENDORF, CHRISTOPH VON
1943   The Chenchus: jungle folk of the Deccan. London. Macmillan.
1945   The Reddis of the Bison Hills. London: Macmillan.
1967a   Morals and merit: a study of values and social controls in South Asian societies. Chicago: University of Chicago Press.
1967b   The position of tribal populations in modern India. In India and Ceylon: unity and diversity, P. Mason, editor, pp. 182–222. New York: Oxford University Press.

GADGIL, D. R.
1965   Women in the working force in India. Bombay: Asia Publishing House.

GAIT, E. A.
1913   Census of India, 1911, Volume 1, part 1. Report. Calcutta: Government Printing Office.

GALANTER, MARC
1963   Law and caste in modern India. Asian Survey 3:544–559.
1964   Hindu law and the development of the modern Indian legal system. Mimeographed, 32 pp.
1965   Legal materials for the study of Modern India. Appendix: Hindu law and the modern Indian legal system. Mimeographed. The College, University of Chicago.
1966a   The modernization of law. In Modernization: the dynamics of growth, M. Weiner, editor, pp. 153–165. New York: Basic Books.
1966b   The problem of group membership: some reflections on the judicial view of Indian society. In Class, status and power, R. Bendix and S. M. Lipset, editors, pp. 628–640. Second edition. New York: Free Press. (Reprinted from The Journal of the Indian Law Institute, 1962, 4:331–358.)

GANDHI. MOHANDAS K.

1940   An autobiography or the story of my experiments with truth.
(Translated from the original in Gujarati by Madadev Desai.)
Ahmedabad: Navajivan Publishing House.

GANGARADE, K. D.

1963   Dynamics of a panchayat election. Avard (Journal of the Association of Voluntary Agencies for Rural Development, New Delhi)
5:5–8.

1964   Conflicting value system and social case work. The Journal of Social Work 24:247–256.

GARDNER, PETER M.

1966   Symmetric respect and memorate knowledge: the structure and
ecology of individualistic culture. Southwestern Journal of Anthropology 22:389–415.

GEERTZ, CLIFFORD

1960   The Javanese kikaji: the changing role of a cultural broker. Comparative Studies in Society and History 2:228–249.

1963   Agricultural involution: the process of ecological change in Indonesia. Berkeley and Los Angeles: University of California Press.

GHURYE, G. S.

1953   Indian sadhus. Bombay: The Popular Book Depot.

1959   The scheduled tribes. Second edition. Bombay: The Popular Book
Depot.

1960   After a century and a quarter: Lonikand then and now. Bombay:
The Popular Book Depot.

1961   Class, caste and occupation. Bombay: The Popular Book Depot.

GIDEON, HELEN

1962   A baby is born in the Punjab. American Anthropologist 64:1220–
1234.

GIST, NOEL P.

1953   Mate selection and mass communication in India. Public Opinion
Quarterly 17:481–495.

1954   Occupational differentiation in South India. Social Forces 33:129–
138.

1955   Selective migration in South India. Sociological Bulletin 4:147–160.

GNANAMBAL, K.

1960   Ethnography of Gannapur. Cyclostyled, 127 pp.

GOODE, WILLIAM J.

1963   World revolution and family patterns. New York: The Free Press
of Glencoe.

GOPALASWAMI, R. A.

1953   Census of India, 1951, Volume 1, India, part 1–A. Report. New
Delhi: Government of India Press.

GORE, M. S.

1961   The husband-wife and the mother-son relationships. Sociological
Bulletin 11:91–102.

1965   The traditional Indian family. In Comparative family systems,
M. F. Nimkoff, editor, pp. 209–231. Boston: Houghton Mifflin.

1968   Urbanization and family change. Bombay: Popular Prakashan.

GOUGH, E. KATHLEEN
 1955 The social structure of a Tanjore village. *In* Village India, M. Marriott, editor, pp. 36–52. Chicago: University of Chicago Press.
 1956 Brahmin kinship in a Tamil village. American Anthropologist 58: 384–853.
 1960 Caste in a Tanjore village. *In* Aspects of caste in South India, Ceylon, and North-West Pakistan, E. R. Leach, editor, pp. 11–60. Cambridge Papers in Social Anthropology, No. 2. Cambridge: Cambridge University Press.
 1961a Mappilla: North Kerala. *In* Matrilineal kinship, David M. Schneider and Kathleen Gough, editors, pp. 415–442. Berkeley and Los Angeles: University of California Press.
 1961b Nayar: Central Kerala. *In* Matrilineal kinship, David M. Schneider and Kathleen Gough, editors, pp. 298–384. Berkeley and Los Angeles: University of California Press.
 1963 Indian nationalism and ethnic freedom. *In* The concept of freedom in anthropology, David Bidney, editor, pp. 170–207. The Hague: Mouton.
 1965 A note on Nayar marriage. Man 65:8–11.
GOULD, HAROLD A.
 1958 The Hindu jajmani system: a case of economic particularism. Southwestern Journal of Anthropology 14:428–437.
 1959 The peasant village: centrifugal or centripetal? The Eastern Anthropologist 13:3–16.
 1960a Castes, outcastes and the sociology of stratification. International Journal of Comparative Sociology 1:220–238.
 1960b The micro-demography of marriages in a North Indian area. Southwestern Journal of Anthropology 16:476–491.
 1961a A further note on village exogamy in North India. Southwestern Journal of Anthropology 17:297–300.
 1961b Sanskritization and westernization: a dynamic view. The Economic Weekly 13:945–950.
 1961c Some preliminary observations concerning the anthropology of industrialization. The Eastern Anthropologist 14:30–47.
 1964 The jajmani system of North India: its structure, magnitude and meaning. Ethnology 3:12–41.
 1965a Lucknow rickshawallas: the social organization of an occupational category. International Journal of Comparative Sociology 6:24–47.
 1965b Modern medicine and folk cognition in village India. Human Organization 24:201–208.
 1965c True structural change and the time dimension in the North Indian kinship system. *In* Studies on Asia, 1965, R. K. Sakai, editor, pp. 179–192. Lincoln: University of Nebraska Press.
GRAY, R. M. AND MANILAL C. PAREKH
 1931 Mahatma Gandhi: an essay in appreciation (fourth impression). Calcutta: Association Press.
GRIGSON, W. V.
 1949 The Maria Gonds of Bastar. London: Oxford University Press.
GROSS, NEAL, W. S. MASON, AND A .W. MCEACHERN

1958   Explorations in role analysis: studies of the school superintendency role. New York: John Wiley.

GUHA, UMA

1965   Caste among rural Bengali Muslims. Man in India 45: 167–169.

GUHA, UMA AND M. N. KAUL

1953   A group distance study of the castes of U. P. Bulletin of the Department of Anthropology 2:11–32. Calcutta: Department of Anthropology, Government of India.

GUMPERZ, JOHN J.

1957   Some remarks on regional and social language differences in India. *In* Introducing Indian in liberal education, Milton Singer, editor, pp. 69–79. Chicago: University of Chicago Press.

1958   Dialect differences and social stratification in a North Indian village. American Anthropologist 60: 668–682.

1961   Speech variation and the study of Indian civilization. American Anthropologist 63:976–988.

1964   Religion and social communication in village North India. The Journal of Asian Studies 32:89–98.

GUMPERZ, JOHN J. AND C. M. NAIM

1960   Formal and informal standards in the Hindi regional language area. International Journal of American Linguistics 26:92–118.

1964   Religion and social communication in village North India. The Journal of Asian Studies 23:89–97.

GUPTA, RAGHURAJ

1956   Caste ranking and inter-caste relations among the Muslims of a village in North Western U. P. Eastern Anthropologist 10:30–42.

GUPTA, T. R.

1961   Rural family status and migration: study of a Punjab village. The Economic Weekly 13:1597–1603.

GUPTE, B. A.

1919   Hindu holidays and ceremonials. Second edition, revised. Calcutta and Simla: Thacker, Spink and Co.

HARDGRAVE, ROBERT L., JR.

1964   Caste in Kerala: a preface to the elections. The Economic Weekly 16:1841–1847.

1966   Varieties of political behavior among Nadars of Tamilnad. Asian Survey 6:614–621.

HARPER, EDWARD B.

1957a   Hoylu: a belief relating justice and the supernatural. American Anthropologist 59:801–816.

1957b   Shamanism in South India. Southwestern Journal of Anthropology 13:267–287.

1959a   A Hindu village pantheon. Southwestern Journal of Anthropology 15:227–234.

1959b   Two systems of economic exchange in village India. American Anthropologist 61:760–778.

1961   Moneylending in the village economy of the Malnad. The Economic Weekly 13:169–177.

1963   Spirit possession and social structure. *In* Anthropology on the march, Bala Ratnam, editor, pp. 165–197. Madras: The Book Center.

1964   Ritual pollution as an integrator of caste and religion. The Journal of Asian Studies 2:151–197.

1968   Social consequences of an "unsuccessful" low caste movement. *In* Social mobility in the caste system in India, James Silverberg, editor, pp. 36–65. Comparative Studies in society and history. Supplement III. The Hague: Mouton.

HARPER, EDWARD B. AND LOUISE G. HARPER

1959   Political organization in a Karnataka village. *In* Leadership and political institutions in India, Richard L. Park and Irene Tinker, editors, pp. 453–469. Princeton: Princeton University Press.

HARRISON, SELIG S.

1956a   Caste and the Andhra communists. The American Political Science Review 50:378–404.

1960   India: the most dangerous decades. Princeton: Princeton University Press.

HAYE, CHOWDHRY ABDUL

1966   The Freedom movement in Mewat and Dr. K. M. Ashraf. *In* Kunwar Mohammed Ashraf: an Indian scholar and revolutionary, 1903–1962, Horst Krüger, editor, pp. 291–336. Berlin: Akademic-Verlag.

HAZLEHURST, LEIGHTON W.

1966   Entrepreneurship and the merchant castes in a Punjab city. Duke University Program in Comparative Studies in Southern Asia. Monograph No. 1.

HEIN, NORVIN

1958   The Rām Līlā. Journal of American Folklore 71:279–304.

HITCHCOCK, JOHN T.

1958   The idea of the martial Rājpūt. Journal of American Folklore 71:216–223.

1959   Dominant caste politics in a North Indian village. Mimeographed, 59 pp.

1960   Surat Singh: head judge. *In* In the company of Man, J. B. Casagrande, editor, pp. 234–272. New York: Harper and Brothers.

HOCKINGS, PAUL

1965   Cultural change among the Badagas: a community of South India. Doctoral dissertation, University of California, Berkeley.

HOMANS, GEORGE C.

1950   The human group. New York: Harcourt, Brace and World.

HONIGMANN, JOHN J.

1960a   South Asian research: a village of renown. Research Previews 7:7–14.

1960b   Education and career specialization in a West Pakistan village of renown. Anthropos 55:825–840.

HOPKINS, EDWARD W.

1884   The ordinances of Manu. London: Trübner and Co.

HSU, FRANCIS L. K.

1963   Clan, caste, club. Princeton: D. Van Nostrand Company.

HUTTON, J. H.
   1941   Primitive tribes. *In* Modern India and the West, L. S. S. O'Malley, editor, pp. 417–444. London: Oxford University Press.
   1961   Caste in India: its nature, function and origin. Third edition. Bombay: Oxford University Press.
IBBETSON, DENZIL
   1916   Panjab castes. (Reprint of chapter in Census of the Panjab, 1883.) Lahore: Government Printing Press.
INGALLS, DANIEL H. H.
   1954   Authority and law in ancient India. Journal of the American Oriental Society, Supplement, No. 17:34–45.
   1958   The Brahmin tradition. Journal of American Folklore 71:209–215.
IRSCHIK, EUGENE F.
   1969   Politics and social conflict in South India: the non-Brahmin movement, Tamil separatism 1916–1929. Berkeley and Los Angeles: University of California Press.
ISHWARAN, K.
   1965   Kinship and distance in rural India. International Journal of Comparative Sociology 6:81–94.
ISAACS, HAROLD R.
   1965   India's ex-untouchables. New York: The John Day Company.
IYER, L. K. ANANTHA KRISHNA (ANANTAKRISHNA AYYAR, L. K.)
   1909–1912   The Cochin tribes and castes. Madras: Government Printing Press.
IZMIRLIAN, HARRY JR.
   1964   Caste, kin and politics in a Punjab village. Doctoral dissertation, University of California, Berkeley.
JACKSON, A. V. WILLIAMS, editor
   1907   History of India. Volume 9. London: The Grolier Society.
JAGALPURE, L. B. AND K. D. KALE
   1938   Sarola Kasar: Study of a Deccan village in the famine zone. Ahmednagar: L. B. Jagalpure.
JAY, EDWARD J.
   1959   The anthropologist and tribal warfare. Journal of Social Research (Ranchi) 2:82–89.
   1961a   A comparison of tribal and peasant religion with special reference to the Hill Maria Gonds. Mimeographed, 60 pp.
   1961b   Social values and economic change: the Hill Marias of Bastar. The Economic Weekly 13:1369–1372.
   1964   The concepts of 'field' and 'network' in anthropological research. Man in India 64:137–139.
KALIDASA
   1959   Shakuntala and other writings. (Translated by Arthur W. Ryder.) New York: E. P. Dutton.
KANE, PANDURANG VAMAN
   1941   History of Dharmaśāstra. Volume 2, part 1. Poona: Bhandarkar Oriental Research Institute.
   1946   History of Dharmaśāstra. Volume 3. Poona: Bhandarkar Oriental Research Institute.

KANNAN, C. T.
1963   Intercaste and inter-community marriages in India. Bombay: Allied Publishers.

KAPADIA, K. M.
1947   Hindu kinship: an important chapter in Hindu social history. Bombay: The Popular Book Depot.
1956   Rural family patterns. Sociological Bulletin 5:111–126.
1957   A perspective necessary for the study of social change in India. Sociological Bulletin 6:43–60.
1958   Marriage and family in India. Second edition. London: Oxford University Press.
1959   The family in transition. Sociological Bulletin 8:68–99.
1961   The growth of townships in South Gujarat: Maroli Bazar. Sociological Bulletin 10:69–87.
1962   Caste in transition. Sociological Bulletin 12:73–90.
1963   The passing of the traditional society. Fiftieth Indian Science Congress, Delhi.
1966   Marriage and family in India. Third edition. Bombay: Oxford University Press.

KARAKA, DOSABHAI FRAMJI
1884   History of the Parsis. Volume 1. London: Macmillan.

KARANDIKAR, S. V.
1929   Hindu exogamy. Bombay: Taraporevala.

KARIM, A. K. NAZMUL
1956   Changing society in India and Pakistan. Dacca: Oxford University Press.

KARVE, IRAWATI
1953   Kinship organization in India. Poona, Deccan College Monograph Series, No. 11. Poona: Deccan College.
1958a   The Indian village. Bulletin of the Deccan College 18:73–106.
1958b   What is caste? (1) Caste as extended kin. The Economic Weekly 10:125–138.
1961   Hindu society: an interpretation. Poona: Sangam Press.
1962   On the road: a Maharashtrian pilgrimage. Journal of Asian Studies 22:13–30.
1965   Kinship organization in India. Second revised edition. Bombay: Asia Publishing House.

KARVE, IRAWATI AND Y. B. DAMLE
1963   Group relations in village community. Deccan College Monograph Series. Poona: Deccan College.

KARVE, IRAWATI AND VISHNU MAHADEO DANDEKOR
1951   Anthropometric measurements of Mahārāshtra. Deccan College Monograph Series, No. 8. Poona: Deccan College.

KAUTILYA
1961   Kautilya's Arthaśāstra. (Translated by R. Shamasastry.) Seventh edition. Mysore: Mysore Printing and Publishing House.

KENNEDY, BETH C.
1954   Rural-urban contrasts in parent-child relations in India. Indian Journal of Social Work 15:162–174. (Reprinted by the Bureau of

Research and Publications, Tata Institute of Social Science, Chembur, Bombay.)

KENNEDY, MELVILLE T.
1925   The Chaitanya movement. London and Calcutta: Oxford University Press.

KETKAR, SHRIDHAR VENKATESH
1909   The history of caste in India. Ithaca: Taylor and Carpenter.

KHADDURI, MAJID AND H. J. LIEBESNY
1955   Law in the Middle East. Volume 1. Washington: The Middle East Institute.

KHAN, KHAN AHMAD HASAN
1931   Census of India, 1931, Volume 17. Punjab.

KHARE, R. S.
1960   The Kanya-Kubja Brahmins and their social organization. Southwestern Journal of Anthropology 16:348–367.

KHEDKAR, VITHAN KRISHNAJI
1959   The divine heritage of the Yadavas. Allahabad: Parmanand.

KLASS, MORTON
1966   Marriage rules in Bengal. American Anthropologist 68:951–970.

KOCHAR, V. K.
1963   Socio-cultural denominators of domestic life in a Santal village. The Eastern Anthropologist 16:167–180.

KOLENDA, PAULINE MAHAR
1958   Changing caste ideology in a North Indian village. Journal of Social Issues 14:51–65.
1959   A multiple scaling technique for caste ranking. Man in India 39: 127–147.
1963   Toward a model of the Hindu jajmani system. Human Organization 22:11–31.
1964   Religious anxiety and Hindu fate. The Journal of Asian Studies 23:71–82.
1967   Regional differences in Indian family structure. In Regions and regionalism in South Asian Studies: an exploratory study, R. I. Crane, editor, pp. 147–226. Duke University Program in Comparative Studies in Southern Asia. Monograph No. 5.
1968   Region, caste, and family structure: a comparative study of the Indian "joint" family. In Structure and change in Indian society, M. Singer and B. S. Cohn, editors. Chicago: Aldine Publishing Company.

KOSAMBI, D. D.
1955   The basis of ancient Indian history (2). Journal of the American Oriental Society 75:226–237.
1965   The culture and civilization of ancient India in historical outline. London: Routledge and Kegan Paul.

KOTHARI, RAJNI AND RUSHIKESH MARU
1965   Caste and secularism in India: case study of a caste federation. The Journal of Asian Studies 25:33–50.

KRIPALANI, KRISHNA
1962   Rabindranath Tagore: a biography. New York: Grove Press.

KROEBER, A. L.
1944   Configurations of culture growth. Berkeley and Los Angeles: University of California Press.
1947   Culture groupings in Asia. Southwestern Journal of Anthropology 3:322–330.

KUDRYAVTSEV, M. K.
1964   On the role of Jats in North India's ethnic history. Journal of Social Research (Ranchi) 7:126–135.
1965   Musul'manskie kasty (Muslim castes). *In* Kasty v Indii (Castes in India), G. G. Kotovskii, editor, pp. 214–232. Moscow: Akademiia Nauk SSSR. Institut Narodov Azii.

LACEY, W. G.
1933   Census of India, 1931, Volume 7, part 1. Report, Bihar and Orissa. Patna: Government Printing Press.

LALL, R. MANOHAR
1933   Among the Hindus: a study of Hindu festivals. Cawnpore: Minerva Press.

LAMBERT, RICHARD D.
1958   Factory workers and the non-factory population in Poona. The Journal of Asian Studies 18:21–42.
1962   The impact of urban society upon village life. *In* India's urban future, Roy Turner, editor, pp. 117–140. Berkeley and Los Angeles: University of California Press.
1963   Workers, factories, and social change in India. Princeton, New Jersey: Princeton University Press.

LEACH, EDMUND R.
1960   Introduction: What should we mean by caste? *In* Aspects of caste in South India, Ceylon and North-West Pakistan, E. R. Leach, editor. Cambridge Papers in Social Anthropology, No. 2. Cambridge: Cambridge University Press.
1967   Caste, class and slavery: the taxonomic problem. *In* Caste and race: comparative approaches, A. de Reuck and J. Knight, editors, pp. 17–27. London: J. and A. Churchill.

LEACOCK, SETH AND DAVID G. MANDELBAUM
1955   A nineteenth century development project in India: the cotton improvement program. Economic Development and Cultural Change 3:334–351.

LEARMONTH, A. T. A. AND A. M. LEARMONTH
1958   The regional concept and national development. The Economic Weekly 10:153–156.

LENSKI, GERHARD
1966   Power and privilege: a theory of social stratification. New York: McGraw-Hill.

LEVINSON, DANIEL J.
1959   Role, personality and social structure in the organizational setting. Journal of Abnormal and Social Psychology 58:170–180.

LEWIS, OSCAR
1955   Peasant culture in India and Mexico: a comparative analysis. *In* Village India, M. Marriott, editor, pp. 145–170. Chicago: University of Chicago Press.

1958   Village life in Northern India: studies in a Delhi village. Urbana: University of Illinois Press.

LEWIS, OSCAR AND VICTOR BARNOUW
1956   Caste and the jajmani system in a North Indian village. Scientific Monthly 83:66–81.

LEWIS, OSCAR (assisted by Victor Barnouw and Harvant Dhillon)
1956   Aspects of land tenure and economics in a North Indian village. Economic Development and Cultural Change 4:279–302.

LOKANATHAN, P. S.
1965a   All India rural household survey. Vol. II. New Delhi: National Council of Applied Economic Research.
1965b   All India rural household survey, 1962. A summary statement on income distribution by rural and All India. Occasional Paper 13, National Council of Applied Economic Research. New Delhi.

LYNCH, OWEN M.
1967   Rural cities in India: continuities and discontinuities. In India and Ceylon: unity and diversity, Philip Mason, editor, pp. 142–158. London: Oxford University Press.

McCLELLAND, DAVID C.
1961   The achieving society. Princeton: D. Van Nostrand.

McCORMACK, WILLIAM
1956   Changing leadership of a Mysore village. Mimeographed, 9 pp.
1957   Mysore villager's view of change. Economic Development and Cultural Change 5:257–262.
1958a   The forms of communication in Vīraśaiva religion. Journal of American Folklore 71:325–335.
1958b   Sister's daughter marriage in a Mysore village. Man in India 38: 34–48.
1959   The development of Hindu law during the British period. Mimeographed, 65 pp.
1960   Social dialects in Dharwar Kannada. International Journal of American Linguistics 26:79–91.
1963   Lingayats as a sect. Journal of the Royal Anthropological Institute 93:59–71.

McCRINDLE, J. W.
1877   Ancient India as described by Megasthenes and Arrian. London: Trübner.
1901   Ancient India as described in classical literature. London: Constable.

McDONALD, ELLEN E.
1968   The modernization of communication: vernacular publishing in nineteenth-century Maharashtra. Asian Survey 8:589–606.

MacLACHLAN, MORGAN E. AND ALAN R. BEALS
1966   The internal and external relationships of a Mysore chiefdom. Journal of Asian and African Studies 1: 87–99.

MADAN, B. K.
1951   The economics of the Indian village and its implications in social structure. International Social Science Bulletin 3:813–822. Paris: UNESCO.

MADAN, T. N.

1962a   The Hindu joint family. Man 62:88–89.
1962b   The joint family: a terminological clarification. International Journal of Comparative Sociology 3:7–16.
1962c   Is the Brahmanic gotra a grouping of kin? Southwestern Journal of Anthropology 18:59–77.
1965   Family and kinship: a study of the Pandits of rural Kashmir. New York: Asia Publishing House.
1968   Caste and development. Economic and Political Weekly 4:285–290.

MAHAJAN, MEHR CHAND
1963   Looking back. Bombay: Asia Publishing House.

MAHAR, PAULINE M. (see Kolenda, Pauline Mahar)

MAINE, HENRY
1861   Ancient law. London: J. Murray.
1881   Village-communities in the East and West. Fourth edition. London: John Murray.

MAJUMDAR, DHIRENDRA NATH
1944   The fortunes of primitive tribes. Lucknow: Universal Publishers.
1958a   Caste and communication in an Indian village. Bombay: Asia Publishing House.
1958b   Races and cultures of India. Bombay: Asia Publishing House.

MAJUMDAR, D. N., M. C. PRADHAN, C. SEN, AND S. MISRA
1955   Inter-caste relations in Gohanakallan, a village near Lucknow. The Eastern Anthropologist 8:191–214.

MAJUMDAR, R. C.
1960   The classical accounts of India. Calcutta: Firma K. L. Mukhopadhyay.

MALAVIYA, H. D.
1956   Village panchayats in India. New Delhi: Economic and Political Research Department. All India Congress Committee.

MANDELBAUM, DAVID G.
1938   Polyandry in Kota society. American Anthropologist 40:574–583.
1939a   Agricultural ceremonies among three tribes of Travancore. Ethnos (Stockholm) 4:114–128.
1939b   The Jewish way of life in Cochin. Jewish Social Studies 1:423–460.
1941   Social trends and personal pressures. In Language, culture and personality, L. Spier, A. I. Hallowell, and S. Newman, editors, pp. 219–238. (Reprinted in Anthropology of folk religion, C. Leslie, editor, 1960, pp. 221–255. New York: Vintage Books.)
1947   Hindu-Moslem conflict in India. The Middle East Journal 1:369–385.
1948   The family in India. Southwestern Journal of Anthropology 4:123–139.
1949   Population problems in India and Pakistan. Far Eastern Survey 18:283–287.
1954a   Fertility of early years of marriage in India. In Professor Ghurye felicitation volume, K. M. Kapadia, editor, pp. 150–168. Bombay: The Popular Book Depot.
1954b   Form, variation and meaning of a ceremony. In Method and perspective in anthropology, R. F. Spencer, editor, pp. 60–102. Minneapolis: University of Minnesota Press.

1955   The world and the world view of the Kota. *In* Village India, M. Marriott, editor, pp. 223–254. Chicago: University of Chicago Press.

1956   The Kotas in their social setting. *In* Introduction to the civilization of India, Milton Singer, editor. Chicago: University of Chicago Press.

1959a Concepts and methods in the study of caste. The Economic Weekly Annual, Volume 2:145–149.

1959b Social uses of funeral rites. *In* The meaning of death, H. Feifel, editor, pp. 189–217. New York: MacGraw-Hill.

1960   A reformer of his people. *In* In the company of man, J. Casagrande, editor, pp. 273–308. New York: Harper.

1962   Review of M. Marriott, caste ranking and community structure in five regions of India and Pakistan. Journal of Asian Studies 21: 434–436.

1964   Introduction: process and structure in South Asian religion. *In* Religion in South Asia, Edward B. Harper, editor, pp. 5–20. Seattle: University of Washington Press. (Also published in The Journal of Asian Studies 23:5–20.)

1965   Alcohol and culture. Current Anthropology 6:281–292.

1966   Transcendental and pragmatic aspects of religion. American Anthropologist 68:1174–1191.

MARRIOTT, McKIM

1955a Western medicine in a village of Northern India. *In* Health, culture and community: case studies of public reactions to health programs, Benjamin D. Paul, editor, pp. 239–268. New York: Russell Sage Foundation.

1955b Little communities in an indigenous civilization. *In* Village India, M. Marriott, editor, pp. 171–222. Chicago: University of Chicago Press.

1959a Changing channels of cultural transmission in Indian civilization. *In* Intermediate societies, social mobility and communication, Verne Ray, editor, pp. 66–74. Seattle: American Ethnological Society.

1959b Interactional and attributional theories of caste ranking. Man in India 39:92–107.

1960   Caste ranking and community structure in five regions of India and Pakistan. Poona: G. S. Press.

1962   Communication: rejoinder to Metraux. Journal of Asian Studies 21:263–265.

MARTEN, J. T.

1924   Census of India, 1921, Volume 1, part 1. Report. Calcutta: Government Printing Press.

MARTIN, MONTGOMERY

1838   The history, antiquities, topography and statistics of Eastern India. London: Allen and Co.

MATHUR, K. S.

1958a Caste and occupation in a Malwa village. Eastern Anthropologist 12:47–61.

1958b The Indian village: is it a structural unity? Journal of Social Research (Ranchi) 1:50–53.

1959   Caste and occupation in a Malwa village. Eastern Anthropologist
        12:47–61.
1964   Caste and ritual in a Malwa village. Bombay: Asia Publishing
        House.
MAYER, ADRIAN C.
1952   Land and society in Malabar. London: Oxford University Press.
1956   Some hierarchical aspects of caste. Southwestern Journal of An-
        thropology 12:117–144.
1957   An Indian community development block revisited. Pacific Affairs
        30:35–46.
1958a   The dominant caste in a region of Central India. Southwestern
        Journal of Anthropology 14:407–427.
1958b   Local government elections in a Malwa village. Eastern Anthrop-
        ologist 9:189–202.
1960   Caste and kinship in Central India: a village and its region. Berke-
        ley and Los Angeles: University of California Press.
1962   System and network: an approach to the study of political process
        in Dewas. In Indian anthropology, T. N. Madan and G. Sarana,
        editors, pp. 266–278. Bombay: Asia Publishing House.
MAYER, ALBERT AND ASSOCIATES
1958   Pilot project, India: the story of rural development at Etawah, U.
        P. Berkeley and Los Angeles: University of California Press.
MAYNARD, H. J.
1917   Influence of the Indian king upon the growth of caste. Journal of
        the Panjab Historical Society 6:88–100.
MENCHER, JOAN
1963   Growing up in South Malabar. Human Organization 22:54–65.
1965   The Nayars of South Malabar. In Comparative family systems, M.
        F. Nimkoff, editor, pp. 163–191. Boston: Houghton, Mifflin.
1966   Kerala and Madras: a comparative study of ecology and social
        structure. Ethnology 5:135–179.
MENCHER, JOAN P. AND HELEN GOLDBERG
1967   Kinship and marriage regulations among the Namboodiri Brahmins
        of Kerala. Man n.s. 2:87–106.
METCALFE, CHARLES T.
1833   Appendix 84 to the report of the Select Committee of the House
        of Commons on the affairs of the East India Company. III-Review,
        pp. 328–334. Minute on the Upper Provinces. London, 1833.
        (House of Commons sessional papers 1831–32. XI, superscribed
        enumeration pp. 692–698.)
MILLER, ERIC J.
1954   Caste and territory in Malabar. American Anthropologist 56:410–
        420.
1960   Village structure in North Kerala. In India's villages, M. N.
        Srinivas, editor, pp. 42–55. Second revised edition. London: Asia
        Publishing House.
MINTURN, LEIGH
1963   The Rājpūts of Khalapur, Part II, child training. In Six cultures:
        studies of child rearing, B. B. Whiting, editor, pp. 301–361. New
        York and London: John Wiley and Sons.

MINTURN, LEIGH AND JOHN T. HITCHCOCK
  1963   The Rājpūts of Khalapur, India. *In* Six cultures: studies of child
         rearing, B. B. Whiting, editor, pp. 203–361. New York and Lon-
         don: John Wiley and Sons.
  1966   The Rājpūts of Khalapur, India. New York: John Wiley. (Six
         cultures series, Volume 3.)
MINTURN, LEIGH AND WILLIAM W. LAMBERT
  1964   Mothers of six cultures. New York: John Wiley and Sons.
MISRA, SATISH C.
  1964   Muslim communities in Gujarat. New York: Asia Publishing
         House.
MITRA, A.
  1965   Levels of regional development in India, being part 1 of General
         Report on India. Census of India, 1961, Volume 1, part 1-A (i).
         Delhi: Government of India Press.
MONGA, VEENA
  1967   Social mobility among the Potters: report of a caste conference.
         Economic and Political Weekly 2:1047–1055.
MOON, PENDEREL
  1945   Strangers in India. New York: Reynal and Hitchcock.
MORGAN, LEWIS H.
  1871   Systems of consanguinity and affinity of the human family. Wash-
         ington: Smithsonian Institution.
MORRIS, MORRIS DAVID
  1960   Caste and the evolution of the industrial workforce in India. Pro-
         ceedings of the American Philosophical Society 104:124–133.
  1967   Values as an obstacle to economic growth in South Asia, The
         Journal of Economic History 27:588–607.
MORRIS-JONES, W. H.
  1967   The government and politics of India. Anchor Books edition. New
         York: Doubleday and Co.
MORRISON, WILLIAM A.
  1959   Family types in Badlapur: an analysis of a changing institution in
         a Maharashtrian village. Sociological Bulletin 8:45–67.
MUKERJI, A. B.
  1957   The bi-weekly market at Modinagar. The Indian Geographer 2:
         271–293.
MÜLLER, FREDRICH MAX
  1868   Chips from a German workshop. Volume 2. Second edition. Lon-
         don: Longmans, Green and Co.
MULLICK, BULLORAM (BALARAMA MALLIKA)
  1882   Essays on the Hindu family in Bengal. Calcutta: W. Newman
         and Co.
MURDOCK, GEORGE P.
  1949   Social structure. New York: Macmillan.
MYRDAL, GUNNAR
  1968   Asian drama: an inquiry into the poverty of nations. New York:
         Random House (Pantheon).
NADEL, S. F.
  1951   The foundations of social anthropology. London: Cohen and West.
  1954   Caste and government in primitive society. Journal of the Anthro-
         pological Society of Bombay, pp. 9–22.

NAIR, KUSUM
 1963   Blossoms in the dust. New York: Frederick A. Praeger.
NANDI, PROSHANTA KUMAR
 1965   A study of caste organizations in Kanpur. Man in India 45:84–99.
NANDI, SANTIBHUSHAN AND D. S. TYAGI
 1961   Forms of villages. In Peasant Life in India, pp. 1–6. Anthropological Survey of India, Calcutta. Memoir No. 8.
NANDIMATH, S. C.
 1942   A handbook of Virasaivism. Bangalore: Basel Mission Press.
NARAIN, DHIRENDRA
 1957   Hindu character (a few glimpses). Bombay: University of Bombay. Sociology Series No. 8.
NARAYAN, JAYAPRAKASH
 1958   Toward a new society. New Delhi: Congress for Cultural Freedom.
NATH, KAMLA
 1965   Women in the new village. The Economic Weekly 17:813–816.
NATH, V.
 1961   The village and the community. In India's Urban Future, Roy Turner, editor, pp. 139–154. Berkeley and Los Angeles: University of California Press.
 1962   Village, caste and community. The Economic Weekly. 14:1877–1882.
NAVALAKHA, SURENDRA KUMAR
 1959   The authority structure among the Bhumij and Bhil: a study in historical causations. The Eastern Anthropologist 13:27–40.
NAYAR, UNNI
 1952   My Malabar. Bombay: Hind Kitabs.
NEALE, WALTER C.
 1962   Economic change in rural India: land tenure and reform in Uttar Pradesh, 1800–1955. New Haven and London: Yale University Press.
NEALE, WALTER C., HARPAL SINGH AND JAI PAL SINGH
 1965   Kurali market: a report on the economic geography of marketing in Northern Punjab. Economic Development and Cultural Change 13:129–168.
NEHRU, JAWAHARLAL
 1941   Toward freedom: the autobiography of Jawaharlal Nehru. New York: John Day.
 1946   The discovery of India. New York: John Day.
NEHRU, S. S.
 1932   Caste and credit in the rural area. London:
NEILL, STEPHEN
 1934   Builders of the Indian church. London: Edinburgh House Press.
NEWELL, W. H.
 1963   Inter-caste marriage in Kuzti village. Man 63:55–57.
NICHOLAS, RALPH W.
 1961   Economics of family types in two West Bengal villages. The Economic Weekly 13:1057–1060.
 1962   Villages of the Bengal Delta: a study of ecology and peasant society. Doctoral dissertation, University of Chicago.

1963   Ecology and village structure in deltaic West Bengal. The Economic Weekly 15:1185–1196.

1965   Factions: a comparative analysis. *In* Political systems and the distribution of power, Max Gluckman and Fred Eggan, editors, pp. 21–61. London: Tavistock Publications; New York: Frederick A. Praeger. A. S. A. Monograph No. 2.

1966   Segmentary factional political systems. *In* Political anthropology, M. S. Swartz, V. W. Turner, and A. Tinden, editors, pp. 49–59. Chicago: Aldine Publishing Co.

1967   Ritual hierarchy and social relations in rural Bengal. Contributions to Indian Sociology, New Series 1:56–83.

NICHOLAS, RALPH W. AND TARASHISH MUKOPADHYAY
1962   Politics and law in two West Bengal villages. Bulletin of the Anthropological Survey of India 11:15–39.

NIEHOFF, ARTHUR
1958   A study of matrimonial advertisements in North India. The Eastern Anthropologist 12:73–86.

NIKITIN, AFANASY
1960   Khozhenie za tri moria Afanasiia Nikitina, 1466–1472. (Afanasy Nikitin's voyage beyond three seas, 1466–1472.) B. Kumkes, editor. Moscow. (Text in Russian, Hindi and English.)

O'MALLEY, L. S. S.
1913   Census of India, 1911, Volume 5, part 1. Report, Bengal, Bihar, Orissa and Sikkim. Calcutta: Bengal Secretariat Book Depot.

1934   India's social heritage. Oxford: Clarendon Press.

1941   Modern India and the West. London: Oxford University Press.

OPLER, MORRIS E.
1956   The extensions of an Indian village. *In* The Indian village: a symposium. The Journal of Asian Studies 16:5–10.

1958   Spirit possession in a rural area of Northern India. *In* Reader in comparative religion, W. A. Lessa and E. Z. Vogt, editors, pp. 553–566. Evanston: Row, Peterson.

1959a   Family, anxiety and religion in a community of North India. *In* Culture and mental health, Marvin K. Opler, editor, pp. 273–289. New York: Macmillan.

1959b   The place of religion in a North Indian village. Southwestern Journal of Anthropology 15:219–226.

1960   Recent changes in family structure in an Indian Village. Anthropological Quarterly 35:93–97.

OPLER, MORRIS E. AND RUDRA DATT SINGH
1952   Two villages of eastern Uttar Pradesh (U. P.), India: an analysis of similarities and differences. American Anthropologist 54:179–190.

ORANS, MARTIN
1965   The Santal: a tribe in search of a great tradition. Detroit: Wayne State University Press.

1968   Maximizing in jajmaniland. American Anthropologist 70:875–897.

ORENSTEIN, HENRY
1959   Leadership and caste in a Bombay village. *In* Leadership and political institutions in India, Richard L. Park and Irene Tinker, editors, pp. 415–426.
Princeton: Princeton University Press.

1960   Irrigation, settlement pattern and social organization. *In* Selected papers of the fifth international congress of anthropological and ethnological sciences, Philadelphia, Anthony F. C. Wallace, editor, pp. 318–323. Philadelphia: University of Pennsylvania Press.

1961   The recent history of the extended family in India. Social Problems 8:341–350.

1962   Exploitation or function in the interpretation of jajmani. Southwestern Journal of Anthropology 18:302–316.

1963   Caste and the concept "Marātha" in Maharashtra. The Eastern Anthropologist 16:1–9.

1965a   Gaon: conflict and cohesion in an Indian village. Pinceton: Princeton University Press.

1965b   Notes on the ecology of irrigation agriculture in contemporary peasant societies. American Anthropologist 67:1529–1532.

1965c   The structure of Hindu caste values: a preliminary study of hierarchy and ritual defilement. Ethnology 4:1–15.

ORR, W. G.
1947   A sixteenth-century Indian mystic. London and Redhill: Lutterworth Press.

PANIKKAR, K. M.
1956   Hindu society at the cross roads. Second revised edition. Bombay: Asia Publishing House.

1961   Hindu society at the cross roads. Third edition. Bombay: Asia Publishing House.

PARSONS, TALCOTT
1953   A revised analytical approach to the theory of social stratification. *In* Class, status and power, R. Bendix and S. M. Lipset, editors, pp. 92–128. Glencoe: Free Press.

1961   An outline of the social system. *In* Theories of society, Talcott Parsons *et al.*, editors, Volume 1, pp. 30–79. New York: Free Press of Glencoe.

PATNAIK, NITYANANDA
1953   Study of the weekly market at Barpali. Geographical Review of India 15:19–31.

1960a   Assembly of the Mahanayaka Sudras of Puri District, Orissa. *In* Data on caste: Orissa, pp. 81–118. Anthropological Survey of India, Calcutta. Memoir No. 7.

1960b   Service relationship between barbers and villagers in a small village in Ranpur. The Economic Weekly 12:737–742.

PATNAIK, NITYANANDA AND A. K. RAY
1960   Oilmen or Teli. *In* Data on caste: Orissa, pp. 9–80. Anthropological Survey of India. Memoir No. 7.

PATTERSON, MAUREEN L. P.
1958   Intercaste marriage in Maharashtra. The Economic Weekly 10:139–142.

PILLAI, N. KUNJAN
1932   Census of India 1931, Travancore Vol. 28, Part I. Trivandrum: Government Press.

PLANALP, JACK MILAN
1956   Religious life and values in a North Indian village. Doctoral dissertation, Cornell University.

POCOCK, DAVID F.
1954   The hypergamy of the Patidars. *In* Professor Ghurye felicitation volume, K. M. Kapadia, editor, pp. 195–204. Bombay: The Popular Book Depot.
1955   The movement of castes. Man 55:71–72.
1957a   Bases of faction in Gujerat. British Journal of Sociology 8:295–317.
1957b   Inclusion and exclusion: a process in the caste system of Gujerat. Southwestern Journal of Anthropology 13:19–31.
1962   Notes on jajmani relationships. Contribution to Indian Sociology 6:78–95.
1964   The anthropology of time reckoning. Contributions to Indian Sociology 7:18–29.

POFFENBERGER, THOMAS
1964   The use of praise. University of Baroda, Department of Child Development. Working papers in Indian personality. MS., 6 pp.

POFFENBERGER, THOMAS AND BIHARI J. PANDYA
n.d.   The effect of the dowry system on endogamy among Leva Patidar in a low status village. MS., 8 pp.

PRABHU, PANDHARI NATH
1954   Hindu social organization. Bombay: The Popular Book Depot.

PRADHAN, M. C.
1965   The Jats of Northern India: their traditional political system. The Economic Weekly 17:1821–1824, 1855–1864.
1966   The political system of the Jats of Northern India. Bombay: Oxford University Press.

PRASAD, RAJENDRA
1957   Autobiography. Bombay: Asia Publishing House.

Pyarelal (Nair)
1965   Mahatma Gandhi, Volume 1: the early phase. Ahmedabad: Navajivan Publishing House.

RAGHAVAN, V.
1965   Variety and integration in the pattern of Indian culture. Far Eastern Quarterly 15:33–41.

RAGHUVANSHI, V. P. S.
1966   The institution and working of caste in the latter part of the eighteenth century from European sources. *In* Kunwar Mohammad Ashraf: an Indian scholar and revolutionary 1903–1962, Horst Krüger, editor, pp. 147–175. Berlin: Akademie Verlag.

RAJ, HILDA
1959   Persistence of caste in South India: an analytic study of the Hindu and Christian Nadar. Doctoral dissertation, American University, Washington, D.C.

RANADE, RAMABAI
1938   Himself: the autobiography of a Hindu lady. (Translated and adapted by Katherine van Akin Gates from a book wirtten in the Marathi language by Mrs. Ramabai Ranade.) New York, Toronto: Longmans, Green and Co.

RANGACHARI, DIWAN BAHADUR K.
1931   The Sri Vaishnava Brahmans. Bulletin of the Madras Government Museum. Volume 1, part 2. Madras: Government Press.

RAO, C. V. H.
1966   The fifth steel plant: Andhra's case. The Economic and Political
       Weekly 1:534.
RAO, M. S. A.
1955   Symposium on caste and joint family: in Kerala. Sociological Bulle-
       tin 4:122–129.
1957   Social change in Malabar. Bombay: Popular Book Depot.
1961   The jajmani system. The Economic Weekly 13:877–878.
1964   Caste and the Indian army. Economic Weekly 16:1439–1443.
RAO, V. L. S. PRAKASA AND L. S. BHAT
1960   Planning regions in the Mysore State: the need for readjustment
       of district boundaries. Calcutta: Indian Statistical Institute. Re-
       gional studies No. 1.
RAO, Y. V. LAKSHMANA
1966   Communication and development: a study of two Indian villages.
       Minneapolis: University of Minnesota Press.
RATH, R. AND N. C. SIRCAR
1960a The cognitive background of six Hindu caste groups regarding
       the low caste untouchables. Journal of Social Psychology 51:295–
       306.
1960b The mental pictures of six Hindu caste groups about each other
       as reflected in verbal stereotypes. Journal of Social Psychology 51:
       277–293.
REDDY, N. S.
1952   Transition in caste structure in Andhra Desh with particular ref-
       erence to depressed castes. Doctoral dissertation. University of
       Lucknow, Lucknow.
1955   Functional relations of Lohars in a North Indian village. The East-
       ern Anthropologist 8:129–140.
1963   Spatial variance of custom in Andhra Pradesh. In Anthropology
       on the march, Bala Ratnam, editor, pp. 283–296. Madras: The
       Book Centre.
REDFIELD, ROBERT
1955   The little community: viewpoints for the study of a human whole.
       Chicago: University of Chicago Press.
RENOU, LOUIS
1953   Religions of ancient India. London: Athlone Press.
RETZLAFF, RALPH H.
1962   Village government in India. London: Asia Publishing House.
REYES-HOCKINGS, AMELIA
1966   The newspaper as surrogate marriage broker in India. Sociological
       Bulletin 15:25–39.
RISLEY, H. H.
1892   The tribes and castes of Bengal. Calcutta: Bengal Secretariat Press.
1915   The people of India. Second edition. London: W. Thacker and
       Co.
RIVERS, W. H. R.
1921   The origin of hypergamy. In The Journal of the Bihar and Orissa
       Research Society 8:9–24.
ROOKSBY, R. L.
1956   Status in a plural society: seminar on social and cultural problems

of India, School of Oriental and African Studies, University of London. Mimeographed, 15 pp.

Ross, Aileen D.
1961   The Hindu family in its urban setting. Toronto: University of Toronto Press.

Rosser, Colin
1960   A "hermit" village in Kulu. *In* India's villages, M. N. Srinivas, editor, pp. 77–89. Second revised edition. London: Asia Publishing House.

Rowe, William L.
1960   The marriage network and structural change in a North Indian community. Southwestern Journal of Anthropology 16:299–311.
1963   Changing rural class structure and the jajmani system. Human Organization 22:41–44.
1964   Caste, kinship, and association in urban India. MS., 24 pp.
1968   The new Cauhāns: a caste mobility movement in North India. *In* Social mobility in the caste system in India, James Silverberg, editor, pp. 66–67. Comparative Studies in Society and History, Supplement III. The Hague: Mouton.

Roy Burman, B. K.
1960   Basic concepts of tribal welfare and tribal integration. Journal of Social Research 3:16–24.

Roy, Ramashray
1963   Conflict and co-operation in a North Bihar Village. Journal of the Bihar Society 49:297–315.

Roy, Sarat Chandra
1934   Caste, race and religion in India: inadequacies of the current theories of caste. Man in India 14:75–220.

Rudolph, Lloyd I.
1965   The modernity of tradition: the democratic incarnation of caste in India. The American Political Science Review 59:975–989.

Rudolph, Lloyd I. and Susanne H. Rudolph
1960   The political role of India's caste associations. Pacific Affairs 33: 5–22.
1967   The modernity of tradition: political development in India. Chicago: University of Chicago Press.

Rudolph, Susanne Hoeber
1965   Self-control and political potency: Gandhi's asceticism. The American Scholar 35:79–97.

Russell, R. V. and Rai Bahadur Hīra Lāl
1916   The tribes and castes of the Central Provinces of India. Volume 1. London: Macmillan and Co.

Sachchidananda
1964   Culture change in tribal Bihar. Calcutta: Bookland Private Limited.
1965   Profiles of tribal culture in Bihar. Calcutta: Firma K. L. Mukhopadhyay.

Sangave, Vilas Adinath
1959   Jaina community: a social survey. Bombay: Popular Book Depot.

SARMA, JYOTIRMOYEE
1951   Formal and informal relations in the Hindu joint household of Bengal. Man in India 31:51–71.
1955   A village in West Bengal. In India's villages, pp. 161–179. West Bengal Government Press.
1959   The secular status of castes. Eastern Anthropologist 12:87–106.
1960   A village in West Bengal. In India's villages, M. N. Srinivas, editor, pp. 180–201. Second revised edition. London: Asia Publishing House.
1964   The nuclearization of joint family households in West Bengal. Man in India 44:193–206.
SCHWARTZBERG, JOSEPH E.
1965   The distribution of selected castes in the North Indian plains. Geographical Review 55:477–495.
1967   Prolegomena to the study of South Asian regions and regionalism. In Regions and regionalism in South Asia studies: an exploratory study. R. I. Crane, editor, pp. 85–111. Duke University Program in Comparative Studies in Southern Asia. Mimeograph No. 4.
SEN, LALIT KUMAR
1965   Family in four Indian villages. Man in India 45:1–16.
SENART, ÉMILE
1930   Caste in India. London: Methuen.
SENGUPTA, SUNIL
1958   Family organization in West Bengal: its nature and dynamics. The Economic Weekly 15:384–389.
SHAH, A. M.
1955a   Caste, economy and territory in the Central Panchmahals. Journal of the Maharaja Sayajirao University of Baroda 4:65–91.
1955b   A dispersed hamlet in the Panchmahals. The Economic Weekly 7:109–116.
1959   Social anthropology and the study of historical societies. The Economic Weekly 11:953–962.
1964a   Basic terms and concepts in the study of family in India. Indian Economic and Social History Review 1:1–36.
1964b   Political systems in eighteenth century Gujarat. Enquiry (Delhi) 1:83–95.
SHAH, A. M. AND R. G. SHROFF
1958   The Vahāvancā Bārots of Gujarat: a caste of geneologists and mythographers. Journal of American Folklore 71:246–276.
SHAH, B. V.
1960   Joint family system: an opinion survey of Gujarati students. The Economic Weekly 12:1867–1870.
1964   Social change and college students of Gujarāt. Baroda: M.S. University of Baroda.
SHAHANI, SAVITRI
1961   The joint family: a case study. The Economic Weekly 13:1823–1828.
SHARMA, KAILAS N.
1956a   Urban contacts and cultural change in a little community. Doctoral dissertation, Lucknow University, Lucknow.

1956b Hypergamy in theory and practice. The Journal of Research 3: 18–32.

1961a Hindu sects and food patterns in North India. Journal of Social Research 4:47–58.

1961b Occupational mobility of castes in a North Indian village. Southwestern Journal of Anthropology 17:146–164.

1963 Panchayat leadership and resource groups. Sociological Bulletin 12:47–52.

SIEGEL, BERNARD J. AND ALAN R. BEALS

1960a Pervasive factionalism. American Anthropologist 62:394–417.

1960b Conflict and factionalist dispute. The Journal of the Royal Anthropological Institute 90:107–117.

SILVERBERG, JAMES

1959 Caste-ascribed 'status' versus caste-irrelevant roles. Man in India 39:148–162.

SINGER, MILTON

1956a Cultural values in India's economic development. Annals of the American Academy of Political and Social Science 305:81–91.

1956b Introduction. In The Indian village: a symposium. The Journal of Asian Studies 16:3–5.

1958 The great tradition in a metropolitan center: Madras. Journal of American Folklore 71:347–388.

1963 The Radha-Krishna bhajans of Madras City. History of Religions 2:183–226.

1964 The social organization of Indian civilization. Diogenes, Winter issue 1964, pp. 84–119.

1966 The modernization of religious beliefs. In Modernization, Myron Weiner, editor, pp. 55–67. New York: Basic Books, Inc.

1968 The Indian joint family in modern industry. In Structure and change in Indian society, Milton Singer and Bernard S. Cohn, editors, pp. 423–452. Chicago: Aldine Publishing Co.

[1969] Modernization, ritual and belief among industrial leaders in Madras City. In Modernization in India: studies in social-cultural aspects, Amar Kumar Singh, editor. Bombay: Asia Publishing House.

SINGH, AMAR KUMAR

1967 Hindu culture and economic development in India, Conspectus 3:9–32.

SINGH, INDERA P.

1958 A Sikh village. Journal of American Folklore 71:479–503.

1961 Religion in Daleke: a Sikh village. Journal of Social Research (Ranchi) 4:191–219.

SINGH, BALJIT

1961 Next step in village India. Bombay: Asia Publishing House.

SINGH, INDERA P. AND H. L. HARIT

1960 Effects of urbanization in a Delhi suburban village. Journal of Social Research (Ranchi) 3:38–43.

SINGH, KHUSHWANT

1953 The Sikhs. London: George Allen and Unwin.

1963– A history of the Sikhs. Two volumes. Princeton: Princeton University Press.
1966

SINGH, RUDRA DATT

1956 The Unity of an Indian village. In The Indian village: a symposium. The Journal of Asian Studies 16:10–19.

SINGH, YOGENDRA
1959   Group status of factions in rural community. Journal of Social
        Sciences 2:57–67.
SINHA, D. P.
1963   The role of the Phariya in tribal acculturation in a Central Indian
        market. Ethnology 2:170–179.
1967   The Phariya in an inter-tribal market. Economic and Political
        Weekly 2:1373–1378.
SINHA, SURAJIT
1957a   The media and nature of Hindu-Bhumij interactions. Journal of
        the Asiatic Society: Letters and Science 23:23–37.
1957b   Tribal cultures of peninsular India as a dimension of little tradition
        in the study of Indian civilization: a preliminary statement. Man
        in India 37:93–118.
1958a   Changes in the cycle of festivals in a Bhumij village. Journal of So-
        cial Research (Ranchi) 1:24–49.
1958b   Tribal cultures of peninsular India as a dimension of little tradi-
        tion in the study of Indian civilization: a preliminary statement.
        Journal of American Folklore 71:504–518.
1959   Bhumij-Kshatriya social movement in South Manbhum. Bulletin
        of the Department of Anthropology, Government of India 8:9–
        32.
1962   Status formation and Rajput myth in tribal Central India. Man in
        India 42:35–80.
1963   Levels of economic initiative and ethnic groups in Pargana Bara-
        bhum. The Eastern Anthropologist 16:65–74.
1965   Tribe-caste and tribe-peasant continua in Central India. Man in
        India 45:57–83.
1967   Caste in India: its essential pattern of socio-cultural integration. In
        Caste and race: comparative approaches, A. de Reuck and J.
        Knight, editors, pp. 92–105. London: J. and A. Churchill.
SINHA, SURAJIT, BIMAR KUMAR DASGUPTA, AND HEMENDRA NATH BANERGEE
1961   Agriculture, crafts and weekly markets of South Manbhum. Bulle-
        tin of the Anthropological Survey of India. Volume 10, No. 1.
SMITH, DONALD EUGENE
1963   India as a secular state. Princeton: Princeton University Press.
SMITH, MARIAN W.
1952   The Misal: a structural village group of India and Pakistan. Amer-
        ican Anthropologist 54:41–56.
SMITH, WILFRED CANTWELL
1957   Islam in modern history. Princeton: Princeton University Press.
SOVANI, N. V.
1961   The urban social situation in India. Artha Vijnana 3:85–224.
SOVANI, N. V., D. P. APTE AND R. G. PENDSE
1956   Poona: a re-survey: the changing pattern of employment and earn-
        ings. Poona: Gokhale Institute of Politics and Economics. Publica-
        tion No. 34.
SPATE, O. H. K.
1954   India and Pakistan: a general and regional geography. New York:
        E. P. Dutton.

SRINIVAS, M. N.
1942   Marriage and family in Mysore. Bombay: New Book Co.
1952a   Religion and society among the Coorgs of South India. Oxford: Oxford University Press.
1952b   A joint family dispute in a Mysore village. Journal of the Maharaja Sayarijao University of Baroda 1:7–31.
1954   A caste dispute among washermen of Mysore. Eastern Anthropologist 7:148–168.
1955a   The social structure of a Mysore village. In India's villages, pp. 15–32. Calcutta: West Bengal Government Press.
1955b   The social system of Mysore village. In Village India, M. Marriott, editor, pp. 1–35. Chicago: University of Chicago Press.
1956a   A note on sanskritization and westernization. Far Eastern Quarterly 15:481–496.
1956b   Regional differences in customs and village institutions. The Economic Weekly 8:215–220.
1959a   The dominant caste in Rampura. American Anthropologist 61: 1–16.
1959b   The case of the potter and the priest. Man in India 39:190–209.
1962   Caste in modern India and other essays. Bombay: Asia Publishing House.
1965   Social structure. The National Gazeteer 1:1–77.
1966   Social change in modern India. Berkeley and Los Angeles: University of California Press.
SRINIVAS, M. N. AND ANDRÉ BÉTEILLE
1964   Networks in Indian social structure. Man 64:165–168.
SRINIVAS, M. N. AND A. M. SHAH
1960   The myth of the self-sufficiency of the Indian village. The Economic Weekly 12:1375–1378.
SRIVASTAVA, RAM P.
1962   Tribe-caste mobility in India and the case of Kumaon Bhotias. London: Department of Anthropology, School of Oriental and African Studies, University of London. Mimeographed, 80 pp.
SRIVASTAVA, S. K.
1963   The process of desanskritisation in village India. In Anthropology on the march, Bala Ratnam, editor, pp. 263–267. Madras: The Book Center.
STAAL, J. F.
1963   Sanskrit and sanskritization. The Journal of Asian Studies 22:261–275.
STEED, GITEL P.
1955   Notes on an approach to a study of personality formation in a Hindu village in Gujarat. In Villiage India, M. Marriott, editor, pp. 102–144. Chicago: University of Chicago Press.
STEIN, BURTON
1960   The economic function of the medieval South Indian temple. Journal of Asian Studies 19:163–176.
1967   Comment on Bernard S. Cohn's paper. In Regions and regionalism in South Asian studies, R. I. Crane, editor, pp. 41–47. Duke University Program in Comparative Studies in Southern Asia. Monograph No. 4.

1968   Social mobility and medieval South Indian Hindu sects. *In* Social
        mobility in the caste system in India, James Silverberg editor, pp.
        78–94. Comparative Studies in Society and History, Supplement
        III. The Hague: Mouton.

STEPHEN, LESLIE
1921   Henry Sumner Maine. *In* The Dictionary of National Biography,
        Vol. 12. pp. 787–790. London: Humphrey Milford.

STEVENSON, H. N. L.
1954   Status evaluation in the Hindu caste system. Journal of the Royal
        Anthropological Institute 84:45–65.

STEVENSON, MRS. SINCLAIR
1920   The rites of the twice-born. London: Humphrey Milford.

STRIZOWER, SCHIFRA
1959   Jews as an Indian caste. Jewish Journal of Sociology 1:43–57.

STROOP, MILDRED LUSCHINSKY
1960   The impact of some recent Indian government legislation on the
        women of an Indian village. Mimeographed, 9 pp.

TANDON, PRAKASH
1961   Punjabi century, 1857–1947. London: Chatto and Windus.

THAPAR, ROMILA
1966   A history of India. Volume 1. Baltimore: Penguin Books.

THOOTHI, N. A.
1935   The Vaishnavas of Gujarat. Bombay, London: Longmans, Green
        and Co.

THURSTON, EDGAR
1909   Castes and tribes of Southern India. Seven volumes. Madras: Gov-
        ernment Press.

TILAK, LAKSHMIBAI
1950   I follow after. (Translated by E. Josephine Inster.) Madras: Ox-
        ford University Press.

TRIVEDI, R. K.
1965   Fairs and festivals: Gujarat. Census of India, 1961, Volume 5, part
        7-B.

TUMIN, MELVIN M.
1967   Social stratification. Englewood Cliffs, New Jersey: Prentice-Hall.

ULLAH, INAYAT
1958   Caste, patti and faction in the life of a Punjab village. Sociologus
        n.s. 8:170–186.

UNDERHILL, M. M.
1921   The Hindu religious year. Calcutta: Association Press.

UNNI, K. RAMAN
1956   Visiting husbands in Malabar. Journal of the Maharaja Sayajirao
        University of Baroda 5:37–56.

VAN BUITENEN, J. A. B.
1966   On the archaism of the Bhāgavata Purāna. *In* Krishna: myths, rites
        and attitudes. Honolulu: East-West Center Press.

VIDYARTHI, LALITA P.
1961   The sacred complex in Hindu Gaya. Bombay: Asia Publishing
        House.
1967   Some preliminary observations on inter-group conflict in India:
        tribal, rural and industrial. Journal of Social Research 10:1–10.

VOGT, EVON Z.
    1960   On the concepts of structure and process in cultural anthropology. American Anthropologist 62:18–33.
VREEDE-DE STUERS, CORA
    1962   Mariage préférential chez les Musalmans de l'Inde du Nord. Revue de Sud-est Asiatique 1962:141–152.
    1963   Terminologie de parenté chez les Musalmans Ashrāf de l'Inde Nord. Bijragen tot de taal-, land- en Volkenkunde 119:254–266.
WALLACE, ANTHONY
    1961   The psychic unity of human groups. In Studying personality cross-culturally, Bert Kaplan, editor, pp. 129–164. Evanston: Row, Peterson and Co.
WARD, WILLIAM
    1822   A view of the history, literature and mythology of the Hindoos. London: Kingsbury, Parbury and Allen.
WATTERS, THOMAS
    1904   On Yuan Chwang's travels in India, 629–645 A.D., T. W. Rhys Davids and S. W. Bushnell, editors. London: Royal Asiatic Society.
WEBER, MAX
    1958   The religion of India. Glencoe, Illinois: The Free Press.
WEINER, MYRON
    1967   Party building in a new nation. Chicago: University of Chicago Press.
WHEELER, MORTIMER
    1953   The Cambridge history of India. Supplementary volume: the Indus civilization. Cambridge: Cambridge University Press.
WHITING, BEATRICE B.
    1963   Introduction. In Six cultures: studies of child marriage, B. B. Whiting, editor, pp. 1–13. New York: John Wiley.
    1965   Sex identity, conflict and physical violence: a comparative study. In The ethnography of law, Laura Nader, editor. American Anthropologist 67 (part 2):123–140.
WILLIAMS, A. HYATT
    1950   A psychiatric study of Indian soldiers in the Arakan. The British Journal of Medical Psychology 23:130–181.
WINSLOW, J. C.
    1923   Narayan Vaman Tilak: the Christian poet of Maharashtra. Calcutta: Association Press.
WISER, WILLIAM H.
    1936   The Hindu jajmani system: a socio-economic system inter-relating members of a Hindu village community in service. Lucknow: Lucknow Publishing House.
WISER, WILLIAM H. AND CHARLOTTE VIALL WISER
    1963   Behind mud walls. Berkeley and Los Angeles: University of California Press.
WOLF, ERIC R.
    1966   Kinship, friendship and patron-client relations in complex societies. In The social anthropology of complex societies, Michael Banton, editor. London: Tavistock Publications.

WRIGHT, THEODORE P., JR.
  1966   The Muslim League in South Indian since independence: a study in minority group political strategies. The American Political Science Review 60:579–599.

YALMAN. NUR
  1962   The structure of Sinhalese kindred: a re-examination of the Dravidian terminology. American Anthropologist 62:548–575.
  1967   Under the Bo tree: studies in caste, kinship and marriage in the interior of Ceylon. Berkeley and Los Angeles: University of California Press.

Index

Place-Names and Group Names
A SELECTION OF THOSE MENTIONED IN THE TEXT.

Name	State	Author
1. Aggarwals	Har.	(Gore)
2. Ahupe	Mah.	(Karve and Damle)
3. Badagas	Mad.	(Hockings)
4. Baderi	Or.	(Bailey)
5. Badlapur	Mah.	(Morrison)
6. Bhotias	U. P.	(Srivastava)
7. Bhumij	Bih., W. Ben.	(S. Sinha)
8. Bisipara	Or.	(Bailey)
9. Bolpur	W. Ben.	(N. K. Bose)
10. Chandipur	W. Ben.	(Nicholas)
11. Chenchus	A. P.	(Fürer-Haimendorf)
12. Cochin Jews	Ker.	(Fischel, Mandelbaum)
13. Coorgs	Mys.	(Srinivas)
14. Daleke	Pun.	(I. P. Singh)
15. Dalena	Mys.	(Epstein)
16. Deoli	Raj.	(Carstairs)
17. Dewara	A. P.	(Dube)
18. Dimiria	Or.	(Patnaik)
19. Gamras	U. P.	(K. L. Sharma)
20. Gannapur	Mys.	(Gnanambal)
21. Gaon	Mah.	(Orenstein)
22. Garos	Assam	(Burling)
23. Gayawals	Bihar	(Vidyarthi)
24. Gopalpur	Mys.	(Beals)
25. Haripura	Mys.	(Dhillon)
26. Hijalna	W. Ben.	(Sarma)
27. Iravas	Ker.	(Aiyappan)
28. Jatavs of Agra	U. P.	(Lynch)
29. Jats	U. P., Har.	(Pradhan, Kudryavtsev)
30. Jhabiran	U. P.	(R. Gupta)
31. Jitpur	Pun.	(Nath)
32. Kadduhalli Nad	Mys.	(Beals and MacLachlan)
33. Kanchanpur	W. Ben.	(Basu)
34. Karimpur	U. P.	(Wiser)
35. Karul	Mah.	(Karve and Damle)
36. Kasandra	Guj.	(Steed)
37. Khalapur	U. P.	(Hitchcock, Minturn, J. Gumperz, P. Kolenda)
38. Kishan Garhi	U. P.	(Marriott)
39. Kotas	Mad.	(Mandelbaum)
40. Kothuru	A. P.	(Y. V. L. Rao)
41. Kugti	H. P.	(Newell)
42. Kumbapettai	Mad.	(Gough)
43. Lamepur	Delhi	(M. S. A. Rao)
44. Lonikand	Mah.	(Ghurye)
45. Madhupur	W. Ben.	(S. Sinha)
46. Mahuva	Guj.	(Desai)
47. Malana	H. P.	(Rosser)
48. Maroli Bazar	Guj.	(Kapadia)
49. Mayur	Ker.	(Aiyappan)
50. Meos	Raj.	(Aggarwal)

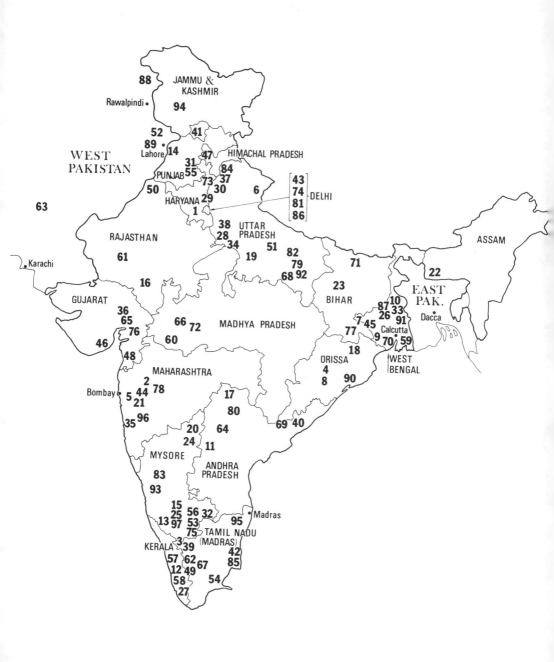

WEST
PAKISTAN

JAMMU &
KASHMIR

88

Rawalpindi •

94

52
89
14

41

47

HIMACHAL PRADESH

31
55

84
37

73
30

6

43
74
81
86

DELHI

PUNJAB

50

HARYANA

29
1

38
28

UTTAR
PRADESH

34

ASSAM

Karachi •

63

RAJASTHAN

61

16

19

51

82
79
68 92

71

22

GUJARAT

36
65
76

46

48

66 72

60

MADHYA PRADESH

23

BIHAR

EAST
PAK.

87
26

10
33

Dacca •

7 45
77
9

91

Calcutta •

70 59

MAHARASHTRA

2
44 78

Bombay •

5
21

35 96

17

80

18

ORISSA

4
8

90

WEST
BENGAL

20
24

11

69 40

MYSORE

83
93

ANDHRA
PRADESH

15
25
97

13

56 32
53

75

95

• Madras

TAMIL NADU
(MADRAS)

KERALA

3 39

57
12
58

62
49

67

42
85

27

54

Place-Names and Group Names
A SELECTION OF THOSE MENTIONED IN THE TEXT.

Name	State	Author
51. Mohana	U. P.	(Majumdar)
52. Mohla	W. Pak.	(Eglar)
53. Morsralli	Mys.	(McCormack)
54. Nadars	Mad.	(Hardgrave, Raj)
55. Nalli	Pun.	(Izmirlian)
56. Namhalli	Mys.	(Beals)
57. Nayadis	Ker.	(Aiyappan)
58. Nayars	Ker.	(Gough, Unni Nayar)
59. Nehalpur	W. Ben.	(U. Guha)
60. Nimar Balahis	M. P.	(Fuchs)
61. Palana	Raj.	(Bose and Malhotra)
62. Paliyans	Mad.	(Gardner)
63. Pat	W. Pak.	(Honigmann)
64. Pathuru	A. P.	(Y. V. L. Rao)
65. Patidars	Guj.	(Pocock)
66. Potlod	M. P.	(Mathur)
67. Pramalai Kallars	Mad.	(Dumont)
68. Ramapur	U. P.	(Opler and R. D. Singh)
69. Reddis of Bison Hills	A. P.	(Füror Haimondorf)
70. Radhanagar	W. Ben.	(Nicholas)
71. Radhanagar	Bihar	(Roy)
72. Ramkheri	M. P.	(Mayer)
73. Ram Nagar	Har.	(Hazlehurst)
74. Rampur	Delhi	(Lewis)
75. Rampura	Mys.	(Srinivas)
76. Samiala	Guj.	(Fukutake, Ouchi, Nakane)
77. Santals	Bihar, W. Ben.	(Orans, Culshaw, Datta-Majumdar, Kochar)
78. Sarola Kasar	Mah.	(Jagalpure and Kale)
79. Senapur	U. P.	(Opler, Cohn, Planalp, Rowe, Reddy)
80. Shamirpet	A. P.	(Dube)
81. Shanti Nagar	Delhi	(Freed)
82. Sherurpur	U. P.	(Gould)
83. Shivapur	Mys.	(Ishwaran)
84. Sirkanda	U. P.	(Berreman)
85. Sripuram	Mad.	(Béteille)
86. Sungpur	Delhi	(Gangrade)
87. Supur	W. Ben.	(Fukutake, Ouchi, Nakane)
88. Swat Pathans	W. Pak.	(Barth)
89. Tararwala	W. Pak.	(Ullah)
90. Telis	Or.	(Patnaik)
91. "Ten Villages"	W. Ben	(Klass)
92. Tezibazar	U. P.	(Fox)
93. Totagadde	Mys.	(Harper)
94. Utrassu-Umangiri	Kash.	(Madan)
95. Vanniyars	Mad.	(Rudolph)
96. Varkute	Mah.	(Karve and Damle)
97. Wangala	Mys.	(Epstein)